PENGUIN BOOKS

CONNEMARA

A native of Yorkshire, Tim Robinson studied maths at Cambridge and then worked for many years as a visual artist in Istanbul, Vienna and London, among other places. In 1972 he moved to the Aran Islands. In 1986 his first book, *Stones of Aran: Pilgrimage*, was published to great acclaim. The second volume of *Stones of Aran*, subtitled *Labyrinth*, appeared in 1995. He has also published collections of essays, and maps of the Aran Islands, the Burren and Connemara. Since 1984 he has lived in Roundstone, Connemara.

Connemara

Listening to the Wind

TIM ROBINSON

PENGUIN BOOKS

PENGUIN BOOKS

Published by the Penguin Group
Penguin Books Ltd, 80 Strand, London WC2R ORL, England
Penguin Group (USA) Inc., 375 Hudson Street, New York, New York 10014, USA
Penguin Group (Canada), 90 Eglinton Avenue East, Suite 700, Toronto, Ontario, Canada M4P 2Y3
(a division of Pearson Penguin Canada Inc.)
Penguin Ireland, 25 St Stephen's Green, Dublin 2, Ireland (a division of Penguin Books Ltd)
Penguin Group (Australia), 250 Camberwell Road,
Camberwell, Victoria 3124, Australia (a division of Pearson Australia Group Pty Ltd)
Penguin Books India Pvt Ltd, 11 Community Centre,
Panchsheel Park, New Delhi – 110 017, India
Penguin Group (NZ), 67 Apollo Drive, Rosedale, North Shore 0632, New Zealand
(a division of Pearson New Zealand Ltd)
Penguin Books (South Africa) (Pty) Ltd, 24 Sturdee Avenue,
Rosebank, Johannesburg 2196, South Africa

Penguin Books Ltd, Registered Offices: 80 Strand, London WC2R ORL, England

www.penguin.com

First published by Penguin Ireland 2006
Published in Penguin Books 2007
2

Copyright © Tim Robinson, 2006
All rights reserved

The moral right of the author has been asserted

Set by Rowland Phototypesetting Ltd, Bury St Edmunds, Suffolk
Printed in England by Clays Ltd, St Ives plc

ISBN: 978-1-844-88066-9

Contents

Author's Note

Hundreds of Connemara people have helped me in my explorations over the last third of a century. In relation to the areas treated in this volume I would particularly like to thank Mícheál King and Paddy Folan of Inis Ní, Tommy O'Donnell of Cúgla, and John King, Joe Rafferty, Máirtín O'Malley, Paddy McDonagh and his father, Pat, all of Roundstone, for their knowledgeable company on land and sea. Conal O'Toole and Tom Woods instructed me in turf-cutting, and the late Mícheál Breathnach was generous with Irish-language lore, as were Willie O'Malley of Ballinafad and John Barlow, originally of Seanadh Chaola, with local history. Some of these are among the Connemara friends who figure in these pages; other portraits are composites or chimeras, not to be identified with any single person alive or dead.

Among the many experts who have overseen my amateur efforts in various fields I am especially grateful for the cooperation of Liam Mac Con Iomaire in translations from Irish sources, and the advice of Dr James White and Dr Micheline Sheehy-Skeffington on botanical matters, Professor Michael O'Connell on the changing environments of prehistoric times, and Professor Paul Mohr on the rocky basis of it all. I thank Dominic Berridge for the loan of Berridge family papers, and Patrick Gageby for furnishing me with old ecclesiastical books. Finally, I deeply appreciate Brendan Barrington's trusty editing. The book is for M, as always.

TR

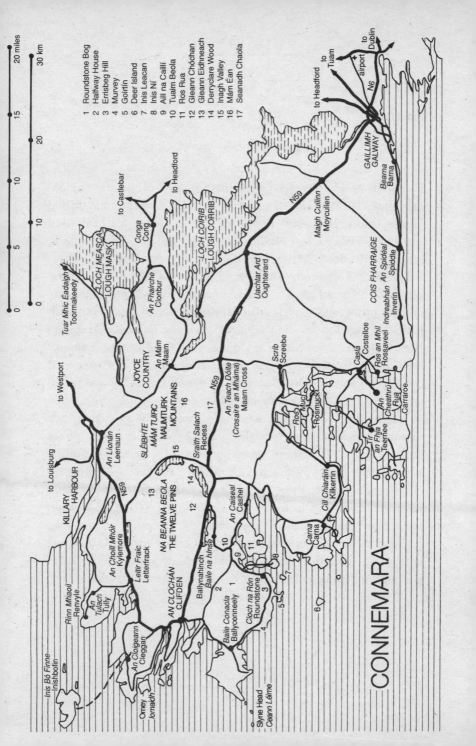

CONNEMARA

1 Roundstone Bog
2 Halfway House
3 Errisbeg Hill
4 Murvey
5 Goirtín
6 Deer Island
7 Inis Leacan
8 Inis Ní
9 Aill na Cailli
10 Tuaim Beola
11 Ros Rua
12 Gleann Chóchan
13 Gleann Eidhneach
14 Derryclare Wood
15 Inagh Valley
16 Mám Éan
17 Seanadh Chaola

20 miles
30 km

to Dublin
to Tuam
airport
to Headford
N6

GAILLIMH
GALWAY

Bearna
Barna

Maigh Cuilinn
Moycullen

N59

to Headford

Conga
Cong

LOCH MEASCA
LOUGH MASK

Tuar Mhic Éadaigh
Toormakeedy

to Castlebar

An Fhairche
Clonbur

LOCH COIRIB
LOUGH CORRIB

Uachtar Ard
Oughterard

COIS FHARRAIGE

An Spidéal
Spiddle

Indreabhán
Inverin

Ros an Mhíl
Rossaveel

Casla
Costelloe

Scríb
Screebe

An Teach Dóite
(Crosaire an Mháma)
Maam Cross

An Mám
Maam

JOYCE
COUNTRY

SLÉIBHTE
MÁM TUIRC
MAUMTURK
MOUNTAINS

16

17
N59

Ros Muc
Rosmuck

An
Cheathrú
Rua
Carraroe

Tír
an Fhia
Teernee

Carna
Carna

Cill Chiaráin
Kilkerrin

An Caiseal
Cashel

10

9
11

8
7

6

5
4

Baile Conaola
Ballyconneely

Cloch na Rón
Roundstone

1
2

3

Ballynahinch
Baile na hInse

NA BEANNA BEOLA
THE TWELVE PINS

12

13

14

15
Sraith Salach
Recess

An Lionán
Leenaun

An Choill Mhóir
Kylemore

Leitir Fraic
Letterfrack

AN CLOCHÁN
CLIFDEN

N59

KILLARY
HARBOUR

An Tulach
Tully

Rinn Mhaoil
Renvyle

An Clóigeann
Cleggan

Omey
Iomaidh

Inis Bó Finne
Inishbofin

to Louisburg

to Westport

Slyne Head
Ceann Léime

0   5   10   15   20 km
0   10   20   miles

Preface

The Sound of the Past and the Moment of Writing

A small concrete cross stands by the road that follows the river from Ballynahinch to the sea. The proprietor of the Angler's Return, two bends of the road and the river further on, told me it marks the place where one of the gillies was found dead of a heart attack. 'Wasn't it good that he died looking out at the river he'd worked on all his life?' she added. But from the time of the tyrannical Tadhg O'Flaherty, who forbade fishing in the lake by his castle, to the fish-ins of the Gaelic Civil Rights Movement in the sixties, the fisheries of Connemara have been occasions of resentment. Perhaps the man died cursing the river that had brought him a lifetime of midge bites and the condescension of the rich.

Whatever the burden of the gillie's last breath, it was dispersed into the air to be degraded by the hiss of rain or eroded molecule by molecule in the Brownian fidget of drifting pollen grains, and captured, a little of it, by the tilting, spilling cups and saucers of the water surface, dissolved, hurried under the old bridge at Tuaim Beola and added to the sea. So one can imagine it infinitesimally present in, and persuasively interpreting, the sough (which we should not delude ourselves is a sighing) of the Ballynahinch woods, the clatter (not a chattering) of the mountain streamlets, the roar (not a raging) of the waves against the shore.

These indefinite but enormous noises are part of Connemara. Sometimes from my doorstep on a still night I become aware that the silence is set in a velvet background like a jewel in a display case, a hushing that, when attended to, becomes ineluctable. It is compounded of the crash of breakers along distant strands, variously delayed, attenuated, echoed and re-echoed. A frequently falsified but never quite discredited forewarning of gales, it is an effect that, from our perspective here, precedes its cause: a depression moving across the Atlantic and advancing its concentric rollers towards our coast. By the morning, perhaps, a tumult of air will be battering the windows, all its wavelengths, from the vast heft of gusts over the hill that half shelters us, to the spasms of the garden shrubs and the fluting of a dry leaf caught between two stones, merging into one toneless bulk noise. Going here and there in thought through the pandemonium, only the most analytic listening can disengage its elements: shriek of sedge bent double out on the heath, grinding of shingle sucked back by the reflux, slow chamfering of a stone's edge by blown sand grains.

Such vast, complex sounds are produced by fluid generalities impacting on intricate concrete particulars. As the wave or wind breaks around a headland, a wood, a boulder, a tree trunk, a pebble, a twig, a wisp of seaweed or a microscopic hair on a leaf, the streamlines are split apart, flung against each other, compressed in narrows, knotted in vortices. The ear constructs another wholeness out of the reiterated fragmentation of pitches, and it can be terrible, this wide range of frequencies coalescing into something approaching the auditory chaos and incoherence that sound engineers call white noise: zero of information-content, random interference obliterating all messages, utterly dire, a metaphysical horror made audible, sometimes dinned into prisoners' heads to drive them mad in the cells of their brains.

Similar too is the sound of the past, the wreck of time's grand flow in tortuous passages. It includes and sometimes drowns the sound of history. History has rhythms, tunes and even harmonies; but the sound of the past is an agonistic multiplicity. Sometimes, rarely, a scrap of a voice can be caught from the universal damage, but it may only be an artefact of the imagination, a confection of rumours. Chance decides what is obliterated and what survives if only to be distorted and misheard. Of the gillie who died by the river, I know nothing more, but may yet find out something. But who, for one of the crowding shades besieging my book, was Cuach na Coille, the 'cuckoo of the wood'? I hear of her from a single source only, and only this: that she was a beautiful horse-woman who lived in Derryclare Wood. I fear that nobody living can tell me more. Even in the ancient forest itself, where slender shafts of sunlight look almost material enough to cast a greenish shadow and sometimes in the restless canopy a cuckoo claims to be 'here/there', the mysterious horsewoman does not appear, tantalizing with her untold tale. Hers, with his, may stand for all Connemara's abolished voices.

*

A preface represents the moment of writing, a fictive moment in which the book is declared complete, or abandoned as incompletable within the limits of time and talent available, and is delivered to that longed-for response, the moment of reading, which stands in the same labyrinthine relation to hearing as writing does to speech. The moment of writing, outcome of the potentially endless reshapings of sense and intricate adjustments of word to context that true writing allows and indeed consists in, is a fractal construction out of all the subsidiary moments in which words, phrases, paragraphs, chapters, have been completed.

Whatever curse or blessing the gillie may have uttered, on someone or on everyone who was not there to receive it, it would have been true speech, spontaneous, out of the unfathomable depth of personhood. As such it would have been the very opposite of true writing. (The material differences between speech and writing are immaterial to this opposition; rehearsed speech is writing, and a dashed-off love-note can be true speech.) How can writing, writing about a place, hope to recuperate its centuries of lost speech? A writing may aspire to be rich enough in reverberatory internal connections to house the sound of the past as well as echoes of immediate experience, but it is also intensely interested in its own structure, which it must preserve from the overwhelming multiplicity of reality. I am aware of the selectivity of my written response to living in Connemara. I concentrate on just three factors whose influences permeate the structures of everyday life here: the sound of the past, the language we breathe, and our frontage onto the natural world. I don't propose these as philosophical categories, merely use them as organizing principles, interplaying with the general topographical drive of the work. And if, as seems possible, this book becomes three books, each might privilege one of these factors while remaining open to all of them. The fact of language (not 'the language question', which scarcely interests me) might predominate in writing about the conflictually bilingual southern region of Connemara. The ocean, inescapable symbol of the ever-changing, almost-eternal, other-than-human setting of human affairs, would especially direct me when I come to the cliffs and isles and promontories of the Atlantic seaboard. The present book concerns a huge tract of south-west and central Connemara; after wandering in Roundstone Bog for a while it works its way from the beaches west of Roundstone, where I live, by Ballynahinch, for centuries the heart of Connemara and the seat of its various masters, to the eastern extremity of Roundstone Parish, the legendary mountain pass of Mám Éan; the sound of the past is particularly insistent throughout this territory.

That is the schema emerging under my hands, at the moment of writing. I may have to abandon it if subsequent volumes lead me another way. And as to this volume, I am aware that, even leaving out of account the writer's ignorance and misapprehensions, the truest of writing about the past can hardly offer more than an appalled recognition of the injustice of time, its brutally hasty recourse to mass graves for irreplaceable individualities and to landfill for delicate discriminations.

Tim Robinson
Roundstone, 2006

Scailp

Of recent years my explorations in Roundstone Bog have repeatedly led me to a place called Scailp. There are several distinct ways
of getting to it, none of them easy, from the seaside village of
Roundstone itself. Bogland is an obstructive, argumentative, quib-
bling, contentious terrain; it demands step-by-step negotiations. I
am left tired but exhilarated by the feat of getting to Scailp and
back again in an afternoon; I catch myself admiring my ability to
move fast over such a tricky surface, and have to remind myself
that this is a loan from fortune and will be soon withdrawn. Ideally,
I feel, a walk should be undertaken with the respect for its own
timescale and structures and ceremonies of mood one brings to
the hearing of a piece of music. Conversation, except on what's
to hand or underfoot, is redundant, inopportune. Solitude is best.
I cannot dance, perhaps because dancing takes place on the flat,
on a surface that suggests no rhythms and leaves my will floundering
in self-consciousness; instead I aspire to a compensating gift of
walking, not in a way that overcomes the land but in one that
commends every accident and essence of it to my bodily balance
and my understanding. Sometimes, though, after one of these almost
ceremonial or ritual walks I am disappointed to find very little in
my mental knapsack; I have taken the distance only in my stride
and not in my mind. But perhaps that is for the best in the case
of a walk with a goal like Scailp, where there is nothing, or almost
nothing; I go out there to wrestle with emptiness, and success
would be to bring exactly nothing home with me, not even a
catalogue of finds and observations or that rather exciting ego-
whiff of sweat and wilderness.

Because Roundstone has spread so far along the coast road in
both directions the quickest way out of the village is to strike
inland, up the lane from the harbour past the back premises of

O'Dowd's bar and Fair Green, the neat little estate built by the County Council in the 1980s. Soon I have to choose between going straight on towards the ragged steeps of Errisbeg Hill, or taking a turning to the right along a track that rises slowly across the flanks of the two lesser and more rounded heights, Roundstone Hill and Letterdife Hill. This time I will take the road ahead. It leads past a scattering of cottages and some recently built bungalows with many dormer windows and smooth lawns that alternate strangely with rough fields overgrown with thickets of furze; the village has clearly staked its claim to this triangle of underused farmland between the built-up coastal zone and the line of hills. Telegraph poles lean into the branches of alders along the margins of a dark little wood; there is a wind-tousled rusticity about the scene; it needs to comb its hair and tuck in its shirt-tail before returning to the main street. The drainage channels along the roadsides are crammed with a plant life that mixes the native-born and the feral intruder; tall ranks of reeds that bow and scrape and whisper among themselves as one passes alternate with dense brakes of the rattling bamboo-like stems of Japanese knotweed, an invasive alien that can drive its shoots through cracks in concrete. I remember passing an elderly man with a long-handled rake laboriously dragging masses of sodden vegetation out of the drainage channels of a damp roadside field; he wiped his surly brow and swore, 'This is the last time I cut rushes and leave them to grow after me!' meaning that in future he would poison them. But he went into the old folks' home in Clifden the next year, and his field is full of rushes again. The small farmer is dying out and tall straggling furze bushes overrun the former pastures; sometimes someone sets a match to them and blackens an acre or two, but the next June they are as golden as before; there is nothing for it but to sell off the land as building sites.

Further up, the narrow road becomes a boreen hedged with fuchsia and berberis, and climbs to a rickety old gate constructed of odds and ends tied together with twine, which gives onto the boggy commonage hillside, the 'mountain', as such land is called in Connemara, whether it be upland or lowland. Outside one of the last cottages I often used to meet Tommy O'Donnell, a sheep farmer, from whose nearly forgotten Irish and obscurely mouthed English I tried to make out placenames and local histories. Tommy was half a head taller than me, cadaverous and hollow-cheeked, nothing but skin and tendons and bones. In his weather-darkened work clothes he was a dreadful silhouette, all height and edges, with no thickness to him, a memento mori from bad times, an apparition from the famine graves he told me of in the bushes behind his cottage. When he stood before me with one lanky arm stretched out at right angles to grasp his long staff, he framed a door-shaped view of the hill beyond. I used to think he was the ideal farmer, as he knew his sheep individually and remembered their mothers and grandmothers too, or so he told me once when he was grumbling about the fox that had come down from the hill and savaged a lamb. (He suspected me of tending to favour the fox, which I did not, since it had also taken every one of the guineafowl I was trying to keep at the time.) But I am told that in his last few years, whether it was because he was getting too arthritic and scatterbrained to mind them, or because the headage payment schemes with which the failing way of life of the West was being artificially prolonged had tempted him into taking on too many, his sheep suffered dreadfully. Once when a little girl from London was holidaying with us I brought her up here, hoping that she would be charmed by the sights and sounds of rural life. We stopped to chat with Tommy while his scraggy yellow-eyed sheepdogs sniffed suspiciously at her, and Tommy held forth in such horrid detail about how after days of ceaseless rain he'd found a ewe stuck in a ditch, all waterlogged and maggoty, that I was glad the child was indifferent to the countryside, to the point of deafness and blindness.

The path leading on from O'Donnell's mountain gate points one in the right direction, towards the pass between Errisbeg Hill to the west and Roundstone Hill to the north, but very soon becomes indistinguishable from the numerous little watercourses that come braiding down to meet the climber. The going is difficult, stony and steep in places and in others soft and slippery, often combining both qualities into one pace. The central areas of the saddle – An Gleann Mór, the big glen – are crossed here and there by the broken-down trenches of long-abandoned turf-cuttings, and are usually so wet that it is best to keep to the hillsides on one side or the other. On the left, clinging to the skirts of Errisbeg Hill, which comes stepping down in little precipices here, is the Path of Afola; at least, John King, another sheep farmer with whom I have often walked the hills, tells me it is a path, but it is not readily distinguishable from the wayward and interrupted slots worn by sheep into the heather. I have written down the name as it sounds; the second element is probably the Irish *athbhuaile*, 'former milking place', for, as I will explain, in the old days cattle would be grazed on isolated grassy patches in mountain land like this during the summer milking season. There is a pleasant Irish phrase for a nostalgic return: *Cuairt an lao ar an athbhuaile*, the calf's visit to the old milking place, which I am reminded of every time I pass this way to revisit Scailp.

At the top of the pass – ill-defined, the terrain being so irregular – a view of the low-lying tangle of land and water beyond begins to open up. A flush, a spongy patch of sphagnum moss collecting the run-off from the hillside, feeds a tiny stream that rapidly grows in volume and volubility as it falls northwards to the first of Roundstone Bog's hundred lakes. A hundred yards further down a few clumps of a heather taller than the common sorts appear on its banks, and where the stream makes a dog-leg to the east between two knolls before continuing its downhill course it is densely overgrown with heather three or four feet tall. This heather is one of Roundstone Bog's famous rarities, the Mediterranean heath, *Erica erigena*, which grows here in the Gleann Mór and in a few scattered localities near the west Mayo coast, and is otherwise absent from Europe north of the Iberian peninsula. Whether it is a true native of Ireland is debatable, since its pollen, unlike that of Connemara's other rare heathers, has not been found in peat deposits from pre-Christian times, and the earliest notice of the plant is due to Edward Lhwydd, the Welsh enthusiast for all things Celtic, who visited Connemara in about

1700. It may in fact have been brought to Ireland as packing around wine casks; both the O'Flahertys of Connemara and the seafaring O'Malleys of west Mayo carried on a flourishing smuggling trade with Portugal and Spain. It was rediscovered by J. T. Mackay of Trinity College, Dublin, in 1830, and although he noted the location as being 'on a declivity, by a stream, in boggy ground, at the foot of Urrisbeg mountain . . . on its west side', I think this hollow in the Gleann Mór, on the north-east flank of the mountain, is its *locus classicus*, as the botanists say, for the place is called French Heath Tamhnóg by the very few people who have names for such out-of-the-way (and egregiously unclassical) spots these days. A *tamhnóg* is a little grassy patch or formerly cultivated patch in a bog, and the other part of the name must be due to a local misremembering of what some visiting botanist had to say about the remarkable heather that had overgrown it. Mackay sent off 150 specimens of the plant to the master-botanist of Kew, Sir W. J. Hooker, and the following year sent a young friend of his to collect a cartload of it; all this must have impressed the Roundstone people with its importance. They had their own interest in it too: in 1900 a visiting botanist found that 'the heath had in many places been ruthlessly uprooted and was lying around in withered heaps', as it was being harvested for use as brushes, both in the home and for spattering the potato fields with copper-sulphate solution against potato blight. Nobody disturbs the heather nowadays, or searches out French Heath Tamhnóg, which, quite apart from the charm of its odd name, is one of the most attractive hidey-holes of Roundstone Bog. When I visited it on a sunny day in mid February recently the heather was a vivid pale green against the wintry grey of the surrounding slopes, and a few mounds of it were already covered in tiny pale-lilac flowers. The tubular blossoms are only a few millimetres long, and with a hand lens one can see the chocolate-coloured anthers just showing in their mouths like the tips of velvet-gloved fingers. It is best to keep to the eastern rim of the hollow while examining the heather, though, and not to tread into it, for this is treacherous ground: the stream divides and subdivides here to flow through the leg-deep clefts of a boulder-bed completely hidden by the waist-high shrubs.

Beyond the *tamhnóg* the stream gathers itself together again, and even where invisible it becomes increasingly audible, flinging itself onwards as if rejoicing in its name, the Róig, the attack or onrush. That day in February the lake at its foot was as darkly brilliant as blue-black ink, and two whooper swans were sailing in and out of its reed-beds. Loch Roisín na Róige, the lake of the small headland of the Róig, is well known to local anglers, but I have never met anyone there. After skirting its banks, which are delicately fringed with little bushes of Mediterranean heath and bog myrtle, one crosses a third of a mile of low rocky ridge separating it from the next lake, Loch Bólard, which is immense (on the local scale) and spreads arms in all directions. An isolated hill, unnamed on Ordnance Survey maps, rises eastwards from Loch Bólard. In the days of the Penal Laws the Mass used to be celebrated secretly in this remote spot, according to a collection of folklore published in 1941. The editor of this work, Seán Mac Giollarnáth, writes the name of the hill as 'Cnoc na gCorrbhéal' but does not explain its meaning (*corrbhéal* looks as if it means 'projecting mouth'), and in documentation of the post-Cromwellian settlement it occurs as 'Knocknagurveele'; perhaps the last word is *corrmhíol*, in which case the name means 'the hill of the midges', although since midges are a torment to shepherds, anglers and turf-cutters throughout the region it is not obvious why they should be especially invoked by this placename. My goal, Scailp, is on the lowest slopes of this hill, four or five hundred yards up the eastern shore of the lake.

Alternatively, one can find one's way to Scailp by keeping to the right or eastern side of the Gleann Mór. This involves scrambling up and down some abrupt knolls of rock and plunging through some foot-swallowing quags, but one has an unexpected guide in the form of a low ridge, the worn-down remains of an old sod fence. I have come across nothing comparable to this fence in Connemara. It stretches for two miles over hill and dale, in three lengths each as straight as a ruler. The first runs from the limits of cultivation near O'Donnell's gate across the shoulder of Roundstone Hill to a turret-like prominence called An Meall Mór, the big hummock, near the saddle-point of the pass; the second, from there for a mile down into and across a very soggy bottom called Gleann an Uisce, the glen of water, and up to the little summit-cairn of Cnoc na gCorrbhéal; the third, from that point down the north-eastern side of the hill to the shores of a lake, Loch Dúlach. Comparing the view of it as seen from An Meall Mór with an old six-inches-to-the-mile Ordnance Survey map one sees that it follows the boundary of a townland called Letterdife. Townlands are the smallest administrative land divisions of Ireland; there are about three hundred of them in Connemara (which itself is a vaguely defined and unofficial entity), of sizes ranging from a few dozen to over five thousand acres; Letterdife with its 1,595 acres is typical, being mainly open mountainside and bog apart from a strip of cultivated land hugging the shore-line and divided into little stone-walled fields, with a dozen or so houses scattered along the coast road. 'Letterdife' is the angli-cized form of the original Irish name, Leitir Daibhche, the rough hillside of the *dabhach*, which could mean a barrel, or a spring well, or a cave (there is a small cave on its foreshore, now blocked up). Most townlands are of ancient origin and their boundaries were maintained solely in memory passed down from generation to generation; not until the Ordnance Survey of the 1830s were they given precise mapped-out limits, and Letterdife is the only case I have come across in which those limits have been drawn on the land itself in such a way, imposing a rectilinear abstraction on such recalcitrant reality. The Moot, people call it, from the Irish *móta*, an earthen embankment. Who built this extraordinary boundary fence, which to have been of any use must have stood high enough to stop cattle from straying? There seems to be no tradition about it, but clearly a team of men must have worked on it for some years, no doubt under a relief-work scheme of one of the hungry decades of the late nineteenth century. And by whose orders? Most probably those of Henry Robinson, the landlord's agent (and no relative of mine), whose mansion was in

Letterdife, just north of Roundstone village, and who would have had cattle on the hillsides inland of it. Weather and the trampling of stock have reduced it to a soft bank a foot or two high, which one could easily step across without seeing it in the general irregularity of the ground, but which, once noticed, perhaps as the westering sun picks it out as a dark seam across the crumpled tissue of the land, is still an eye-compelling anomaly, a fading rebuke to this entropic chaos of stone and water.

Having followed this marker across the valley bottom one has only to cling to the skirts of Cnoc na gCorrbhéal around to the left for a quarter of a mile, past some haphazardly piled clutches of blackish boulders – gross geological monstrosities, thundercloud eggs – to find Scailp. And so, having reached it by one route or another, what is this place? A steep little coomb of the hillside, tumbling down to the lakeside; a roughly built stone hut, roofless and full of bracken, crouching in the shelter of a lumpy rock outcrop; a patch of green grass on top of a knoll where sheep sometimes lie beside a hollowed-out stone-heap, the remains of a pen for lambs; a silvery tree trunk, almost branchless, rising out of a split rock; a wind off the lake and the bog beyond it stretching to the horizon, a presence of pure space. A *scailp* can be a cleft or small cliff, a clump of bushes or briars, a hut roofed with sods of turf, and so on – any one of a variety of poor nesting places. And, the lake being Loch Bólard, this hillside must be the *buaile ard*, high 'booley' or milking pasture, from which it derives its name. 'Booleying', a small-scale version of the ancient life-pattern of transhumance practised in the Pyrenees and other regions where nomad shepherds used to move flocks of thousands of sheep a hundred miles or more between lowland and upland, has been recorded in Connemara from centuries ago. Roderick O'Flaherty mentioned it in the book on West Connacht he wrote in 1684:

They dwell for the most part next the borders of the countrey where commonly is the best land, and in Summer time they drive their cattle to the mountaines, where such as looke to the cattle live in small cabbins for that season.

Two magical dates: May Day, the first of May, and All Saints' Day, the first of November, delimited the summer of the ancient Celtic year, the months of nomadism, the hunting season of the wandering warrior bands of the Fianna. Roderick O'Flaherty's kinsmen, the former lords of Connemara, with their herds, their womenfolk, harpist, priest and wolfhounds, used to remove from their seaside castles to large temporary wooden dwellings in the glens of the Maumturk Mountains for the summer. Among the peasantry the custom of booleying persisted into the early years of the twentieth century, and there were more immediate and practical reasons for it than the pressures of ancient tradition. Land near the shore was often unenclosed and it was difficult to keep cattle out of the growing crops, so the grassy patches of the mountain, accessible in the better weather, were a resource not to be neglected. Since cattle in calf could not be driven long distances to and fro every day, the womenfolk would stay with them, living in makeshift huts, while the menfolk were busy with fishing, kelp-burning and tillage nearer home. Here is an account of life in the booley taken down from an elderly Irish-speaker, Peadar Mac Thuathaláin, in south Connemara some time in the 1920s or 1930s:

There used to be booleys on the mountains from Slyne Head to Galway. The men of the villages would go at the beginning of summer and make little huts at the booleys beside *clochair* [natural heaps of glacial boulders], with a wooden rafter and a covering of oak wattle and reed scraws. Bog-oak timbers are found in the mountain *clochair*. The sort of door they had on the hut was a bundle of heather or a bundle of sticks. They had sheep and lambs on the booley as well as cattle. They used to build stone fences for cornering the sheep. The fences would be built crookedly, with angles in and out.

The women would stay in the hut at night without coming home, five or six of them sleeping together with a fine bed of young heather under them – the healthiest bed anyone ever slept in – a new flannel blanket for each woman and her pair of linen sheets; a good fire at the head of the hut; the best of food for them; oatmeal bread and milk, and porridge now and again; their dinner: potatoes when autumn came. After the women had weaned the lambs, they used to heat up the sheep's milk. They would drink that until they were glutted. Each woman, once she had the milking done, knitting and sewing all day long until the evening milking time.

The menfolk would come in the evening and take the milk home. They used to put it in a tub to settle. They would wash their tankards and *lámhóga* [wooden vessels holding six or seven gallons] with boiling water. They would lay them on a wall with their mouths to the wind until it was time to take them to the women on the booley. A man might take three tankards with him, to oblige two other men.

When the men at home had let the milk go sour, it was put into a churn and churned. When it had become butter two or three of the women would come from the booley to put it in wooden kegs and salt it. They used to have hundredweight kegs and they would fill the hundredweight keg and the men would go to Galway with it, the keg down in a basket on one side of the horse and two tankards of butter-milk on the other side. The butter was sold to sweet-makers in Galway, and most of it went by sea to England. A man they called Tim of the Butter was always on the quay to buy it. You'd rather have a bite of the butter that was going then than seven bites of the stuff that's going nowadays.

Is it just nostalgia that dresses those damp hillsides in the golden light of Arcadia? Peadar Mac Thuathaláin recalls their simple enter-tainments: 'For a couple of hours every evening they had songs, dancing and lilting. There was an old saying: "You brought the dance from the booley with you." ' And other accounts, such as that recorded from a Donegal man born in 1874 by the folklorist Seán Ó hEochaidh, concur as to the joyousness of life at the booley, dwelling especially on those long summer evenings when the lads would come out from the villages to sing and dance with the girls. Of course, such hours, welcomed in and made much of, flattered and cajoled into expansiveness, stayed by hospitality of word and note, naturally would stand out in memory from the days of dank mist spent huddling around a moribund fire on the slopes of the Hill of Midges, or of rain battering in from the Atlantic, or of a 'skinning wind' as they say in Roundstone, days on which the senses would shrink like snails into their shells and the body would round itself to shed time like rain trickling off a boulder. At night the unlimited darkness beyond the little glow of the fire would have been prolific of fears. Mac Thuathaláin tells of a woman who always took her father's rapier with her to the booley of Clochar Éidín in south-east Connemara and kept it stuck in among the scraws of the roof of her hut. One night while she and the other women were chatting they heard an ugly cry outside. She drew out the rapier and pulled the bundle of heather from the doorway. At first she thought the dark shape outside was a sheep, but when it made for her she thrust the rapier in at its ear so that it came out of its mouth, and left the creature dead. In the morning they found it was a wolf – the last one that was ever seen on the 'mountain' of Cois Fharraige.

All animals can threaten the boundaries of the human psyche if not the body; for country folk, hares were particularly dubious beings. According to Mac Thuathaláin, the women of a booley on the hills of Formaol, near Casla, were sitting out on a hillock one day, knitting and sewing, when they saw a hare going to and fro among the cattle until it found one that had recently borne a calf and began to suck its milk. When they threw a stick at it, the hare ducked and let the stick go by, and then ran after it, picked it up and carried it off, which scared the women so much that they sent word home. Their menfolk came with hounds and hunted the hare unsuccessfully on several occasions; then they sent for Micíl Mag Cearra, the owner of the finest of hounds, but he called his hound off after he saw the hare escape it by leaping eight feet into the air. Some time later Mag Cearra was in County Clare searching for a little grey mare that had been stolen from him, when he was greeted by an old woman who mysteriously knew all about him and his business. She invited him in for a meal and reminded him of the hunt. 'You whistled off your hound,' she said, 'because you knew it wasn't a right hare. It was I that was there that day. When a year of want comes on me, I turn myself into a hare and go off into the country to fend for myself. And now, eat up your dinner while I fetch your little grey mare.' And with three jumps she was out of the door in the shape of a hare, and was back with the mare before he'd finished his meal.

The only bit of history I have heard about this booley at Scailp is that one night something black came up from the lake and made the dogs bark. Raftery, the blind, wandering versifier of south Galway, once composed some verses criticizing an old thorn-bush that had given him inadequate shelter from a storm, and in reply the bush recited to him the entire history of Ireland from the Deluge to the Battle of the Boyne. The wind-blasted tree of Scailp, which I'm told by an elderly shepherd, who himself never saw a leaf on it, was a holly, has not been so well placed as Raftery's roadside hawthorn to observe the cumulative disasters of history; all I hear from it when I place my ear against its naked timber is an amnesiac whimpering. The bog-lore I get from Roundstone people, and which I will lend to this tree, consists of stories that drift over Roundstone Bog like patches of mist, sometimes merging and becoming indistinguishable, sometimes fading into thin air for a time and then re-forming themselves out of nothing. 'As I sat down in Camden Town / I heard the ferocious voice of hounds' are the only lines of an old song to survive in the memory of an elderly turf-cutter I met once near the deserted village of Aircíní, by the river that forms the north-eastern boundary of the bog. Aircíní, he told me, was nicknamed Camden Town, and the song concerned a man on the run who called in for food at a cottage there. One of the two brothers who lived in the cottage was in the pay of the police, and when the fugi-tive saw him slipping out secretively he feared betrayal and took himself off into the bog. He hadn't gone far when he heard the tracker dogs, but he threw them off the scent by swimming out to an islet in a lake, and eventually he got out of the country. So much seems clear in the telling, but the time-setting is obscure. The lake is called Loch Reddington after this hunted man, said my turf-cutter. Now, old records tell me that a Patrick Reddington had a hedge school by Toombeola Bridge near Aircíní in the 1830s; was he the outlaw? But could Camden Town have been a familiar name to the villagers so long ago?

Such ghosts of stories perhaps transmute into stories of ghosts. Half-forgotten stories haunt the Halfway House, a ruined cottage by the one road that crosses the bog to Ballinaboy near Clifden. It is said that at some period before the Famine the brother and sister who lived there used to welcome in packmen going the lonely road to the fair at Ballinaboy, and murder them and throw their bodies in a lake. People still don't like to pass the place at night. I also hear of the seven-year-old girl of a family living in an isolated farmhouse near the far end of the Bog Road who saw her father's ghost crossing the bog once, before she even knew he was dead. The previous day he had collected a bucket of mussels as bait off the shore below Ardagh, in preparation for a fishing expedition, and when he looked at the mussels in the morning they were all open, which was unusual. But he ignored the sign and went off with his bucket across the bog to Murvey, five miles to the south, where he kept his currach in a cleft of the shore. That evening when the family were waiting for him to come home the little girl looked out of the window and saw the figure of a man a long way off in the bog, carrying a sack or net of fish on his back, as she had often seen her father returning from Murvey, and she said to her mother, 'You may put on the potatoes now; he's coming.' But her father never arrived at the house, and later his body was recovered near where he had been drowned, a mile out to sea off Murvey Rock.

Two of Tommy O'Donnell's stories involve members of his family who could cross the bog in incredibly short times; when I retell them to other Roundstone people they shake their heads and say, 'You may cross out those stories!' Tommy used to boast of an uncle of his who worked at Marconi's Telegraph Station, which was operative in the 1910s on the far corner of the bog near Ballinaboy. People crossing the bog from Roundstone would follow the Moot for the first part of the way, especially if it was misty. Tommy O'Donnell's uncle used to go that way to work, and according to Tommy he could leave home at six in the morning and be there by seven. (Tommy added that this uncle of his was the strongest of all the five hundred men working at Marconi's; he could lift six hundredweight 'and a bit with that'. He eventually went to America to lift weights. Once he was challenged to lift six hundredweight and hold it up. The next morning he was paralysed and couldn't even lift himself up in the bed. They brought him home to Roundstone, but he died soon after, at the age of twenty-four.) Another great bog-walker was Tommy's grandfather Mattie. He was an active man, said Tommy; he would never lay his foot on a gate but vault across it. He used to do odd jobs for the Franciscans in Roundstone, and he could mow all the grass within the monastery walls in four days, a job his son after him used to take eight days for, and his grandson, Tommy himself, three weeks. Once when Mattie was walking home to Roundstone from the fair at Clifden, Henry Robinson, the agent, came by in his pony-drawn side-car and offered him a lift. They took the Bog Road, and when they were passing the Halfway House O'Donnell said, 'Let me down here and I might get a hare.' Robinson was sceptical: 'How would you get a hare, without a dog or a gun?' he asked. O'Donnell replied, 'If I don't get him on the run I'll get him some other way.' 'Well,' said Robinson, 'if you meet me at Kelly's Bridge with a hare, I'll give you five shillings!' (Kelly's Bridge is where a stream off the bog goes under the coast road just north of Roundstone.) O'Donnell was eleven in family, and in those days five shillings would have made him a millionaire, as Tommy put it. So he went off into the bog, to a place where he knew a hare would be resting in its 'form', the hollow in the heather a hare makes to fit itself, and he came up very quietly and grabbed it. Then he carried it, kicking and roaring, held out in his two hands, across the bog to Kelly's Bridge. He reached the bridge just as Robinson came by on his side-car, which was fast walking, as Tommy said, even though Robinson had had to follow the road round the north-east corner of the bog. Robinson looked at him in amazement and said, 'That's not Mattie O'Donnell. It must be his ghost!' He was as good as his word, though, and the next time he called into his bank he got out the five shillings for Mattie.

The O'Donnells used to build their field walls with little gaps in them for the hares to get through, and hang snares in them. One day Tommy's father was up on the edge of the bog cutting sedge, and Tommy and the other children came up to see him. He'd just killed a hare he'd snared, and they wanted to take it home, but he wouldn't let them, and he brought it himself when he came home in the evening. Usually hares were not gutted until they were to be cooked, so they left it hanging by the legs on a bush by the house. But while they were having their tea they heard a thump, and when they looked out the hare was gone. This convinced them that the creatures are 'haunted', and never since have they eaten another hare.

Another of Tommy's hare stories concerned an old man who was caught by a terrible storm out on the bog while coming home from the workhouse at Clifden, went astray and died. Some say it was a woman crossing the bog from the Red Gate in Murvey on her way to Inis Ní who found his body, but Tommy used to claim that it was found by his grandfather Mattie O'Donnell, with the help of a hare. Mattie was out beyond Scailp looking for missing sheep when he saw this hare behaving oddly. Instead of running off when it saw him, it sat up and looked at him, and then lowered its head and pointed its ears at him. Then it went in under a rock. Mattie went to the place and looked in after it, and there in a little hollow was the corpse. The old man had wrapped himself in heather to keep warm. His body was very decayed; they had to bury him at the spot. Later on somebody brought out sacks of cement and sand on donkey-back, and made a slab to mark the grave. The place is still called Mícheál's Grave, or the Dead Man's Grave.

The arena of all these tales and many others lies before me when I lean against the tree at Scailp. The calm mosaic of land and reflected sky reaches away to a distant gleam of the Atlantic in the west, the foothills of the Twelve Pins, Connemara's mountain core, in a blue-grey withdrawal to the north, and Errisbeg Hill rearing up its dark, angry-looking peaks to the south. Under and around all, water feels its way to the sea. Roundstone Bog is a stage, in both senses: people enter it and exit again, and their time in it is an interval between two periods of social existence. They are solitaries, patches of mist, almost ghosts already. Old Mícheál's exhausted stumblings and baffled changes of direction end as a crawl into a hole. Even the shepherds of old times for whom the bog was a familiar workplace, who strode out vigorously and climbed on boulders to scan the levels, and shouted to each other, had to struggle with its distances. The bog is not for me an emblem of memory, but a network of precarious traverses, of lives swallowed up and forgotten. I plan to revisit every part of it and rescue all its stories, and write them into this book. But today it looks as if nothing and nobody had ever crossed it, apart from patches of sunlight picking their way from knoll to knoll, or the tremendous footprints of storm clouds rushing in from the west. Once again I turn back towards the village, bringing too much or too little from Scailp.

Dead Man's Grave and Halfway House

I could, I suppose, turn to my reference books and scientific offprints and write sensibly about Roundstone Bog, outlining its topography and hydrography, its archaeology and ecology, history of land-use and current problems of conservation. But I prefer to imagine walks across it, enmeshing the reader in its textures, letting the generalities emerge when the pressure of detail compels them. And so, once again, to Scailp. This time I follow the little road up from the harbour for only a hundred yards or so before turning right into Farrell's Road, the lane that climbs gently between meadows half-lost to whitethorn and furze bushes, with a few large new houses set back on the rising ground inland of it. The low drystone walls and ditches of the wayside are overgrown with fuchsia and willow and brambles; I know them foot by foot from blackberrying every autumn. Four hundred yards along on the left is a thicket topped by a storm-battered ash tree, and if one peers through the hedge one can just make out a shadowy squarish recess in the bank beyond, with some stonework showing in its sides. Here Farrell lived, a tailor; here he sat with his scissors, thimble and, instead of a tape measure, a bit of sheepskin, according to what I have been told of the work methods of Connemara tailors, who used to record the measurements of each client by holding up a straight edge of a sheepskin against him or her and marking off the lengths on it with little snips. When the garments were finished a strip would be cut off the sheepskin to leave a fresh edge for the next job. Similarly Time, the tailor of all things, snipped strips off Farrell's lifespan until nothing was left, and then off that of his house, and then off all remembrance of him or his house, of which I hereby salvage this one narrow strip.

Half a mile further on is a gate, from which the lane continues, unsurfaced now, across unfenced heath, with the rough slopes of

Letterdife Hill rising on the left. This is the commonage land pertaining to Letterdife, which means that the households of that townland each have the right to graze a certain number of beasts on it. Sheep, it seems, do not like to stray too far from where they are first put onto the 'mountain', and so the flanks of Letterdife Hill are dotted with the hardy little black-faced ewes of Connemara, whereas one sees few of them further out into the bogs beyond the hill. Sometimes there are a dozen or so heifers and young bullocks lying in the road or on little knolls close by it, enjoying the comparatively dry surface under them while chewing the cud. There may also be a statuesque group of Connemara ponies silhouetted on the skyline of the hill; left to run wild for their first two years, they will take off into the fastnesses of the bog if approached too closely.

Not far past the gate, the road crosses a shoulder of the hill and begins to descend towards its eventual meeting with the coast road. Just beyond its highest point, and a hundred yards up the hillside to the left, is a level patch of ground called Clochairín, which means a small stone structure or a stony place. Most of the stones have been carted off long ago for building fences, but one can make out the foundations of a one-roomed dwelling a bit more substantial than a booley hut, measuring about fifteen feet by eight inside, with traces of little enclosures nearby, and a ruinous sheep-pen built in the shelter of a rock outcrop. This, I am told, was the home of the Woods family, a sister and two brothers – one of whom, his descendants believe, was an itinerant pig-castrator – who came from east Galway to be shepherds for the Robinsons. Old maps show that the house was roofless by the 1890s, but if the Woods were still there in the 1880s they would have looked down at their master's mansion then being built, at the bottom of the slope to the east of them. At any period they would have had an endlessly interesting outlook over the branching waterways of Roundstone Bay, busy with turf boats and fishing boats working out of dozens of little creeks of its tangled coastline. Above and beyond all that, a vast unstable panorama of hills and skies, full of the sort of vision-like realities I have seen myself from that airy height. I remember, for instance, a kestrel facing into a southerly gale and effortlessly holding its place for a minute or two, and then turning to let itself be flung far away across the bog; a cirrus cloud like a cosmic feather lying across all the southern sky, and a raven measuring its length with slow wingbeats, slipping from bar to bar of it all the way from its territory up on Errisbeg until it was a dot over the hills of Carna; and, most spectacular of all, a rainbow, its interior filled with light and dark spokes radiating from the summit of Cashel Hill a few miles away across the bay. It took me some time to understand this last phenomenon, which I have never seen described. The sun at that moment was shining through a small gap in clouds behind me and casting shadows of their ragged edges into the mass of raindrops that was emptying itself onto Cashel; these shadows were of course parallel, having their geometric origin in the sun, and if I had looked at them to the south-west they would have appeared to diverge in the familiar fan shape, whereas in the north-east they were converging in vanishing perspective towards a point exactly opposite the sun, which was the centre of the rainbow's arc and also, by chance, the summit of the hill. In the past the shepherd's duties, one feels, included care for the minor arcana of the skies such as these; nowadays the farmer drives up the road and checks on his sheep through binoculars without getting out of the car, and drives down again, leaving cloud-herding to writers and artists.

From Clochairín the lane falls gently north-eastwards to its junction with the coast road at a place called the Sedge Gap; people cutting sedge for thatch on the hillside used to bring it down and stack it by the roadside here for collection. A few hundred yards before that point there is a turning off the lane to the left, running northwards over level bog. This is a turf-cutters' road; there are turf stacks beside it here and there, and the bog on either side is scored by turf banks old and new, so that the original ground surface is reduced to long narrow strips separating rectangular pits a yard or two deep, often waterlogged and difficult to negotiate. The vertical sides of these hollows are of dark-brown or blackish peat, patterned with the marks of the spades with which the turfs have been sliced off them. In summer thousands of white tufts of cotton-grass redeem the grimness of the terrain. There used to be one or two old cars, rusting away but not quite abandoned, on muddy tracks between these cuttings, that the turf-cutters would run for shelter in when heavy showers swept across the bog. It is worth diverting down one of these tracks that leads eastwards towards a long thin lake called Loch Caimín, from its shape, a *caimín* being a shepherd's crook. The squarish islet in the middle of this lake, about fifty feet across, has some rough drystone work to a height of four feet along its western and southern shoreline, the remains of a wall defending its landward side. There are twenty or so known crannogs or lake dwellings like this in Connemara, and they probably date from the Bronze Age or Iron Age. This one was first recorded by a geologist of fine general curiosity, G. H. Kinahan, in the *Proceedings of the Royal Society of Antiquarians of Ireland* for 1872. The role of the inhabitants of this island dwelling and of others like it, in the creation of the treeless wilderness all around them, I will write about later on.

Just over a mile from its beginning the turf road brings itself to an end with a little turning place for cars, as if the Caimín River just ahead of it were an insuperable obstacle. In fact the river, which delivers the outflow from Loch Caimín to a lake further into the bog to the west, can be jumped in places, but with care, as it has cut a deep, dark slot in the peat. Turning to follow this stream westwards, one is orienting oneself towards the unscathed heart of the bog and away from its cut-about fringes. Cnoc na gCorrbhéal lies a mile and a half to the south-west, with the taller hills near Roundstone half hidden behind it, but for a distance of over five miles ahead the land does not rise more than eighty feet above sea level. There are a hundred or more lakes in the twenty-five or thirty square miles of Roundstone Bog, most of them lying in rock-basins, the work of the glaciers that came down out of the mountains to the north and pushed across this region, dragging away most of its soil and loose stone, in the last Ice Age. This is what the geologists call knock-and-loughan topography, from the Irish words *cnoc*, hill, and *lochán*, lakelet. Hillocks

of bare rock stand out among acres of sodden sedgy ground; even
the more walkable stretches are a mosaic of heathery hummocks
and wet holes. It is an extreme environment, with very high rainfall and wind exposure, utterly treeless except on some lake islands
and with scarcely a bush apart from the occasional juniper clinging
as if in desperation to the lee side of a boulder, or a dwarfed holly
tucked into a sheltery niche of a lake shore.

To put this bog into the context of Irish bogs in general, one
first has to distinguish 'blanket bogs' from the 'raised bogs' of the
midland plains. The latter originated in overgrown fens in which
sphagnum moss could flourish and, over thousands of years, build
up deep deposits of sphagnum peat, which, being thicker in the
middle where the original lake was, give these bogs their characteristic slightly domed formation. Blanket bogs, on the other hand,
are draped over the land, moulding its contours like a blanket; in
Roundstone Bog, under the smooth soft surface and masking a
craggy underlay of rock, there may be anything from a few inches
to fifteen or more feet of peat, the detritus of thirty or forty centuries
of plant life compressed into a dense blackish material under its
own accumulated weight and preserved from decay by its own
acidity. Secondly there is a distinction, in terms of vegetation,
between mountain blanket bog, covering vast areas of high ground
throughout Ireland, and lowland or Atlantic blanket bog, found
principally in the rainy west of Galway and Mayo. Roundstone
Bog is the finest example of this last sort, and one of the few such
areas with a substantial core untouched by turf-cutting or forestry.
Its inlay of lakes makes it almost unique; certainly there is nothing
like it in Ireland, or nearer than the Outer Hebrides.

Looking into the distance on heading into the bog, one's first
impressions are of monotony and uniformity, but experience soon
undoes that, through the constant recalling of attention to what is
underfoot or immediately ahead by the difficulties of progress. The
most serious obstacles are the flat areas where water glints between
clumps of sedge; one is tempted to hop from tussock to tussock,
but is forced to backtrack when they become too far apart; then
one detours onto a hummocky area pitted with bog-holes and,

after struggling with that for a while, scrambles onto a promising-looking ridge of rock and heather, which turns out to be a promontory ending in more sedge swamp. All this can produce weariness and anxiety, but it is pure delight when the weather is good, the evenings are long and there is no need to hurry. Sometimes I come back from such a walk with my head so empty it seems not a single thought or observation has passed through it all day, and I feel I have truly seen things as they are when I'm not there to see them.

I have never met anyone out here, in dozens of expeditions, but I have occasionally persuaded friends to join me so that I might revivify my apprehensions of the place through their reactions to it. Thus I have appreciated the company of the sheep farmer who will note with disapproval the fox slinking off round the shoulder of a hill, and who will assure me that if a fog should creep up on us his dog would be able to lead us home; of the poet who will bring back like a sprig of heather some epiphany of wilderness and grow it into a poem; of the ornithologist who can alert me to the merlin's low, swift-vanishing flight towards its nesting place on one of the lake islands; even of the entomologist who might point out some small horror: a long-legged, shiny black ground-beetle voraciously hollowing out the fat abdomen of a still-fluttering goat moth. But to be alone out here is my delight too. As a precaution nowadays I bring a mobile phone – it would not do to break an ankle in this fastness – and then it is a sweet pleasure occasionally to surprise my partner, M, busy in our garden or the studio back in the village, with a call – about nothing, about everything – out of this vast space brimming with changeable light and pristine breezes and murmurous silences.

But when the wildflowers are in bloom on every variety of surface from wet-shiny black peat to grey lichen-covered rock, one feels the need of an ecologically inclined botanist to make sense of the chaos of visual impressions. Each of these different terrains is the habitat of a relatively well-defined type of vegetation, a community of several species of plants with its individual ecological preferences. Scientists have drawn up elaborate classifications of such 'plant associations', as I shall explain later in this book; the categories of their systems reflect as abstractions modalities of one's hands-and-knees-on experience of such a landscape as Roundstone Bog, but their lumbering terminology is not spry enough for the present context. However, in informally introducing some of the main participants in the biotic dance, I am following in the footsteps of such scientists. I will start with the drier and work towards the wetter environments.

First, on the better-drained slopes of hills such as Errisbeg and Cnoc na gCorrbhéal, the sumptuous purple-and-gold patchwork of bell heather and the low-growing western gorse – one might think the two plants had chosen each other for musical reasons, their colours sing together so bravely. In Connemara and south Mayo a lovely local addition to this widespread community is St Dabeoc's heath, with rosy bells half an inch long nodding on thin, weak branches that often straggle up through its supportive neighbours. This is one of four rare heaths found in Roundstone Bog whose principal populations are in Spain, Portugal or France, and how they come to be flourishing in this almost tundra-like terrain is much debated. Moving on to the bog itself, a dominating feature of large areas is the tall purple moor grass; *fiontarnach* is the Irish word for it in its spectacular autumn decay, when its blond (*fionn*) colouration together with the reddish-brown of bracken and the dusky purple of bare bog-myrtle twigs gives the mountain land the appearance of luxurious furs piled up in gigantic ostentation. In winter, leaves of purple moor grass are torn away by the wind and sent streaming over the land, catching and accumulating in wire fences to such an extent that a gale will drag them down. Various sedges, tawny, amber and rufous – language is inadequate to their subtle and changeable tints – occur in profusion, including the so-called black bog-rush, a constant signatory of Atlantic blanket bog, recognized by the little tuft of blackish flowers near the top of its slender stem; acres of wet peat are covered in it. Hare's tail cotton-grass, another sedge, with its single flowerhead like a tuft of cotton, and common cotton-grass with its three or four flowerheads, turn parts of the bog into a wind-stirred sea of white in late summer.

Two heathers are particularly widespread: cross-leaved heath, so called because its leaves are arranged in whorls of four and form little crosses, and ling, *Calluna vulgaris* (I give the scientific name since the common names of this and *Erica cinerea*, bell heather, are hopelessly variable from book to book). Bog myrtle often occurs in similar areas, a wizened-looking shrub only two or three feet high – folklore says it was once a tree, until its wood was used in the making of the Cross and a curse was placed on it; nevertheless it is not wholly accursed, for the shepherds used to rub its aromatic leaves on their faces to repel the midges that on heavy days torment man and beast. Among the many flowers of the Atlantic boglands, the bright yellow stars of bog asphodel, a small lily, look too refined and delicate for this rough world of wind and rain. Tormentil, its four yellow petals as neatly symmetrical as those of a heraldic rose, and the bright blue flowers of heath milkwort show as sparks of colour among the heather stems. The reddish-pink blossoms of lousewort will attract a continental botanist's attention, for this little plant used to be common throughout Europe but has lost ground as the wild bee that pollinates it has become rarer, so that it is now a noted feature of Ireland's mountainy land. It is parasitic, its rootlets penetrating those of heathers and stealing their juices, a response to the problem of living in a place where several feet of impermeable peat seal off the nutrient supply from the rocks below. Another solution to the scarcity of nutrients is that of the carnivorous plants, such as the butterworts and sundews with their flat, sticky leaves that curl up and close like fists upon midges and suchlike morsels that alight on them. In bog-holes and lake margins grow the most extraordinary of the little killing machines of the bog: bladderworts, rootless aquatic plants that look like scraps of moss. On their leaves are tiny transparent bladders closed by valve-like flaps. These bladders can expel water through their skin, forming a partial vacuum inside; when some little pond-creature comes along, attracted by an exudation of sugar on the outside of the flap, and touches a bristle there, the trap springs open, the bladder expands and the victim is sucked in, all in a hundredth of a second.

Every year I relearn the names of some of the mosses and liverworts of the bog, and forget them again. But I do remember the smooth, glossy black hummocks of *Campylopus atrovirens*, having heard student botanists rather unfeelingly call it 'drowned dog moss'. *Pleurozia purpurea*, a liverwort, is unforgettable too; it looks like masses of deep-red worms. These two plants, together with black bog-rush, are in fact the characteristic species of typical Atlantic blanket bog. Other species serve the scientists as discriminating features of plant communities restricted to more particular ecological niches. In sloping areas where there is water flowing in runnels or moving through the upper layers of the peat, and in the depressions of hummock-hollow systems, particular sedges and rushes occur, while others prefer places where water is flowing on the surface, or where there has been regular grazing. Bog sedge, carnation sedge, bulbous rush – they may be distinguishable only by an expert, but, unnoticed, they add their characteristic textures and colours to the understated variousness underfoot. The white beak-sedge, however, cannot be missed: its pale, tan-coloured flowerheads, like little stars borne on slender grass-like foot-high stalks, form a floating layer above flat acres of the very wettest of bog, across which one advances like a walker-on-water of imperfect faith, swaying as the surface quakes and threatens to give beneath one's weight, and from which one staggers onto firmer ground with relief. This sedge is a staple of the diet of the Greenland white-fronted geese that formerly wintered in Roundstone Bog, and perhaps still do in small numbers, finding territory here not too different from their natal tundra. National Park rangers, who keep note of where these rare and reclusive birds feed, tell me they learn first to recognize the birds themselves, then their grey-white tubular droppings, and then the sedge that they have twitched out of the ground to get at its succulent bulbils. Wildfowlers too know these signs, I fear.

Sphagnum moss, through its peculiar structure and chemistry, is constantly at work, or at play, in the slow self-inhumation and self-resurrection of the bog. Its leaves are partly composed of large cells that fill with water through their pores, so that the plant acts like a sponge; also it can secrete organic acids into the surrounding water in exchange for potassium, magnesium and calcium, the nutrients it needs. These two properties allow the plant to grow above the water table, because it drags the bog-water up with it, recreating the acidic, waterlogged, nutrient-poor habitat it is adapted to. There are many species of sphagnum, each favouring its own range of wetness; some are usually completely submerged in bog-pools, with others growing on them to form islands; further species colonize these islands and grow into relatively dry hummocks, which may be invaded by sedges and heathers and purple moor grass. So from year to decade the wet becomes dry, and, since the rainwater has to go somewhere, the dry becomes wet; the microgeography of the bog is a flux, too slow for the human eye but continually rearranging its intricate textures and colours.

Such are the more striking plants of Roundstone Bog; books and papers on them and on a hundred other species, not to mention innumerable lichens, single-celled algae and other dots of life, are piled on my table. And then one comes to the lakes, which offer another suite of habitats, each with its own plant associations, its specific floral mix, as recognizable as a family face. If I follow the Caimín River westwards for a quarter of a mile I come to the first large lake, Loch na bhFaoileann (the anglicized form Lough Wheelan gives a rough idea of the pronunciation), meaning the lake of the seagulls. This lake is all arms; the river flows into one of its northern ones, and the eastern one will force a detour on me so that I will have walked a mile by the time I reach the end of its western arm. (What fantastical shapes these lakes have! Their complex angularity, even on a map, is in extreme contrast to the flowing curves of contour lines, and when one reflects that lake margins are themselves actual contours as measured with drop-by-drop accuracy by water level, one realizes what smooth liars maps are in their representation of relief.) Like many of the larger lakes this one has many islands, most of them thickly covered in shrubs and even trees. But the first island I pass is not wooded; it comes to within a shallow yard or two of the main-land, and its name, Oileán na nUan or Lamb Island, together with a trace of a wall across its nearest point, suggests that it has been used for penning ewes in the lambing season. So, it is the exclu-sion of sheep and cattle and goats that has allowed these little woods to form on the other islands – an observation in its turn suggesting that all the drier parts of the bog, and especially its rocky knolls, would look like this if it were not for their long history of grazing. The islands, then, are a glimpse into some distant past of the bog. Their vegetation has been described by David Webb, in his day Ireland's leading botanist and part-author of the standard work on the flora of Connemara, and his colleague E. V. Glanville; their paper, though scrupulously scientific, betrays the excitement of setting foot in *terra nova*:

The first point to be emphasized is that the island vegetation is completely untouched by man, and almost completely by animals; this produces a fascinating and unfamiliar atmosphere of primeval jungle . . . The wood-land zone . . . is of the greatest interest. One has only to penetrate into it for a yard or two to realize how much it differs from the majority of 'natural' woods on the mainland. Here on the islands seedling trees are abundant on every side, and at almost every step one's foot crunches through rotting, moss-covered branches to the deep layers of humus below . . .

Webb and Glanville looked at lake islands in central Connemara, as well as some in Roundstone Bog, finding a total of 39 woody species and 132 herbs. In general the lake islands have a zone of heath on the windward, western side, grading eastwards into wood-land, the whole sculpted by wind into a single dome. On the Roundstone Bog islands the most frequent tree is rowan. Other commonly occurring ones are birch (of the downy variety, *Betula pubescens*), holly, yew and common sallow, which often leans out over the water on the lee shore. There are sometimes a few hawthorns on the outskirts of the wood, and an occasional sessile oak. Bramble and broad buckler fern grow in the deep shade, another fern, common polypody, on branches and rocks, ivy and honeysuckle twine everywhere, and bilberry is abundant in the less shady parts. Around the exposed western rims of the heathy side one finds dwarf juniper, creeping willow and bog myrtle. Such was the normal state of vegetation, but on two islands in Loch na bhFaoileann Webb and Glanville found that the presence of large numbers of cormorants during the early summer was causing an ecological disaster:

About 150 pairs at present nest on the larger island investigated (Crow Island). The other (Big Island) was formerly used as a nesting-ground but has recently been abandoned; it is much visited, however, by the birds for feeding. Both islands present an extraordinary scene of disorder and desolation. Nearly all the trees have been killed by the corrosive effect of the birds' droppings, and only their dead and slowly rotting skeletons persist. Most of the ground is covered by a coarse scrub of gorse and brambles, by bracken, or by rank herbs; on the areas most constantly occupied by the birds the peaty soil is largely bare, with a partial cover of weeds, seedlings and trampled grass. Everywhere there are thick deposits of fresh guano, rotting fish, dead young birds, eggshells and the remains of crabs and molluscs. Finally on the central ridge of Crow Island is the extraordinary array of nests, which are columnar structures 30 cm. high, made of stems of Ling, Reed Grass and Bramble, fronds of Bracken, and leaves of Woodrush.

'Coarse scrub', 'rank herbs', 'weeds' – such emotive language is rare in botanical texts. But not all humans were as disapproving of this destruction of Eden as the botanists: I am told that farmers from Inis Ní used to dig out the guano and bring it home, presumably by donkey, for use as fertilizer. However, about ten years after the above account was written (in 1961), the local anglers' association decided that the cormorants were damaging the brown-trout fishing for which the Roundstone Bog lakes are well known, and put a bounty on their heads; so people started blasting away at them with shotguns, and the birds shifted to another island a mile deeper into the bog to the north-west, in Loch Scainimh (where they flourish, and in the opinion of our champion Roundstone angler Joe Creane are actually improving the fishery through the nutriment they bring into it from the shore — whereas the Loch na bhFaoileann trout have declined in quality). When I first visited the lake, in the 1980s, the Loch na bhFaoileann islands were still blasted and haggard; now Big Island is verdant, but with one or two dead trees raising their heads above the newer growth like stags alerted, while Crow Island looks like parkland with shrubs and rowan trees scattered over a smooth green sward, answering well to its Irish name, An tOileán Glas, the green island.

A hundred yards or so of drainage channel links the south-western arm of Loch na bhFaoileann to the next lake, which looks rather different from it even on a map, having more rounded outlines. The reason is soon apparent: unlike the last with its stony banks, this lake is set into a level area of deep bog and has a rim of soft peat like a little cliff a foot or so high (depending on the water level) all around it, and so far as I can see its bottom is of peat too. The anglicized map-name of this lake is Lough Doolagh, and John King, my Roundstone guide to this area, tells me the land along its southern shore is called Dúlach; the word is not in the dictionaries but if it were, it would mean 'black place'; so I deduce that the proper (i.e. original Irish) name of the lake is Loch Dúlach, or, if it is more fussy about its own grammar than is many a placename, Loch an Dúlaigh. It is not fished: trout from black-bottomed lakes, or even from the peaty parts of otherwise stony-bottomed lakes, are poor malnourished things, 'smutty' in skin colour and pallid of flesh, says Joe Creane.

Stand at the right point in Dúlach — about a hundred paces from the eastern end of the lake — and you suddenly catch sight of the last section of the Moot, an almost healed dark scar in the land, running straight up from the lake shore to the summit of Cnoc na gCorrbhéal half a mile away. But I prefer not to follow it and then have to scramble down the far side of the hill; instead I work my way around its northern fringes, keeping close to the shore of Loch Dúlach and then along the drain connecting it to yet another lake, locally called the Dry Lake because part of it is overgrown with reeds, and officially known as Kerryhill Lake – an unaccountable name, until one realizes that 'Kerryhill' was probably the surveyors' attempt at *corrbhéal*, whatever that means, which in its turn must have been the name of the locality comprising both the hill and the lake.

From here I turn my back on the wide, level loneliness stretching away beyond these lakes, and follow the lower reaches of the hillside round towards Scailp, only half a mile away to the south. But I am not destined to reach it this time, for just fifty yards or so from the shore of the Dry Lake I arrive at another magnetic pole of the bog, one so seldom visited and so often referred to by Roundstone people as an almost fabulously distant and hard-to-find place that I begin to associate it with Childe Roland's Dark Tower itself: Mícheál's Grave. 'Did you ever see Mícheál's Grave?' was the usual response in the village whenever I mentioned that I'd been exploring the bog, and for a long time the answer was 'No', despite the detailed and contradictory directions I'd been given to it by various men too old to guide me there themselves. Eventually I asked a farmer who I knew occasionally went that way looking for strayed sheep to mark it for me with a little cairn; the next time I was out there I spotted a pile of a few stones on top of a boulder, and near it found the rough nameless concrete slab that had been made on the spot, and, a few yards to the south-west, the hole under a rock the old man had crawled into to shelter from the storm and in which he died. He was an Ó Dónaill from Ervallagh, a cluster of cottages by a little harbour just west of Roundstone village, and his misadventure probably occurred around the end of the nineteenth century. The story goes that a hare directed a passing shepherd to the hole the old man's corpse was eventually found in, as I have told. Also I hear that some American relatives of his arranged for a proper tombstone to be cut and delivered to Roundstone, where it lay on the quayside for a long time, but it was never brought out to the grave – not surprisingly, if it was one of the massive Aran limestone slabs favoured at that period, which would have been impossible to carry so far – and it is now probably lying in the mud of the harbour bottom. Mícheál, one hopes, died in his sleep, tucked up in warm heather, while the storm raved and convulsed outside. As a fisherman and farmer of those days he would have been inured to cold, to wet clothes, to long days on little food. That he was coming from the workhouse means that he had been reduced to penury in his old age. Perhaps all he had to leave was his name, which he bestowed on the spot, the acre or two of rugged heath between the lake and the bottom of the hill being generally known as Mícheál's Grave. But just as often it is called simply the Dead Man's Grave, as if the utter solitude of that particular death was a reflection into local anecdotal history of a universal principle regarding all our futures: for each one of us, there will be just one death, that of the self, which is not necessarily more to be feared or lamented than deaths of loved ones, or of the irreplaceable great, but uniquely inconceivable, a metaphysical darkness as incomprehensible as the light of consciousness it extinguishes.

Where do I go from here, this mental dead end? The way back to Roundstone by Scailp and southwards over the hills seems suddenly too long and arduous; to the east and north and west the bog is for the moment directionless. As bog-water gropes and puzzles, sensing no outlet, and settles for stillness, so the will flags. If a hare were to appear, watching over me, suggesting the way with its ears . . . Instead, a cormorant comes arrowing overhead, its target Loch Scainimh a mile to the north. Every spring when we see them from our sea-windows in Roundstone, heavy-looking angular black birds with, in the breeding season, a badge of white on the thigh, hurtling up the bay at a height of a hundred feet or so, with rapid decisive wingbeats and long necks urgently outstretched, we know that this is where they are heading. I will follow nature's signpost, more commanding than any sense of purpose, deeper into the bog.

To get to the cormorant's lake from Mícheál's Grave one has to cross the very heart of the bog, a seldom-visited labyrinth of

flat wetland and lakes called Tulach Lomáin Mór, a name that
used to puzzle me. John O'Donovan, the Irish scholar who was
in charge of the collection and anglicization of placenames for
the Ordnance Survey of 1839, opined that this meant 'Lomond's
Big Hill', but of course there is no big hill here. However, when
the sheep farmer John King and I were sitting near Mícheál's
Grave once, he pointed out a rocky knoll a few hundred yards
beyond the Dry Lake and said, 'That's Tulach Lomáin!' – and all
became clear, for on the nearer face of the knoll was a rather
striking bare outcrop (a *lomán* in Irish), providing the only landmark in this exceptionally featureless terrain. A *tulach* is a hillock,
not a hill; and the area has at some stage been divided into two
townlands, one big (*mór*) and the other small (*beag*). (O'Donovan
would not have set eyes on the place; while he visited Connemara's
ancient churches, its uncouth soaking deserts didn't tempt him
into long excursions, and he did his etymology by the fireside in
a Clifden hotel or in his friend James Hardiman's library in Galway,
on the basis of notes taken by the 'sappers' in the field.)

Once past the hillock one skirts around Loch na Súdairí (a
name that recurs three times in the bog; the lake of the leaches,
perhaps, or of the swamp-holes; something deriving from *sú*,
suction or absorption, for certain), and then the little domed
woods of islands in Loch Scainimh appear a quarter of a mile
ahead, well before one gets a glimpse of the lake itself. This is the
largest of the Roundstone lakes, being a mile long and three or
four hundred yards wide in most places. The name, anglicized as
Lough Skannive, means 'gravel lake' and refers to its stony bottom.
The cormorants' island is pale with excrement, the skeletal trees
heavy with nests. In the breeding season the birds – two or three
hundred of them – stand around on the rocks with hardly room
to stretch their black-umbrella wings; when they all take off at
once they sound like the wind. In winter there are small groups
of whooper swans on these central lakes, sailing slowly to and fro
as if in a trance. I have never seen an otter out here – they are
more frequent, or perhaps just more easily seen, on the seashore
– but I have occasionally noticed an otter-run, a groove a few

inches wide worn into the grass. People think that sea-otters and land-otters are separate species, but that is not so; they come and go between bogland and coastline via stream-beds and culverts. Sheep also make their own paths, trekking to and fro in single file, but these are wider and lead from dry patch to dry patch or to the crossing place between lakes, whereas the otter-runs go as straight as possible from lake to lake. One could map these overlapping networks of trails and use them as guides in the flat parts of the bog where the lakes are not visible until one is close to them, or at least have them as a reassurance that life finds its ways and establishes its customs even in this wilderness.

To extract oneself from Tulach Lomáin it is probably easiest to make for the one road that crosses the bog, just over a mile to the north; I could probably find my way round either end, east or west, of Loch Scainimh, but by going eastwards I keep to slightly more familiar territory. The lake sprawls and ramifies and is surrounded by smaller lakes, but one can pick one's way through all its complexities to a short length of stream linking it to the long, narrow, north-western extension, like a skeletal arm, of Loch na bhFaoileann. In this stream there are a few stepping stones, put in position by the shepherds no doubt, but so long ago that they look like a random effect of time. The name of the place, as I wrote it down from one of the few Roundstone men who would ever visit it, is Casheldrine. Nothing in the vicinity suggests a cashel, so I understand the first part of the name to be *casla* or *cuisle*, a narrow water-channel. The last part could well be from *draighean*, a blackthorn; if so, the name is Casla an Draighin, the watercourse of the blackthorn. It is one of a handful of keys to crossing the bog; if you miss it you will have to walk an extra mile or two around one or other of the lakes linked by the stream. If Mícheál, coming from the north on his way home from the Clifden workhouse, intended to cross here but missed the place in the murk of a gathering storm and turned to his right along the lake shore, he would have entered a many-forked tongue of land, and by the time he had found his way back to where he went wrong he would have been exhausted. From here I can hop and splash and trudge on northwards, past lakes nameless on the maps or whose map-names are only dubiously confirmed by local people, very few of whom would ever have seen them. Two contrasting images from this vague terrain come back to me as I write: in I-forget-which lake, tens – perhaps hundreds – of thousands of tiny black whirligig beetles seething up through the sunlit water to cavort on the surface in such density as to propagate little squalls of life across it, and the skeleton of a horse reclining like an antique warrior on his tumulus while surveying the emptiness through empty eye sockets; I tried to photograph it, but later found that my camera had been empty of film.

The goal of this traverse is a low ridge, along which the Bog Road makes its way, and which rises to two eminences, Na Creagaí Móra, the big crags, to the south-east, and Na Creagaí Beaga, the small crags, to the north-west. At 201 and 150 feet respectively, these are mountains after the day's level going. Arbitrarily, I will make for the first-named, and scramble up the steep twenty-foot scarp of its southern aspect. Na Creagaí Móra form a rough little plateau covered in shin-high bushes of the cross-leaved heath, *Erica tetralix*, a common heather that is immediately distinguishable from the other heathers by its flowers, which grow in a little bundle at the end of its stems rather than spread out along the stems. But no! On closer examination the heather on the plateau, or some of it, is not quite the same as that familiar species; its needle-like leaves are arranged in whorls of four, as in the cross-leaved, but the whorls are set closer together and the leaves stand out more nearly at right angles to the stem. With a lens one can also see that the sepals in this heather are hairless except on their margins, whereas in the cross-leaved heath they are covered in woolly hairs. Are these differences, which only a heather-fancier would notice, enough to make it a separate species? (They certainly were enough to cause a mighty row in Connemara in the 1980s, when the presence of this rarity on the north-western corner of Roundstone Bog, near Clifden, became an argument against the proposal to build an airport there – but that is a story I have told in another book.) This heather, *Erica mackaiana* or Mackay's heath, was unknown to science until it was discovered almost simultaneously in the summer of 1835 in northern Spain and here on Na Creagaí Móra. It is now known to occur sporadically in Roundstone Bog from Loch Roisín na Róige to Ardbear near Clifden; there is also a small colony near Carna, and one in Donegal, but otherwise it is virtually confined to the Spanish province of Asturias. Its Irish discoverer was a young Roundstone man out gathering litter for his father's cattle. His life story is intriguing, and sadly brief.

William McAlla was born in 1814, the son of a Scottish soldier who after service in the Peninsular War had retired to Roundstone to keep an inn. A patron of McAlla's later wrote: 'The old man is so addicted to drinking that his house must be a very unhappy one. The son is in this respect the complete contrast of his father and never tastes any kind of liquor.' This exemplary youth was still at school, destined for a career as a teacher, when James Mackay of Trinity College, Dublin, made his discovery of the Mediterranean heath on the hill behind the village in 1830. It is likely that Mackay was staying at his father's inn, as would have other botanical visitors to the district, which was already well known for its St Dabeoc's heath and other rarities, and young McAlla soon became an enthusiast and a guide to these local specialities. In 1835 a Cambridge botanist, Charles Babington, visited Roundstone; McAlla, he recorded in his diary, 'took us to the station of *Erica mediterranea* in Glan Iska on Urrisbeg mountain', and the next day they 'crossed the bogs for two or three miles to Graigha Moire [an attempt to spell the name of the hill in English phonetics] on which he showed us a new heath nearly allied to *Erica tetralix*'. McAlla sent specimens of it to Mackay, who forwarded them to that keystone of the botanic hierarchy, Sir William Hooker of the Botanic Gardens at Kew, informing him that its discoverer 'promises to be a useful person in the country. He is now in Dublin and I intend to give him my assistance in the prosecution of the study of botany.' Hooker soon realized that this was the same plant as had just been found in Spain. It was Babington who named the new species, rather confusingly, *Erica mackaiana*, Mackay's heath, after McAlla's new patron and discoverer of the Mediterranean heath, *Erica mediterranea* (now known as *Erica erigena*).

In the following year McAlla was employed by the Ordnance Survey, which was covering Connemara at the time and (in those intellectually omnivorous days) was interesting itself in botany, but he was dismissed after seven months under a cloud, apparently for having given away some specimens to Babington. Thereafter he made a little money by supplying specimens to Professor John Scouler for the museum of the Royal Dublin Society, and then, ambitiously, he wrote to Sir William Hooker at Kew, informing him that he intended to go out to New Zealand to collect plants, adding that, 'I have made no arrangements with regard to how I am to be provided with funds when out.' Hooker made enquiries of his colleagues in Ireland about McAlla, with satisfactory results, and soon agreed to pay the would-be discoverer for new plants, at the going rate of £2 per hundred species. By October 1841 McAlla was in Dublin, but that was as near as he ever got to New Zealand. Scouler, who had probably initiated the idea of the expedition and had raised £50 to outfit him, was annoyed to find that McAlla was collecting seaweeds for another botanist and had caught a feverish cold from being constantly wet. Sailings to New Zealand were infrequent, and McAlla showed no signs of preparing himself; nevertheless, Scouler continued to plan for his departure, though now he had to warn Hooker that in financial matters he had no faith in 'this wild man I have caught in Cunnemara . . . although perfectly honest he is far too simple and from his ignorance of business habits apt to be imposed on . . .' But Scouler finally gave up and withdrew his support:

His incorrigible habits of procrastination and his cowardice . . . have worn out my patience. He made it a point to do nothing today which could be deferred until tomorrow and to do nothing for himself while there was a chance of someone else doing it for him. I am sorry for it for with all his faults he is the most general naturalist and algologist in this place and also of a literary and philosophical turn of mind. In a letter I had from him a few days since he candidly acknowledged that I am justified in the step I have taken and thanked me for all I had done for him and promised to repay the money I had advanced for him.

McAlla came home and continued his botanizing, selling sets of specimens to visitors and publishing a two-volume collection of pressed specimens of seaweeds, *Algae Hibernicae*, in 1845 and 1848. In 1849, aged thirty-five, he was carried off by the cholera epidemic which swept the region in the aftermath of the Famine. His tombstone is in a little field, formerly the Presbyterian grave-yard, by the lane running inland from Roundstone harbour.

There is one other episode in McAlla's history that concerns the Creagaí area (I am being deliberately vague about the locality): the identification of yet another heather, the rarest of them all. One small and constantly threatened patch of the Dorset heath, *Erica ciliaris*, grows uncomfortably near the side of the road – uncomfortably because of the dangers to the plant, and also for any certainty as to its status. This is the only place it is known in Ireland; in England it is found very sparingly in a few places in the south-west, but it is principally a Pyrenean plant. A Thomas Bergin came across it here in 1846, and McAlla confirmed his identification of it. Mackay was informed, but did not publish the find until 1859. Another visitor claimed to have seen the plant in 1852, but later could not find the spot, and Babington and others searched in vain and came to suspect a misidentification, or even an 'imposition', perhaps on the part of the 'wild man' of Connemara botany. But in 1965 the plant came to light again: David Webb was told by one of his students of a 'very large *Erica mackaiana*', visited the spot, and found that the unusual heather was in fact *Erica ciliaris*. Wide searches in the vicinity have not turned up any other specimens of it. Whether this present patch is the one last seen over a century earlier is debatable since the records are rather ambiguous as to location, but most researchers think that it is. Unlike the Mediterranean heath, the Dorset heath is known to have occurred in Ireland in prehistoric times; its fossilized pollen grains, together with those of Mackay's and St Dabeoc's heaths, have been identified in peat deposits dating from a warm period between Ice Ages some 220,000 years ago. Probably the patch near Na Creagaí is its last stand. How strange, then, that this one known occurrence of it is by the road! But, if it had not been by the road, how would it ever have been noticed in the twenty-five square miles of the bog? McAlla might well have been in correspondence with English plant-collectors with access to specimens of *Erica ciliaris*; could Babington have been right in suspecting fraud? Does the guilty shade of Roundstone's great botanist haunt the crags, planting heather in the night?

From Na Creagaí Móra north-westwards to Na Creagaí Beaga is a mile of the Bog Road. These 'small crags' rise from the shores of Loch Dhoire Chunlaigh, or Derrycunlagh Lough, below the road, to the south. Doire Chunlaigh, meaning 'the wood or thicket of moss', or possibly 'of stubble', is the name of a townland of over two thousand acres, nearly all bog, but more particularly of a patch that was once cultivated, a few little fields tilted to catch the best of the sun on the slope from the lake shore up to the road and the ruins of a deserted herd's cottage beside it to the north. The cottage is roofless, and its gables and broken-down side walls have been rejigged with the aid of old timbers and broken iron gates into a makeshift cattle-pen. This was the notorious Teach Leath-Bhealaigh, the Halfway House, whose occupants are said to have committed many murders at some period before the Famine. They worked in conjunction with a robber called Liam Dearg (Red Liam) who lived on an island in another lake, still known from him as Loch an Ghadaí, the lake of the thief, a mile further along the road to the north-west. Here is a scrap of *seanchas* or traditional lore taken down from an Irish-speaker in the Carna area in the 1920s or 1930s:

It was on this island [in Loch an Ghadaí] that Liam Dearg, the thief, used to live, and he had a small boat to come in and out. He used to watch the road until he'd see someone coming alone from Clifden or going there. If he failed to get a hold of someone going west he would get a hold of them going east, and he would take their money from them or the goods that they had bought. At that time no respectable woman would go that way without two or three people to accompany her, for fear of Liam Dearg.

Another Carna man, recorded at the same period, told how Liam Dearg met his death:

There were two thieves outside Clifden. Liam Dearg was one of the Mannions, and Seán na gCannaí [Seán of the cans] was of the [?] Lowry family. There was another man, of the Conneely clan, nearby. He was related by marriage to Seán na gCannaí. Conneely had a daughter, a little girl. One evening Liam Dearg and Seán na gCannaí had a large sum of money on the table. The little girl of Conneely's was in the room but they didn't notice her. When there was a big heap laid out for Liam Dearg and a big heap for Seán na gCannaí, Seán got up from the table and got a beetle [a wooden paddle for beating washing]. He came up on Liam Dearg from behind and killed him with a single blow of the beetle. Then he put him under the bed, and he and his wife buried him that night.

The little girl went home to her father and mother's house. She stayed at home that evening. The next day a priest was to come to hear confessions. 'I won't go there again,' says the little girl, 'until I go to confession with that priest.' The little girl went to confession with the priest and told him all that she had seen, and that her parents wanted to send her to Seán na gCannaí's house. When the Mass was over the priest spoke to Conneely and told him not to send his daughter to Seán na gCannaí's house any more. She didn't go there again.

'You're as bad as Liam Dearg' was a saying people had, that they'd say to a contrary person.

The legend of the Halfway House became well known through the writings of a James Berry, who was born near Louisburgh in 1842, settled in Carna as a farmer and died there in 1914. He used to publish a column based on stories picked up locally, spiced with a deal of bombast and Irishry, in the *Mayo News*, and these were collected into a book, *Tales of the West of Ireland*, in 1966. The title of his version of the matter is 'The Horrors of the Half-Way House':

In the centre of the moor there was a hillock on which there stood a house, nor was there any other house near it within a radius of five miles. This was Derryconly, the home of Anna More or Anna Connelly, who defeated the Claddagh fishwives in Dick Martin's election fight in Galway. Here she lived with her sister, Kathsha. In crossing the vast moor, this house was a landmark, for there was no road through the region in those days. In wintertime, of course, many peddlers and others asked for lodging in this house, where they were received cheerfully.

But any person who ever entered that house never left it alive, for the inhabitants murdered them at midnight. This terrible havoc continued until the inhabitants of that house of horror were far advanced in years. One evening, a peddler asked for lodgings, and was, as usual, cheerfully received. He seemed to be wealthy, so they murdered him and found that he had a large sum in gold and silver. In dividing the money they quarrelled, and the two sisters and a brother named Columb (called More-na-Irka, big Columb with the horn, for he had a lump on his skull as large as an inflated bladder) killed another brother, the arch murderer, Breen Dharag. Then they bound his corpse with straw ropes to which they attached heavy stones, and cast it into the lake, which lay just beside the gable.

The following summer, when the lake's level was lowered in hot weather, some little boys and girls were tending cattle when they saw something white at the lake's margin. They imagined it might be a large fish or a dead swan, so with the inquisitiveness of youth they went to investigate, and were horrified to see that it was the corpse of a man. They hurried home to tell their parents, who went to Mr. Martin. Yeomen were sent out, and they were greatly astonished to find that the corpse was that of Breen, the red murderer. They arrested Big Anna, Kathsha and Columb, who were taken to Galway, where they were hanged some time later.

I have collected a few more details and variants of what passes for tradition (nowadays a mixture of half-forgotten oral lore and half-remembered reading matter) about these killings, such as that Liam Dearg had a wooden raft and used to drag the corpses of his victims onto it and dispose of them in his lake (not in Loch Dhoire Chunlaigh, the lake nearest to the Halfway House); also that the children saw many skeletons in the lake. One old man I spoke to, well regarded as a storehouse of memory, believed that the rich man who was murdered came by on a bicycle, which seemed to jerk the whole scenario nearer to our own times by a century or so – until it turned out that this picturesque detail was due to a misunderstanding of the word 'peddler' in Barry's book.

It sounds to me as if there might be a scrap of history in all this, rattling around like a coin in an empty can. The Mr Martin whom Barry mentions would be Thomas Martin of nearby Ballynahinch, landlord of two-thirds of Connemara in the years leading up to the Famine of the 1840s. There might be old records from Galway Gaol or leases in archives of the Martin estate that could throw a glimmer of light on the faces of those who lived and died here. Or it may all be a dark absurdity, words put together to conjure up all the shudderings and black treachery of the bog and condense them into a tale. Even today there is still enough ghastly talk about the Halfway House to frighten the benighted passer-by, but nobody now walks out so far in the dark, and in our cars we pass the place too quickly to see anything more uncanny than our own headlights reflected in the eyes of the sheep that rest on the dry road surface here. We still like gruesome stories, though. I have myself been guilty, when leading minibuses of students around Connemara, of stopping here at twilight to show them the twisty hawthorns and the gaunt roofless gables and try to make them experience a moment or two of the strangeness of Roundstone Bog, to hear its rumorous breezes, while holding them quiet with the legend of the Halfway House.

In daylight, however, it is as if the story has soaked up the gloom of the place like a sponge, so that one can throw it away, leaving Doire Chunlaigh as the brightest-feeling place in the bog. The rock here is the same dark stuff as that of Errisbeg, but every outcrop, boulder and fallen building stone is encrusted with an only-just-off-white lichen. One can step over the field walls, which are too far gone to be barriers but are enough to accentuate the tiny subdivisions of the land, wriggling around all its dells and declivities, curling up to big boulders to form sheep-pens in their shelter, framing a green slope of sheep-nibbled sward in which one can make out the low parallel ridges of an old potato patch. Above all there are trees, scattered singly, bent double and forged by the prevailing wind into long eastward-streaming bundles of crooked sticks: two or three glinting green hollies, a dozen hawthorns all fantastically bearded with lichens, and a moderate-sized ash away down in the most sheltered recess of the slope, its wide-spreading branches bowed almost to the ground. To visit the place at any other season is to feel its invitation to revisit in spring, when there will be primroses among the bracken shoots, violets in the lea of the walls, honeysuckle in the crevices of the rocks.

Best of all, while waiting here for a lift back to my base in Roundstone after a long ramble in the bog, I can stand on the little summit just above the ruined house for an overview of all the complications of land and water I have described – dazzling when the sun is in the south, as if half a sky had been shredded and strewn over black earth, impossible to read as a geography of named and storied places, and scarcely to be believed in as a reality, an interweave of death and life, that can, with care, be walked across in safety.

Superincumbent Intellect

A bog is its own diary; its mode of being is preservation of its past. The current page is the brightest and fullest, but whatever grows and dies on the surface, together with whatever is blown into it from neighbouring areas, will be pickled in the acidic waters, buried under the remains of future years' growth and added to the layered record. Changes of climate, periods of flooding and of drying out, the coming and going of woodland, even the origination of the bog itself at some period after the end of the last Ice Age, are recorded, but in a compressed shorthand that science has had to learn, and is still learning, to decipher. Roundstone Bog, in 1935, was one of the schools in which Irish botanists first acquired the newly developed skill from their continental colleagues. Robert Lloyd Praeger initiated this contact, as he describes:

It is now many years since in my pet subject of plant distribution I found progress held up owing to absence of knowledge of the history of our flora: which history, or at least that fragment of it which we can hope ever to elucidate, lies buried in and under our bogs and other superficial deposits. More recently, finding that in the domain of archaeology Dr. Mahr was similarly handicapped, I joined forces with him. We persuaded Knud Jessen, a foremost worker in Glacial and post-Glacial floras, to undertake researches in Ireland: a strong committee was formed, the Government and various learned institutions gave money, and for two seasons Jessen dug and explored in many parts of the country, and also trained Irish workers to continue the investigations which he initiated.

In Connemara Jessen's first probings were just a few hundred yards north of the guesthouse he stayed in, formerly the land agent's residence, at Letterdife. As he no doubt noticed on his arrival, the shoreline there consists of black cliffs of peat several feet high, and the intertidal zone exposed at low water is also made of peat. In fact he estimated that sea level must have risen by 2.5 metres since the beginning of peat formation. Similar evidence of a relatively recent transgression of the sea had been noted in various places on the Irish coast, as in other parts of north-western Europe and Greenland; it is one of the localized adjustments of the earth's crust to two contradictory effects of the melting-back of the ice fields, which eased the land of the huge burden of the glaciers and at the same time swelled the oceans.

The second site investigated by Jessen, as near as I can work out from his description, was in the low-lying area one or two hundred yards north-west of Na Creagaí Móra. Here he was joined by several botanists for an impromptu discussion. Praeger gives a memorable picture of it in his evergreen book *The Way That I Went*:

That great bogland behind Urrisbeg recalls a quaint scene on a very wet day in August, 1935. A number of botanists had forgathered at Roundstone, and the particular occasion was a kind of symposium on bogs, held in the middle of one of the wettest of them. There were A. G. Tansley from Oxford, H. E. Godwin from Cambridge, Hugo Osvald from Stockholm, Knud Jessen and H. Jonassen from Copenhagen, G. F. Mitchell from Dublin, Margaret Dunlop from Manchester. We stood in a ring in that shelterless expanse while discussion raged on the application of the terms soligenous, topogenous and ombrogenous; the rain and the wind, like the discussion, waxed in intensity, and under the unusual superincumbent weight, whether of mere flesh and bone or of intellect, the floating surface of the bog slowly sank until we were all half-way up to our knees in water. The only pause in the flow of argument was when Jessen or Osvald, in an endeavour to solve the question of the origin of the peat, would chew some of the mud brought up by the boring tool from the bottom of the bog, to test the presence or absence of gritty material in the vegetable mass. But out of such occasions does knowledge come, and I think that that aqueous discussion has borne and will bear fruit . . .

The fruit of Praeger's initiative has undoubtedly been a vigorous tradition of 'palaeoecology' in Ireland, to which Frank Mitchell was central throughout his long career, and to which important contributions are being made today by researchers from the National University of Ireland, Galway. The knowledge that has come out of such occasions is a source of wonder, but it has a bitter truth in its depths, to which I shall return. Mitchell, in his autobiographical *The Way That I Followed* (and he was of the very few scientists who could be forgiven for stepping on the heels of Praeger's famous title), also describes that rare day in Roundstone Bog, adding that he arrived back at Roundstone after it so wet that he decided a swim in the harbour would freshen him up, despite the continuing rain, and was nearly shot by the local doctor, who thought he was a seal. These botanists were a hardy lot, Praeger famously so with his liking for twenty-mile hikes with diversions into tangled and wet places. A young archaeologist has described to me with awe how Frank Mitchell in his latter days rambled all over Inishbofin in foul weather looking for prehistoric hut sites, outwalking field-workers a third of his age. Jessen, in a little photograph in Harry Godwin's 1981 book *The Archives of the Peat Bogs*, looks heavy-featured, tough and weatherbeaten, as well as fiercely concentrated on whatever specimen he is examining; Godwin comments, 'How he resembles his Jutish predecessor!', referring to the famous Iron Age sacrificial victim found preserved in a Danish bog. And as a group they certainly did bring intellect as well as flesh and bone to bear on the bog. Mitchell, who at the time of the 'symposium' was 'a fledgling quaternary botanist' acting as courier to Jessen, went on to become Professor of Quaternary Studies at Trinity College, Dublin, a chair specially created for him with regard to the wide spread of his work in the geology, botany, archaeology and human ecology of the Quaternary period, i.e. the last two million years or so, covering the Ice Ages and thereafter. Tansley, one of the founders of the science of ecology, was present because he was preparing the section on bogs in his *magnum opus* of 1939, *The British Islands and their Vegetation,* and had asked Hugo Osvald, who had studied the raised bogs of Sweden, to visit the

Irish bogs with him. Godwin, a junior colleague and disciple of
Tansley, was travelling with them to extend his knowledge of
watery terrains, having already studied the English fens; he was
later to become Emeritus Professor of Botany at Cambridge. Knud
Jessen was the focus of this extraordinary conjunction of heavyweight botanists; Godwin describes him as 'the great pioneer
archivist of the Irish peat bogs'. Mitchell tells us that Jessen was
his 'father in science', while Godwin, already an established botanist,
and Tansley stood in the relationship of nephew to uncle. It had
been agreed that Tansley's party would meet up with Jessen's somewhere, and since Praeger and his wife and Margaret Dunlop were
holidaying in Roundstone, all came together very satisfactorily to
provide us with this rainswept scene, so emblematic of the generational continuity and human fibre of science, and of its simple
love for its object. I shall describe (in briefest outline and to the
extent that they speak to me, an envious bystander to the com-
munality of science, a mere picaro of the intellectual sphere, but
always ready to risk a tumble) the methods and findings of those
early soundings of Roundstone Bog, and then of the more advanced
studies made in recent years by Jessen's intellectual heirs in Ireland.

Jessen's procedure was to bore through the peat and whatever
deposits underlay it down to bedrock with a long, hand-operated
auger, and extract a core that he could sample at various depths.
Seeds, roots and bits of leaves could be identified in these samples,
and, under a microscope, pollen grains, for even after thousands
of years of burial these are almost as species-distinctive as flowers.
At both his sites Jessen found that the upper layers of peat were
largely derived from the sorts of grasses, sedges and mosses that
grow on the bog today. Below this on the shore site was a peat
derived from birch wood and containing large stumps of pine
trees; at a corresponding level the inland site, which had once
been a lake, had no pine stumps, but plentiful pine pollen indicated that pines had grown nearby. Further down, the peat was
of reeds with sphagnum and pondweeds. Below that, resting on
rock, was brown mud and sandy clay, with leaves of dwarf willow,
juniper, crowberry and, at the inland site, a rare arctic-alpine moss.

Jessen was particularly elated to find this basal gritty layer, which he had come across elsewhere in Ireland and which represented the landscape of late glacial times.

Reversing his sequence and interpreting it, one sees whole ecosystems flowing across the land like cloud shadows on a breezy day: first, the raw stony desert left by the Ice Age; next, the tundra following on the heels of the retreating glaciers, and its colonization by birch and dwarf willow; then lakes with beds of reeds, invaded by sphagnum and filling up with peat to form a bog; a birch wood taking over the bog surface as it dries out, and becoming a pine forest; finally bog again, overwhelming the pines and preserving their roots. A series of epochal transformations condensed into a few metres of dirt.

Since Jessen's day two techniques have been developed for determining the age of samples from such deposits: radiocarbon dating and dendrochronology. The first, invented in the 1940s, utilizes the fact that although most carbon atoms have nuclei containing six protons and six neutrons, some have six protons and eight neutrons; and these are unstable and at some random moment of their existence will break up. While the behaviour of any given carbon-14 atom is unforeseeable, the statistics of a large collection of them are perfectly regular: half of them will decay in 5,730 years, half of the remainder in the next 5,730 years, and so on. New carbon-14 atoms are being created all the time out of nitrogen atoms in the atmosphere as a result of the constant bombardment of the earth by cosmic rays. Plants incorporate carbon into their tissues by absorption of atmospheric carbon dioxide, and animals acquire it by eating plants or other animals. If part of the plant or animal is preserved as a fossil, its carbon-14 content will decline regularly with time, while its carbon-12 content will remain constant, and so the time that has elapsed since the carbon was incorporated into the living creature can be calculated from the ratio of carbon-14 to carbon-12 found in its fossil today. Modern technology can separate the two carbon isotopes in even the tiniest samples of wood, charcoal or bone, count them atom by atom and so date them with great accuracy.

All this assumes that the ratio of the two carbon isotopes in the atmosphere, and therefore in living creatures, remains constant from age to age. However, this scientific truth has turned out to be not so true as scientists would like it to be, and so dates established by this method are stated in 'radiocarbon years', and the correction factors used to covert these into ordinary years are complicated and arguable. What one needs is a Rosetta Stone with parallel texts in radiocarbon dates and calendar dates – and for the period we are concerned with in this prehistory of the bog we have just such a key to the decoding of the past, in the form of timber. Every year a tree puts on a new ring of wood, a thicker one in good times and a thinner one in lean times. The sequence of rings laid down over a given range of years is as unique as a fingerprint. From trees cut down today the sequence is known back to some centuries ago; from posts and beams in old buildings, further back still, and from fossil tree trunks, it is known as far back as the end of the Ice Age. And since samples from specific rings of these timbers can also be radiocarbon dated, a graph can be drawn relating the two sets of dates, so that any radiocarbon date can be translated into a real date – with the usual doubts and ambiguities that arise in every attempt of the intellect to calibrate reality, in this case concerning some periods for which the curve is very irregular.

In Ireland one of the leading practitioners of Jessen's methods, amplified by the two techniques described above, is Michael O'Connell of NUI, Galway. Weighty research papers by him and his colleague Karen Molloy land on my desk from time to time; I struggle with their long lists of plant species and complicated diagrams of how each species' contribution to the spectrum of fossil pollens waxes and wanes through time, and have come to appreciate that, like high-resolution photographs, these studies are all the more dramatic for being so scrupulously precise. Much of their work has been done on bog in the National Park in the north-west of Connemara and near Spiddle to the east, but their findings in general are valid for Roundstone Bog. Michael O'Connell has written a layperson's account of them, which I follow here, jettisoning its freight of detail.

Plant life began to re-establish itself as the glaciers retreated about 14,000 years ago, suffered a setback 2,000 years later when the ice sheets expanded again, and got into its stride with rising temperatures from about 11,000 BP ('before present'). So much water was still immobilized as ice that sea levels were much lower than they are today, and plants were able to migrate across land-bridges from Europe into Britain and from Britain into Ireland. Sedges and grasses, docks and sorrels, pinks, saxifrages, stonecrops, all showed up for this millennial springtime. Then came low arctic shrubs: dwarf birch, which has long moved on northwards from Ireland, and dwarf willow, still to be found in the Connemara mountains. Meadowsweet, crowberry and juniper followed, while the lakes filled with pondweeds and lilies. The first trees, silver birch, transformed the look of the land and, as the climate improved further, were replaced by hazel. From 9,700 BP Scots pine dominated the forest, with oak (probably the sessile oak as found here today), and some elm. After 8,000 BP alder flourished in response to the beginning of what is called the Atlantic period, which was warmer and wetter than today. Lakes began to fill with reed swamp; in wet valleys peat began to form and the peaty areas to be invaded by sphagnum moss, acidifying the waters. Brown bears, wolves, boars, foxes, hares and humans had all crossed the land-bridges by this time. The little flint barbs and scrapers used by the pioneers of the Middle Stone Age have been found near Oughterard at Connemara's eastern gateway, and it seems unlikely that these hunter-gatherers did not work their way around the seashore and from lake to lake into the ultimate west. I list them together with the wild beasts because they had no more effect on the balance of natural forces than any other large mammal; it was not until the New Stone Age or Neolithic revolution that disequilibrium between humans and their habitat manifested itself.

The pollen record of the Neolithic period in Connemara has several dramatic features. After 5,930 BP wheat pollen puts in occasional but momentous appearances, marking the beginnings of cultivation, while holly and ribwort plantain make themselves known, suggesting that trees have been felled and that domestic animals are being grazed in open woodland. A sudden fall-off in levels of elm pollen can be dated to around 5,850 BP. This 'elm decline' is a feature of such records throughout northern and western Europe; it was first noted by Danish scientists in the 1940s, and Frank Mitchell's studies in the Irish midlands highlighted it as a significant event. But what is that significance? It seems probable that something like our present-day Dutch elm disease, a fungal disease carried from tree to tree by wood-boring beetles, was to blame, but the fact that early indications of farming precede its outbreak by only a century suggests that human traffic had much to do with its spread. Right at the birth of agriculture the sound of the axe has an ominous ring.

In north-western Connemara, where there is an impressive concentration of Neolithic tombs, the advance and then the retreat or temporary defeat of agriculture is well marked in the pollen record, and since there are tombs from the same period quite near its northern margins Roundstone Bog is likely to have gone through some similar history. In cores from a lake bottom in that area Michael O'Connell and his team found a rapid decline in tree pollens and a rise in weed pollens at a depth corresponding to a date of around 5,820 BP, indicating widespread clearance of the forest in favour of pasture. But intensive farming lasted a mere hundred and fifty years – five or six generations – before the woods began to regenerate, after which there seems to have been no human activity in that locality for another seven hundred years. Perhaps those five or six generations, if as preoccupied with the afterlife as their tomb-building suggests, were long enough for a pre-literate community to have forgotten that their landscape was ever, and might be again, other than as they knew it.

In general at this time the woodlands were changing, birch replacing hazel, ash replacing elm, yew and oak coming to dominate the canopy. In valleys and on poorly draining flatlands lakes were filling up with reed-beds and bog was forming. By 4,500 BP these bogs were drying out in response to a brief climatic improvement. Plants typical of wet areas, such as bog asphodel, gave place to heaths and then to the forests of pine whose stumps are to be found in the bogs today. By 3,300 BP there had been partial clearance of the oak and yew forest. A new and sinister indication appears in the cores at a level corresponding to this period: a layer of humus black with soot. This was the Bronze Age, a time of growing populations, of more efficient tools, of regular burning of the land to encourage grass production, and so of environmental degradation, perhaps coinciding with a climatic deterioration. Carbon particles clogging the pores of the soil would have impeded drainage; as a result rushes invaded wet pastures and within a century or two woods gave way to heath, and heath to bog. As bog won out, farming declined again and was at its lowest at AD 100 to 400, in the late Iron Age.

So we owe the bogs to the axeman, the arsonist, the greedy grazier. Those Iron Age people living on the *crannóg* of Loch Caimín and other such little island homesteads were surrounded by bog already so ancient that it must have seemed to them as much a datum of nature as the sky above it. Whatever stock of cattle they raised was enough to keep it grazed down and prevent the invasion of scrub and woodland; they handed it on, part of the inalienable heritage of want, to the medieval clans and the religious foundations, to the nineteenth-century landlords and their famished tenantry, and to the grant-driven sheep farmers of today. Or perhaps, of yesterday – for the days of headage schemes, by which the farmer of these 'disadvantaged' regions is supported by a cheque in the post in proportion to the number of animals he or she owns, are coming to an end; now the grants are for reducing sheep flocks, and new regulations emanating from Brussels forbid the wintering of stock on the 'mountain', which means that many farmers will give up sheep altogether as they don't have the grassland to feed them and bought-in feeds are too expensive to make the business worth the effort. Once again the land is in crisis. A cessation of grazing will allow heather to regenerate and the grouse to return; already in protected areas within the National Park the wildflowers are attaining a renewed glory after decades of overgrazing. But after a while scrub will make the leap from lake islands to the lake shores and migrate into the hearts of the bogs from their margins, and something will be lost. Ecologists tend to value a landscape according to its biodiversity: the more species of plants and animals the healthier is the environment. But the monotonies of impoverished terrains have their own grandeur, as do ruined cities; desert is magnificent in its life-denial. Our desires are utterly contradictory, incapable of reduction to order and coherency, in this matter of land-use and landscape values.

As to our own effects on the ground we stand on, our powers of creative destruction and destructive creativity are enmeshed inextricably. Intellect calls on the remotest fields of knowledge – even the mysteries of cosmic rays and quantum physics – to let us look into the depths of the bog. What was darkness and burial is opened into views of an *ur*-landscape, a clean-scoured world of rock, quickly enveloped in flowers and forests; then a shadow is glimpsed between the trees; one can feel the ground quake at the fall of a grain of wheat pollen. A new species has arrived, carrying a dreadful weapon, the intellect. An arms race has begun, the axe evolves from stone to bronze to iron to steel. Great woods with all their sighs and cries go down into silence; the animals succumb: yesterday the bear, wolf, boar, deer, eagle, and today the grouse, the golden plover. The soil is coerced into fruitfulness for a while and abandoned when it falls exhausted. Cultures and religions succeed one another; the coming of intellect (borrowing that word to stand for symbolic communication, communal memory, cumulative innovation) tumbles us into a rate of development beyond the adaptive capacities of biological evolution. Intellect is a new factor, arising out of nature but wrecking its equilibria. Ice Ages were so slow-moving that animals and plants could retreat before them and survive, but intellect is a raging fire. And now intellect, discovering its own effects, acquires a guilty self-consciousness. At the last moment we try to conserve some shreds of nature, which are in fact the waste products of our economy. Our wastelands are so beautiful and so tender we wonder if we should enter them at all. Should we stand here discussing the origins of the bog, knowing that a footprint in sphagnum moss lasts a year or more, that the tuft of lichen we crush unseeingly has taken decades to grow? Sometimes when a snipe leaps from under my feet and goes panicking up the sky, I am appalled at my own presence in a place so old and slow and long-suffering as Roundstone Bog.

The Last of the Turf

'It comes in on people's shoulders and it goes out as a thread of silk — *Téann sé isteach ar ghuaillí daoine agus tagann sé amach ina shnáithín síoda*,' says an old riddle, the solution of which is 'turf'. One morning many years ago, watching a tiny whirlwind play with the fine dust left on the hearthstone by the previous night's fire, I decided that I would write the story of this magical substance, from its dark gestation in the depths of the bog to its brilliant assumption in flame. Since then I have often talked with turf-cutters out on the bog, heard their stories and noted down their lore, but I very nearly left it too late to try my hand at turf-cutting, for this ancient practice is reaching its last days. Year by year fewer and fewer people cut their own turf, because it is hard work and because other fuels give more heat and less flying ash. Also, there is some official recognition of the fact that lowland blanket bog is too rare and distinctive a landform to be strip-mined for low-grade fuel. Turf-cutting by machine is forbidden on most of Connemara's bogs, and hand-cutting is being phased out. So, when I eventually laid aside other matters and started to ask who among my neighbours could take me out and show me how to handle a turf spade, I found that nearly all of them had given up the time-honoured springtide chore. And then I missed a few opportunities because I was away, or the weather was bad, or my promised mentor was ill, and it was not until June 2004 that Jimmy, a humorous old bachelor ripened by the sun and wind of many seasons on the bog, proposed to bring me out for a few hours' work on his young married friend Connor's turf bank. Connor was working on the local Social Employment Scheme, Jimmy explained, and so, by the time he got off work at three, went home, washed, made love and so on, it might be nearer five before they came for me; however, since it was St John's Eve and the days were long, we agreed on the belated start.

The pair of them turned up to collect me that evening; I sat in the back of Connor's car with the turf spades, and within a few minutes we were bumping cautiously along one of the turf-cutters' unsurfaced roads, and then even more cautiously along a soggy and rush-grown track over the bog surface, to a turf bank in the low-lying eastern flatlands of Roundstone Bog near Loch Caimín. A lark far overhead was screwing a song into the deep blue nothing-ness. To the west the bog seemed to go on for ever, and in the huge luminous spaces to the north the Twelve Pins looked dwarfed, domesticated, rounded, piled together, a litter of brown puppies. Close at hand, a little cliff-face of bare peat a few feet high and a hundred feet long separated the area Connor had cut the turf from in previous years and the untouched bog surface that was to be broached today. We flung out the spades and jumped over the road-side ditch on to the near end of the bank, delighted to be so far out in the sunlight and silence and scent of the bog. 'Roundstone is gone,' cried Connor – we had been deploring the shoddy modern buildings overlooking the harbour – 'but this place will never change!' He was wrong in that, though; all around us were turf banks whose owners they identified for me – 'That's Seáinín's bog over there; that's Marty's bog just beyond it . . .' – but none of these had been worked for years, and as they remembered the old turf-men, and Johnny McD., who just wandered from bank to bank chatting and drinking tea and delaying everyone, the breeze seemed to fill with gossiping shadows. I remembered that when I first walked the bog twenty years ago there were a few wrecked cars lying here and there along the turf roads, which affronted my envi-ronmental sensibilities until I realized that the rusty hulks were still in use: the turf-cutters used to run to them for shelter when thunder-showers came striding over the bog. Even the skeletons of these old cars have long been tidied out of the landscape, as have their owners.

But, whatever about the rest of them, we were here and alive and well, to work this bank. First, the 'scraw' or top layer of bog, full of living roots of sedge and heather, had to be removed. Jimmy had a curious old spade with a broad pointed blade the shape of a poplar leaf, with which he made a cut six or so inches deep along the top of the bank and a foot or so in from its face, to mark out the first strip of scraw, and then he cross-cut it into big cake-like slabs which Connor, with his own spade held horizontally, quickly and energetically sliced and levered off and flung down into the water that had accumulated at the foot of the bank. Neither of them was an Irish-speaker by birth, nor had their parents been, but they used the Irish term, *lagphortach*, 'bog-hollow', for the wet cut-away area below the bank. Jimmy told me that by rights they should be using pegs and a stretched string to keep the cutting straight; some of the old turf-men were very 'tasty' that way, he said. Connor looked critically along the line Jimmy was cutting to mark out a second strip of scraws, and said, 'You've got a nurse's bend in it there!' and seized the spade to correct it. I was agog to record this term of the art, which turned out to derive from the dangerous bend just north of the village where the road passes the former public nurse's cottage.

When three strips of scraw had been removed, leaving a bare area about three feet wide along some thirty feet of the top of the bank, Connor started to cut the first layer of sods out of it with his *sleán*. This was a spade with a long blade about four inches wide and an extra little blade like the sail of a boat sticking up at right angles from its left-hand edge. Standing on the bared bank or 'bench' and driving the *sleán* down into the soft bog-stuff at rather less than thirty degrees to the vertical, Connor rapidly cut out a long sod about four inches square and flung it up onto the top of the bank, the cutting and the throwing constituting one continuous motion. Then he cut out another sod and another, working across the bench from the outside edge to the face of the bank, stepped back a bit to take out another row of sods, and so on, until the whole layer, the first 'spit' of the bog, had been removed, leaving another bench ready for cutting about eighteen inches lower than the first.

'I know all this is hundreds of thousands of years old,' said

Connor, stamping on the bare peat of the new bench, as eager to learn from me as I from him, 'and they say it was all forest here long ago; but what is this stuff? Compressed trees?' I explained that the bogs started to grow perhaps three thousand years ago and were only intermittently forested, and that the peat is the remains of much the same sorts of plants that grow on the bog today. That prompted a curious thought: if the bottom of, say, a six-spit-deep bog is three thousand years old, then one end of a sod of turf is five hundred years older than the other. Suddenly the sods appeared to me as compass needles torn out of their natural alignment in the time-field, their orientation to the centre of the earth. To the Roundstone folk of old, too, they had some strange power in them; Jimmy remembered hearing of a witch living in Murvey who used to fly into Roundstone on two sods of turf.

Then it was my turn to learn. The *sleán* slid easily into the butter-soft peat, but my first few sods tended to slip sideways off the blade and fall into the *lagphortach*, or to break in the middle as I tossed them onto the bank; however, I got the hang of it by degrees. Connor showed me how to give a split-second jab of the tip of the *sleán* into the lower bench between each cut, to wipe the root fibres off its edge and keep it keen. If we had continued work to the end of the bared area, that would have been a second spit of the bank cut; then we could have cut a third out of the newly formed bench, and so on. Connor's bog is rather shallow and waterlogged, and does not yield more than three spits, whereas Jimmy's, a mile away on the lower slopes of Letterdife Hill, is about five spits deep. In the old days there would have been a *meitheal* or working party of men cutting one member's year's supply of turf and then moving on to cut another's. Often the team would consist of a man at either end of the bench, one using a left-handed and the other a right-handed *sleán*, cutting the sods and throwing them onto the bank, where two more men would use pitchforks to toss the sods further back, onto the spreading area, to undergo the various stages of drying-out. Sometimes the turf would be 'breast-cut', that is, the cutter would stand in the *lagphortach* and cut the sods horizontally out of the face of the bank. This method is more suitable than the other for peat deriving from reeds, which tends to break up if cut vertically, but it is hard work throwing the sods up onto the bank. Jimmy told me about a champion turf-cutter working for the Turf Board during the war years who could breast-cut and throw so quickly that he would have six sods in the air at the same time! We hardly emulated him that day; we wasted time taking photos of each other at work, trying to capture the flight of the sod, and we talked. We congratulated ourselves on the fact that there weren't even any midges to spoil the golden evening. Especially in May dense clouds of midges can drive turf-cutters demented; they are not so prevalent in high summer, but reappear in September – though I have been told that the autumn midges are not so bad, because they only have one eye.

The further stages of harvesting the turf, and the rich vocabulary associated with them, I know mainly from reliving his turf-cutting days with Mícheál Bairéad, a now wheelchair-bound friend of mine in Roundstone. After a few days lying on the spreading ground or *ionlach* the sods acquire a hard skin, if the weather favours, and are firm enough to handle without breakage. Then they are 'footed', that is, put together into the little heaps called footings or *gróigíní*. The sort of footing I see on Roundstone's bogs consists of three or four sods stood on end and leaning together, with another laid across their tops. Another south Connemara man tells me that if the sods are still too wet and flexible to stand up another sod can be placed lying on the ground in among them as a support; this hidden sod is the *fóidín shionnaigh*, the fox's sod. According to Mícheál, the right way to make a *gróigín* is to lay one sod on the ground, lay another with one end propped on the first, and stand four other sods like a little tent around the first two. The damper faces of the sods should look outwards so that they dry better. If dry ground is in short supply one can economize on space with the *gróigín Francach* or French footing, made by laying down a pair of sods parallel to each other and three inches apart, another pair across them, a third pair across those, and a single sod across these last. This type of footing is built on the edge of the turf bank, so that as much wind as possible can blow through it. Mícheál also drew for me a footing made up of a long zigzag tail of sods each with one end resting on the previous sod; I can't find my note of what he called it, but my south Connemara consultant referred to it simply as a *rang* or row, and felt that it was the lazy man's solution. Another elementary footing is the *meandar*, consisting simply of two sods leaning up against a third (the word means 'a tick', as in 'I won't be two ticks').

After nine or ten days of good drying weather the turf can be refooted, *athgróigthe*, that is, arranged in heaps about twice as big, with all the sods standing on end leaning against each other, the driest ones being placed in the middle, and left for a few more days. Next, the sods are put into small conical ricks or *dúcháin*, about four feet across at the base. The interior of a *dúchán* is of sods 'all standing on tiptoe', as one man put it, and the outer layer or *gríobh* is carefully built up out of sods laid radially and slanted a little so as to shed water. A small *dúchán* is called a *gúigín*. The expert turf-men of old would think ahead to the *gríobh* when cutting the sods; they would finish the downward stroke of the *sleán* with a little scooping motion which would give the lower end of the sod a backwards curve with the fibres combed back in the same direction; then they would be careful to lay the sods in the *gríobh* with the curved end outwards so that the fibres would conduct the raindrops off it. These niceties were a measure of the importance of turf as a life-resource; in a wet year they could make the difference between saleable and unsaleable turf, and between a cold, damp house and a cosy one.

Later in the season the turf would be brought to the roadside in wheelbarrows or in baskets on donkey- or human-back, and, if it was to be left there over winter, piled into bigger ricks or *cruacha*, again with a carefully constructed outer layer of sods to keep out the rain. If one miscalculated and still had sods left over when the *gríobh* was completed, the rest could be built into a smaller rick called a *glamba*. The same construction is used in turf stacks built at home. (Once when M and I bought a load of turf and painstakingly built a *cruach* in our woodshed, a neighbour complimented us by saying that it was well 'sciobolled', adapting the Irish word *scioból*, a barn.) After all these stages, the turf is in position to be brought into the house and burned. And since by then each sod has shrunk to around half of what it was when fresh out of the earth, the harvest is a perennial disappointment. All that work, for so little heat? As a London woman who fell in love with Connemara's ways and traditions, to the point of marrying into a small farm near Roundstone, said to me once, with a sort of rueful wonder at her laborious and alien lifestyle, 'Every time I put a sod of turf on the fire I remember that I've already handled it seven times.'

The turf we cut in Connor's bog that day was what Mícheál would have called *donn-mhóin*, brown turf, and it was not of the best, for there are of course various types and qualities of turf. The best, the least ashy and most heat-giving, is the dense black *cloch-mhóin*, literally 'stone turf', found at the lower levels of the bog near bedrock, and where the black bog-rush grows. *Fíor-mhóin*, true or right turf, a black, stiff turf from deep swampy bogs, is also desirable, but is hard to cut because there are stringy lumps in it of a stuff called *feoil chapaill*, literally 'horse-meat', which no *sleán* can penetrate; turf-cutters surmise that these deposits have formed out of the tussocks that stood up out of the surface of the swamp. *Móin feoil chapaill* and *móin bhán*, the pale sods cut from the upper-most layers of the bog, are good for lighting the fire in the morning, I am told, but burn so quickly that you would be kept very busy feeding the fire all day with them. When left out on the bog in stacks, *cloch-mhóin*, *donn-mhóin* and *móin bhán* stand up to frost and rain better than other sorts, whereas *móin ghiolcaí*, cut from reedy or sedgy bogs, can crumble to little lumps (*caoráin*) and dust over winter. Last year's leftover turf, *sprémhóin*, is better than nothing, I am told, while *spairteach*, soft soggy turf, is good for nothing at all.

Towards the end of that summer, as I was passing down the old road across the skirts of Letterdife Hill, I stepped off the track to nose around Jimmy's own turf bank for a few moments. Evidently he had long finished cutting and footing, and the last of the turf was roughly piled near the roadside. The turf face exposed by this year's cutting was short and shallow, and it was clear that the productive days of this bog were more or less over. The cuttings of previous years had filled in to various extents and were reduced to vaguely rectangular wet hollows floored with sphagnum moss, cotton-grass and the buttercup-flowers of lesser spearwort. A few damsel flies with electric-blue tails hovered indecisively over the remaining small trenches of standing water, and yellow tormentil blossoms twinkled among the heather tufts on the drier bank tops. A sun-bleached bog-oak root like a great sprawling silver octopus seemed to preside over Nature's slow reclamation of the place. The remains of a little turf barrow, its rubber wheel, triangular bed and sides of dried-out, splintery wood, lay absolutely flat on the ground like a fossil leaf in a rock. I was amused to note a wooden rack, evidently for drying turf on, about six feet long, A-shaped in section and a foot or so high, roughly cobbled together out of bits of an old cargo pallet; I had never seen one like it in the bogs, nor had any local person I mentioned it to later on. At this late stage in his career and in the very autumn of the turf era, Jimmy had made a technical innovation! Looking at these things in the silence of the bog, I imagined the never-to-be-cut sods of turf, heads down in the darkness, so much fossilized nostalgia, rehearsing all the fading and soon-to-be-forgotten words and ways of generations of turf-cutters.

Climbing Errisbeg

Because I have climbed Errisbeg Hill some fifty times I rarely head for the top nowadays, but prefer to wander to and fro on the lower slopes, just above the 'mountain wall' that divides enclosed and cultivated land from open commonage, looking at oddly shaped rocks and the twisty paths sheep have made between the roundish clumps of western gorse, as if I could never sate myself with detail. Along the south flank of the hill the boundary between enclosure and commonage coincides with that between the pale granite of the coastal strip and the dark gabbro above it, and the latter must be much the harder as the slope steepens markedly at this level. But geology calls for overviews and is better left for hilltop consideration; in fact any hill suggests a progression from close-up observations of what is immediately under the climber's hands and feet, through rests for breath-catching and retrospection and glances ahead at intermediate delusive skylines that hide the ultimate goal, to the triumphal horizon-sweeping outlook from the summit and the crushing realization of the depths of time that weigh on a mountain top and even on the mere 987 feet of Errisbeg.

I usually come onto the hillside through O'Donnell's mountain gate, and turn south-west from it along the mountain wall; here I am following what used to be the main road of the district, before the 1820s when the engineer Alexander Nimmo came to found Roundstone and its harbour and to build the present road, which keeps lower down and nearer the coast. The original road, which would never have been more than a rough track, came southwards from Ballynahinch, where the Martins, landlords of most of Connemara, had their seat; it climbed across the eastern flanks of Letterdife Hill and Roundstone Hill, and then round Errisbeg Hill to Murvey, from which it followed the same line as today's road to Ballyconneely and, more importantly in those days, to the harbour and the old castle of Bunowen. Here and there along this route are traces of habitation, now deserted in favour of houses nearer the shore and today's coast road. Half a mile south of O'Donnell's gate is the old settlement of Cúgla (a name that trails more history than I can cram into a digression here), now consisting of five or six small farmhouses along a quiet side road; the old Ordnance Survey map shows dozens of open rectangles representing roofless buildings scattered among the filigree of field walls around them. Here my contact is another Tommy O'Donnell, as it happens; but this one is very different from the scarecrow figure I used to meet on the way to Scailp. Tommy O'Donnell of Cúgla is a neatly built and neatly dressed man, full of information but unfortunately too lame to accompany me onto the hillside, on which he has pointed out from his house a dozen or so places with interesting names, most of which I have had difficulty in relocating in subsequent explorations by myself. The Malthouse, for instance, where *poitín*, the illicit spirit from barley, used to be distilled; the Fairy Woman's House, of which no story survives that I can come to hear of; Meall Daing, the first word meaning 'a knoll', and the second being unknown to me.

One of the difficulties of locating these places from Tommy's descriptions is the sheer complexity of the hillside above Cúgla, of which I am only beginning to assemble a mental map after many years of rambling it. There are six or seven narrow gullies running down south-eastwards towards the village, deeply incised and edged with low cliffs further up but all quite shallow and tending to the boggily indeterminate near the foot of the hill. Some of these have minute streams in them, trickles only a few inches across that disappear into boggy patches or widen into shallow puddles here and there, by which I sometimes stop to watch the whirligig beetles – shiny-black, apple-pip-sized, each one paired by its shadow on the stream-bed – dashing about the surface as if madly scribbling their names on water. On one of these occasions I was distracted from my exploration by another tiny shadow on the stony bottom of a pond, which had a

completely different pattern of behaviour from the frantic cursive
of the beetles; it moved in short darts, resting immobile for a
second or two, shifting almost instantaneously a couple of inches,
resting again for an instant, and flicking away in another direction. This shadow was much more noticeable than the tiny
grey-brown water-skater that was casting it, on the surface of the
streamlet. Small enough to have been drawn on the nail of my
little finger, the shadow was shaped like a four-leaved clover, and
each lobe of it had a delicate golden rim. Looking at the water-
skater itself I could see that its front and hind pairs of legs were
flexed as if to support its weight, in which case each of four feet
would have been slightly depressing the surface film; these depressions were evidently acting like concave lenses, dispersing the
sunrays falling through them and concentrating them into a narrow
band around the dark circles projected onto the stream-bed.
Peering more closely again at the clover-shape I could see two
other even smaller dots of shadow on either side of it: the impressions of the creature's middle pair of legs, which were longer or
straighter and did no more than touch the water surface, and with
which presumably it propelled itself like a rower in a skiff. It
seemed at least marginally comprehensible that this minute display
of clockwork jewellery should be staged by sunlight and insect
and the laws of refraction to the delight of my eye, since I happened
to be passing by, but not that it should be happening unobserved
in a million sun-drenched pools all over the bogs at that moment;
to be an ambulant point of view is a familiar mystery, but the
existence of infinities of untenanted potential points of view is a
destabilizing thought.

Tracking these little streams up and down the hillside, I eventually managed to associate one of them with the Malthouse. From
his house Tommy had pointed out to me a notably smooth, slanting
rock outcrop some forty feet square as marking this place, and
when I made my way up to it I found that the outcrop formed
the north side of one of the gullies, the south side being a massive
glacially moulded outcrop like a recumbent dinosaur, with the
stream flowing in a slot a few feet deep in the peat against its

flank. A few stones had been placed in the stream to dam it, so that it widens into a pool at this point – one of the few pools on this hillside big enough for its purpose, which would have been to supply plenty of water to cool the 'worm', the coil of copper piping in which the distilled whiskey was condensed. In fact the whole place was well suited to its function: the vertical rockface by the stream providing shelter for the men tending the turf fire under the pot and topping up the barrel containing the worm, and the slanting outcrop commanding a wide outlook down to the village and the main road for the man on the watch for the police. Having found this splendid rock sheet I lay on it for a time, feeling myself as closely applied to it as lichen, and let my eyes rove over the fields and houses below, the deserted island of Inis Leacan just offshore, as flat on the water as I was on the rock, and the mysterious low domes of St Macdara's Island and Deer Island further out, all these places being replete with memories and stories for me, and I planned how, if time allows, I would someday write them into another book, place by place and page by page.

Conscious of work to be done, and driven by my paranoia of place, I soon got up, followed the stream three hundred yards downhill until it disappeared under the mountain fence and became a ditch in Cúgla, and, having pinpointed that end of it, followed it uphill again for a couple of hundred yards past the Malthouse, where I came upon traces of a little hut or pen, nothing more than two rows of stones a few feet long extending from the foot of a low cliff, which answered to what I had been told of the Fairy Woman's House, and which revealed nothing more of itself on that visit. To fix its position I pressed on, rather breathlessly, up the steepening gully to where it narrows between rock walls and is almost blocked with a mass of scree. It is the prominent knolls of rock between the upper ends of these gullies that give the hill its characteristic gap-toothed skyline. Three of these projections are especially salient; Tommy names them, from left to right, as An Goibín Géar (meaning the small, sharp beak), Clochaí Whitewash (a slight garbling of Cloch an Whitewash, the stone of the whitewash), and Aill na gCuinneog (the cliff of the

churns). These are one's intermediate goals in climbing the hill
from the direction of Cúgla, and each is worth scrambling around
in detail. An Goibín Géar sticks out like a canted pyramid, the
south face of it being an almost vertical drop of twenty or thirty
feet into the gully passing below it, and its north face an easy
scramble. I stood on the point of it once with a compass, trying
to take bearings of some landmarks in order to fix its position
for my map of Connemara (it is too insignificant a feature to
figure on the official maps), but I found that the compass needle
was completely disoriented and eventually settled down pointing
south rather than north, probably because the point had been
struck by lightning at some time, magnetizing the rock. Clochaí
Whitewash is a smaller pyramid overhanging a gully, with a patchy
crust of whitish quartz on its southern face; for some reason the
Cúgla men used to scratch their names on it with a stone, I am
told by the grandson of one of those obliterated signatories. Aill
na gCuinneog is a substantial cliff forming the north side of the
deepest of the gullies, and once sheltered a booley or summer
milking pasture. There is a ruinous little building, hardly more
than a heap of stones now, under this cliff, called Púirín Chúgla,
a *púirín* being a hut or hutch. The 'cliff of the churns' always
reminds me of a little anecdote told by a Connemara man in the
1930s of his childhood:

I saw my mother churning milk at the booley. One day she couldn't
get the butter to set with the churn-dash. She put the churn on her
back (there would be a rope round the churn and a breast-sling) to
take the churning home. When she was coming down Leitir Chaisil
[near Carna], she let the churn down off her back and took the lid off
it. When she looked into the churn the butter was made. I was with
her. 'Come here,' she said, 'and see what I've got.' There was nothing
to be seen in the churn but butter.

The womenfolk and children booleying by Aill na gCuinneog
would have had only a short trot down the gully to reach home,
clearly visible half a mile below. They would have been able to

watch their menfolk at work in the little fields or even on the shore beyond, where wavering towers of smoke would have been rising from the kelp kilns. They would have been able to identify each of the scores of currachs and hookers fishing around the islands sacred to the boatman's saint Macdara and to his rival Coelan, and the turf boats sailing out to the Aran Islands, which appear from this height as a grey-blue plume laid along the horizon. It was a homespun, hard-worn world, as closely woven, rough-textured and ragged as their everyday garments, but above and around it the sea and sky flaunted silks of a splendour beyond the reach of envy. Today there are no potato-diggers in the fields or kelp-burners on the shore; in summer, streams of cars head along the coast road to and from the beaches. On the hillside one very occasionally meets a man checking where his sheep have wandered to; a woman or a child, never. The sound of churning is not to be heard at Aill na gCuinneog.

But these brief evocations of other times and of places to which I hope to return someday are interim views, hastily drawn like the breaths one takes when resting for a moment in a climb, turning away from close-up engagement with the next step of the slope to look back into the distances already traversed, as if a draught of space were as necessary to the body as air. Then one goes on, as in this particular walk I go on, picking my way over the scree to where the glen opens out into a boggy arena surrounded by the many peaks of Errisbeg Hill. The very highest is straight ahead; Tommy O'Donnell and the few others who still know the hill call it the Windmill because in about 1950 the Electricity Supply Board planned to install a wind turbine here, and mounted an apparatus for measuring wind speeds, like a windmill about ten feet high, says Tommy, who was paid to go up to take readings from it every day. Whether there was too little or (more likely) too much wind, Tommy does not know, but the plan came to nothing. The Ordnance Survey trigonometrical point, a four-foot concrete pillar, is not on this highest point but on another peak only a few feet lower but a hundred yards or so to the south-west, where it is more easily seen from the corresponding points on the offshore islands. West of this last is another high point with two small stone cairns on it, called the Two Towers. To the east of the Windmill, just above Aill na gCuinneog, is a roughly domed knoll that looks as if it is the real summit as one toils up towards it from Roundstone; it is called Tower an Phúca, but what story connects it with the *púca*, the goatish hobgoblin, I have not learned. Looking back east from this eminence one sees Roundstone, just over a mile away, as a clustering of white and grey and ochre flecks, then the narrow waters of Roundstone Bay between it and the long, arthritic finger of Inis Ní, and more distant branchings of the sea surrounding and penetrating further lowlands to which Cnoc Mordáin forms a lazy recumbent skyline. The coast to the south and west of Errisbeg Hill is best surveyed from the Two Towers. Directly below are the two famous back-to-back beaches of Goirtín and Dog's Bay, one on either side of a sandy spit joining a low island of grey granite and green pasturage to the mainland. This unusual mushroom-shaped landform is the *iorras beag* or small peninsula from which the hill and the townlands that share it, Errisbeg East and Errisbeg West, get their name. To the west lies the district called Iorras Mór or Errismore, the big peninsula, a wide low wedge of land driven into the Atlantic; the lighthouse of Slyne Head is just visible at its furthest tip.

Finally, it is from the topmost peak that Roundstone Bog becomes visible as a whole for the first time, stretching away to its indeterminate limits, which are often blurred with haze: the coast road with its scattered holiday homes to the west, the outskirts of Clifden six miles to the north-west, the main road to Galway skirting the foothills of the Twelve Pins to the north. Alexander Nimmo, who carried out a survey of the bogs of west Galway in 1813, was the first to give an overall description of what then was a nameless wilderness:

From Mannin Bay to the river of Ballynahinch is an extensive flat moor of a singular appearance: from one of its principal districts I have named it the Moor of Orrismore. This tract is about seven miles by four, and, generally speaking, is a plain, not much elevated above the sea; it is however intersected by many low ridges of mica slate, and in the hollows between them are a multitude of lakes. I have an exact survey of the moor, and find the number of the lakes to be about 143, of different sizes, many of them having numerous and intricate arms. When viewed from an elevation, this appears to be a complete labyrinth, in which it is difficult to perceive the direction of the drainage.

Nimmo was reporting to a commission set up by the House of Commons 'for enquiring into the Nature and Extent of the Bogs in Ireland, and the Practicality of cultivating them', and his recommendations might have presaged the end of this particular bog:

The ridges aforesaid prevent any navigation from being easily led into these lakes from the limestone tract [of central Connemara], but in the event of an extended cultivation, something of that kind might be effected; for example, a dam upon the stream near Ballinaboy would throw it into one narrow sheet of water to the upper end of Lough Fadda, with various arms penetrating the moor, so that limestone or calcareous sand loaded at Ballinaboy, might be transported over most of a tract of about two miles long. A similar instance occurs on the north of Orrisbeg hill, where a great congeries of lakes are all nearly on one level, and from which a navigable cut might be brought very near to the Roundstone bay where lime coral and sea weed may be easily procured . . .

However, in those torpid post-Union years when most of Ireland lay 'unimproved', he could not recommend throwing money into this morass:

With the exception of a few of the smaller lakes, which are mere bog pools, and may be easily bled, the most of them are high in the bank, and have rocky mouths, so that they cannot be drained at moderate expense; and where so much land is still to be reclaimed, such an application of labour would at present be unadvisable. The best purpose to which they can be applied, is by the judicious position of farm steadings, to derive all the benefit possible from them in the way of water-carriage through the arable grounds. And in the mean time it is obvious that they greatly facilitate the business of drainage and enclosure.

The ending of the Napoleonic Wars soon after the date of this report, and the consequent collapse of agricultural prices, initiating a sequence of crises culminating in the Great Famine of 1845–9 and continuing into the last century, meant that such 'farm steadings' never were established; so, it is to human suffering and failure that we owe the preservation of the unique terrain visible from Errisbeg.

I have tried several times to describe this landscape. Not long ago I went up to look at it again from the top of Errisbeg, trying to find an adjective for it, and the one that came spontaneously to mind was 'frightened'. For a moment I felt I had identified the force that drives the expansion, the self-scattering, of the universe: fear. The outline of each lake bristles with projections, every one of which is itself spiny; they stab at one another blindly. There is a fractal torment energizing the scene, which is even more marked in aerial photographs, in which the lakes seem to fly apart like shrapnel. Of course all this is purely subjective and projective: I was the only frightened element of the situation. But when I collect myself and try to analyse the view from Errisbeg and relate what forms I discern in it to what I read in geological texts on Connemara, the results are deeply perturbing to my sense of the human scale. Studying the apparently random distribution of land and water, of rocky hillocks and sodden levels, one regularity at least is soon identified: a chain of long, narrow lakes and reed-beds, with lengths of stream linking them, running north-north-westwards from the western foot of Errisbeg and including the largest of all the lakes, Lough Fadda or Loch Fada, which simply means 'long lake', near Ballinaboy. On a map this alignment of linear features is very striking. A geologist would immediately know that its cause is a fault, or a bundle of parallel faults, cutting through the underlying rock and making it more vulnerable to erosion along a narrow zone. In fact this 'Murvey

Fault', as it is called, runs from Dog's Bay to Clifden and beyond to Cleggan Bay in north-west Connemara, and has been traced on the seabed as far as the straits between Inishbofin and Inishshark. And it is not just a crack in the rock; the land to the west of it has been shifted southwards along it relative to the land on the east, by nearly half a mile. This is hardly noticeable at first glance because erosion and bog growth have long ago obliterated differences between the terrains on either side of the fault, but on a geological map of the area it is clear that various boundaries between rock types make sudden jumps southwards where they cross the fault line. One evidence of this relative displacement is visible from the top of Errisbeg: a stream flowing westwards from near Loch Roisín na Róige marks a lesser fault that intersects the Murvey Fault just below the hill, and the continuation of this lesser fault can be seen as a long hollow following the same westwards direction but offset to the south. The work of giants, one might think, but it is a relatively minor effect of the earth-shaking forces that have shaped this landscape. A much greater, if less visible, one is the Mannin Thrust, a roughly horizontal fault plane across which a huge block of land – most of what is now western Connemara – has slid southwards and now rests on rocks that used to lie many miles offshore from it. In one area of seven or eight square miles to the north-west of Errisbeg, all the rock above the fault plane has been eroded away in the millennia of millennia since this movement took place, so that the rock that was overridden now forms the surface. This area is called the Delany Dome after the geologist, Frances Delany, who first identified it. Seen from Errisbeg it is all flat bog like the rest, but on walking across it and examining the rock wherever it shows above the peat one can see that it is very fine-grained, all the crystals in its structure having been milled to dust and reconsolidated by the enormous pressures and stresses to which they have been subjected. To understand something of the nature of these rocks and of the forces that shuffled mountain ranges one across another, one has to look into the births and deaths of lands and seas, the history of geography, in which, as it happens, the terrains constituting what is now Ireland have repeatedly been in the thick of the collisions of continents.

Because of the heat of radioactivity in its interior, most of the Earth's substance is plastic enough to flow in convection currents that ascend, spread and descend in a perpetual rolling motion, the brittle crust forming the continents and the ocean floors being spat out, carried to and fro, torn apart, piled up and swallowed again by these currents like flakes of scum on a boiling pot. All this happens so slowly that the distances between continents have changed by a hundred paces or less during the whole of human history. The Earth is something like four and a half billion years old, and the oldest rocks of Connemara were formed around 700 million years ago. Rocks of the same types and origins occur in Mayo, Donegal, Antrim and Scotland, and are called Dalradian (from the medieval Scottish and Ulster territory of the Dál Riada); they are mainly sedimentary rocks that have been much meta- morphosed − altered and recrystallized − by all the folding, crushing, stretching and heating that has happened to them since they were first deposited. At that period nearly all the continental masses of the globe were gathered together as one supercontin- ent, which was just beginning to be ripped in two by the ascending and diverging currents of hot material beneath it. As the crust thinned and sagged below sea level an incipient ocean formed along the zone of tension, and rock eroded from the surrounding lands was washed into it grain by grain, piling up into great thicknesses of sands and muds, and slowly consolidating into stone. As rifting of the supercontinent began, volcanoes pierced through the crust and layers of molten gabbro − a coarsely crystalline rock rich in iron and magnesium − were forced between the strata of sedimentary rocks. By 500 million years ago the new ocean, which geologists have named Iapetus, was perhaps as wide as the present Atlantic and was beginning to narrow again. To the south of it lay Baltica (the present-day Scandinavia) and the vast continent of Gondwana, while the land mass to the north of it, called Laurentia, comprised what are now North America and Greenland. Two smaller fragments of continental crust on opposite sides of the ocean were pushed together as the ocean ceased to exist; this new conjunction hardly formed an entity as yet, being only a small part of a continent put together out of the old Laurentia, Baltica and other pieces of the jigsaw, but another few hundred million years would make it Ireland.

The terrain that was to become Connemara was part of the northern fragment of this future Ireland; initially it was adjacent to what is now Donegal, but as the continental margins drove together it was chipped off and squeezed southwards, to dock against what is now Mayo. In the last stages of the collision of continents, not only were the Dalradian sedimentary rocks metamorphosed by heat and stress, folded and buckled in ridges hundreds of miles long and several miles high, but in Connemara a huge block of these metamorphic rocks and the sheets of gabbro intruded into them were rammed outwards over an arc of volcanic islands that had lain off the southern coast of Laurentia. So it comes about that the rock now exposed in the Delany Dome is in origin a rhyolite, an igneous rock like a fine-grained granite, representing the roots of those long-annihilated volcanos, while the rock surrounding it and underlying most of Roundstone Bog is amphibolite, which is gabbro that has been highly metamorphosed in the course of its movement across the Mannin Thrust – in fact the amphibolite strata have been completely inverted like a rucked-up carpet, so that older layers lie above the younger. Errisbeg Hill itself is of a less extremely reworked gabbro; both sorts of rock originated as molten intrusions emplaced deep in the Dalradian rocks below a volcanic arc, perhaps the same one that gave rise to the Delany Dome rocks.

The compaction of these marginal terrains during the fusion of the two continents not only piled up mountains but forced rock far down into the hot depths, where it melted and rose again as a light magma that cooled some way below the surface to form huge domes and bulbs of granite, a coarsely crystalline rock chiefly composed of quartz and silicates of alkali metals. At this stage, one has to remember, the Atlantic had not yet come into existence, and the new 'Caledonian' mountain chain, perhaps as huge as the Himalayas, ran from the present Appalachians through the northern parts of Ireland and Scotland to Norway. Soon after its creation exposure to all weather regimes from the tropical to the glacial wore the Irish mountains down to a plain; the Twelve Pins, a tenth or less of the height of their bygone ancestors, are the glacially carved remains of a plateau raised in a much more recent period of mountain-building. Similarly, erosion has bared several of the granite rock-domes and levelled them off to form most of the present southern coastal region of Connemara, including the lower slopes of Errisbeg.

That, in rudimentary summary, is the geologists' understanding, or my limited understanding of their understanding, of how the main elements of this apparently eternal and peaceful scene, the view from Errisbeg, have come into their present and temporary conjunctions. Rereading what I have written, I note the use of a rhetoric of violence: collision, stress, tearing, crushing. The timescale of the world's building and unbuilding of itself can only be related to the scale of lived experience by the chilly abstractions of arithmetic, of powers of ten, or by metaphor. The same processes could be presented as constructive: the continents dance together and conjoin, or in parting scatter the seeds of new countries; the chemistry of the depths concocts the subtle colours of minerals and the perfection of crystals; soil is provided out of stone. If metaphors of destruction predominate it is because the geological timescale threatens our sense of our own significance. Our awarenesses as individuals last between, say, a tenth of a second and a century; we can just about catch the dart of a water-skater and the symptoms of global warming. Outside that range, scientific instrumentation and the collective resource of historical record mediate a secondary and ever more interpretative access to the milliseconds and the millennia. But as single biological entities we sail on a tiny raft of timescales between the atomic and the cosmic; we know that in a tenth of a second a world of things happen, and in the century virtually nothing. To Pascal's two spatial abysses of the infinitely great and the infinitely small, between which the human being is suspended, we have added two abysses of time.

The inner abyss is closed to our imaginations; only calculation can open it. As to the outer abyss, I can intuit something of it through a survey of its works in the landscape seen from the top of Errisbeg, but its reality weighs upon me more intimately when I think of the layers of rock, thousands of feet thick, that once lay overhead here and have been worn away by the winds that blow out of that abyss, to free the peak I stand on.

Murvey

and a note on Costa del Sod

Murvey is the name of the next townland west of Errisbeg Hill . . .

That statement, forced on me by the hurry of time, is not false, but profoundly unsatisfactory. To resist the betrayal of reality it enacts, I have to call to mind two of the prime words of the Irish language, the language of a culture for which topographical terms once had the weight and resonance of cathedral bells: *muir*, 'sea'; *magh*, 'plain'. The first is obviously the equivalent of Latin *mare*, French *mer*, etc., but to my ear there is a more powerful swell and surge in it. The second is indissolubly associated with Ireland's mythic dimensions. According to ancient traditions recorded in the medieval compilation known as *The Book of Invasions*, during the time of the early bands of invaders led by such divine heroes as Partholon and Nemed, certain lakes burst forth and certain plains were cleared; that is, the land was brought into accordance with human needs. Plains are named again and again in these legends as sites of foundational events or aspects of the Otherworld: Magh Tuireadh or Moytirra, the plain of the pillars, is where the epic battle of the magical Tuatha Dé Danann and the demonic Fomhóire was fought; Magh Meall, the delightful plain, was an island of enchantments.

Micro-echoes of powerful significances such as these persist in even the most customary and familiar of today's placenames. 'Murvey' is the anglicized form of the Irish *muirbheach*, or more accurately of its old dative form *muirbhigh*; it connotes a level stretch of sandy land by the shore, and figures in the names of hundreds of places characterized by such a feature. The first syllable is obviously from *muir*, the second, less certainly, is thought to relate to *magh*, giving 'sea-plain' as the literal meaning of the word. 'Murvey' is as good an approximation to the proper pronunciation as can be expected from the colonialist attempt to render the sounds of one language in the spelling of another, but in comparison to the Irish it is insipid. Irish placenames dry out when anglicized, like twigs snapped off from a tree. And frequently the places too are degraded, left open to exploitation, for lack of a comprehensible name to point out their natures or recall their histories.

The defining feature of Murvey, eighty acres or so of grassed-over dunes and sandy levels called the White Beach, endlessly tousled and combed by the wind off the sea, lies at the western extremity of the townland and faces onto a wide shallow bay. Since this bay marks the western limit of the parish of Roundstone, and of the territory treated in this book, I shall visit it first, and then work my way back eastwards along the shoreline. One approaches the White Beach by a quiet side road that branches off to the south from the main road and winds this way and that between lichen-mottled drystone walls, around hillocks with great granite boulders nested in heather and little fields with damp hollows full of yellow irises. After passing one or two small farm-houses and holiday cottages it straightens itself out and heads west, becoming softer and softer underfoot with blown sand, and eventually delivers one to a gate in the last field wall, beyond which is open grassland sloping gently down to the dunes rimming a spacious, blonde beach. In summer the turf is brightened by a sparse pointillism of chrome yellow bird's-foot trefoil and white clover, together with catsear, yarrow, yellow-wort, wild pansy, centaury, and the tiny spiral orchid called autumn lady's tresses. The wind, and the constant nibbling of cattle and rabbits, keep the vegetation cover as closely fitted to the slight swells and slopes of the ground as a worn carpet. The onshore breeze sends sand grains flying inland at ankle-level, tirelessly reconfiguring the terrain in detail. Some of the dunes are reduced to mesa-like plat-forms with vertical faces of sand crossed by two or three dark horizontal bands that represent former land-surfaces on which generations of prehistoric folk had their fires, grazed their cattle and dumped a litter of periwinkle and oyster shells.

My most recent visit was on a vigorous spring morning when the Atlantic was a bed of seething amethyst to the southern horizon. The past winter's war with the land had excavated craters and canyons out of the dunes near the shore. Inland of these blowouts the thin carpet of grass and herbs was half-drowned in pallid sheets of sand. In one place little cracks were opening in the sand layer, and when I felt into them I found the stiff little blade-like leaves of buckshorn plantain thrusting up vertically; in some cases they were already spread like the feathers of a shuttle-cock, pushing the sand back into a formation like a minute volcano rim, and soon they would be lying on the surface as flat as a lace doily. I also noticed a bare patch of a hundred square yards or so with a regular microtopography of half-inch-high conical sand-hills, each topped by a snail shell that protected the sand under it from erosion. There were live snails too, small flattish ones like spirally patterned buttons, in their thousands, for the blown sand contains a high proportion of broken seashells, the lime of which encourages the proliferation of land-snails, who need it to build up their own shells.

Ecologists have borrowed the Scots Gaelic word *machair* for this type of habitat characterized by level expanses of closely grazed turf on a lime-rich soil derived from sea-sand. (The Irish equivalent is *machaire*, and both derive from *magh*.) It is restricted to the western coasts of the Scottish Highlands and Islands, and especially the Hebrides, and around fifty small sites on the western Irish coast, from the north of Donegal to the Aran Islands, but nowhere further south than Fanore in County Clare. It is there-fore a rare landform, and what there is of it is in danger of being eaten away by caravan parks and golf links. The *muirbheach* of Murvey is one of the finest examples in Connemara, and the least known, being so well hidden away beyond settlement and fieldscape. Thus the placename, if one attends to it, invites one to be aware of the place's (literally irreplaceable) qualities, its light-flooded, free-breathing expansiveness, and its precarious stability founded on constant random change.

In winter and spring the wild music of seabirds draws one

southwards along the shore of the Trá Mhóir, the 'big strand' below the dunes, where flocks of oystercatchers, sanderlings and ringed plovers forage on the wet, ripply sands at low water. Unfortunately a rocky hook of land here traps all the litter of a vast stretch of the Atlantic, which the unchoosy forces of nature sort out and assemble into tidelines. At Dog's Bay, the better-known beach to the east, the Roundstone Youth Club organizes a spring clear-up and removes dozens of bagfuls of rubbish before the tourists arrive, but Murvey, less visited and further from the village, is neglected. However, as it turns eastward the coast rises a little and one is soon out of sight of the necropolis of plastic bottles. Humans of all times since the Stone Age have sorted and assembled what's of interest to them. Near the south-west corner of the shore several acres of sand are carpeted with empty seashells, the contents of middens that must have been in use for millennia, and I notice that a recent beachcomber has collected hundreds of fish-net floats and piled them into the broken-down remains of a little stone hut. To the east the beach is replaced by boulder banks and low cliffs, and another pattern, on a bigger scale, becomes apparent, the interruption of the granite coastline by deep vertical-sided inlets, which one comes across with discon-certing abruptness. These canyons have been eroded by the endlessly crashing waves into the fault zones and dykes of softer rocks that cut north–southwards through the granite, and they are floored with big, pale sea-rounded boulders of rhyolite and quartz. The inner ends of two or three of them are prolonged into small caves. The Irish term for a cliffed creek or sea-cave of this sort is *fuaigh*, and in collecting the west Connemara place-names I have written this as it is pronounced: *fó*. The first one, marking the eastern limit of the *muirbheach*, is Fó Mhór, the big creek, and the next, a few minutes' walk further on, is Fó Scardáin, because during and after southerly gales the waves surging up it leap high into the air in a *scardán* or spout that can be seen from the cottages a quarter of a mile inland of it. Then comes Fó Chapaill, the horse's creek, and towards the eastern end of the townland is Fó na gColm, the creek of the rock doves, the wild progenitors of our city pigeons. This last is a blowhole; part of the roof of its cave has collapsed and one can look down a gaping hole among the grasses and bushes on the cliff-top into a dank and echoing rock chamber below. When waves rush up the inlet and cram into the cave their spray comes up through the hole like a fountain and is blown far and wide. A Murvey man whose farm is a mile inland from it tells me that when his sheep are tormented by midges getting into their eyes and ears they assemble on a hillock that apparently captures the salty breeze from the 'puffing-hole', as he calls it. There is a story to be told about this cave, to which I shall return shortly. Finally the last of the Murvey creeks, where the eastern end of the townland overlooks Dog's Bay, is Fó na Crí, which gives its name to a village of a few cottages on the hillside above it. I have never seen the name written down except in my own map and sources deriving from it, but I am fairly sure it means 'the creek of the boundary' (*críoch*), as it marks the eastern limit of the townland. This is where the Murvey Fault, which I have described as seen from Errisbeg, comes down to the shore. It is a very substantial feature with house-high craggy cliffs that make its waters look dark and dangerous, and it is prolonged for half a mile inland by a narrow fault valley which the coast road runs through and which shelters enough sycamore trees and alders to have won the name of Murvey Wood.

According to folklore collected in Murvey in 1937 or 1938, Fó na gColm played a part in a curious and pitiful incident that took place some two generations earlier, in January 1873, which is still dimly remembered in the locality and is famous in world literature. A man called Willie Maley or William O'Malley, living about two miles to the west in the townland of Callow, quarrelled with his overbearing and drunken father over the preparation of a potato patch:

He had the spade left in the garden and the father threw out the spade and the son went for it and put it in the garden again. The father threw it out a second time. The son caught the spade and brought it in and kept a hold of it. The father came up to him to take the spade from him and in the struggle they had with the spade between the two of them, the son swung the spade and split the father's head. He caught him and carried him into the house and said to his step-mother: 'anios a Chailleach nach bhfuil sé sinte agat.' ['Now, old woman, isn't he stretched out for you.'] He then ran to the mountains and the step-mother went up to the barrack and reported him to the police. The dispatch was sent all over and the guards were in search of him. Willie was in the mountains and it was cold frosty weather and he hid himself out in a lake named 'loch beitheanach' [in Roundstone Bog]. He was under furze and the guards walked right over him and the dogs which were on his track never smelled him. He used to go to some houses up in the hills and he got food but where he was tonight he would be miles away further the night after.

One night he was up in Errisbeg hill and the snow and frost made him come down to the shore in Murvey for a refuge, and he went to a shore called 'Fo na Goillin' [Fó na gColm] in a place called 'Poll na Caiteoga' ['the hole of the spray', i.e. the blowhole] and when the night came he crawled up half dead with the hunger and nearly dead with the cold to a house and he rapped at the door of the house. Joyce asked who was there and Willie said some sort of talk but Joyce could not catch onto it and he opened the door and let him in and the man of the house was ready to go to bed and his mother was already gone. The man of the house got food for him and put him sitting by the fire and Joyce put him in his own bed and watched the night for him.

Before the dawn he left the house and went to the shore in the same place and he passed three or four nights that way. At last he went to the mountains again and he made his way through the mountains until he came to Carrowroe and there he went on board a boat and sailed to Aran . . .

The rest of the story is well known in the Aran Islands. O'Malley stayed with some relatives of his in Cill Rónáin, but when the police got word of him he was taken across to Inis Meáin. After some narrow escapes there he was smuggled out in a boatload of potatoes to Tralee, and he eventually took ship to America, where his wife joined him after a year or so. The Aran Islanders seemed to have relished their part in the adventure. When W. B. Yeats and Arthur Symons visited Aran in 1896 they were brought to meet the oldest inhabitant, who told them, 'If any gentleman has done a crime, we'll hide him. There was a gentleman that killed his father, and I had him in my own house six months until he got away to America.' J. M. Synge heard the story too, on his first visit in 1898, from an old man of Inis Meáin:

He often tells me about a Connaughtman who killed his father with the blow of a spade when he was in a passion, and then fled to this island and threw himself on the mercy of some of the natives with whom he was said to be related. They hid him in a hole – which the old man has shown me – and kept him safe for weeks, though the police came and searched for him, and he could hear their boots grinding on the stones over his head. In spite of a reward which was offered, the island was incorruptible, and after much trouble the man was safely shipped to America.

This impulse to protect the criminal is universal in the west. It seems partly due to the association between injustice and the hated English jurisdiction, but more directly to the primitive feeling of these people, who are never criminals yet always capable of crime, so that a man will not do wrong unless he is under the influence of a passion which is as irresponsible as a storm on the sea. If a man has killed his father, and is already sick and broken with remorse, they can see no reason why he should be dragged away and killed by the law.

Here we have the seed of Synge's scandalous masterpiece *The Playboy of the Western World*, which occasioned a riot when first performed at the Abbey Theatre in 1907. According to Aran oral history, O'Malley acquired the nickname 'the Playboy' because his hosts tried to shake him out of his depression by organizing parties and card games to amuse him.

To create his contradictory hero Christy Mahon, Synge fused elements of the story and character of the woebegone hangdog

O'Malley with those of another fugitive, the mercurial and irre-
pressible James Lynchehaun, whose exploits were much discussed
at the time, and who, by an odd coincidence, seems also to have
been connected with Murvey. The Lynchehaun, as he was called,
was born in Mayo in 1858 or 1860, and became a teacher in a
school at Achill Sound, from which he was soon dismissed for
falsifying accounts and insulting an inspector. He then obtained
a post in the Roundstone area, and a tradition has been recorded
that this was in Murvey National School. All ran smoothly there
for a year or so, until, as he himself tells it:

Money, the source of evil, began to get flush with me. I got into
company and spent more freely, but, to my sorrow, when wine is in
wit is out with me.

About this time I got into serious trouble by assaulting a native who
attempted to pick my pocket which contained my quarter's salary. This
would-be robber had a bottle of whiskey, and while putting it in a
seemingly friendly manner to my mouth with one hand, he was manip-
ulating my pocket with the other. But he suffered for the attempt, for
I danced on his body, although I had to pay the piper afterwards. This
man's friends pursued me in order of getting even with me, so I had
to act the fugitive and desert the school and parish. After hiding for a
few days I was discovered and arrested, brought before a Justice of the
Peace, and confined in the bridewell at Clifden to await my trial in
Galway at next sessions.

Two influential friends took compassion on me and bailed me to
stand my trial. When I got out I gave them 'leg-bail' and left them to
settle their accounts with the law authorities.

On his way home to Mayo the Lynchehaun called in at another
school pretending to be an inspector, terrified the teacher with
threats of a bad report and 'borrowed' three pounds off him. But
Roundstone heard no more of him until 1894, when news spread
of a sensational crime perpetrated in Achill, where he had found
employment with a Mrs Agnes MacDonnell and then had been
dismissed. Mrs MacDonnell threatened to have him evicted, and

in a sequence of violent, obscure and confused incidents he burned down her house and stables, and assaulted her, nearly biting her nose off. He was arrested, but while being transported to prison in a jaunting car he persuaded the constable who was holding on to him to light his pipe for him, and while the man's grip was relaxed he 'bounced off the car like a hare' and disappeared into the bogs. He found shelter with a young woman, his cousin, who hid him in a hole in the floor under a dresser, so that on his discovery he became celebrated in ballads and newspaper reports as 'the Achill troglodyte'. Condemned to life imprisonment, he made a most ingenious escape from gaol by doctoring an indicator on his cell door so that it appeared to be locked when it was not. After a series of brushes with the police, the defiant and improvisatory wit of which made him a popular hero, he got away to America. In Chicago he claimed that his crime had been political and with the support of the Irish nationalist community managed to resist extradition. He twice revisited Achill in disguise, was arrested for a break-in and talked his way to freedom again. It seems he died in Scotland in about 1937.

The Lynchehaun's victim, Mrs MacDonnell, may have had a romantic attachment to him, for even after being nearly battered to death by him she described him as 'a fine, young, strong, dark, animal-looking man'. As such he seems to have been the opposite of the pathetic Christy Mahon of the beginning of Synge's play, whom we first hear of as 'going mad or getting his death, maybe, in the gripe of the ditch', like the poor parricide Willie O'Malley shuddering with cold and remorse in the watery cell of the puffing-hole. Synge's genius was to make Christy's apparent parricide a comedic error and so release him from his family tragedy to evolve into the sexually attractive, ready-worded, devil-may-care Playboy who goes off 'romancing through a romping lifetime' at the end of the play.

Murvey National School is no longer extant, and no one in the locality remembers hearing of its once notorious teacher. Even its site, on the south side of the road a few hundred yards beyond the turn to the village of Fó na Crí, has been obliterated by a stone quarry. But the cottage O'Malley crept up to can still be pointed out, and the sea still sighs and groans like a repentant criminal in the puffing-hole down on the shore.

★

It's a difficulty for the topographical writer trying to sculpt his text that places have accidental connections as well as essential features. My bias is towards trusting the place's name to indicate its essence, as does the name 'Murvey' when it is brought home to the Irish language; but only a part of the townland is *muir-bheach*, and I have resorted to its fortuitous and tenuous links with both of Synge's sources for *The Playboy* to knock my account of the rest of it into shape. And finally, when I climb the low heathery hill bitten into by the quarry where the school was, to take a last and hopefully unifying look around Murvey before turning back towards Roundstone, my attention is distracted by the view opening up behind me. Roundstone Bog, which stretches away in stillness and silence from the other side of the road below, fades into vague distances to the north but is rimmed to the west by a tidemark of little white rectangles. The latter area lies outside the bounds of the present book, and if I write about it someday I will approach it from the wild and legendary coastline beyond it; but it intrudes here and now, for in its banality it threatens all that attaches me to Connemara. What I see from Murvey is the inland aspect of the proliferation of buildings along the coast road to Ballyconneely, and I know that, further west along the side roads running down the Iorras Mór peninsula to the golf course and beyond, the pressure of development is even more intense.

The selling-off of Connemara is immensely profitable to landowners and developers, and as a result planning regulations are flagrantly subverted, with the connivance of clientele-dependent politicians. It corrupts our eyes; we see every field as a potential house site, flaunting a price tag instead of its ragged hawthorn tree. All year round, the sound of the rock-drill is heard in the land. One by one the hummocky patches full of yellow irises and buttercups are bulldozed and turned into level lawns, the ditches brimming with purple loosestrife and meadowsweet go under tarmac as boreens are widened to accommodate SUVs, and the crooked old field-boundaries of lichen-patched stones give way to trimmed hedges and concrete-block walls. A suburb without an *urb* is coming into existence, a centreless anywhereville.

About two-thirds of the houses in these areas are holiday homes and stand empty for most of the year; their contribution to the local economy in the brief summer season is small, and their seasonal demand on the overstretched rural water, electricity and road systems inordinate. Of course our transient summer neighbours bring invaluable stimuli into the community, economics apart; 'We love to see them come, and we love to see them go!' is a frequently heard sentiment in Roundstone. But the sheer number of new houses is threatening all the traits of Connemara that attract the summer-folk in the first place. Will they tire of the raddled countryside of Costa del Sod, as I named it in a bitter moment? But then they never see it out of season, when the anarchic scattering of buildings with their trailing electricity and telephone wires wrecks the magnificence of its bogland setting and leaves it intolerably bleak.

The worst example, the one that stirs me to this diatribe, is an estate of fifteen or so box-like holiday homes on a low hill well-named Leitir Seasc, the barren slope, utterly unsheltered from the wind off the Atlantic, half a mile out into the otherwise almost uninhabited open space east of Ballyconneely. In estate agents' parlance, they enjoy an unrivalled outlook across Roundstone Bog. But many a view enjoyed is a view stolen. By their intrusive presence on the skyline they invade the bog, erode its otherness, clip its wings. They are visible even from Scailp, a fact I couldn't bring myself to mention when writing up that quintessentially solitudinous spot. Nothing can be done. I have not attempted to find out the reasons for this particular failure of the planning system.

Literally as I write, it comes back to me that this hill figures in a story I heard from Jim O'Malley, the old blacksmith of Bunowen, in the 1980s when I was rambling around making my map of Connemara. I will tell it now, to get myself out of the deadlock of sterile anger I feel concerning this violation of the bog.

Ballyconneely, as the name suggests, was the settlement of the Conneelys in olden times, until they were massacred by the Ferocious O'Flahertys. Just one of them escaped alive, a woman called Una, who was pregnant and in due time bore a son. She brought him up in some other place and would not tell him where she was from until he forced her to do so by fasting. When the lad was grown up, he went to his mother's native territory and found that the O'Flaherty tyrant of the day lived on an island in a lake near Bunowen. Joining some reeds together end to end, young Conneely measured the distance from the shore to the island, and then, on the flank of the Leitir Seasc hill called Colbha (meaning 'edge' or 'side') he set up two stones that same distance apart and practised the long jump, first with the slope and then against it, until he could jump from one stone to the other. When the O'Flaherty's daughter saw him returning to the lake she fell into the water; this was the beginning of their love. Conneely jumped onto the island and stabbed out the eyes of her father, and then, when the blind man offered to shake hands with him, the girl gave Conneely a horse's leg bone to hold out to him, which the O'Flaherty crushed to powder. Conneely then killed the O'Flaherty and married his daughter, and, I suppose, they lived happily ever after and repeopled the village with Conneelys.

That is the tale, and this is the place called Colbha. At the time of my researches an old man of the vicinity told me that the two stones were still to be seen, and gave me directions to them, but as he could not accompany me across the fields I was never quite sure that the stones I found, among many and many a stone, were the right ones; therefore I do not know if they have survived the clearance of this hilltop for building. Tales, however, can outlast stones, and this tale still lies around to be used. Taking it as a parable for our times, I interpret it thus: the O'Flahertys, whose name means something like 'lordly in action', stand for the forces of construction, and the Conneelys, who legend says are descended from seals, for the spirit of nature. Nature can be pitchforked out, but a seed always survives and blows back in again. In the end there is reconciliation and fruitful marriage between the polarities. May Roundstone Bog live to see that bright day.

The Boneyard

There should always be flowing water between consecrated ground and a plot set aside for the burial of unbaptized infants. That was the belief in the old times, according to an elderly man of the locality with whom I was discussing the children's burial ground at Goirtín, two miles west of Roundstone village. Indeed there is a little stream between the hillock topped by a stone bearing the words 'In memory of the deceased infants' and the wall of the official cemetery just west of it. This memorial is a recent mark of reconciliation with the past; it was erected by the Roundstone Development Committee as a Millennium Year project, and the spot was consecrated by the parish priest, Fr McCarthy, on 2 January 2000.

When I was exploring Connemara for my map in the 1980s I was shown about forty children's burial grounds, only a very small number of them marked on official maps or recorded in any way other than in folk memory, and most of them known only to people of the immediate vicinity. A few of them are noticeable scatterings of small set stones, uninscribed but obviously not a random assemblage; others I would discover only because some oddity of the terrain would attract my attention: why does the little road down to Lettermore, near Renvyle, have a kink in it? Why are there so many small boulders under the thorn-bushes on a tiny peninsula of the shoreline of Camas Íochtair? Why does the boundary wall between the townlands of Canower and Rosroe, near Cashel, bisect a small hummock a few yards from the high-water level? Many of these burial places are totally obscured by bracken and brambles; an old man pointing out one such meagre memorial in the corner of a field behind his cottage added, 'Some of my own are buried there.' Often a stillborn child would be buried by night in some ancient earthwork whose origins as a stockyard around a dwelling had been forgotten for centuries and which bore an anomalous otherworldly repute as a fairy fort, or under a fence between two properties, as if neither side would accept responsibility for it, or on the no man's land of the seashore. Although disused for some decades now, children's burial grounds are still tender spots of the rural landscape and have to be approached with tact.

In their obscurity and ambiguity these sites match the Catholic doctrine of limbo, that shadowy province of the afterworld reserved for those who, through no fault of their own, have not been saved by the word of Christ. As the *Catholic Encyclopaedia* of 1912 explains in its article on baptism:

The Catholic teaching is uncompromising on this point, that all who depart this life without baptism are perpetually excluded from the vision of God . . . Many Catholic theologians have declared that infants dying without baptism are excluded from the beatific vision; but as to the exact state of these souls in the next world they are not agreed. In speaking of souls who have failed to attain salvation, these theologians distinguish the pain of loss (*paena damni*), or privation of the beatific vision, and the pain of sense (*paena sensus*). Though these theologians have thought it certain that unbaptized infants must endure the pain of loss, they have not been similarly certain that they are subject to the pain of sense. St. Augustine held that they would not be exempt from the pain of sense, but at the same time he thought it would be of the mildest form . . . Since the twelfth century, the opinion of the majority of theologians has been that unbaptized infants are immune from all pain of sense. This was taught by St. Thomas Aquinas, Scotus, St. Bonaventure, Peter Lombard, and others, and is now the common teaching in the schools . . . As to the question, whether in addition to freedom from the pain of sense, unbaptized infants enjoy any positive happiness in the next world, theologians are not agreed, nor is there any pronouncement of the Church on the subject. Many, following St. Thomas, declare that these infants are not saddened by the loss of the beatific vision, either because they have no knowledge of it, and hence are not sensible of their privation; or because, knowing it, their will is entirely conformed to God's will and they are conscious that they have missed an undue privilege through no fault of their own. In addition to this freedom from regret at the loss of heaven, these infants may also enjoy some positive happiness . . . While the opinion, then, that unbaptized infants may enjoy a natural knowledge and love of God and rejoice in it, is perfectly tenable, it has not the certainty that would arise from a unanimous consent of the Fathers of the Church, or from a favourable pronouncement of ecclesiastical authority.

Nevertheless, in its article on limbo the *Catholic Encyclopaedia* is confident in asserting that 'as a result of centuries of speculation on the subject, we ought to believe that these souls enjoy and will eternally enjoy a state of perfect natural happiness.' And the 1992 *Catechism of the Catholic Church* takes an optimistic, if rather vague, view:

As regards children who have died without Baptism, the Church can only entrust them to the mercy of God, as she does in her funeral rites for them. Indeed, the great mercy of God who desires that all men should be saved, and Jesus' tenderness toward children which caused him to say: 'Let the children come to me, do not hinder them,' allows us to hope that there is a way of salvation for children who have died without Baptism.

That was the mellow mood of Vatican II, and in its aftermath some retrospective measures are being taken for the sake of the poor souls whose mortal remains went into the children's burial grounds before these mild modern understandings. Fortunately (and after a mere 1,500 years of reflection) theologians have found ingenious ways out of their own trap; for instance, Christ's general will to save all may be deemed equivalent to a baptism by desire. Thus those formerly regarded as the unbaptized can be disinterred and reburied in a proper cemetery, or a proxy baptismal service may be conducted on their behalf. In 1994 a children's burial ground in Rusheenduff, Renvyle, was consecrated, as a result of a campaign led by Mary Salmon, whose two stillborn children lay there, having been denied Christian burial some sixty years previously. By courageously exposing the depth of her anguish and resentment she made herself the spokesperson for the generations of women who had been so cruelly misled by their spiritual fathers:

I felt very let down by the Catholic Church . . . I remember one priest saying to me 'surely you did not cry for that baby', to which I replied 'I did cry for that baby and I think there's no God in heaven to take him away from me'. I told him my baby was not in purgatory or limbo and that I did not believe in such places. I also told him that I would see my baby very soon. I had taken the baby's death so hard that I felt like dying. In those days it was customary for the local priest to bless a pregnant woman before giving birth and to consecrate her with oil two or three weeks after the birth. After I had the dead babies the priests never came near me and because of this I stopped going to the church to be consecrated after giving birth of my other children. I was very bitter towards the clergy, because I believed at the time that they wanted almost to pretend that nothing had ever happened. I stopped attending Mass and it was only after Fr. Keane visited me and pleaded with me to return to Mass that I eventually agreed to go again. In recent years I have had many visits from priests in America who knew my sons over there. These priests have all talked to me about my loss and these conversations have brought me some consolation but they will never fully make up for the clergy's uncaring attitude back then.

Since then children's burial grounds have been blessed by the local priest in a few other places in Connemara, but these gestures of atonement and reclamation have been prompted by the parishioners; the Hierarchy remains silent on them and offers no guidance. As one priest said to me, 'The cardinals do their own thing. They work out the logic of the doctrine, and it's the logic of the head, not of the heart. They despise emotions. So we do this discreetly. Say too much about it and you'd get a rap from Rome. It comforts people today, but it's too late for all those in the past. The Church will never admit that it was wrong. It fears that if it did so the whole structure would crumble – which might be no great harm.' So priests and the leaders of congregations improvise the inauguration of a more humane regime, and not always without discomfiting those they would comfort. Some elderly parishioners may not want anything to do with such matters even today, their feelings being understandably confused and embittered. Very few people turned out for the ceremony at Goirtín in the year 2000.

It would not be right to blame solely the Church for the stream of tears that flows between the children's burial ground and the cemetery. Death is mysterious, and so is birth; doubly so is death-in-birth. Suspicion lurked around it, of abortion, infanticide, witchcraft. Up to a few generations ago, a question would have shadowed the mind of the sorrowful parents: did the envious fairies steal away our lovely vigorous baby and leave this wretched limp thing in its place? The decline of such superstitions, the medicalization of childbirth, the pressures of secularism and feminism, have all contributed to the abandonment of the old ways and the evolution of a charitable assumption that all infants are baptized, by the very fact of their parents' having desired them to be so. Nevertheless, I cannot pass by the burial place of these failed attempts at life without registering my amazement and distress over the persistence of the gargoyle-logic of limbo into such recent times. Stony throats continued for centuries to roar forth the consequences of their false premises high above the heads of suffering humanity, oblivious to the fact that what matters once an infant is dead is not the welfare of a non-existent entity in a fictional hereafter, but the feelings of the parents, and perhaps particularly of the mother, who brought this scrap of humanity so briefly, or so nearly, into the world. A funeral, with the words set down to be spoken over each of us in our turns, and burial in the ground set aside for all our corpses, would have been a communal recognition of the little body's attempt at personhood, and would have helped the bereaved to begin to let their loss fall into the past. When at a child's funeral I hear our kind-hearted parish priest say, 'God must have loved little Jane so much that He called her to Him so soon', and the parents repeat the formula to themselves and even to me, I recognize once again that what to me is a sentimental inanity is a source of strength to others and is not to be despised. So, the centuries-long Catholic ban on burying the unbaptized in consecrated ground, necessitating the furtive, unceremonious spading-in of the dead baby or foetus under a boundary wall, in the haunted rath or among the stones of the seashore, was a bitter wrong.

The stream, this little Jordan of such millennial consequence, a mere trickle in dry weather but quite busy after a downpour, carves a miniature valley around the western side of the knoll on which the memorial now stands, then spills through a culvert under the path leading to the cemetery gate and makes its way down to meet the tide through improvised canyons a few inches deep in the sand of the beach. A few yards to the west of it, the consecrated ground within the walls of salvation is hummocky, sandy and grassy. The graves are in irregular close proximity, almost as neighbourly or as mutually intrusive as those of *Cré na Cille*, Máirtín Ó Cadhain's famous novel that imagines an eternity of gossip, flirting and backbiting between the corpses in a south Connemara graveyard. But in compensation Goirtín cemetery is awash with spacious colours: often, the blue-grey of the Atlantic blowing over it from the south; sometimes, the severe enamel blue of Mary's mantle; occasionally, that Mediterranean quintessence of blue, the *azur* of Valéry's *Cimetière Marin*. In winter the mourners cower under blasts of slanting rain; in summer the graves are self-strewn with the low nodding blossoms of sand-dune flora.

I like fossicking and yoricking about in graveyards, scanning the headstones, stopping for a closer look at one or another, as one takes down a book from a bookshop shelf to see if its opening words live up to its title. One of my desiderata for a well-run world would be that every tombstone carry a brief biography (and, at the foot, 'For notes and sources, see over'). But how reductively uninformative are the inscriptions here! John Barlow, fondly remembered; Margaret Dundass, sadly missed. Mr Barlow I knew as the deaf, mannerly old gentleman who sold me my newspaper every day, and who once told me that he had not expected to spend his life behind the counter of a shop. He exercised great caution in stocking the shop; a phrase I several times heard from him, for instance when I suggested he might get in a few guide-books, or even some of my own maps, was 'You could have a lot of money tied up in those things!' This most peaceable of men often held me there for half an hour reminiscing about his glory days as a member of the Local Defence Force; he would explain to me that in manning a machine gun 'you need to be able to work all around you', and his whole frame would shudder with the imagined recoil as he directed a withering spray of bullets into every corner of the shop. Miss Dundass, a schoolteacher retired for many a year, was in her nineties when I used to call in on her with queries about village history; I remember her sitting crouched like a cricket by a smoky fire in her rather derelict little house on Marine Terrace, which she would allow no one to repair or tidy up because she was losing her sight and could only manage in unchanging circumstances. The last time I saw her she was mooching about outside the house on a sunny after-noon; 'I'm mooching about,' she said, as if she were taking the opportunity of teaching me the word, the reflexes of her calling as prompt as ever.

The cemetery also houses the bones of some notable person-alities that figure in history books: Bulmer Hobson, the gentle Quaker revolutionary who retired to the house at the bottom of the road down to Goirtín after the debacle of the Easter Rising, and wrote his book *Ireland Today and Tomorrow* there; Maurice McGonigal, President of the Royal Hibernian Academy and painter of many Roundstone landscapes; the Duchess de Stacpoole, local patron of the Lady Dudley Nursing Scheme and chatelaine of Errisbeg House. All three died before I came to live in Roundstone, but local people remember them and have given me the odd non-historical particular about them. Hobson had a bicycle fitted with a little petrol motor, and Joe Rafferty, who kept a shop on the coast road not far away, placed a stone by its door to help him mount and dismount. When Hobson's sight was failing he studied the mechanism of the eye and devised a reading aid, a sheet of glass of some kind suspended from his forehead so that it would swing out of the way if he nodded off. McGonigal, I am told, was buried with his palette, which had been given to him by Paul Henry, who had it from Sir William Orpen – a nice emblem of the continuity of Roundstone's artistic tradition. The Duchess, I hear, was a ruthless and erratic motorist; when a local lad was buying his first car, his father warned him of the three terrors of driving in Connemara: 'the ditches, the donkeys and the Duchess'.

One of the deepest difficulties of disbelief in a hereafter is the implication that so much suffering remains for ever unrevenged and uncompensated; but such is the case, or so it appears to me. I think here of Fidelma, a kindly, obsequious, shapeless old lady who did some cleaning jobs, and was married to a sly, malicious and probably marginally deranged joker from Mayo, who it is said sometimes beat her and threw her out of her house at night, and for some years before her death dragged her off to live here and there far away from her familiar neighbours. When the hearse bringing her remains from that distant town was approaching the village and her husband heard that people were waiting in the street there to follow it to the cemetery in the customary procession, he persuaded the driver to detour around by Ballyconneely, avoiding Roundstone, and so cheated her of respect to the last and beyond. But all graves are memorials to time's disrespect; the knowledge even of who lies in the older ones is mouldering in the newer, just as library shelves are filling with books on other books, which will never be opened and must eventually be pulped to give room for more. Cemeteries themselves get buried in cemeteries; the Ordnance Survey map of 1839 shows a burial ground at Goirtín as a roughly oval unenclosed patch about thirty yards by fifteen; on the 1899 map it is seventy yards long by thirty across; today's cemetery is a walled rectangle about two hundred yards by a hundred, and is fully occupied, while a new tract to the west, recently taken in, is sparsely tenanted as yet, a green forethought.

★

The terrain out of which the cemetery is taking successive bites is a stretch of *muirbheach* or machair, a smooth sward kept trimmed by exposure and grazing, based on long-consolidated sand. It spans the base of a peninsula, the *iorras beag* or little headland, from which the townlands of Errisbeg East and Errisbeg West, extending inland from it, derive their names. The peninsula consists of a narrow sandbar, with a beach on either side of it, linking the mainland to what would otherwise be an island about a mile offshore. The whole area is loosely called Goirtín, anglicized as Gorteen and meaning 'small field', a name that perhaps primarily applied to the head of the peninsula, on which there used to be potato fields. Seen from the slopes of Errisbeg Hill rising just inland of it, the whole landform looks like a long arm bone and a knobbly fist thrust out into the sea. The beaches rimming the bays on either side of the sandbar – Dog's Bay to the west, and Port na Feadóige (bay of the plovers), also known as Gorteen Bay, to the east – are themselves bone-white and consist of minute shards of mollusc shells and the exoskeletons of the single-celled sea-creatures called foraminifera. The whole formation is a place of bones. Buried in it or exhumed by scouring winds are the remains of humans and their kitchen refuse. George Petrie, in the early 1830s, was the first to take note of the abundant traces of early settlement here:

A few years since on the shore of Roundstone Bay, a bank of sand 300 feet high, being removed by a storm, discovered on the strand beneath a cluster of nine oval houses of stone in perfect condition including their roofs; they have since been reburied by a new accumulation of sand.

Although not exactly part of the shoreline of Roundstone Bay, Goirtín is the only nearby location where great movements of sand occur, and Petrie must be referring to the duneland west of the graveyard or the sandbar south of it (although his '300 feet' is surely a mistake, perhaps for '30 feet'). In 1895 F. J. Bigger discovered hut sites on the mainland close to the neck of the peninsula, presumably the remains of Petrie's 'stone houses', and

investigated them in the following year in the company of Robert
Lloyd Praeger and others:

A hasty survey of the place would show here and there small clumps
of stones which indicated the positions of hearths that were probably
the centres of hut sites . . . Where we found a good site from which
the covering had not long been removed and from which the remains
had not been collected, it was a most instructive sight, as we could see
the hammer-stones just as they had been last used by their prehistoric
owners, the flakes lying probably on the spots where they had fallen
on being struck off, or where they had been laid down after being
used; and amongst these objects broken and split bones and small heaps
of shell fish, the remains of their meals, were also visible.

The description of Bigger's finds suggests the Neolithic period,
and it is clear that humans have occupied the Goirtín peninsula
at least intermittently since then. Until recently two or three
blackish layers could be seen in the faces of the dunes where
westerly storms had carved them into low cliffs all around Dog's
Bay. These soot-blackened 'soil horizons' with their spills of
seashells showed very graphically that at various periods in the
distant past people had foregathered here, perhaps seasonally, to
live off the harvest of the sea, and that after a time each of these
habitation surfaces had been buried by a further building-up of
the dune system. They have largely been obscured by loose sand
again, as a result of coastal protection work. In one area, near the
south end of the bay, an archaeological dig was carried out in
advance of this work, in 1991, by a team led by Erin Gibbons.
The oldest remains were found at the level of the beach and
represent human activity here in the Neolithic, before the dunes
began to form. They included a small scraper and some worked
flint, and two stretches of drystone wall. In a soil horizon about
half a yard above the beach there were plentiful signs of occu-
pation: animal and fish bones, burnt stone and charcoal, pits
containing shells, and holes left by wooden posts. On an exposed
shelf of sand about three yards above the beach, among severely

eroded dunes, more considerable structures were found. A well-constructed drystone wall could be traced for some fifty yards southwards, with an intact kiln on the seaward side of it. The kiln seemed to have been used for drying corn, as carbonized oats were found in it and elsewhere nearby. It was built into the sandy soil and consisted of a bowl lined with cut granite stone and a flue. It had been abandoned when the stones began to flake from repeated firings, and had been backfilled with soil and stones including a large fragment of a saddle quern. Finally the place had been reused as a children's burial ground; three little burials were excavated, one of them in the flue of the kiln itself.

A puzzling feature of the shell middens seen by Bigger and his colleagues is that some of the shells had been gathered into separate heaps according to their species, which included limpets, oysters, flat periwinkles, mussels and common whelks. Similarly, separate deposits of limpet, periwinkle and whelk shells were found here in 1944 when F. J. O'Rourke opened a trial trench near the north end of the dunes. It is difficult to imagine why these common food-species should have been segregated; perhaps they were gathered at different times of the year. Even more interesting is Bigger's find of a deposit, fifty-five yards long and up to fifteen yards broad, of dogwhelk shells, in which all the shells were broken, the topmost whorls having been smashed, leaving the lower whorls and the mouth intact. The dogwhelk (*Nucella lapillus*, until recently known as *Purpura lapillus*), like the closely related *Murex* that was the source of the famous Tyrian purple of classical times, has, just under the point of the shell, a gland that secretes a whitish slimy substance rich in potent chemicals including a nerve poison and an antibiotic; the substance may play a role in carrying extraneous particles out of the shell, in rendering the animal or its eggs unpalatable, or in protecting the eggs against disease. From the human point of view its important constituent is a pigment chemically similar to indigo, which turns a rich purple colour on exposure to light and air. This substance was the foundation of the prosperity of the Phoenician city of Tyre (now known as Sur, to the south of Beirut); according to the Greek geographer Strabo, writing some two thousand years ago, 'Although the great number of dye works makes the city unpleasant to live in, yet it makes the city rich through the superior skills of its inhabitants.' The original discovery of shellfish purple is of course lost in prehistory, but it was important enough to have its representation in Greek myth. One day Hercules was walking on the beach with a Tyrian nymph whose favours he hoped to win. His dog came across a *Murex* and devoured it, and the nymph, seeing the stains on the dog's mouth, bargained with Hercules for a robe of that same glorious colour. So Hercules took the shellfish, extracted the dyestuff and made her the first robe of Tyrian purple. Since it took about 25,000 shellfish to provide a tenth of an ounce of dyestuff, Tyrian purple was literally worth its weight in gold and was used only for the most prestigious and luxurious garments. In Rome only the Emperor, the highest officials and priests were allowed to wear purple. At the Battle of Actium, it is said, Mark Antony's ship flaunted purple-bordered sails. In the great days of Byzantium, emperors used to sign their names in shellfish purple. The dyers' skills were closely guarded trade secrets, not written down, and it seems that knowledge of them died with the Byzantine Empire after the capture of Constantinople by the Ottomans in 1453.

Was there some reflection of all this oriental splendour in the lives of the unrecorded folk of Dog's Bay? Emily Murray of Queen's University, Belfast, has collected the evidence for a dogwhelk-dye industry in the west of Ireland. Middens of broken dogwhelk shells have been found at Ballyconneely and in various dune systems around the south-western peninsula of Connemara, at Omey Island and at a few places in Mayo, Sligo and Donegal. Recent radio-carbon dating of the surviving sites places them all within a period roughly from AD 360 to 800, that is, in early Christian times. However, there are no known references to the use of shellfish purple in writings of the period. The Venerable Bede in his *Ecclesiastical History of the English People*, written in about 731, states that in 'Albion' there is 'a great abundance of whelks, from which a scarlet-coloured dye is made, a most beautiful red which neither fades through the heat of the sun nor exposure to the rain; indeed the older it is the more beautiful it becomes' – but this passage occurs in a eulogy of 'Albion' that lends it all the charms of ancient days, and is perhaps not to be taken literally. All other medieval references to the use of shellfish purple in Britain or Ireland seem to derive from Bede. Despite many speculations and assertions in twentieth-century sources on the topic, scientific analysis, with one possible very recent exception, has failed to confirm that shellfish purple was used in illuminated manuscripts from Ireland or Britain. In the many accounts of ancient Irish dress, from Giraldus Cambrensis down to contemporary scholars, if purple is mentioned its source is given as a lichen, and technical analysis of old textiles tends to confirm this. But there is substantial written evidence for the use of shellfish purple from the seventeenth and eighteenth centuries. A William Cole offered his 'observations on the Purple Fish' to the Royal Society in 1685:

For in October 1684, there were two ladies of Myne head [Somerset] who told me, there was a certain person living by the seaside in some port or Creek in Ireland, who made considerable gain, by marking with a delicate durable crimson colour, fine linen of ladies, gent. etc. sent from many parts of that island, with their names or otherwise as they please; which they told me was made by some liquid substance taken out of a shellfish . . . these shells, being harder than most of other kinds are to be broken with a smart stroke of a hammer on a plate of iron, or firm piece of Timber (with their mouths downwards) so as not to crush the body of the Fish within: the broken pieces being picked off there will appear a white vein, lying transversely in a little furrow or cleft, next to the head of the fish, which must be digg'd out with the stiff point of the Horse hair pencil.

J. C. Walker, in an essay of 1788 on Irish dress, states that dyeing with shellfish purple 'is still practised in the counties of Wicklow, Wexford and other counties on the east coast of Ireland', while an anonymous writer in the *Annual Register* of 1760 gives us this charming scene from the west:

I happened some years ago, to be at a gentleman's house upon the western coast of Ireland, where I took particular notice of a gown which the lady of the house wore one day. It was a muslin flowered with the most beautiful violet colour I had ever seen. Upon my expressing my admiration of it, the lady told me, with a smile, it was her own work and seeing me wonder at her saying so took me down to the seaside, among the rocks, when the tide was out, where she gathered some little shellfishes ... and to convince me brought a handful of the fishes home with her, and breaking them open, and extracting the liquor with the point of a clean pen, marked some spots directly before me ... Though the fishes were sufficiently plenty, the drop that was extracted from each was so little that I suppose the contents of an hundred would make a drop so large as a small pea.

Finally there is some evidence from placenames of the existence of a dye industry only a few miles from Dog's Bay: a townland near Slyne Head is called Creggoduff, which represents the Irish Creig an Duibh, 'the rocky place of the black stuff', and in a seventeenth-century source the place is named as Creagacorcron, which would mean 'the rocky place of the purple stuff'. The 'black stuff' is probably the intensely black, iron-rich sediment collected from the bottom of bog-holes, widely used for dyeing wool until a couple of generations back and referred to in numerous Connemara placenames; it gives a dull black colour, or, with the addition of oak chips, a glossy jet black. The 'purple stuff' could be from a lichen; but Creggoduff lies close to all the dogwhelk sites of south-western Connemara listed above, and it might be that it was once a centre for producing seashell purple, and that when this luxury item was no longer in demand the dye trade lingered on, dealing in humbler materials. Since a single dogwhelk yields only ten or twenty milligrams of dye, which is much less than the product of the Mediterranean *Murex* species, the Irish shellfish-purple business must always have been on a small scale. Emily Murray suggests that it involved the dyeing of skeins of wool by direct application from the live shellfish, the wool being used in the fringes of mantles and similar sparing applications, rather than the whole-sale production of dyed fleeces and robes. Goirtín, then, was never the Tyre of the West, and traces of whatever eminence it once enjoyed in the trade are hard to find nowadays. Bigger's fifty-yard-long deposit of shells seems to have vanished, lost no doubt to the fierce erosion of the dunes rimming Dog's Bay. I have never even come across a scattering of broken dogwhelk shells here, but a Roundstone lady tells me that in her childhood she and her playmates used to collect them, and string them into necklaces. Nothing goes to waste; the nymph of Tyre needs the juice of the creature, and the girls of Roundstone its bones; both are moments in the Earth's ruthless self-adornment.

Because the wind perpetually dusts the sward of Goirtín with lime-rich seashell stuff off the beaches, and because it is under-lain by more or less consolidated sand, the pasturage here is nutritious and dry underfoot, and therefore is a valuable resource in this region of wet, peaty soils; it 'puts bone' on the cattle, as they say. The whole peninsula is commonage, in the limited sense that each landholder of the townland in which it lies, Errisbeg West, has the right to a share of its grazing. The regulations governing these rights are complicated, and evidently ancient. Each holding is called a 'band'. The holder of a band may put fifteen sheep and one ram onto Goirtín, from the first of November to the first of December; nowadays the agreed total of sheep is 345. Cattle may be grazed here from 15 May to the last Sunday in July and from 15 August to 1 November, the allowance per band being three cows with their calves, or nine yearlings, or a half-collop plus one yearling. (A half-collop is a cow 'with two teeth up', i.e. a one-year-old, I am informed. The Anglo-Irish word 'collop' is from the Irish *colpa*, meaning a full-grown cow or horse, or its equivalent as a unit of grazing, six sheep.) The beasts are counted on to and counted off from the commonage on the assigned days, their owners meeting for the purpose at 3 p.m. by the gate of Thomas Griffin, a farmer of Errisbeg West. The best of the grazing is on the level land just

west of the cemetery and among the granite knolls of the head
of the peninsula; the sandbar joining these two areas has a spine
of rough grassland, now largely planted with marram grass and
fenced to keep cattle and tourists off it.

A sandbar of this sort, connecting an island to the shore, is
called a 'tombolo' by the physical geographers, who have borrowed
the term from the Italian for a sand dune. The dune systems of
Ireland are evidently the result of waves and wind bringing sand
ashore from the ocean bed, and they are thought to have begun
to form after a fall in relative sea level six thousand years ago. A
quirk of geography has led to the construction of the tombolo
here. The one-time island that now forms the head of the peninsula is about a mile long, and lies almost parallel to the shore and
a half mile off it. The dominant wind direction here is south-
west, so the island absorbs most of the shock of incoming waves
and the channel inshore of it is sheltered. Waves refracted around
the two ends of the island meet head to head in its lee and cancel
each other's impetus, so that their cargos of sand are deposited in
relatively still water. As the zone between island and coast becomes
shallower and shallower it becomes more and more effective in
robbing the waves of their energy, and deposition accelerates.
Once the growing sandbar reaches sea level the wind takes over,
scouring sand from the beaches and heaping it above high-water
mark, where vegetation soon begins to bind it into dry land.

But this cumulatively constructive process can be reversed, and
an equally cumulative destruction ensue. Since the lower deposits
of organic material in the dunes have been dated to some two
thousand years ago, the sandbar is at least that old, while the
alternation of blackish strata representing habitation levels with
bright layers representing the burial of those habitation levels
under further depths of sand shows that building of the tombolo
has continued ever since then: so it might appear to be a fixed
and stable item of local geography. However, the huge increase
in human traffic, especially in summer, now amounts to a force
that threatens to undo nature's millennial work. At present the
sandbar is well vegetated, but only through a continuous effort

of conservation. In recent decades it seems to have been denuded by erosion at times, perhaps in a natural and cyclical alternation. Old photographs show that it was virtually all bare sand in the 1950s but had begun to recover in the 1960s; by 1976 there was a good coverage of vegetation all along the core of the spit. Some of this variation may have been due to early attempts to stabilize the spit by planting it with marram grass; this species has the ability to grow upwards through many feet of sand, and if it can be established its stalks and leaves filter the flying sand grains out of the wind blowing through it so that they fall, accumulate and are eventually bound together by the grass's root systems. The Land Commission had certain areas fenced off to keep the cattle out of the marram grass, but the fences were neglected, and spring tides undermined them and dragged them down the beaches. Eventually the Land Commission handed the problem over to the County Council, which had the fences removed. In the 1980s the east side lost most of its plant cover. By 1990 the beaches were encroaching on the vegetated sand from either side, and the grassland was further reduced by blowouts, sandy pits where the cover had been totally worn away and the wind was excavating the underlying dunes. During the January storms of 1991 it looked as if the sea might break through the spit, leading to the wreckage of the famous beaches and the loss of grazing on the headland. The landholders of the townland, advised by Teagasc, the Agriculture and Food Development Authority, formulated the Roundstone Beaches Project and won the support of the County. During spring of that year a lot of reclamation work was done under a community employment scheme. A gang of men went off with lorries to Belmullet to dig up clumps of marram grass, planted the shifting sands with it, fenced off the planted areas, fortified the exposed faces of the dunes by setting rows of pine branches along the tops of the beaches to trap the flying sand, and, later on, armoured the most vulnerable stretch, at the south end of the Dog's Bay beach, with gabions, big boxes of thick wire mesh filled with boulders. All this interference with nature was unsightly for a time, and I was tempted to think that it would have been better to let wind and tide have their way, that perhaps the bar has come and gone many times; but then Erin Gibbons' excavations showed quite uncontrovertibly that it has been in continuous formation for at least two thousand years, and if it is breaking up now it is because of cumulative human interference, from the introduction of rabbits by the Normans down to the pleasure-seeking invaders of our own days. We can no longer delude ourselves that there is a Nature whose wild destructive and constructive forces derive a certain validation in our minds from their impartiality, their independence of our hopes and desires; rather, we are part of the problem and so must be part of the solution, if such there be. In the meantime, piled sand and a healthy coverage of plant life are burying the tattered fences of Goirtín in their depths and restoring a simulacrum of untouched naturalness.

A curious episode in May 1991 underlined for the Roundstone community what an unusual and vulnerable feature of their environment the tombolo is. Word suddenly spread that two large container lorries had arrived at six o'clock in the morning and were parked on the main road above Dog's Bay, that one of the fences protecting the newly planted marram grass had been cut, and that two tractors were driving up and down a gully in the eroding dune face, bringing loads of sand up to a smaller lorry which was transporting it up the side road to the container lorries. The tenants of Errisbeg West immediately blocked the side road with their own tractors and compelled the intruders to replace the sand. It turned out that a contractor from Carna had been employed to collect this material, under a licence issued by the Department of the Marine. The licence limited them to thirty tons, to be gathered from below high-water mark, but they assured the tenants they had been given the nod for the removal of fifty tons. It was also clear that they were saving themselves some effort by taking the loose sand above high-water mark at the foot of the eroding dune. Their employers, we learned to our amazement, included Italian university institutions that needed samples of the sand because, as mentioned, it is largely composed of the shells of foraminifera. Since foraminifera (or forams as scientists call them for short) are single-celled creatures, one might have thought that a sample would be something of the order of a teaspoonful, but it transpired that the Italians – the Technical University of Turin, the Institute for Research on Models and Structures, in Bergamo, and the Italian National Electricity Board – were not studying the beautiful structure of foram shells but the crushability of calcareous sands, as part of a research programme ultimately relating to marine engineering projects, and that the type of sand found in Dog's Bay was unobtainable in bulk onshore anywhere else in the northern hemisphere.

I was called upon by the Roundstone Community Council to draft a letter to the Minister for the Marine, in my grandest manner, demanding that the licence be immediately rescinded since its provisions had been breached, and pointing out that the area had recently been designated as one of Scientific Importance and that its Neolithic-to-medieval archaeology was currently being investigated. Scientists from the Italian institutions hurried to Roundstone to try to placate us; their offers of funding for social development projects and scientific research into the precious terrain were rejected loftily. They even promised to bring the sand back once they had finished with it. We became absurdly obdurate and told them that return of the sand would only be acceptable if we could count the forams off the beach and count them back on again, and that we would not tolerate any breakages. A newspaper report of all this even has me saying grimly, 'A line has been drawn in the sand!', and perhaps I did indeed get carried away to that extent. Eventually the scientists went away and we heard no more of the matter; I don't know how they solved their problem. There may have been more to this affair than met our eyes at the time, for on rereading a document that 'came into my hands' during the controversy I find this annotation: 'The research reported in this document is being sponsored by the U.S. Government through the European research office of the U.S. army. The document is only intended for distribution within the U.S. Government and the above named contractor.'

So the foram is a consequential creature, by reason of its numbers. Single-celled organisms more complex than bacteria, in that their DNA is contained in a nucleus, they are classed as Protozoa and represent a halfway stage of evolution between bacteria and the animal kingdom. The earliest ones in the fossil record are over 550 million years old; nevertheless they share half the genes that define us as human beings. There are about sixty thousand species worldwide, including those known only as fossils; over two hundred species have been recorded from Dog's Bay. Some might be a millimetre across, others a tenth of that. Each species builds shells of a characteristic form, most of them being divided by partitions into several chambers connected by small openings called 'foramina' (from which the creatures get their name). Under the microscope foram shells are of extraordinary variety. Many look like triumphs of the baker's art: plaited bread rolls, fancy cupcakes, tarts with elaborate spiral trelliswork of piped icing. The organism builds the chambers of its shell one by one and occupies all except one or two of the outermost and most recently constructed. It trawls for its food – bacteria, single-celled algae and other tiny floaters – with a network of hairlike extensions of its substance that radiates from the aperture of its outer chamber. Most forams have shells of calcite and extract the material for them from seawater, and therefore are an important part of the 'carbon cycle' that stabilizes the amount of carbon dioxide in the atmosphere and so keeps the Earth habitable. It has been estimated that 1.23 billion tons of foram shells are deposited on the sea floor each year, representing the death of 226 billion billion individuals – each one of which had its own life-history, proposed by its sac of DNA, and disposed by the chaos of the sea, some of them, into such prodigies of order as the tombolo of Goirtín.

Having walked the length of the vast necropolis of forams, along either of the beaches, one can scramble up a little slope onto the broad head of the peninsula. The ground is the smooth swellings of consolidated dunes, covered with a sward that feels elastic underfoot, nibbled as neat as a lawn by rabbits and rich with lime-loving herbs. Outcrops of granite interrupt it here and there, together with big round boulders of granite dropped at random by the retreating glaciers ten thousand years ago, sometimes in piles that make visitors think they have discovered prehistoric dolmens and stone circles. Patches of this fertile terrain were cultivated in harder times; here and there the traces of old potato ridges show in the green turf like ribs in a famished beast. But the field walls have long been reduced to gapped rows of stones, and cattle wander unconstrained by them. The land's edge is low, rocky and intricate. On the south-facing shore of the peninsula is a small sandy bay called An Trá Gharbh, the rough strand, backed by broken dunes that spill prehistoric shell middens. Near the western point of the headland an alert eye might spot some hundreds of beach pebbles a few inches long laid out in a regular pattern on a flat marshy area of the shore; the stones have almost sunk into the soft ground, but the pattern is still just legible, and walkable, as a maze of the classical Greek form known as the Walls of Troy. A well-informed Englishwoman of the locality told me that it was made by the British land-artist Richard Long, but I doubted this, since it was rather untypical of his work, until I found a photograph of it in his book *Walking in Circles*, published in connection with his 1991 exhibition in London. In an interview reported in that book Long said:

In *Connemara Sculpture*, which is that maze, I'd gone to the museum in Dublin and had seen that particular image on an early rock carving, a sacred stone. I drew it in my notebook. Then, a week later, when I was in the west of Ireland and wanted to make a sculpture out of beach pebbles, I had the image in my notebook.

I have enquired of the National Museum and am informed that the carving in question can only be the so-called Hollywood Stone, which is now off display in the Reserve Collections. It is a labyrinth stone of the Christian era originally located by St Kevin's Road, the ancient pilgrims' way to Glendalough in County

Wicklow. The connection with pilgrimage is apposite, for Richard Long's life has been largely devoted to a divinatory worldwide journeying through wildernesses, and his own road has been marked by his sculptural works; I say 'divinatory' because what he divines is the match between site and construct, the latter usually being a rearrangement of whatever the terrain provides, such as sticks or stones, seaweed or mud, in an elemental configuration, frequently a circle, straight lines or a cross. The *Connemara Sculpture* is uncharacteristically complex; it is an early work, dating from 1971. Having intervened in nature thus, he photographs the result in its setting, and passes onwards, leaving its future in the hands of nature. For his audience, the real artwork is a photograph, and perhaps a short text, exhibited in an art gallery, and the persistence or otherwise of what he leaves behind him is apparently irrelevant; but it is not so to me. I have had a brief exchange of letters with Richard Long on the afterlife of the traces of his passage. I had marked the sites of two of his circles on my map of the Aran Islands, and in 1997 his wife, Denny, telephoned my partner, M, looking for a copy of the map to give him for his birthday, which we happily provided. However, the birthday gift was apparently not well received, for soon afterwards we heard from him as follows:

Dear M, As a matter of fact, the edition of the map you kindly sent Denny didn't have my sculpture on it – which is fine by me, as it was never my intention for my sculptures to be marked 'sites'. I was originally very surprised and aghast when someone told me years ago that my work was marked on a map. (It was without my knowledge or intention.) Anyway, it's good it has been deleted. Also the way my 2 works are mentioned in the book [*Stones of Aran: Pilgrimage*] is appropriate & fitting to the spirit in which they were made.

Naturally I sprang to the defence of my cartography:

Actually your circle of upright stones *is* marked on the Aran map M sent Denny (the little fig 3 at the east end of the island, south of Túr

Máirtín); but in this new edition the note on it is in the companion book rather than on the map itself as in the previous edition.

I'm sorry to learn that you were aghast when someone told you it had been marked on a map. If I had been reproducing one of your photos of it I would have looked for permission, naturally; but marking its position on a map is a different matter. I would never treat one of your works with anything less than great respect, but the primary loyalty of maps is to what is there. Think of it this way: once an artist has made a visible intervention in the landscape and left it there, it contributes to other people's experience of the place, which may well be expressed in someone else's work of art. Placelore will start to accumulate around it – and my subject matter is the web of placelore. Just as a text is relinquished to other people's interpretations once it has left the writer's hands, so your marks on the landscape will have a career of their own; they are no longer defined by their origin in your creativity. If they are of a persistent substance like stone they may play roles other than that of a work of art (fox's den, pilot's landmark), or revert to being mere stones. Your other Aran circle on the coast a mile or so further west actually functioned as a fairy circle once, I see from my diary . . .

. . . and I finished with a reminiscence of taking two children to visit the circle, and jumping into it hand-in-hand with them. Richard Long was clearly mollified by this, and his next letter was purely friendly, which is why I have not hesitated to pinpoint his *Connemara Sculpture* and raise the question of the role of his artefacts in their natural setting. The essence of his works is, according to his intentions, what he brings home to the artworld: a photographic image in many cases, not primarily of value for its merits as landscape photography or as a record of a site-specific sculpture, but as the entrypoint to a concept, the idea of a journey, the passage of a particular human being through certain places. But if the spirit of the work has flown off into the realms of thought, its bones, remaining in actuality for at least a time, have equally complex destinies. If identified, as I have identified a few of them in Aran, the Burren and Connemara, they may even be preserved as memorabilia, objects imbued by touch with the charisma of the artist, contemplation of which might reveal the stages of his or her self-creation as a creator. One might take them as markers of exemplary terrains in which the formative processes of Nature are particularly clearly displayed at work. Unidentified, their origins unknown to the passer-by, they are minor enigmas of the landscape. As they slowly founder in the interplay of the elements, their status as the product of an intention becomes as hard to be sure of as those of the nearly effaced potato ridges or the random clutches of glacial erratics. Eventually they will be anonymous contributions to the compilation of the Earth, like the soft bones of stillborn babies rotted into that knoll by the seashore, or the husks of uncountable forams heaped onto the tombolo. We find ourselves in a world compacted out of our forebears. In art we take responsibility for this fact, or at least recognize our ineluctable complicity in its processes. It is as if we choose that our parents have to die; it is our fault. In growing out of childhood we drive them on before us into middle age; in adding a birthday to our lives we burden them with another year; finally, one more day packed with hours and minutes for us is enough to push them over the edge. This is how we make room, make time, make the world, for ourselves. This is the gargoyle-logic of creation.

Ogygia Lost

Whether islands from the creation of the world have been situated in the sea, or whether they have been afterwards separated from continents, by the intervention of inundations, is a subject of debate.

This is the first sentence of Roderick O'Flaherty's *Ogygia*, written in 1685, and in some moods it is all one needs to know of the geological theory of islands. Ogygia is the island on which the nymph Calypso hid and protected Odysseus and by her wiles delayed his homecoming for seven years. The name 'Calypso' means something like 'she who conceals'. According to Plutarch this island is situated not in the Mediterranean but in the Atlantic, 'five days of navigation from Britain'. O'Flaherty's book is a history of Ireland, and he justifies his choice of title thus:

Whether Ireland be Plutarch's Ogygia, which he places to the west of Britain, in his book of the Moon's appearance in her course, as some assert; or whether it be the contrary, as others think, is all the same to me. For I have intitled my book Ogygia, for the following reason given by Camden: 'Ireland is justly called Ogygia, i.e. very antient, according to Plutarch, for the Irish date their history from the first eras of the world; so that in comparison to them, the antiquity of all other countries is modern, and almost in its infancy!'

Ireland, then, is uniquely ancient, a place of mystery and concealment, from which it is difficult for the wanderer to part. And if its enduring fascinations arise from its being an island off the west of Europe, then islands lying off the west of Ireland itself can be expected to exert a superior power of enchantment.

From the promontory of Goirtín or the hill slopes above Roundstone one sees, about four miles offshore, an uninhabited island called Cruach na Caoile. According to O'Flaherty this name is a corruption of 'Cruagh Coelann' (in his seventeenth-century spelling), Coelann being a saint who had his chapel there. A *cruach* is a stack or a stack-shaped hill, and this island is a flat-topped hill like the lower stages of a shallow pyramid in building. Because of its symmetry and, frequently, its purple-grey gloom against the southern brightness, it has an air of being withdrawn into itself, as befits a hermit's retreat. Its granite slopes descend without interruption into the ocean, offering no beach or natural harbour. Because of its exposed position it is usually beset by waves, and there are few days in the year when it is easy to land on it. The first two times I went out to explore it, on what seemed very suitable calm days, with an Inis Ní boatman and his son who tend to the island's little automatic lighthouse, we found that the surf was roaring all the way round it; on the second occasion, when my companions tried to edge in close enough for me to jump ashore, a thole-pin broke under their strenuous muscle-work with the oars and we had to back off hastily before the boat was thrust by waves onto the rocks. Because of these rebuffs and the strange lore I had gathered about it, Cruach na Caoile had become Ogygia itself for me by the time of my first successful landing, in the autumn of 1989.

Some years previously the island had been sold by the Mylottes, publicans and farmers of Carna, to a German, who had landed some mouflon sheep and a ram on it by helicopter, with the intention of letting them breed and then having a shoot there, or so it was rumoured – a horrible idea, which came to nothing; little more was heard of the German, and eventually the great wild creatures died without human intervention over several years, from wind, rain and longing for the scent of herbs of their native Sardinia. A Roundstone man, Paddy McDonagh, used to go out now and again to see how they were faring, and on one Sunday afternoon of flat calm I accompanied him. As we left Roundstone Bay in Paddy's wooden currach with its chugging outboard engine we exchanged shouts and laughter with an elderly couple in a rowing boat from a neighbouring village, who were out inspecting their lobsterpots, and they lobbed a great spider crab at us; I remember vividly the weird black blot of spines and legs momentarily splashed on the sky. A little further out near Inis Leacan, the now-deserted island Paddy was born on, we visited a net he had set the day before, in which were enough fish for our dinners, including a male cuckoo wrasse, a stumpy multicoloured fish called the *bod gorm* in Irish, *bod* being slang for the penis and *gorm* meaning blue – a name that promotes much simple fun among fishermen. Otherwise the passage was without incident. The glass had been high for days and the sea was as calm around Cruach na Caoile as Paddy had ever seen it. We hopped onto the rocks and moored the boat with ropes stretched between boulders and the anchor so that it floated some way offshore and wouldn't get knocked if a swell arose. Paddy paused for a while, bending forward with hands on knees, observing the boat keenly to see that it was behaving itself, before we set off into the interior.

The island is thick with bracken, gorse, heather and long grass. On the sheltered eastern side there are traces of cultivation, broken field walls and the ruins of a keeper's cottage, dating from a century ago or more, when the Berridges of Ballynahinch and their predecessors the Martins had a breeding herd of red deer on the island, which in English is still called Deer Island. (This name posed a problem for fishermen, to whom four-footed animals bring bad luck. Old Miss Dundass once told me that when her brother was taken out in a boat as a little lad, he piped up as they passed the island, 'I want to see the deer!', so that the fishermen had to shut him up and make him repeat the phrase 'Cold iron, cold iron', which it seems was an antidote to the mention of the animals.) I am told that the last of the deer, a doe in kid, was shot in the hungry years of the 1940s or 1950s. In the days of the Berridges there used to be over a hundred of them. A Mícheál Phádhraic Dhonnchadha Ó Clochartaigh held the lonely post of *maor* or bailiff. He had no boat; when he needed to visit the mainland he would light a signal fire, and a boatman from Leitir Árd, who also brought out his supplies of turf, would come and fetch him. Ó Clochartaigh's offspring emigrated to America; they knew no

English when they left, according to the old Carna man from whom this oral history was recorded in the 1930s. A story taken down from another Carna man, about a woman giving birth on the island, conveys the contiguity of the Otherworld, the night world, to the daily life of the deer herds. I translate literally from the Irish, to give the starkness of the telling:

A woman was in Cruach Chaolainn who went into labour. There was nobody in the house or on the island but herself and her husband. When the birthpangs came on her the husband went out by boat to the mainland to the north to get a wise woman. The wife was alone in the house and in labour. When night came she was lying down by the fire with her face towards it. A big dark man she had never seen before came in, a huge monstrous black thing.

'Get up, girl!' says he.

She didn't get up. The cock crowed and he had to go.

'Ah, it's well for you,' says he, 'if it wasn't for that male thing outside, your life would have been short!'

When the husband and the wise woman came in the morning she'd had a baby boy. The baby was sound and she was safe. The cock has great power if it has a good voice.

Roundstone people tell me that the last inhabitant of Deer Island was a Marcus Clogherty, whose son settled in Loch Conaortha, north of Cill Chiaráin. I also hear rather vague reports of a family who moved into Roundstone from Deer Island and settled near the lane up to Errisbeg Hill, and who were so isolated by shyness that nobody realized that they were in a very bad way until they died in a state of terrible neglect. From further inland, in Emlaghmore near Ballynahinch, I have picked up a mention of a cross of some sort marking the spot where a man, perhaps of the King family, was stabbed by a wild fellow who was nick-named 'the Fia' (from the Irish word for a deer) because he had been resettled in the area from Deer Island; his brother had some similar name, perhaps 'the Cat'. In noting such almost obliterated communal memories, I sometimes feel like a priest bending his ear to the mouth of a dying man to capture the profound and determinative sense of his last breath.

Buried in rampant brambles a few hundred yards south-west of the ruined cottage, Paddy and I thought we could make out the fallen stones of the little chapel said to have been built by the island's saint. The site was ideal for a hermit's oratory, tucked into the shelter of a low inland scarp and looking out at a vast unworldly delight of islands and bays and mountains, with the long grey band of the Aran Islands almost closing the southern horizon, the low honey-coloured granite dome of St Macdara's Island two miles away to the east, and to the north all the silver-headed peaks of Connemara looking over each other's shoulders. In O'Flaherty's time the memory of Coelann was celebrated in the parish of Moyrus (the present-day parishes of Roundstone and Carna) on the third of February. According to some less authoritative local lore I have heard, Caolann (as he is now spelled) was brother to all the Connemara saints, Macdara, Macduach, Cáillín, Flannán et al. Legend associates Caolann's island particularly with that of his neighbour Macdara. An old man of Cill Chiaráin told me that a tyrant stole all the male animals off Macdara's island to Caolann's island, and that they leaped back again. The ram left its hoofmarks where it landed on the island's shore, and they can still be seen when the tide is out. The bull fell short of the island and came bursting up through the rocks, leaving a hole called Spout an Tairbh, the spout of the bull. This is actually a blowhole; foam is flung high into the air from it as waves rush into submarine passages below. Even on calm days it can be seen from the mainland as a little white feather on the western tail of Macdara's island, appearing and disappearing with the rhythm of the sea. '*Da mba míorúilt é, ba mhíorúilt cheart é!*' commented my storyteller – 'If it was a miracle, it was a proper miracle!'

Next, Paddy and I made a circuit of the island – a walk of a couple of miles – and pinpointed all the places I had learned the names of from various fishermen. Among them: Scothach na nGiuróg, the reef of the terns, which thrusts out into the Atlantic from the southern point of the island; Fó na gCacannaí, the creek of the droppings, where cormorants roost; Duirling na Roilleachaí, the stonebeach of the oystercatchers; Tobar an Ghiolcaigh, the well of the reed, a seepage of fresh water down a rockface at which fishermen would come to drink, sucking the precious water through the hollow stem of a reed. Finally we climbed just over two hundred feet to the highest point of the island, Caorán na nGall, the moorland hill of the foreigners, and searched through the bracken but could find no trace of the cairns under which these 'foreigners' are said to have been buried. According to the nineteenth-century Galway historian James Hardiman, the incident concerns an Abbot O'Donnell, on the run after the suppression of the White Friars monastery in Donegal in the time of Queen Elizabeth. He was finally captured by the English soldiery in Coillín near Carna. The rest of the story I translate from the Irish version recorded in Carna about eighty years ago:

The soldiers said that he'd pay dearly for the trouble he'd given them. The priest said he had no objection to death, that he would be as happy to be on the other side as to be in this life. 'But if I am to die,' says he to them, 'my mind is greatly troubled about the bag of gold I had and that I buried on that island out there, and nobody would be able to find it but me.'

'If there's a lot of gold in it you needn't die at all. We wouldn't kill you at all if there's enough in it to satisfy us,' says the soldiers' officer.

'I am happy to give you the gold and then to die,' says Father O'Donnell.

'How will we get to the island?' says the officer.

'I'll get a boat,' says the priest, 'and we'll tell nobody where we're going.'

The priest got a boat and he sailed to the island with them. They came to land on the lee side of the island. He got out and got a grip on the boat. He held the boat while they got out. When they were all out and had walked up onto the land he gave the boat a push and leaped into it, and lay down in the bottom of the boat. The wind was with him and he took the boat out. They began to fire bullets at the boat. They couldn't see him: he was in the bottom of the boat. When he was far enough out he raised the sail and sailed home again. He sent word throughout Iorras Aintheach, Iorras Beag and Iorras Mór that no boat was to take them off. For seven or eight days the people of the region could hear one of them shouting and yelling. (There is the odd person in the world and nothing is so wonderful as the distance they can make themselves heard from. There were such, long ago.) The priest himself was listening to them. After fourteen or fifteen days they were not to be heard. Said the priest, 'No more calling will be heard out of John from the Hill of the Foreigners.'

A week after that a boat went in, and they had died. They were all dead together on the hillock, and they were buried together, and the place they are buried is called Caorán na nGall from that day to this.

The island is of course haunted, if only by the echo of that terrible shouting. Again from Carna a scrap of doggerel was recorded, composed by one of a group of women who were landed on the island to pick *creathnach* or dulse, a sweet edible seaweed, and were frightened by voices:

> If I live to see the boat arrive
> And my hand reaches its nose
> There'll be no sign of Kate
> On Caorán na nGall any more.

From the now silent summit of Caorán na nGall Paddy and I surveyed the taut line of the horizon between those ultimate outposts of Connemara, Slyne Head to the west and Na Sceirdí to the south. These latter are a scattering of reefs and shoals and two islands of bare rock one or two hundred yards across, about five miles south of Deer Island. The islands are called Dún Godail, cuttlefish fort, and An Sceirde Mór, the big *sceird*, a most expressive word meaning a bleak, windswept place. Roderick O'Flaherty's description seems to situate them on the very horizon of reality:

There is, westwards of Aran, in sight of the next continent of Balynahynsy barony, Skerde, a wild island of huge rocks, the receptacle of a deale of seals thereon yearly slaughtered. These rocks sometimes appear to be a great city far off, full of houses, castles, towers, and chimneys; sometimes full of blazing flames, smoak, and people running to and fro. Another day you would see nothing but a number of ships, with their sailes and riggings; then so many great stakes or reeks of corn and turf; and this not only on fair sun-shining days, whereby it might be thought the reflection of the sun-beames, on the vapours arising about it, had been the cause, but alsoe on dark and cloudy days happening.

Women from Carna used to go gathering dulse there too, and once were cut off by bad weather and almost given up for lost, according to the Carna *seanchaí* already quoted:

Nine women went out to Na Sceirdí picking dulse. The boat that landed them on the rock went off fishing. She was to come back for them in the evening. She wasn't able to come back or to come alongside them because of the working of the sea. She had to go home. No boat came for them for nine nights and nine days, the sea was so wild, and every man who had one of his family out there said they must certainly have been lost. On the morning of the tenth day the sea had calmed, and this woman, a woman of the Faherty family, the mother of Seán an Chóta, said she had seen them. She was standing on Caorán na hÁirde [a small hill near Carna] and she told the relatives not to be anxious, that the women were alive, that she herself was watching them going down when the surf fell back and picking a handful of dulse, and going back up to the top of the rock when they saw the surf coming.

A boat went out with four men to collect the women. The nine were alive, as the woman who sat on the hill had said. Their jaws were swollen from chewing the dulse all the time. They weren't as good as they used to be until a fortnight after coming home.

That happened in the autumn. The Fairhaired Merchant put his curse on anyone who trusted an autumn night. An autumn night had defeated the Fairhaired Merchant.

This mysterious personage, the Fairhaired Merchant (an Ceannaí Fionn), figures in the folklore of the west of Ireland, according to which he and a companion once set off by boat to discover *bun na spéire*, the foot of the sky, as the horizon is called in Irish; eventually they reached walls of brass they could not climb, which they agreed must be the foot of the sky. It is said that the Fairhaired Merchant 'was very sharp and effectual and could understand things of every sort but could never understand the length of autumn nights, the mind of woman, or the tide when it ebbs'.

By the time we had admired and commented on everything visible within the rim of the sky, all three of these tricky matters were on our minds. Was the autumn day closing down, were our wives wondering when we would return, was the boat pulling at its anchor? It was time to go. On the way down the hill I picked up a skull, not of one of the starved foreigners but of a mouflon sheep – the only sign we had seen of them so far. The storm-beach near where we had landed was of heaped granite boulders a foot or more across and worn by centuries of pounding seas into ellipsoids and near-perfect spheres; we manhandled a few of them into the bottom of the boat to take back for our gardens. As we cast off we caught sight of two or three of the mouflons for the first time, or at least of their great horns sharp against the sky high on the hillside.

On the return voyage we landed briefly on one of the two satellite islets of Cruach Chaoláin called Oileáin na Cruaiche, the islands of the Cruach, mistranslated into English as the Hard Islands, as if from *crua*, hard. A shaggy white seal pup lying on its shore goggled at us intruders, and a flight of barnacle geese took to the air. We photographed each other on the bare summit of the islet, with the big island itself in the background, as if to prove we had been there. Back in Roundstone harbour we disembarked our cryptic trophies: four globes of granite, and a staring skull. Perhaps Cruach na Caoile wasn't Ogygia after all, for, even if it had not been entirely open with us, it had not delayed our return beyond reason.

*

In the summer of 2001 Cruach na Caoile went on fire. At night, seen from the higher parts of Roundstone village, the flames working their way through the dense vegetation looked like a delicate sparkling necklace slowly tightening, choking the life out of the island. By day the southern sky was a murky disaster. The skin of peat on Caorán na nGall smouldered for weeks; the hill was reduced to bare rock. Perhaps it was a coincidence that this unparalleled clearance of scrub happened when rumours were circulating about a proposal to install a wind farm of twelve wind turbines on the island. Nothing more was heard of this scheme, but the smoke and the rumour announced that an alien world of financial calculation, innovative technology, dubious statistics and unfamiliar acronyms was making its bid for the horizon. Later in that year we learned through the local newspaper that two rival companies, one based in Spiddal and the other in Portlaoise, were investigating the possibility of siting wind turbines on An Sceirde Mór. It transpired that Na Sceirdí, which one might have thought must be the for ever inalienable patrimony of the cuttlefish and the dulse, were in fact privately owned. They had been bought by Martin Mylotte, together with Cruach na Caoile, from the Berridges in 1940, and the Portlaoise firm, which had already erected a mast to measure wind speeds on An Sceirde Mór, had agreed to buy the rock from the Mylottes if it seemed worthwhile to go ahead with the project. The Spiddal company applied to the Department of the Marine and Natural Resources for a licence to carry out preliminary studies; their ultimate aim was to erect a 25-megawatt wind farm of twenty turbines on the foreshore of the island. Although the other company objected that their own project would be hindered by any other wind-farming activity there, the Spiddal company were granted their licence, on the basis of the Government's policy of promoting the use of renewable energy, and the fact that the site lay outside the five-kilometre offshore limit recommended 'to minimise visual intrusion'. To be profitable a wind farm sited so far offshore would have to be large; it would also necessitate the construction of a high-voltage power line from wherever the electricity was to be brought ashore, across the hills and bogs to Screeb, some sixteen miles away, to connect with the Electricity Supply Board's grid. An investment of €70 million was mentioned. In 2003 the company submitted its tender for a power purchase agreement with the ESB, under the terms of AER VI, the sixth round in the Alternative Energy Requirement Competition, without success. But the project is still under discussion, and is likely to be revived as the technology of wind power in such extreme environments develops.

The State's support for alternative energy projects arises because electricity generation by the burning of fossil fuels is a significant source of the gases that are causing global warming. Under the Kyoto Protocol of 1997 Ireland is committed to limiting the rise in greenhouse gas emissions in the period 1990–2010 to 15 per cent, and faces financial penalties if it fails. Demand for electricity is predicted to increase by 50 per cent over the same period, and the question as to whether that demand should be satisfied seems not to be on the public agenda, whereas if the demand for crack cocaine threatened to rise by some comparable figure, steps would be taken both to thwart the satisfaction of that demand and to tame it. Our civilization is addicted to energy, increasingly dependent upon it and vulnerable to any shortfall in supply. Instead of entering into a deep engagement with the struggle against this craving we have invented a whole new industry, as polluting and energy-thirsty as many another, that denatures landscapes by the square mile yet dresses itself in green and is heavily subsidized because it offers comfort to our environmentalist consciences.

The generally accepted solution to the wind farm industry's land-hunger is to build massive offshore installations. Although An Sceirde Mór is about ten miles out in the ocean there is no doubt that turbines on it would be visible from the mainland in the Carna and Roundstone regions; the relatively small turbines of the Inis Meáin wind farm can be clearly seen from County Clare, a slightly longer distance away. But perhaps that tiny busy flickering on the horizon would disturb so few that democracy would have the right to overrule their tender feelings in this critical campaign against global warming. Perhaps, to the fishermen and summer yacht-people sailing by, the installation would look magnificent in its lonely commerce with the elements, a reapparition of Roderick O'Flaherty's 'great city far off, full of houses, castles, towers, and chimneys; sometimes full of blazing flames, smoak, and people running to and fro'. What of the disturbance to wildlife? Dúchas, the Heritage Service, who were at the time our statutory guardians of the natural environment, offered no objections to the Sceirde proposal; perhaps they knew whereof they did not speak, although I never heard of any study being done on the bird life of Na Sceirdí. Not a word of the place's folklore would be lost, for it has already been written down, and much of what still is to be heard in people's mouths has often already been recirculated through tourist literature; also, stories that have outlasted centuries can fly through wind turbines unscathed. The question is not to be fought out in the usual arena of cultural conservation versus economic development; the local community is going neither to lose the heritage of its past nor to gain a more prosperous future through the installation of turbines on An Sceirde Mór. As the owner of the rock put it to me, the Sceirde turbines would be 'out of everyone's way'. But would they be out of mind, and does it matter?

The wind-farming industry's mechanization of great tracts of open countryside is a profound tragedy, whether or not it is necessitated by the onset of global warming. Like any other extractive industry, mining the wind produces spoil heaps; in them lie foregone landscapes of fenced-off hillsides, closed paths, culverted streams, plant life bulldozed aside. This is a sudden additional encroachment of the machine world on the natural world. Ever increasingly, the old, wild, weird places become inaccessible except to the imagination. And now the sea is not inviolable. The desert isle becomes a factory in which the wind itself, no longer the spirit of freedom, is condemned to drudge like Caliban. Experience and the imagination can no longer accompany one another on the voyage to Ogygia, and both suffer and decline, the latter starved of sensory detail, the former chilled by its own indifference.

Do I cry out too soon? I write to express the heart's unreason-ableness, not to convict the world of its wrongs. Deer Island and Na Sceirdí are untouched as yet, except by that sinister fire and that premonitory mast, but in my mind they have lost their secretive reclusiveness, their precious strangeness. The horizon has been fingered and smudged. The walls of brass contract around us.

Holiday Island

Master of summer's informal ceremonies in Roundstone harbour is Máirtín O'Malley, whose dark locks and eyes and sea-eagle profile, which he shares with his sister Mary the poet, his swash-buckling way of swirling about the bay in a RIB or rigid inflatable boat, creating a huge curling wash, all commend him to the tourist in hopes of traces of Connemara's fabled wildness. The island of Inis Leacan, too, is an attractive invitation to a taste of the old days; it can be reached in minutes on a speedboat, one can dawdle round its rim in an hour, it has beaches for sunbathing, picturesquely ruined cottages, little stone-walled fields full of wildflowers – and yet it lies upon the threshold of the Atlantic, and the rough stone gables of its deserted homes accuse a pitiless history. 'We used to live on the island when time had no value,' one of the island's farmers, now living on the mainland, explained to a holiday-home owner, 'but now time has value. That's why people have all left the island.' To refresh my impressions of the place for this piece of writing I determined to revisit it in the holiday season, when time might at least be picked up at summer-sale discount.

For four years now, Rosie McGurran, a young Belfast artist resident in Roundstone, has been leading a group of painters, some of them quite well-known professionals, some skilled amateurs, others absolute beginners, out to Inis Leacan to learn from her and each other in its archetypally moody west-of-Ireland scenery. This year Máirtín had been engaged to ferry them out, so I joined them on the quayside, on a June morning of sunshine and occasional scudding showers. It promised to be a day of coincidences useful to me in my drive for Connemaran omnis-cience. Máirtín told me that he had been approached on the quayside the previous evening by an American couple; the man had introduced himself as Greg Broughton, explained that his great-grandfather had been the landlord of Inis Leacan, and wondered if it was possible to visit the island. To their surprise and delight, Máirtín had invited them to join Rosie's outing, and had also referred them to me as local antiquary. (What is my role in Roundstone's community? A square fish in a round pond, I sometimes think.) They had not found me at home that evening, but I was looking forward to meeting them on the island, as historical information about the Broughtons is hard to come by. However, they had not shown up by the time I was scrambling into the boat with the first batch of artists.

Máirtín's RIB actually belongs to the composer Bill Whelan, who owns the big house known as the Fort just north of the harbour, employs Máirtín as marine factotum and generously allows use of the boat for many social occasions. Clinging to its slippery bulges, we accelerated out of the harbour with the exciting power of wealth behind us, and were soon besting a headwind and choppy currents in the mouth of the bay, banging into each wave like a wheelbarrow going down steps. The tide being too far out for easy use of Inis Leacan's little nineteenth-century harbour, we were delivered, rather jolted, onto the north shore of the island at Aill an Chipín, the rock of the little stick (why so called I am yet to learn), and had to scramble over seaweed and rocky slopes to reach dry land. Inis Leacan means roughly 'shelving flagstone island', which well describes its shores. Above the rocks at our landing point is a steep beach of white shell-sand. Its grassy crest has been undermined by rabbit burrows and when I trod on it my foot went down into a three-foot layer of densely packed whelk, limpet, oyster and scallop shells, for much of the beach is a huge shell-midden, which has hardly been more than glanced at by archaeologists as yet, but has clearly been built up over all the island's generations, probably from the late Stone Age to medieval times.

The harbour, with its narrow entrance between the old Congested Districts Board pier and a smaller 1950s pier at right angles to it, is at the north-eastern and most sheltered corner of the island. Two buildings stand in open ground just inland of it:

one with a high ridge roof and a plaque above the door that identifies it as 'Inishlacken National School A.D. 1908', and the other, a small traditional cottage, whitewashed and slate-roofed. Rosie had arranged for the use of both of these for her artists, and was soon lighting turf-briquet fires in them, for there were occasional showers gusting off the sea. The school, which closed in 1925 when the number of pupils fell below twenty-five, had lain derelict for a long time but was reroofed a few years ago by the Ashes, a family who have kept up their connections with Roundstone since the days of the Revd James Ashe in the 1840s, and who celebrated the renovation of the building with a party that must have rocked the island, helicoptering in countless visitors and locals from Ervallagh, the nearest point of the main-land. The interior, apart from a corridor-like cloakroom inside the door, is one bare, lofty room with tall sash windows on three sides, and four bunk beds, adapted more to roughing it for a day or two than to residence. The little cottage close behind it has a central room open to the roof rafters, with a hearth wide enough for a person to sit in it on either side of the fire. This was the cottage used by the Belfast artist Gerard Dillon in the spring and summer of 1951, and to which he invited his colleague George Campbell and a younger artist, James MacIntyre, as described in the latter's book *Three Men on an Island*. Rosie's Inis Leacan Project this year was dedicated to Dillon, an artist she particularly admires; one of her own paintings, entitled *Homage to Gerard Dillon*, shows herself wearing the island as a fantastic hat, or, if not the whole island, a representative patch of it, a tip-tilted field that tenderly cups a little white cottage. Dillon's *faux-naif* Inis Leacan scenes also show a landscape of cosy, rounded enclosures: a donkey twiddles its ears in a womb-like field; a painter going home with a completed work under his arm is almost hugged by the curves of a boreen; two islanders lounge in the shelter of a wall; a seagull perches sedately on a rounded boulder. Space is a cluster of nurturing cells, and time has no value, or is more valuable than anything that could possibly be earned in it.

And, in part and in summer, Inis Leacan answers charmingly

to this description. Most of the land is divided into little meadows, many of them bowls of yellow irises or fleabane or ragged robin. There are a few loitering donkeys, sheep stand ready to defend their lambs, wheatears and stonechats flit along the rambling stone walls, a swallow threads silently through the window of a half-ruined barn. The shoreline is a necklace of incidentals; old Pat McDonagh, a former islander, once conducted me on a circuit of the coast and named forty-four of its features for me: Barr na Leapa, meaning 'the head of the bed', a rock in the harbour mouth; Lochán na mBallach, 'the small pool of the rockfish'; Fuaigh na Móna, 'the creek of the turf', a natural harbour from which what little turf the island had was shipped in hookers to the Aran Islands; and so on, each placename as compact and some-times as cryptic as a clue in a treasure hunt. No point of the island is much more than fifty feet above sea level, but it has several little heights Pat thought worth pointing out to me, Cnocán an Ghreasaí, the cobbler's hillock, and Cnocán an tSagairt, the priest's hillock, among them. A grass-grown boreen runs south from the harbour to a crescent of cottages, all in ruins now, around a small bay of the east shore, from which the southern section of the island is called Trawvally; I think the Irish of this must have been Trá an Bhaile, the beach of the village. (None of the former islanders still living has more than scraps of Irish, but their parents would have been fluent speakers.) A field on the east of this boreen, two hundred yards south of the harbour, is called the Lawn – and this brings one back to the history of the island, for a slight swelling in the Lawn is the sole remaining trace of the Broughtons' residence, Mountain View Lodge – a banal name, but validated by the glorious panorama of Errisbeg darkly arching in the north-west, the Twelve Pins glistening far away to the north, and the smooth swell of Cnoc Mordáin along the eastern skyline.

Inis Leacan, like most of Connemara, had been part of the former O'Flaherty clan territory and was confiscated by the Cromwellians, who granted the island to a branch of the Blakes of Galway, along with Inis Ní and more extensive lands around Indreabhán in south Connemara. Colman Robert Broughton acquired Inis Leacan from

Patrick Blake in 1835. The Broughtons were a Yorkshire family, I have been told by Rosaleen Mills, a descendant, but she could not tell me why he made such a move in that dire epoch. The annual rent of the island was at the time £80, and the population 190 or 200. The Broughtons' coming was not a happy event for the island, which, according to a Fisheries Report, 'in July 1835 obtained relief from the Western Committee owing to potato failure and change of landlord, distressing people for rent'. However, in the decade of the Great Famine the population was virtually unchanged, being 126 in 1841 and 125 in 1851, unlike that of misfortunate Inis Ní, which was still in the hands of the extortionate Blakes and was almost depopulated by deaths and evictions. Records show that in 1856 Colman was leasing out nine small houses in Inis Leacan, where his son Christopher Robert Broughton had his own house and was leasing out another five smaller ones. By then Colman had also enlarged a cottage into the two-storey house known as Ellistrum Lodge, in Ervallagh, and was leasing it out. But it seems Colman was still living on the island, for a visitor wrote an account of staying with him there in 1866. The writer was D'Arcy Wentworth Thompson, Professor of Greek at Queen's University, Galway, and for him Inis Leacan was a 'craggy Ithaca' in which Broughton, 'a wanderer in earlier years like Ulysses', exercised 'an old paternal chieftainship' over his 'thirty vassals'. Broughton entertained him with reminiscences of the Famine and the subsequent cholera epidemic, and showed him the gold medal he had been awarded for repeated heroism in sea rescues. Thompson stayed overnight, and was kept awake by a braying donkey until Colman opened his bedroom window and flung his boots at it. The Broughtons were Catholics, and I have read somewhere of Colman and his family coming out by boat day after day to attend a Franciscan mission in Roundstone. It is also remembered locally that on a very low spring tide he waded on horseback across the channel to Ervallagh. A very old Roundstone fisherman once told me that Broughton had been a hard landlord, that some of the tenants moved out to Aircíní four miles north of Roundstone, and then to Inis Ní, and eventually returned to Inis Leacan; perhaps this was after the Broughtons sold the island to a Robert Macredy of Recess near Ballynahinch. By 1880 Colman was living in Boolard on the lane running up to Errisbeg Hill from Roundstone village; at that time of hardship he was Chairman of the Roundstone Relief Committee. The Congested Districts Board bought out the estate from Macredy in 1907, renewed the harbour, built the majority of the cottages visible today, divided the land into long 'stripes' and distributed it among the tenants, but could not stem the fall in population. The last inhabitants, Tom and Mary Woods, were rehoused in Roundstone in about 1982, but some of the former islanders or their offspring still bring cattle out to graze on the island, making them swim behind currachs from Ervallagh beach.

As it happened, while I was looking at the hummock in the Lawn, Tom and Mary's son Martin came down the boreen to greet me; he had come into the island from Ervallagh in his currach to shear his sheep. 'Come here,' he said, 'and I'll show you a bit of history.' First he pointed out a rounded knoll forming a little promontory where the Lawn came down to the shoreline; then he led me to the next field north of the Lawn, which belonged to his family, and showed me a deep depression in the middle of it. Broughton had had the earth dug out of it, he told me, to be spread on the rock of the knoll to make a smooth grassy place for the ladies to sit on and enjoy the view. There used to be a ship's figurehead in the form of a mermaid standing on it, which had been washed ashore from a wreck, and from which the place was called Lady Point. 'But is it true the Broughtons are coming here today?' he asked. I said I had heard so. 'Well, I hope I don't meet them,' he said, 'I probably owe them rent!'

Martin also directed my attention to a big boulder near the highest point of the island (Caorán, fifty-four feet), near the ugly old concrete reservoir tank and the collapsed windmill that used to pump water up to it from a walled-in pond close by; the boulder was called the Rocking Stone, he told me, and if you pushed it in the right place you could rock it, but if you pushed it anywhere else 'You could put your ring out trying, but you wouldn't shift it.' I decided to try my hand, and as Martin went on his way down the boreen I hopped over the field wall and walked up to the stone. It was much taller than me, and quite immoveable, but I was rewarded by a constellation of mushrooms growing by it. Then I inspected the rusty skeleton of the windmill, which Martin told me had been beautiful in its day; now it looked like a gigantic praying mantis. From there I set off on a slow anticlockwise circuit of the island. Along the north shore there is a scattering of derelict cottages, two of them neatly reroofed with green metal sheeting and refurbished as holiday homes, but unoccupied at this time of year; here and there among the ruins some of Rosie's painters were hunkered down out of the wind trying to control their flapping sketchpads. Beyond the last of the cottages the shoreline becomes wilder and bleaker as it turns to face the great gap of empty sea horizon between the long pale beach of Goirtín a mile away to the west and the sombre silhouette of Deer Island against the southern sky. The sea has dragged away the track that used to run down this side of the island, and, as I already knew from islanders who had lost grazing to it, a recent storm had toppled the shingle bank and flooded the fields inland of it with big pebbles. An oystercatcher flew around me with increasingly anguished pipings as I neared a little marsh where it must have had its nest; a wailing drift of common gulls conducted me off their territory under a canopy of wings, while offshore a few terns repeatedly stabbed themselves into the waves with melodramatic shrieks. There were white ruffs of foam around various reefs whose names I had learned from boatmen: Carraig na gCon, the rock of the hounds (or, more likely, of the otters), in the straits between Inis Leacan and Ervallagh; An Searrach Mór and An Searrach Beag, the big and little foals, two rocks that follow at the southern heels of the island. Tóin an Oileáin, the backside of the island, is the name of this south-west corner of Inis Leacan, as it is of the corresponding sea-whipped extremities of several other Connemara islands.

Pat McDonagh had shown me a little holy well a little way east of Tóin an Oileáin when he was conducting me round the island, but on subsequent visits I had failed to find it. Like the better-known holy wells in Inis Ní it is not a real spring well but a pothole full of salt water in the intertidal zone. Nearly all the other pothole wells I have been shown along the south Connemara coast are called Tobar Cholm Cille, but this one was dedicated to the Connemara fishermen's patron saint Macdara, whose island, Oileán Mhic Dara, lies low on the horizon to the south of this point. My notes described it as a round depression six inches across and about three inches deep, on the outer edge of a big slanting rock outcrop called Leachta Sheáin Jós, John Joe's flagstone. Looking along the southern coast now, I was faced by a hopeless confusion of big slanting rock outcrops, but, being obstinate in the pursuit of places, I spent half an hour looking for the little saucer-like rockpool, scrambling to and fro between dry land and the sunken tide that was gurgling and groaning in deep clefts and coombs of the lower shore. And I eventually found it, not on a slanting surface as I'd remembered, but on a ledge below a prominent dome of rock. It looked to me as if it had once been a much deeper hole (most of the wells of this type are two or three feet deep) and that a shard of rock had broken off the seaward aspect of the outcrop, shearing away all but the bottom few inches of the pothole and a trace of one of its sides on the rim of the dome. I dipped my fingers into the little font of seawater and anointed my eyes, and then photographed it from all angles, taking care this time to photograph the rock dome too and to pace out exactly how far it is (eighty-three yards) from the western end of the high field wall that runs along the coast here, so that I would never lose the place again.

As I was about to continue my circuit of the island I saw a couple coming along the shore as if to meet me – the Broughtons, as it turned out, with the inevitability of accidental meetings on a small island. Greg Broughton was tall and limber, while Cathryn was petite, with a pretty smile and bright eyes under a close-fitting hat that made me think of the cloches my mother wore before I knew her, in her flapper days. Both were obviously well able to afford eternal youth; later I learned from them that they each had their own business in the Los Angeles area, hers a public relations firm and his an environmental consultancy. I was delighted to be able to show them the holy well, one of the secrets of Greg's lost ancestral domain. Then I sounded them for Broughton history. At first all I got was what they had read up the night before in one of my own publications, an echo-effect that haunts me in Connemara these days; but then some unexpected notes were added. It was only recently, on inheriting a box of old papers from his grandfather, that Greg had learned of the Inis Leacan connection. In the box was the gold medal awarded to Colman Robert Broughton by the Shipwrecked Fishermen and Mariners' Royal Benevolent Society, and letters from his son Christopher Robert Broughton, Greg's great-grandfather, from which it appeared that Christopher had taken ship from Ireland to sail around the world, had visited Santa Barbara en route and liked it, and after his return to Inis Leacan had emigrated there. He became a sheriff of Santa Barbara County and lived in a building, now roofless but preserved as a historical site, the Las Cruzes adobe. When Greg mentioned this fact to a local historian, the historian replied, 'And I'll tell you something you didn't know about your great-grandfather. He ran a whorehouse out of that building!'

After that colourful excursion into another world we continued on our ways round the grey rocky shore, I anticlockwise, they clockwise. Back in the old schoolhouse I watched Rosie imparting technical tips to a group of learners by painting the view from one of its windows of a cluster of old cottages among rocky knolls and little fields, all the lines of the composition drawn together and interwoven as if the brush were nest-building. In the other cottage I found that two of the Back Lane Painters had persuaded a pearl-pale and sedate young art student to sit for them. Between her blacker-than-black hair and her long black skirt, she was a colour-chord as exotic, among all the rest of us dressed for island and weather in jeans and ragged pullovers, as a parakeet flitting across the grey rocks of Inis Leacan would have been: lime-green jacket, pink gauzy scarf, sky-blue knitted cap.

When I remarked on her having preserved this ensemble immaculately through the trip in Máirtín's boat and the clamber up the seaweedy shore, she assured me, with a note of reproof, that it was what she always wore. And I suppose that, being her own work of art and a cause of art in others, she had no need to burden herself with canvases and easel.

As the afternoon drew on most of the artists came out to lounge in the sunshine on the flowery slope leading down to the harbour. Their eyes were on the scenery, which was conducting a master-class in fake west-of-Ireland painting. The fisherman fiddling with nets and lobsterpots on the quay arranged himself into a Seán Keating sketch, the old gables and field walls cuddled together into a Gerard Dillon composition, the changeable light on the Twelve Pins was knocking out Paul Henrys by the minute. But it was the sward we sat on that entranced me. Here and there tiny ground-hugging plants bore jewel-like flowers; most of them in different shades of pink: the slightly wine-flushed white stars of English stonecrop, the shocking pink of storksbill, and the pale pink of sea milkwort (it wasn't until I saw it under a lens, back at home, that I could appreciate the wax-smooth perfection of its minute five-lobed cups); others of various yellows, that of wall-pepper as sharp as its taste, that of lesser hawkbit, a small dandelion-like flower that floats its flowers an inch or two above the rest on slender stalks, a more mellow, afternoon yellow. This vegetation was an attenuated version of the *Plantago* association Praeger described from cliff-tops in Clare Island and elsewhere on extremely exposed shores of the western seaboard, and much of the soil surface, crumbly with blown sand and seashell dust, was bare except for the flat rosettes of buckshorn plantain, which clung to the ground like appliqué decorations, each of them no bigger than a watch face. 'Tell only happy hours' is an exhortation carved on old sundials, but I was happy to let the plantain, with its narrow leaves like a dozen or a score of old-fashioned watch hands, tell all the island's hours at once, the bitter ones with the rest. Somehow the various threads of my expedition were drawing together into a nest for its meaning. On Lady Point I could almost see the Broughton ladies of old at their embroidery, so many Penelopes regarding the porter-dark sea. The Broughtons of today rounded off their own experience graciously by buying Rosie's painting, and I invited them to dine with us that evening on the mushrooms I had gathered. Máirtín turned up on time with the RIB, entering the harbour with a flamboyant swish, and soon, the wind behind us, the day behind us, we were flying back to Roundstone on wings of spray.

The Wind Through the House

The building that presently houses M and myself and our work
has a rather tentative, gull-like stance, with one foot in the sea
and one on land. It is definitely part of the village, being within
two minutes' walk of the street, the shops and the bars, but it is
also set apart, not just at the very end of the quayside but a little
beyond that, the lower portion of it being built upon an angle
of the sea wall that juts out from the back of the old pier, and
the upper portion of it on a little cliff that forms the coast
running south from the harbour. We call it Nimmo House after
the engineer who built the harbour and founded the village in
the 1830s, and who according to old records had a store on this
site or nearby, giving us licence to think that some of his
stonework anchors us here.

Ramshackle extensions and drastic reshapings, adapting the
building to various uses, have left it a puzzle in three dimensions,
with no internal connection between upstairs and downstairs. In
the late nineteenth century the landlord's agents, the Robinsons
(no relatives of ours), had turf stores and stables for carts and
carriages here, an old man has told me, with an upper storey from
which grain was fed through shoots to the mangers below. In the
1900s the Congested Districts Board, a governmental agency
charged with developing industries in the overpopulated and
penurious west, converted the upper storey into a lace-making
school and employed young Margaret Cosgrove from Fermanagh
to teach her skills to the local girls. Next door on the quayside
was the office of Richard O'Dowd, clerk to the landlord's agent;
Richard and Margaret soon met and married, whereupon she had
to give up her post. Their descendants still run O'Dowd's pub,
on the village street overlooking the harbour. When lace-making
failed, the CDB turned to knitting. Several elderly ladies, visiting

what is now the living room of our house, have pointed out exactly where their knitting machine stood, and the glass panels through which Miss McGee, the manageress, kept an eye on them from a little office off the workroom. Then the building became a carpet-making factory; down at sea level it acquired a concrete clutter of boiler houses and storerooms built out to the front and partly resting on the sea wall, while at the upper level a back extension was built on the land above the little cliff, as a residence for the manager, who seems to have devoted himself to drink, judging by the astonishing number of bottles we discovered in the bushes when we took over the premises later on. The carpet factory moved away, and Gaeltarra Éireann, the Gaeltacht development authority at the time, built a hideous big-windowed, blue-panelled knitting factory next door, blighting the look of the harbour and obscuring the older building from view. At this nadir of its fortunes the older building shared a common lobby with the Gaeltarra factory and was hardly visible from the quayside; empty and virtually forgotten, it became a rubbish dump for the defective socks that poured off the knitting machines while the lessee of the factory toured the USA on state-funded sales drives. The ensuing bankruptcy left the factory on the hands of the new Gaeltacht authority, Údaras na Gaeltachta, and the older building on those of the Industrial Development Authority. An attempt was made to sell them both off as a parcel, but when the businessmen proposing to buy the factory seemed to think that they should get the old building thrown in for nothing, the IDA became suspicious and withdrew from the arrangement.

At that time M and I were producing and publishing our maps in one of the units of the little crafts estate run by the IDA at the other end of the village. How had that come about? Previously we had been living and working in a cottage on Árainn, the largest of the Aran Islands (and as to how that, in its turn, had come about, I have written two fat volumes to explain it). That phase of our lives came to an end in 1984, when I was already making my map of Connemara and it had become clear that if ever I was to finish it, and if the map enterprise was ever to be more than a cottage industry, we needed a studio and some financial backing. On learning about the newly established crafts estate in Roundstone we approached the IDA, and to our amazement were welcomed into their fold with no questions asked; in fact they made extraordinary efforts to expedite our move from the Aran Islands, and bemused us with the graphs they drew up for us predicting exponential growth of income and of numbers of employees, based on an ever-widening programme of cartography. The reason for all this enthusiasm became clear soon after our arrival: the official opening of the estate was to take place shortly, the minister would be coming down from Dublin, and it was politically desirable to be able to demonstrate the viability of the estate by having tenants in place and productively at work. The IDA grant-aided us generously and sent M off to Dublin on a start-your-own-business course (which led to the coining of the name Folding Landscapes). But the Connemara map took me years to complete, and although for a while we did indeed try employing assistants we soon had to admit that we had misunderstood the nature of our own enterprise, which could never be other than personal in its methods and subjective in its motivation. However, the IDA stood by us loyally and, I think, adopted us as a kind of mascot, their executives finding it more amusing to call in on us for a cultural chat than to discuss productivity with our neighbours the electronics factory. So, when the decrepit old building on the quayside fell back into their hands, they steered us in its direction. Although it was dank and filthy, and rain dripping through the neglected slate roof had rotted the floorboards in a couple of places, we saw that the glamour of the ocean suffused the former workroom from two sides, that its windows embraced Connemara from tidemark to skyline, and we knew we could make something beautiful of it. Fortunately, just at that time our map project won the Ford European Environmental Award, and the prize money covered a good proportion of the £16,000 price of the building. When it became known that we had acquired it at this very moderate cost the businessmen were taken aback; suddenly, it appeared to be the most desirable site in Connemara.

They offered to pay more, and the IDA felt a thrill of *Schadenfreude* in informing them that they were too late. The village too was amazed, and a large faction of it was covertly delighted that the business interest had been bested by, of all unlikely people, the dreamers and wanderers of Folding Landscapes.

The change in the old lace school's fortunes was soon consolidated when a local builder bought the dreadful factory next door and remodelled it as a set of holiday apartments, demolishing the common lobby that had joined it to what was now our house, studio and workspace, and running a broad flight of steps up between the two buildings. Simultaneously, with the financial help of my father, we had some tatty partitions removed in the upper half of our premises, revealing the good proportions of the former lace-schoolroom with its three big skylights in a lofty, plank-lined ceiling, while wide openings were pierced in the labyrinth of walls downstairs, liberating its spaces from their squalid cells. Nowadays there are so many windows and glazed screens in the building that light wanders through it in all directions and puzzled reflections meet themselves round corners. My writing desk and computer are in a downstairs room that has the sea lapping along two walls of it at high water, and when a yacht rounding the head of the pier looms in a window behind me, two or three simulacra of it seem to manoeuvre and flit from vista to vista in the adjoining map storeroom and M's office. Once when work was still being done in the bedroom and we were sleeping on mattresses under the uncurtained gable window of the old lace-schoolroom, a full moon rose from the further shore of the bay, paving the black waters with shifting fragments of itself and sending slow vague ripples of reflected moonshine down the long perspective of the ceiling. The landscape is folded into the building, not just visually but in respect of all the senses: the cracking and creaking of a hooker's mainsail being raised in the harbour calls us to the windows; the chilly rush of a squall sends us hurrying around to position the rounded beach cobbles we use to stop doors slamming; there is a salty tang of damp (and an obscure, many-legged, skipping shore-fauna) in corners of the storeroom, and a honeyed perfume sometimes wafts through the bedroom from the sweet peas around the door on to the garden. There are more serious incursions of the outdoors too; especially around the equinoxes, a spring tide coinciding with a south-easterly gale can set big waves on us, rushing across the bay, bursting over the sea wall into the courtyard and forcing their way through crevices of ancient stonework in our foundations to well up through floors, occasionally to a depth of some inches. People give us sound advice on dealing with this phenomenon – bulldoze the lower quarters and rebuild, raising the floor level or tank-walling it all round like a swimming pool – but the nuisance the flooding causes us would not justify such an expensive and disruptive procedure, and we prefer to live with the sea rather than fight it; if it comes in, it will go out again, and the carpet will stand a few more soakings before it disintegrates. And although I grumble at having to empty the bottom shelves of the bookcases and stack boxes of map-covers up on top of filing cabinets whenever one of the fishermen calls in to warn us of an exceptionally high tide, secretly I relish the sea's occasional visits.

In fact once a year the house celebrates the sea, blesses it and is blessed by it, with a party that has become a traditional adjunct of Roundstone Regatta. In Connemara's summer calendar this event usually takes place in the third weekend of July, and during the preceding week the traditional workboats, the Galway hookers and their smaller sisters the *gleoiteoigí* and *púcáin*, assemble in the bay, many of them coming on to Roundstone from south Connemara's great marine festival, the celebration of St Macdara's Day on the saint's island near Carna. On the Saturday there are heats for the currach races and the smaller sailboats; the quayside is thronged with massively muscular, dark-faced lads from the Irish-speaking areas, watching the events with silent concentration. The finals are on the Sunday, as are the races for the two sizes of hooker, the *leathbhád* (literally, half-boat) and the *bád mór* (big boat). The big boats are magnificent creatures, full-bosomed and black-hulled, with brown sails the high peaks of which seem to tower above the mountains that form the backdrop to the scene. On that day everyone we know from the village and the wide world is welcome to watch the races from the flat roof of our studio, or, if rain threatens, through the windows of the big schoolroom, to wander and converse in the garden, to listen to the guests who have brought fiddles and flutes playing jigs or the stately airs of Carolan, to drink wine and eat new potatoes roasted with rosemary, or a fruit crumble reminiscent of the previous autumn when I, hunter-gatherer Hiawatha, had picked black-berries with this occasion in mind, 'that the guests be more con-tented'. The billowing triangles of sail fill our windows as the races begin, the boats flit down the bay and are out of sight for a time, then reappear kicking up foam and perilously leaning to the waves if the wind is strong, turn about a buoy and go off again, and come back racing to a finish near the harbour. Since there are overlap-ping heats for various classes of boats, and a system of handicaps, we never know exactly what is happening or who is winning, but the confusion and delay and apparently aimless tacking to and fro, which angry boatmen will be arguing over in the pubs that night, augment and multiply the spectacle for our guests. On one occasion we watched spellbound as twenty-eight traditional boats, the largest gathering of them to be seen in Roundstone Bay since the days when they were the everyday traffic of the Connemara coast, set out together to sail around the south head of Inis Ní and up the next bay to Cashel. The breeze was so light that they moved with solemn slowness and in the deepest silence, their brown sails disposed in sheaves and fans like leaves gifted with a flower-arranger's sensibility, until the wind itself held its breath at the beauty of the sight, the stately progress was abandoned, and with infinite care, as if to avoid ruffling each other's reflections, they all turned about and crept back to their anchorages. Whether the regatta ends in perfect sunset calm or fades into otherworldly mists or culminates with thrills and leaping spray, our windows and doors admit its mood, and when finally the boats have all returned, folded their wings and settled, crow-black, to roost on the water, and M and I, alone again, find that some of our thought-ful friends have done most of the washing-up, and sit down with a last glass of wine, we feel that the house itself has sailed joyously all day and is now peaceably at anchor.

The world beyond the windows sustains the house on our average studious and solitary working days too. There are in particular the tidal doings of the seaweedy shore immediately under the window at my elbow as I write, which I can rest my eyes on by spinning my office chair a quarter turn to the left from the computer screen. There used to be otters here; I haven't seen them for some years although we hear their squeaky whistles on the still nights of drizzle they like, when it is almost as wet above the water's surface as below. When the tide is out, the bold black-and-white oystercatchers come swaggering along to chisel limpets off the rocks with their orange bills. In winter there is often a heron, motionless, a monk worn grey and sinewy by fast and prayer, waiting to stab a fish out of the water as I wait to catch the word I need. Beyond these little theatricals of the tidal zone there stretches the width of the bay, uninterrupted to the shores of Inis Ní half a mile away. When the sun is in the east countless dots of gold, each existent only for an instant, swarm on this surface. There seems to be a repetition, a signature, a rule, behind this dancing dazzle; I lose time trying to catch what exactly is happening before my eyes. Low, slow rollers, the reflections off Inis Ní of whatever billows the Atlantic is breathing into the bay, are coming towards us and being reflected again off our own sea wall, forming an elaborate interference pattern. Superimposed on that is an oblique array of smaller waves driven by a northerly wind down the centre of the bay, and on that again, a network of tiny ripples stirred by the airs circulating in the shelter of the little cliff and the house itself. In response to the moment-by-moment summation of these rhythms, each minuscule patch of the water surface is rolling, pitching and yawing, and when for a split second its angle is right it throws the sun at my eyes. A Fourier analysis of Being-by-the-Seaside! Then sometimes this inexhaustible self-computation of multitudinous reality falls still, and blue prevails. I look into this too, entranced: blue beyond blue, blue behind blue, blue within blue. Vision, the supreme sense faculty, is matched with a vision, a supreme revelation, of one of the absolutes of vision: blue, which, being an ultimate term of description, cannot be described and can only be received into oneself in the perfect solitude and incommunicable privacy of the mind, and yet which it is our faith to believe is the same for all time, all sighted humanity.

Surely this playground of the glorious mystery of light is inalienable! Whatever damage is done to Connemara, the sea cannot be bulldozed, broken up, built upon, surely? 'That's what you think!' sniggers Fate, preparing a little surprise. I went to a public meeting in the Community Hall to find out more about a proposed Roundstone Marina we had heard vague talk of, and discovered that the plan was to locate it within fifty yards of our gable window, exactly in the stretch of water I have described, to divide up that theatre of daily miracles with floating concrete walkways, to pollute its moonlight with security lamps, to irritate its sensitive skin with rattling halliards. The site map produced by the engineer did not even have the courtesy to show our house, although it would have been the only dwelling to be directly affected by the development. A PR consultant spoke rapturously in a deathly jargon about the high-spending Category ABC1 visitors the marina would attract. This shock almost determined us to leave Connemara – and in one way I was glad of it. After all, we had spent nearly thirty years in the west, and so perhaps it was time for another drastic change in our lives; it also appeared that I had made all the maps and written all the books I had in me about the little areas I had explored here, and that whatever I was to create in the future on the terrifying mental blank sheet that confronted me at that time, it would not relate to Ireland. The experience of two previous campaigns on environmental matters had been embittering and stressful, and I felt reluctant to mobilize the considerable but voiceless opposition to the scheme that existed in the village and among regular summer visitors. In any case would it not be too easy for the proponents of the marina to accuse me of having a personal interest in the matter? And perhaps it would be said – it would certainly appear so

– that we were putting our own somewhat precious and arcane interests before the solid economic good of a community whose young, finding no employment locally, have their eyes fixed on Australia. To me it seemed that any economic benefit of the scheme would fall into the hands of those who already had plenty of money – but what did I know of the mysteries of the trickle-down effect?

Not knowing what to do, I fled to London and immersed myself in translation work, being unable to write my own words. M stayed on in Roundstone and, decisive as always, put in an objection to the marina committee's application for planning permission. This caused the planning department to call for a map showing the relationship of the proposed marina to our house, which at least caused a delay, but permission was eventually granted. Since then the scheme has run into financial difficulties, a proportion of the grants its proponents had counted on from the Government are in doubt, and they have perhaps learned not to take politicians' pre-election promises too literally. But another election approaches, and what will be the final outcome we do not know. In the meantime we have become more philosophical about the proposal and less proprietorial about peace and beauty; also, I have started on the present book, finding that there is still an infinity of material on Connemara for me to chisel literature out of to my heart's content or discontent.

And, most importantly, our relationship to the house has changed. Having no biological heirs, we had long thought of leaving it to some institution that could make worthy use of it, rather than have it disappear into private hands to be knocked down and replaced by yet more holiday homes. Now we have arranged for the NUI, Galway, to have it when we are gone, with all its contents of books and paintings, plus the archive of material collected over thirty years of research into the regions I have been concerned with, for use as a small conference venue, as accommodation for writers, thinkers and researchers on sabbaticals or residencies, and for similar purposes in tune with its current ethos. When we tell anyone of this plan, the response is always,

'How generous!' – but as we will not be here to make any sacrifice in the matter, generosity does not come into it. However, this exchange serves to remind us that neither will we be here to share in the delight and fun of other people's discovery of the place; and so we have begun to anticipate that future by opening up the house to such events. Already it has hosted what we called the First Roundstone Conversation, a three-day gathering of American writers and university teachers on the topic 'Place and Story', in which we heard from, among others, Ron Engles on environmental ethics and the Earth Charter, and Jo Meeker, grand old man of ecocriticism, on the interrelationships of ecology and literature. Similarly we have listened in as the poets Moya Cannon and Éamon Grennan discussed their work with twenty-eight students on a creative writing course, all seated around a square parterre in the garden that the tall willows, birches and aspens growing on each side of it have turned into a courtyard. Such occasions bring a breath of new ideas and new words into our rather secluded lives here; also, we feel relieved of the burden of ownership, as if we were now just the temporary caretakers of the house, and we revel in the freshening wind of futurity blowing through it, wafting away the spiderwebs of anxiety. And at the same time it is our creation and our toy. Only a childish desire to live for ever, and ever and again in different places, inhibits me from calling it our home.

The Neighbours

The sea is our nearest neighbour, our house being the last one on the quayside and the holiday apartments next door to it empty for much of the year. A little pier puts out its sheltering arm round the harbour from just outside the gateway we share with the apartments, and each morning when I come out on my way to collect the *Irish Times* and the everyday shopping I am immediately faced with the harbour waters and take note of their mood as automatically as I would exchange some remark on the weather with any villager I pass.

In winter when the sea is a queasy heaving greyness, or set with small sharp teeth like a steel file, the only person I am likely to speak with is Denis, a lanky figure who stands for hour after hour on the pier, as patient as a heron, impervious to the bitterest winds, sorting through the tangles of hundreds of yards of net or welding some rusty gadgetry on his battered old trawler. There used to be half a dozen small trawlers and half-deckers regularly fishing out of Roundstone when we came here twenty years ago, but there are only two or three nowadays. In the shrimp season (October and November) I see Dick O'Toole steering his big wooden currach out into the bay, standing bolt upright at the tiller behind a huge pile of shrimp pots; later in the day he will be filling shallow plastic trays with the fidgety morsels and loading them into a van to go to the buyers in Galway. During the few March weeks in which dredging for scallops is permitted there may be two or three small half-deckers from south Connemara moored in the harbour. When the tide is sunk deep in the harbour and they are hidden by the quayside, I hear the soft mysteries of Irish drifting up over its stone lip from the boatmen's timeless conversations.

A short steep incline leads from the quayside to the village street. At the junction is a ragged cordyline palm growing in a small triangle of ground that a neighbour and myself weed twice or thrice a year and on which we have planted hydrangeas; I frequently step into the bushes to twitch out a beer can or a plastic bag, which I stuff into the rubbish bin nearby, throwing up my eyes to heaven in a mime of environmentalist despair that nobody ever notices. I greet the street dogs, currently Toby, a short-haired terrier, white with black blotches, attached to Mary King's bar, and Fluffy, an amiable nonentity lacking characteristics other than fluffiness, whose home is in the little estate behind the village, but who, even if it is raining hard, prefers to spend his days in the centre of the village where something – anything – might happen. In winter, however, nothing is happening. Too many of the village's windows are of holiday apartments; no one looks out of them at this dead season. Day after day 'everything has a hump on it', as a neighbour put it; cats, dogs, people, even the mountains, are hunched against wind and rain. I walk up the street past Mary's bar, the narrow darkness of which, mid afternoon, might shelter one old bachelor from Inis Ní or Errisbeg. Sweet-natured Mary herself looks up from her knitting and waves to me from her perch on a barstool by the window, the rain trickling down the glass making her look pale and forlorn. A few yards further on are the two shops: Ferron's, grocery and newsagent; and opposite, Woods's, butcher and grocery. There were three others but they closed one by one as their owners retired and no one took them over. The two surviving businesses carry a depleted selection of goods during the quiet season; I look through the dispiriting range of biscuits and vow to learn to bake my own. However, I often bring home some little linguistic acquisition from the desultory conversations that arise as I wait with one or two others for a shower to pass, such as the opinion of an old lady that the crooked politicians we see on television are 'going against the grain of God', or a turn of Hiberno-English I haven't seen noted before, the latest being 'The blackbird's been carting my flowerbed again', meaning that it has been scattering the soil; from the Irish verb *cartadh*, to shovel or scrape aside, to 'root' like a pig.

As well as Mary's there are two more pubs near the shops;

another two have closed during the last few years and show no sign of reopening. Early in the last century one of the surviving pubs, the Shamrock, was a little hotel favoured by artists including Jack Yeats. Nowadays it is bright and welcoming, but when I first knew it, a sleepiness had long fallen on it. Occasionally I would penetrate its dingy gloom to buy a bottle of gin, which would be handed over to me wrapped in brown paper and plastic bags as if my modest purchase were illegal and shameful, and once I had the privilege of overhearing a conversation there that seemed to have formed out of a long afternoon's silence like a stalactite on the roof of a damp cellar. There were two old countrymen at the bar, who greeted me with wordless nods. I spoke in hushed tones with the elderly proprietor, who gloomily withdrew to a back room and then slowly climbed the stairs in search of the gin. In the silence we could hear him moving boxes around overhead. Then one of the two clients suddenly announced, 'I losht my teef after that foksh!' After considering this for a minute or so the other man gave a sort of groan with an interrogative rising note in it. The first expanded on his remark: 'The foksh jumped up out of the bracken and the dog went after it and I shouted "Cummeer!" and me teef flew out.' And after taking another minute to absorb this, the second man groaned again, on a descending note indicating that the story had been heard and understood. By the time the proprietor had reappeared with the gin bottle the resettled silence made it clear that the day's entertainment was over, or at least that its high point had passed.

Beyond the shops and pubs the street continues to rise, passing on the right the recently built Eldon's Hotel (named after a Mrs Eldon who had a shop on its site a generation ago), the Sheep Chandler's gallery (so named by its French owners, Florence and Katerine, out of some unfathomable but charming linguistic confusion), and the long-established Roundstone Hotel; all of these being closed for the winter. Opposite them an open space called the Green Field slopes down to the seashore past tennis courts, netless at this season, and the Community Hall, a 1950s collocation of box shapes. The wind off the bay assails the street here, and greetings between the rare passers-by are cut down to the fewest possible words – 'A hardy one!' – or reduced to a groan and a shuddering of the shoulders. As a black squall marches on the village I might duck into the post office and, while standing in the damp queue, exchange a bit of my half-learned Irish for a scrap of half-forgotten Irish from an old lady of Inis Ní, or hurry round the corner past the Catholic church to Fair Green, the Council-built estate of a dozen semi-detached cottages on the back street of the village, to call on Mícheál Bairéad, an ex-Garda from south Connemara, for more regular practice in the language. When I first knew Mike he was living down near the harbour in a curious house consisting of two wedge-shaped rooms one above the other, squeezed into a gap between a row of houses looking onto the triangular garden, and a laneway above it. The rooms were very small, and as Mike was very tall and broad he was extremely cramped even before the moment of misfortune – a faint, a fall, a blow to the head on the corner of a table – that left him with paralysed legs. Being wheelchair-bound he could not use the tiny twisty stairs in the thin end of the wedge, and so when I stepped in off the laneway I was immediately confronted with the ironwork of the foot of his big old-fashioned bedstead. I never heard him complain, though, and often found him at work confecting some hopeful device such as a set of cardboard rings each inscribed with the alphabet and mounted on the cylindrical core of a toilet roll, to help him with the cross-word puzzles that filled his tedious hours, or a spring stretched between his shoe and a strap round his knee, to support his foot, in a failed attempt to walk again. I admired his serenity enormously, and it is a matter of deep regret that there was some bitterness in him towards me at the end of his life. Here is how it came to pass, this winter's tale.

Mike used to give me old Irish sayings and stories of fairies, ghosts, wicked landlords and strolling poets that he had from his forebears in Irish-speaking Cois Fharraige and Muínis, and when I found these difficult to follow I would get him to write them out. After a year or two these notes began to look like the manuscript of a book. Also one December I found him making a few Christmas cards with lively, naive drawings of boats in the harbour, which impressed me enough to get the cards printed properly, to his delight. This success suggested to me that he should write down all his south Connemara lore in Irish, and illustrate it, for Folding Landscapes to publish. The activity enriched his days for two or three years; he produced essays on turf-cutting, *poitín*-making, boat-building, holy wells and horse fairs, a collection of old riddles, stories of tinkers and folk heroes – all the mental furniture of his traditional south Connemara childhood. The book was to be called *Fadó Fadó*, which means 'long, long ago' and has the elegiac quality of a tolling bell from those repeated long *ó*'s.

But a problem had begun to loom in my mind: Mike's spelling, to put it positively, was as expressive of bygone folklife as the crooked little stone-walled fields of his ancestors' farm. To publish his writing as it stood would have entailed studiously transcribing its countless inconsistent quirks, and might have exposed him to a sarcastic review in a local paper. For me to correct his spelling on the basis of my lately acquired book-learning would have been an intolerable dictionary-labour, so I turned to knowledgeable friends. It occurred to me that Bríd Nic Dómhnaill, the indomitable head of Recess National School, which was then being boycotted by parents who objected to her commitment to teaching through Irish, could do with some project to fill up the week after week she was spending in an empty classroom; and indeed she threw herself into the detailed and delicate task of correcting the text. But the results did not please Mike. Whatever this is, he said, it is not Connemara Irish. Then Liam Mac Con Iomaire, a native speaker of Connemara Irish, found time, in the midst of his busy schedule in the language laboratory of University College, Dublin, and his own writings, to try to dig me out of this hole. It seems that in his Garda life Mike had been posted here and there, and his Irish had picked up tinges of Munster dialect as well as officialese. What were we to aim at, the ragged riches of Connemara Irish or the respectable tone of 'Dublin Irish', as Mike derisively called the standardized language? The project became a nightmare; I spent hundreds of hours typing and retyping drafts. M's expression conveyed a suspicion that we were all giving ourselves hermeneutical hernias over a load of rural idiocies. Obstinately in search of the perfect and definitive dual-text edition, I suggested to Mike that he translate his own work; but when I found that his English prose reduced his frisky rebellious Irish to a policeman's plod, I was tempted to tinker with it, shifting words about, then sentences, and then paragraphs, until it lost all touch with the original. I was drained by this Sisyphean addition to my own overwhelming project of mapping Connemara, and began to call on Mike less frequently and with growing weariness of heart. He was still serene and encouraging; he said there was no hurry, it would all come right in its own good time. But the good time did not come. Once, he allowed himself to say that he wished he'd never started on it. I came home from Fair Green by the shortcut through the damp tree-shadowed graveyard of the Protestant church that day, troubled and harassed. And soon after that, Mike died. His relatives appeared for the funeral and called on me afterwards; they knew someone who spoke Irish, they said, and they'd soon get the work published. I gave them photocopies, but of course the book never appeared. To this day, folders stuffed with Mike's original texts and drawings, and reams of corrected and recorrected typescripts, bulk large in one of my filing cabinets, a heavy reproach.

In summer when I come out of our gate onto the quayside it is frequently with a loud rattle from the trolley on which I lug parcels of maps up to the post office for dispatch to Folding Landscapes' customers and distributors in Ireland and overseas. There are yachts moored in the bay, and a group of sports-fishermen may be swaggering down to board the motorboat that will take them out, uttering expletives that make our own chaste fishermen turn their eyes towards the horizon. Ladies are crouched before their easels, baffled by the speed with which the sunshine and the cloud shadows are endlessly repainting the Twelve Pins. A crowd of pint-drinkers and view-eaters is standing along the wall above the harbour outside O'Dowd's pub, many of them regular visitors whom we have come to know and who will call on us on certain expected dates during the summer holidays. Politicians, barristers, broadcasters, Dublin 4 and its children come in the high season; academics turn up after school has restarted but while the universities are still on vacation. Once when M and I were in our studio trying to work out if it would be to our advantage to deregister for VAT, our turnover being so small, we saw the Minister for Finance passing the window; 'The very man!' we said, and called him in to advise us. There is even a traffic jam on bank holiday weekends, and tour buses decant Germans, French or Italians fifty at a time. Toby the dog races up and down the street chasing the swifts that hurtle along it, and sometimes makes us anxious by swimming far out after them when they go skimming over the bay.

One of my functions in the village is to be a perambulating historical litter basket; anyone who comes across an old account book or remembers a placename their grandparents used to use may rely on me to receive it into my care. Paddy 'Shoulders', who owns a JCB and does street-work for the Council, has several times called me over to his latest trench to show me what he has turned up. Most recently this was a layer of oval pebbles just under the tarmac along the edge of the pavement; it seems that in the old days there were storm drains along either side of the street lined with such pebbles, thousands and thousands of them, all four or five inches long – which explains, he said, why when he had gone down to the shore for pebbles to decorate a plinth in the IDA grounds, he couldn't find any of that handy size.

In her latter years I often used to meet the former village schoolmistress, Maggy Dundass, taking the sun at the corner of Marine Terrace and the road down to the IDA park, opposite the Catholic church. (Half the history of Roundstone lies down those two ways, and I will return to them.) She had been compressed by the weight of the years into a tiny, rounded mouse-shape, and she usually had some anecdote as savoury as a buried hazelnut for me. One of these stories she said she had kept 'under the stones', and she passed it on to me under an oath of secrecy, which I think I may break now, a century or more after the event. There were two brothers in her grandfather's old cottage on the slopes of Cnoc Mordáin near Carna, she told me. A poor scholar, Seán na Scoile, Seán of the school, lived there too, and a sort of instructor called Lydon who taught them the long jump. So the brothers grew up fine men and one of them joined the Dublin Metropolitan Police. Queen Victoria used to send the Prince of Wales to represent her in Ireland, and on one of these visits after he had inspected the DMP he said he'd noticed a fine-looking man, the second-tallest in the ranks. (He was in his cups, Miss Dundass explained; it was all his fault! He was the one with the long tongue!) So they made enquiries and found it was Dundass he meant. Whether it was in the newspaper or not, 'this one' heard of it – she was the daughter of the Lord Mayor or maybe of the Lord Lieutenant (Miss Dundass wasn't sure which) – and she kept on after him. When Dundass came home with a photograph of her everyone said, 'Oh no, it won't do at all!', and Dundass would say that he'd told her he couldn't keep her. When he went back they disciplined him and told him to keep away from her, but one night he was on guard duty and when the other guard came to relieve him, he wasn't there, just his uniform neatly folded and left in the sentry box. He'd gone off with his fair one! They went after them and caught them at Holyhead. They brought her back but they gave him leg-bail. He went to stay with his brother in England. Later on the brother came back to Ireland and the night he arrived he slept at the house of a friend in Dublin. In the middle of the night she came to the door. 'I heard he's come back,' she said. 'No, it's his brother,' said the friend. So she went off again . . .

'Well, I won't delay you!' is the polite formula used to dismiss me by the tellers of such inconsequential tales when my appetite to hear outstays theirs to tell. But Connemara has delayed me inordinately, half a life long, with its rambling histories and inviting airs. If the weather is fine, or interestingly bad, I often walk on from the corner by the church and instead of cutting back home through Fair Green follow the coast road westwards, past the last few cottages and recently built dormer-bungalows of the village to the first fields, full of gorse and rocky knolls and badger setts, and there take a lane running inland that connects with the one coming down from Errisbeg Hill to the harbour, and thus makes a rectangular walk of a mile or so. Errisbeg House is on the west of this first lane, raggedly screened by alder trees and willows growing in the watery ditches that bind its four acres of rather wild garden. It is a three-storeyed, grey-faced Victorian pile with a gesticulatory roofline of gables, valleys and chimney stacks that empathizes with the agitated skyline of Errisbeg Hill just behind it. The house was thrown together by the Cloghertys, merchants and publicans of Roundstone, in 1878 and probably gentrified in 1910 (the stuccoed south façade with its little balustrade and classical urns bears that date and the name of a local builder, T. Creane). Joe Clogherty leased the house periodically to Jesuit and Redemptorist priests on retreat, and, from the 1930s, to the Duchess de Stacpoole, whose grandson Richard eventually acquired the freehold. Passing up the lane and glancing in at the crazy old place, it feels like a dream half-remembered that M and I lived there for nearly three years. Although there were cold and draughty nights, and we had to run to and fro with buckets to catch the drips during rainstorms, it is as a summer story that I remember that time: the pipistrelle bats spiralling silently around the living room in the evenings; the honey that oozed from a bulge in an attic ceiling from the decades of bees' nests under the slates of the roof; the snipe calling me into the garden with the cascade of sweet flute-notes they make with their wing feathers as they let themselves fall through the pre-dawn light.

First, the historical background. (Neither M nor I had a historical background of our own, but we enthusiastically adopted that of the de Stacpooles when we found ourselves playing duke and duchess for a while.) A Richard de Stacpoole fought at the Battle of Hastings, built a castle, Stacpoole Court in Pembrokeshire, and was knighted by William the Conqueror. Two generations later a Robert de Stacpoole came to Ireland with Strongbow. His descendants acquired large tracts of land in Cork and Limerick, and conformed to the Protestant faith in the time of the Penal Laws against Catholics. One of them became High Sheriff of Clare in 1763, before returning to the faith of his fathers and taking up residence in Grosvenor Square in London, where he entertained the exiled French King Louis XVIII. After the fall of Napoleon he was rewarded with the title of viscount, and later of count, and was persuaded to move to France, where he bought a large house in the Faubourg St Honoré in Paris and the Château de Montigny near Fontainebleau. His son Richard, having donated £40,000 for the restoration of St Paul's in Rome, was created a marquis, and later a duke, by Pope Leo XII. (A painting the size of a billiard table, hanging in a passageway of Errisbeg House, in which a few pale faces seem to float like beans in a dark-brown soup, apparently represents the family being presented to the Pope on the occasion of this last ennoblement, which, our Roundstone Duchess used to say, almost beggared the family, but for which they were also rewarded with the second-largest extant fragment of the True Cross.) Richard imported a pack of foxhounds from Ireland to Montigny, and fox-hunting flourished there for a while, but in the end both the château and the Paris house had to go because of his munificence and extravagance, and he retired to Hampshire. His son George Stanislaus bought and restored in romantic style the ancient abbey of St Wandrille de Fontanelle in Normandy, and after the death of his wife Maria (*née* Dunn, of Bath House in Northumberland) took holy orders and became domestic chaplain to the Pope. His son George married Pauline, only child of Edward MacEvoy of Tobertynan in Meath, and wrote an entertaining book of memoirs, from which I have most of this family history. Their son George married Eileen, who was to become our Roundstone Duchess. (I have heard a landed Protestant lady snort, 'That woman, going around calling herself a duchess! She was nothing of the sort!' – for the Ascendancy still exists and recognizes no titles that do not emanate from the British throne.)

Eileen had been born into a rich Protestant flour-mill-owning family, the Palmers of Glenlo Abbey near Galway, had converted to Catholicism, and spent her married life at Tobertynan. She used to bring her children to Errisbeg for holidays, and when she was widowed came to live there permanently. She had the gardens laid out, and used to give garden parties in aid of the Lady Dudley Nursing Scheme, which had been founded by the Lord Lieutenant's wife to provide district nurses in Connemara and other neglected areas. It seems from a radio interview she gave in her latter years that she was also very hospitable to apparitions, and unalarmed, if sometimes annoyed, by mischievous fairies. She spoke of a portrait of the first Duke that leapt off the wall and landed unharmed, leaving its hanger on the picture rail, and of a grandfather clock that fell over, mysteriously ending up on its back. She described a little boy, two and a half feet high with corn-coloured hair cut in a fringe, who came into the house; when she put her hand on his head, he wasn't there. Once, sitting with her niece by the front door, she saw a little goat coming to her, which the niece couldn't see. Naturally her isolated and dishevelled old house was reputed to be haunted.

Eileen, Duchess de Stacpoole, died in 1984, and Errisbeg House now belongs to her grandson Richard. When we came to Roundstone later in that year, the Duchess was a well-established figure of local legend. At that time we were unhappily housed on the IDA crafts estate where we were renting one of the units as our studio; it was a milieu that added all the disadvantages of suburbia to those of rural life. We only knew Richard and Ann de Stacpoole through occasionally calling in to buy fresh eggs from them. There was obviously wealth in their background, but none to hand, due, we speculated, to the creaking armour of trusts and policies and codicils that upper-class families inflict on their rising generations. Ann was a tall, handsome, blonde-haired ex-Sloane Ranger, who had fulfilled the traditional goal of her caste by marrying a viscount and producing an heir. Richard was light-framed and spontaneous, forever borne up by an ebullient optimism. Out of some generous whim he phoned us one evening to say that they were off to live in England for a while, and would we like to move into the house? We accepted the marvellous invitation with alacrity. When the caretaker of the IDA estate heard of it he called on us with a bottle of whiskey, saying, 'You'll need this!' 'Well, at least we'll be meeting a better class of ghost,' we replied.

So Errisbeg House became our perch until we finally got a place of our own, the premises on the quayside. Much of the time we had the run of the house, from the comfortable old kitchen with its big warm range in the back quarters, and the tiled hall hung with the horned heads of beasts of chase, up the wide stairs past supercilious ancestral portraits, to the drawing room, with its overflowing escritoires and worn volumes of Debrett, and then up narrower stairs to the attics, where we had our own rooms. When the family was in residence and the house was rampant with the comings and goings of their frolicsome guests – Proust-reading hard-riding resident of the Isle of Man, serially lovelorn eternal student, gay interior designer, Junoesque creator of towering flower arrangements in the hall – we tried to keep to our quarters but were frequently drawn into the blithe maelstrom, providing cultural chat for novelists at the dinner table and counselling in the nursery for distraught and bewildered au pairs. We even stood as earth-parents to Erris, Richard and Ann's youngest daughter; after the Catholic baptism service I carried her around the garden and showed her ceremonially to the animals, the apple trees, the compost heap and the hill from which she was named, and at each station I whispered to her truths she would not have learned from the priest's missal or her godparents' chequebook. When the high-spirited flock took wing again we expanded to reoccupy the vacuum, or most of it, for the formal dining room with its ghost-white marble busts of the first Duke and his coroneted lady, and the late Duchess's gloomy bedroom with its huge staggering wardrobes, were seldom entered except to rescue explorative kittens and expel strayed robins.

In fact, more than all its human and supernatural frequenters, it is for the house and garden's animal life that I treasure the memory of our Errisbeg days. On moving in we found we had inherited an arthritic but still noble-browed black Labrador called

Sandringham Seal (she had pretensions to royal lineage), a peahen (her mate had flown away but was still to be heard screeching in the gorse-bushes of the hillside), lots of hens and bantams, and a gaggle of speckly silver guineafowl. Soon one of the hens hatched out a clutch of duck eggs that she had been persuaded to sit on, and we enjoyed the traditional farmyard comedy of her anxious running round the pond when the ducklings first took to the water, and later of the ducklings' own amazement when they found themselves sliding about on ice one frosty morning. We had to keep the ducks and hens shut in at night because of foxes slinking down from Errisbeg Hill. The hens used to troop off to the henhouse on their own initiative as dusk fell, but the ducks preferred to linger on the pond, especially if it was raining, and sometimes it would only be as we were going to bed that we would remember them; then we would have to put on raincoats over our dressing gowns and go out in the great darkness under the trees, and shout and beat the waters with Richard's polo clubs to drive them off the pond – a curious spectacle for any late-night passer-by on the lane. The guineafowl roosted high in the trees behind the house; they would start preparing for the night early in the evening by hopping onto the lowest branches, and gradually work their way up with a glorious cacophony of squeals and shrieks, to a height of forty feet or so. There they were safe from the fox, but as they insisted in hiding their nests from us in the shrubberies or the bamboo thicket they were picked off one by one, eggs and all, until we were left with one old male, one hen and one young male. This was a stable hierarchy so long as the youngest knew his place, but by degrees he began to challenge the alpha male, and eventually drove him off from the female. The old fellow was so dispirited that he took to going to bed with the hens while the young couple were still shouting for joy up in the trees. We thought he was going to die, he looked so shrunken and wretched, but it turned out he was merely resting up. One morning when I opened the henhouse door he shot out like a charging bull, seized the young stud by the wattles and dragged him round and round the big circular flowerbed in front of the house until all traces of rebellion had been shaken out of him and the status quo re-established.

We also acquired our own pets and for the first time in our lives enjoyed the privilege of sharing a home and forming a family with non-human creatures. One morning as we were going off to our studio we saw two kittens, one with a damaged eye, in the fernery by the gate, but we hardened our hearts against them as the feral cats a friend had wished on us were already breeding prolifically in the stables. But when we came back that evening, in a rainstorm, one of the kittens, the sound one, ran towards us, and we had to bring her in. With supreme self-confidence she explored the house from top to bottom, tried out each of Seal's dry teats, and crept in at the bottom of our bed to investigate my anatomy with her rough little tongue. So the violet-eyed, silky-furred, irresistibly beguiling Nimma (as we named her, in feminized homage to the great engineer) fell in for a long life of love and luxury, whereas the next day I came across the sodden corpse of her unlucky, unnamed twin. Soon afterwards we were stopped in the lane by an elderly villager we scarcely knew, who announced, 'I have a dote of a little dog for you.' We told him we couldn't take on a dog just then, as we were about to leave Errisbeg for our new premises, but that evening he called round to the house, reached into the breast of his coat and produced a handful of fluff that ran around the garden in a delirium of vitality, until Nimma pranced up to it and clipped it on the ear. We could not help but be totally welcoming of the newcomer. Squig (so named from her randomly angular trajectories) and Nimma were the two inestimable treasures we brought with us when we left Errisbeg to move into Nimmo House down on the quayside.

Forgotten Roundstone

Smugglers and Asylum Seekers

Ever since I was shown it by a Roundstone builder twenty years ago I have been intrigued by the curious markings on a stone set into a wall of a big barn of a building, tending to the ruinous, known as the Old Store. The grim half-derelict structure, which has now been replaced by a palatial holiday home, stood by a little quay at the bottom of the lane that drops steeply down to the shore from the corner of the village street by the Catholic church. It was a two-storeyed building, dank and grimy, surrounded by half-demolished extensions and mangled rusty machinery, with a gapped and sagging slate roof which looked as if it would be ripped off by the next storm. Its rough masonry of local granite was patched with concrete blocks, having been breached repeatedly to adapt it to a long history of varied uses, for in its day it had served as a fish-curing station, as a store for fishing gear, kelp and *carraigín* seaweed, and as a seaweed-fertilizer factory. At the time I was conducted into it to view the interesting stone, the Old Store belonged to a local company, Kerry Shellfish Ltd, and the builder, if I remember aright, was engaged in making concrete tanks in it to hold lobsters and crayfish awaiting the lorries that would take them across to France. The earliest-looking part of it was a rectangular building oriented north–south, perhaps forty yards long and twenty wide, and had been extended to the north; to see the stone we had to pick our way across the detritus of many decades into the darkness of the extension, and crouch at the bottom right-hand corner of the interior wall that would have been the north gable wall of the original building – that is, just where one might expect to see a foundation stone. On first running my finger along the shallow grooves in its face I thought we were dealing with a cross-inscribed stone laid on its side, perhaps robbed from some ecclesiastical ruin; but when I made a rubbing of it I found that the shape was more complex: a horizontal about ten inches long with a small squashed circle or D-shape around one end of it, crossed by three shorter verticals with angular terminations that were difficult to make out. In the bottom left-hand corner, a date, 1731, was fairly clear. I have shown it to various archaeologists; the best they can suggest is that the inscription could be a merchant's mark or guild insignia, perhaps a stylized representation of a plough such as occurs on some Galway gravestones. To me it looks like a key, and as such I shall use it to gain entry into Roundstone's history.

In 1731 neither Roundstone nor the road through it existed, for it was not until the 1820s that Alexander Nimmo designed the harbour and laid out the village along a section of his new coast road. (It is often stated that the name 'Roundstone' is derived, half by translation and half by phonetic imitation, from its Irish name, Cloch na Rón, which means 'the rock of the seals'. This may be so, but on the other hand the two names may be quite independent. The bay is referred to as 'Round-stone haven' by Roderick O'Flaherty, writing in 1684, and the rock from which it is named and which stands like a marker on the west side of its entrance is strikingly round.) William Larkin's map of 1819 shows that the predecessor of Nimmo's road, passing through the district from Ballynahinch to Bunowen, kept to higher ground around the flanks of Errisbeg Hill. It would have been a rough track or bridle-path at best, and it can still be made out in places, along the line of the wall dividing fields from the open commonage of the hillside. Larkin shows very few buildings down by the shore, but one marked 'Store' on his map undoubtedly represents the Old Store or a predecessor on the same site, as does a 'storehouse' marked on an even earlier map in an atlas of charts published in 1775 by Murdoch Mackenzie Senior, who surveyed the bay in 1766.

These dates carry us well back towards 1731; we can assume that there was a store here then, no doubt one a good deal smaller than the Old Store itself. The little harbour by it, a squarish inlet whose banks have been lined with stone and built up to form

the quay beside the store, looks as if it might be of that same age
or earlier. Who was using it? — for official reports agree with the
maps that there were only a few scattered cottages within a mile
of the place even down to Nimmo's arrival. By chance, we can
answer that question; an individual voice from that era, aggrieved,
plaintive, makes itself heard above the susurrus of the forgotten.
In a handful of letters dated 1737 and preserved in the Public
Records Office we read of the smuggling of wool out of
Roundstone Bay and the disgraceful failure of the authorities to
suppress it. One H. Littleton, Town Major, a disillusioned officer
of the garrison in Galway, writes:

It is certain the most part of the wool run out of this kingdom is run
out of Roundston's Bay, 30 mile from this place, it lying very
commodious for that purpose and nobody to hinder it, the Collector
and Surveyor having lived here near 30 years and by that means in
league with the most part of the country . . . The *Spy* man-of-war has
been stationed here for near 4 years and near 100 ships have loaded
with wool in that time and sailed to France from Rolston's Bay, without
any molestation . . .

This claim may well be a gross exaggeration, but one can see why
a store was needed, to house the wool going out, and the brandy,
tea, silks and other goods coming in. Ireland at the time was
suffering under legislation aimed at disadvantaging its trade in
favour of that of England. Since the 1690s Galway had been among
the ports from which the export of wool was forbidden except
to England; however, by our date of 1731 its contraband trade
was flourishing. Because Connemara was almost inaccessible by
land there was a lawful seaborne trade along its coasts, and the
illicit trade could be conveniently combined with this; ships leaving
Galway in ballast or with partial cargos could take wool on board
in dozens of creeks and pools of this ideally complicated coast,
with little fear of detection. Many of the Galway grandees were
heavily involved, and officials winked at the business, according
to the indignant Littleton:

Martin Kiernan, Esquire, and Andrew Morrish, merchants in this town, loaded a ship with wool at Round Stone Bay, and Michael Fearservice, master of said ship which is called the *Ould Margret*; Thomas Blake of Menelough and Jonuck Bodkin and Leo Bodkin, merchants in this town, loaded a ship with wool at Round Stone Bay in the beginning of October last . . . and the said Bodkins runned many hogsheads and ankers of brandy in the said Round Stone Bay and brought it safe to Jonuck Bodkin's and Leo Bodkin's farm to Oranmore . . . James Disney the Collector's son, and James Figgi, the Barrack-master of this town, runs as much wool as any of the gang . . .

In another letter Littleton exposes the comfortable relations between the smugglers and the revenue services:

A ship belonging to Jonuk Bodkin and other merchants sailed, 13 April last, to Roundston's bay and loaded wool for France; I cannot say but she took her leave with good grace, for she saluted the garrison and the man-of-war with seven guns; the man-of-war sailed, 16th April, at 4 o'clock in the afternoon, from New Harbour, about three miles from this garrison, but according to custom went too late . . .

The immediate occasion of Littleton's correspondence was the misfortunes of an ex-smuggler surnamed McDonagh, who had turned informer. McDonagh claimed to have been inveigled into a public house by a priest, kidnapped by 'a great parcel of gentlemen, or ruffians as I may call them', carried off he knew not where in County Clare and, a month later, from place to place in County Galway, kept in fetters and moved by night slung under a horse's belly, until he mysteriously escaped, and endured four days without food on a mountain unable to put his clothes on because of his handcuffs, before 'the great God and a poor countryman' saved his life and he was able to throw himself into the hands of Mr Littleton, 'the sincerest person to the Government that I know in this part of the country, for there is such factions here, that it is but few in employments here but is in favour with all the runners of wool'.

Among the gentlemen-ruffians that carried McDonagh off were the Bodkins, two sailors from the *Spy*, some servants of Thomas Blake of Menlo, and a steward of Anthony Martin of Dangan, near Galway. At this period most of Connemara, including the Roundstone area, belonged to the Martins of Dangan, and Anthony's son Robert was soon to build a house at Ballynahinch which he claimed was an inn and is likely to have been a base for his smuggling operations. Larkin's map shows a path (the present-day Farrell's Road) running northwards and obliquely up the hillside from the site of the Old Store to join the old track leading directly to Ballynahinch; we may visualize a train of Connemara ponies climbing up it laden with hogsheads of brandy and ankers of tea, and poor McDonagh slung underneath one of them.

As has been mentioned, Larkin's map of 1819 shows very little habitation in or near the present village of Roundstone, but it does mark a settlement of five cottages and a chapel just over a mile away to the west, and names it as 'Coogaula'. In those days this hamlet was reached by a track branching off the road across the mountainside above it; nowadays it lies on the north side of the coast road a short way beyond the end of the village. When I went to look for traces of the chapel I met a garrulous and slightly distracted old lady who, on the strength of her Irish, was the sole surviving justification for the townland of Errisbeg's status as part of the Gaeltacht. As I learned later, she was also regarded by the credulous as one of the neighbourhood's two witches; she used to go round enquiring for kittens, which people did not like to give her as they did not know why she wanted them. Old Sorcha pointed out a half-built holiday home just above the road, where the chapel used to be, and told me work had been abandoned on it because of the ill-luck arising from building on such a site. (Of course the house has now long been finished and lived in, without dire consequences.) She was also concerned about another house below the road, which she said had been built on a path leading to the chapel, a thing that should not be done.

From her dark look I intuited that the inconvenience would be resented by otherworldly beings rather than by humans.

As to Larkin's Coogaula (pronounced 'Coogla' these days), in 1959 a visitor to Roundstone, the novelist and future chairman of the Arts Council Mervyn Wall, found that the settlement's own view of itself was that it had been founded by refugees from Down, Armagh and Antrim, driven from their homes by Cromwell. Patrick Bolton, a small farmer of the locality, told him:

My ancestor was expelled from Derry. He was allowed to take as much of his property as would fit in a cart. He put his wife on top and went on foot himself, leading the horse. The way he came was down between Lough Corrib and Lough Mask; and when he came to the sea, he stopped; and my people have been here since.

Mervyn Wall's report of this (in a radio talk) was noted by a Patrick Tohall, who had published an account of the Diamond Fight of 1795 and the subsequent migration of Ulster Catholics to Connacht, and who later came to investigate the Coogla community for himself:

Mr Bolton recounted the surnames as Bolton, King, Lavery, McCahill, McCulla, Moran and Shiel . . . the residents were called 'Na h-Ultaigh' [the Ulstermen]. The only house remaining is the Shiel home, still occupied by Martin Connolly, their descendant in the female line. Six of the seven migrants were Weavers, the exception being McCulla who was a Nailer . . . Mr Bolton refers to a hereditary document describing the original exodus, including reference to wicker curraghs used to cross Lough Cong [an error for Lough Corrib, surely]; but the document cannot be traced . . . On the other hand his approximate calculation by generations which had been surmised as 1675, worked out, when tested by him in conversation, to a revised surmise of 1775, which is near enough to 1795.

Well, as Sorcha said to me, ending one of her old tales with an echo of a standard formula of the oral tradition, 'That was a long time ago, and we weren't in it then, and that's a good thing because if we were we wouldn't be here today!' In the long perspective of time Cromwell has come to stand for all ancient oppressions, and it seems that our Roundstone Ulstermen were not the only refugees in Galway and Mayo to adopt what Tohall calls 'the Cromwell fiction'.

In fact the sparse population of Connemara may have been substantially increased by the events of 1795 in Ulster. The Defenders were an armed and oath-bound organization of rural Catholics, inspired by the recent French Revolution and reacting against increases in taxes and tithes, the shortage of land due to the expansion of the linen industry, and the aggressions of the Protestant 'Peep o' Day Boys'. At the Battle of the Diamond, fought at a crossroads near Loughgall, County Armagh, Defenders took on Peep o' Day Boys and lost; the outcome was the foundation of the Protestant Orange Order, and the expulsion of many Catholic peasants. In Galway too the Catholics had to endure not only the frosts of colonialism but also the blasts of sectarianism. The Catholic Martins had managed to assemble and hold on to their thousands of boggy acres through the period of confiscations following Protestant King William III's triumph over Catholic James II in 1690, but Robert Martin, while remaining the staunchest Jacobite and the leader of the Catholic faction west of Galway, had found it necessary to obtain official certification of his adherence to Protestantism. His son Richard was the first Martin to be educated at a Protestant school, but several incidents of Richard's life show that his heart was with the Catholic cause. According to a Dublin newspaper report of 1796:

The persecution in the county of Armagh is not exhausted, although it has scattered thousands of miserable victims in every direction and left them to the winds of heaven. A computation may easily be formed of the extent of this mischief from the fact that a single gentleman, Col. Martin of the county of Galway, has given asylum to more than a thousand souls on his own estate, all peaceable, inoffensive and living by the labour of their hands . . . We have seen a proof sheet of a print of the refugees coming from the north to Connemara displaying more misery and wretchedness than any man of any religion would wish to see fall to the lot of a fellow creature.

Twenty-eight years later a jocose article in *The Times* attributed Richard Martin's electoral successes to this huge influx:

Mr Martin owes his constant return to Parliament to an act of the greatest virtue and hospitality. When the Orangemen of Armagh were banishing the Catholic peasantry – when they were putting nightly on the doors of the Catholics 'to Hell, or to Connaught,' and if the summons was not obeyed by an immediate disappearance, conflagration and murder were the consequence – Mr Martin received into his wilderness the almost countless multitudes. He did more. He made freeholders of them; for in that free country a tract of mountain or of bog, the fee-simple of which would not seduce 100L [£100] out of the pockets of any man in his senses, was sufficient to constitute some hundreds of electors; and they are grateful. He keeps a storehouse of brogues, which he opens at the time of election to his constituents, and they sally forth in genteel though exceedingly inconvenient style, to vote for the 'veisther' (master.) They regularly deposit the mark of distinction on their return, any thing in the shape of a shoe never having been seen on a human foot, except septennially, in the whole of Connemara.

What truth there is in the contemporary estimates of the numbers driven out of Ulster, I do not know. I have seen it stated that 1,000 came to Galway and 4,000 to Mayo, while 6,000 sailed for America and no fewer than 20,000 for Scotland – but the muse of the history of sectarianism is Exaggeration. I have not come across any traces of other such refugee communities in Connemara. Pat Bolton, I have been told by several who remember him, was an incorrigible fabulist – his account of helping Seán McEntee with the Howth gun-running was a classic – but the basic facts about a settlement of folk from the North seem to be well founded, and so perhaps Pat's ancestor did come grinding along the bridle-way around the shoulder of Errisbeg with his wife on top of a cartload of household goods, sniff the breath of ocean on his face, and turn off down the narrow boreen to where the promised land of Coogla, Cúige Uladh, the Province of Ulster, stands today.

Nimmo and His Brothers

Alexander Nimmo was a phenomenon. He was only forty-nine when he died, and even a bare listing of his works, travels and accomplishments suggests that he must have bowled through life as if in a post-chaise, flinging out plans and proposals that kept hundreds busy for years after he had vanished over the horizon. Little or nothing is known of his private life and even within his short career there are periods of years in which he seems to disappear from view; during one of these he apparently carried out a one-man visual survey of the surface geology of the whole of Ireland. He was born in Scotland and his contributions to British civil engineering are notable, but he spent most of his working life in Ireland and left his mark on every corner of the country. His reports are refreshingly clear of the repetitive complaints about Irish fecklessness and papistry that disfigure so many nineteenth-century commentaries on the woeful island. A technocrat who never thought it needful to mention his own humane intentions, he held that the poor people of Ireland were perfectly capable of relieving their own distress by doing thus and thus according to his succinct recommendations. Connemara received much of his attention. Connemara's poverty, infertility, bogginess and stoniness did not perplex him; he knew just how and where to bridge its gaps and make its crooked ways straight. Thomas Moore had famously referred to 'the houseless wilds of Connemara'; Nimmo knew exactly where houses should arise, and that indeed is where they did arise. Roundstone is uniquely Nimmo's foundation. The inhabitants of the village are obsessed, it sometimes seems to me, by the question of where the great man is buried. Some of them hold, with a certainty more suitable to an article of faith than a detail of history, that he lies in the old Presbyterian churchyard a hundred yards up the steep lane opposite the harbour; and there are reasons to think that they are right, although none of the few remaining graves there bears his name.

The following brisk summary may give something of the tempo of Nimmo's career; I owe the bones of it to a paper by the late Professor Seán de Courcy, of the Civil Engineering Department in University College, Dublin, a courtly and urbane old gentleman whose interest in the subject had been stimulated by his attachment to Roundstone, and whose yearly summer visits we always appreciated.

Alexander Nimmo was born in 1783, the son of a watchmaker and hardware shop-owner of Kirkcaldy in Fifeshire. A precocious lad, he studied at the local grammar school, excelling in Greek, Latin and mathematics, and then at the universities of Edinburgh and St Andrews. Aged nineteen, he was appointed Rector of Inverness Academy. During school holidays he was employed in mapping the county boundaries of Scotland, on the recommendation of the engineer Thomas Telford, that giant of the second Iron Age. He contributed articles on carpentry, land drainage, bridge design and the mathematical astronomer Ruggero Boscovich's natural philosophy to the *Edinburgh Encyclopaedia*. In his twenties he was elected an honorary member of the Geological Society of London and a Fellow of the Royal Society of Edinburgh.

In 1809 a parliamentary commission was established 'to enquire into the nature and extent of the several bogs in Ireland and the practicability of draining and cultivating them', and on Telford's recommendation the Commissioners engaged Nimmo as one of their nine engineers. He started work in January 1811, finished at the end of December 1813, and was paid for 720 days' work including 200 in the field. He first reported on north Kerry and contiguous parts of west Cork, mapping a vast area including the Macgillicuddy Reeks, Mangerton and Sliabh Luachra, travelling on horseback or on foot. His hand-coloured manuscript maps are up to sixteen feet wide and five and a half feet deep; Professor de

Courcy used to tell me how when he unfolded one of them in the reading room of the National Library he had to drape it over the heads of neighbouring researchers, and he has written that they 'convey in their draughting a most compelling sense of the wildness and occasional bleakness and loneliness of the huge moors and mountains which Nimmo and his surveyors traversed'. Nimmo also surveyed parts of the harbours at Valentia and Castlemaine, and established the height of Carrauntoohill by barometer. But Nimmo not only recorded what was, he prescribed what should be, in the way of roads, improvements in the navigability of rivers, and canals to drain the bogs and bring in seaweed and sand to fertilize them.

In 1813 Nimmo was sent to Galway to report on the bogs of Connemara. He argued for the development of the lakes, especially those of the Inagh Valley, recommended that a port be built at the mouth of the Ballynahinch River, and that, among other extensions of the road system, 'the present road through Orrisbeg should be improved and perfected by keeping it on lower ground' – thus preparing the ground for his later project at Roundstone. He completed his Connemara work in one year. His draft map of what we now call Roundstone Bog, with its 143 lakes, has not come to light.

Nimmo then spent two or three years in a tour of the public works of France, Germany and Holland, and became proficient in Dutch, French, German and Italian. Having set up in private practice in Dublin, he designed and consulted on the construction of the mailboat harbour at Dunmore East in Waterford, which won high praise from Telford. Anticipating the foundation of the Geological Survey by nearly two decades, he devoted a year or more, perhaps in 1816–17, to a personal geological survey of Ireland, closely annotating a copy of Alexander Taylor's (1793) map with colour washes indicating rock types and symbols for gold, silver and other metals. In 1818 he was elected a member of the Royal Irish Academy.

In September 1820 Nimmo was appointed by the Commissioners of Irish Fisheries as engineer to survey the coasts of Ireland

and report on 'the most useful lines of communication between the principal harbours and interior of the country through the mountainous districts'. He started in Sligo and worked clockwise round the coast, completing the circuit by the summer of 1821, reporting on harbour sites and producing surveys of Sligo Bay, Port Ballintrae, Strangford River, Killough and Ardglass, the coast of Down, Carlingford Lough, Belfast and Larne. Soon afterwards he began work on the well-known 'Nimmo's Pier' in Galway. In 1822 he was appointed engineer to the 'Western District' (which probably meant Connemara, and Erris in north-west Mayo), and over the next eight years expended £167,000 of public money in its development through famine-relief schemes. He soon had thirteen piers being built in Galway and Connemara, and commenced the main Oughterard–Clifden road. At the Maam T-junction near the head of Lough Corrib he displayed his domination of the landscape of the future by designing himself a symmetrical residence and office, with outside stairs on the left and right to accommodate a file of employees receiving their weekly pay, and siting it exactly opposite the bridge he was building, to enjoy a symmetrical perspective view of his new road from Maam Cross. His private venture at Roundstone (of which, more detail below) grew out of these wide-ranging reorderings of Connemara.

Nimmo's accumulation of knowledge about the practical aspects of Ireland's coastline must have been immense. In 1823 he surveyed Dublin Bay for the Irish Fisheries, and prepared his *New Piloting Directions for St. George's Channel and the Coast of Ireland*, a chart and a fat book of instructions for navigating into all harbours with notes on times and speeds of tides. He also charted Valentia harbour for the Admiralty, and had the first steam dredger in Ireland brought in and put to work on the port of Drogheda. A curious example of his lateral thinking powers is a paper he read to the Royal Irish Academy, 'On the Application of the Science of Geology to the Purposes of Practical Navigation', proposing that pilots be trained in the recognition of materials brought up from the seabed, as an aid to finding their position when astronomical observations were not to be had.

In his private practice he provided Limerick with a monument to its political hero, Thomas Spring Rice, and designed the elegant seven-arched bridge across the Shannon there, modelling it on the Pont de Neuilly, which he had admired in Paris. He also built the dramatic Poulaphouca Bridge in Wicklow, with its single Gothic arch of nearly two hundred feet in height. According to Seán de Courcy there may be numerous other unattributed works of his scattered around the country. He was also much concerned with the development of railways, contributing a paper on the topic to the *Dublin Philosophical Journal and Scientific Review* in 1825 (the year in which the first real railway system, the Stockton and Darlington, opened) and reporting on a proposed Limerick–Waterford line. Outside Ireland he was engaged on the Liverpool and Leeds Railway and the Manchester, Bolton and Bury Railway, and was consulting engineer to the Duchy of Lancaster, the Mersey and Irwell Navigation, and three other railways.

Nimmo died on 20 January 1832 at his Dublin house, 78 Marlborough Street, aged forty-nine, worn out, surmises Seán de Courcy, by many years of overwork.

It was Nimmo's decisions that shaped the theatre of our daily life in Roundstone. In the 1813 report on the bogs he had recommended the building of a port where the Ballynahinch River opens into the head of Roundstone Bay, but later on he decided to situate it a few miles south of the river mouth, where there is a roughly rectangular bight (to use his word for a minor recess of the coastline) under a thirty-to-forty-foot cliff on the western shore of the bay. His new road was to pass this spot; in fact it runs boldly along the very edge of the cliff, so that the village, which has grown up along the road, boasts an almost uninterrupted panorama of the bay and the hills that enfold it. Nimmo's harbour consisted of a 150-foot wharf along the south side of this bight, with a 60-foot jetty running north from its seaward end. The inland end of the wharf was (and still is) rounded off with an ample semicircular curve; so was the end of the jetty, and, as a neighbour pointed out to me, it 'fitted beautifully into the sea'; sadly this feature was lost when the jetty was repaired and lengthened in 1990 after a badly moored trawler had tilted over at low tide and dragged out some of the stonework, and the weakened structure had been neglected until winter storms half ruined it. Most of this harbour is of local granite, but the coping stones along its rims are splendid yard-long blocks of hewn limestone shipped over from the Aran Islands. The fishermen point out a typical Nimmo touch, a thought for the practicalities of the fisherman's trade: in an oblique flight of steps down the face of the wharf, one step is of limestone rather than granite, and marks the half-tide level. There is a low limestone-capped parapet along the seaward side of the jetty, outside which the jetty's granite bodywork swells out in a smooth wave-defying mass to its foundations, like the curve of the belly of an upturned, broad-beamed boat from keel to gunwale. Again, unfortunately, this splendid curve was compromised, and the jetty was resurfaced in concrete, covering its limestone coping-stones, in the repairs or botch-job of 1990.

Like all Nimmo's Connemara marine works, Roundstone harbour was funded as a famine-relief scheme; in 1822 the Fisheries Board allocated £369 4s. 7d. for it, of which a quarter was contributed by the Government and a quarter by the Mansion House Committee, a charitable body. In 1824 the work was still unfinished, further grants totalling £111 2s. 10d. were made, and the Inspector of Harbours, a Mr Donnell, 'deemed it proper to observe that £155 (Irish) is charged to Government for this work by the Government engineer [Nimmo], exclusive of the foregoing sums'. Mr Donnell was not satisfied with the progress of the work, and recommended its recoping and raising, and the addition of a parapet to the jetty, to secure what had been done. In the following year he found that the recoping had been carried out 'in a most substantial manner', but the rest of the job had not been completed although the time agreed had expired; nevertheless, since the undertaker was not entitled to draw any money until the whole work be completed, he 'entertained no doubt of it being soon finished in a permanent and satisfactory manner'.

Having set in motion the building of the harbour, Nimmo went on to originate the village, and if he had a heart – we have no direct evidence of this – he must have invested a little of it in this project. But here is his own curt account (in his 'Coast Survey' of 1826) of how Roundstone was born out of some local row concerning its pier:

In 1824 my assistant, Mr. M'Gill, was employed to make up the defective part of this pier (which was beginning to receive some injury), and subsequently, as the tenant of the farm on which this pier is situated was very clamorous for damages alleged to be sustained by him in the progress of the work, I ventured at my own expense to purchase up his interest in the lease, as the most likely way to settle his claim: I now hold it by lease under Mr Thomas Martin, and expect soon to have a tolerable fishing village; several people are already settled there, and I am building a store for the purposes of the fishery.

By 1829 Mr Donnell, the Inspector of Harbours, could report to the Fisheries Board on the impetus given to this impoverished neighbourhood by Nimmo's work:

Four years back there were only three or four scattered cabins near this quay, and the small quantity of corn produced in the country adjacent, was entirely used for illicit distillation. A substantial slated store has been built on the quay. The building of a new village is rapidly proceeding; many of the houses are occupied, and I am informed that a patent has been obtained for holding markets and fairs. There can be no doubt but that this hitherto sequestered and almost unknown district will shortly give extensive employment in fishery, agricultural and commercial avocations.

Another pier was partly built to form the north end of the harbour in 1830, and a fishery commission sitting in Roundstone in 1836 was told by a former Inspector of Fisheries that 'its completion would render Roundstone harbour the best and safest between Galway and Westport. During a Herring Fishery, there are sometimes six hundred boats in the harbour; and they are all exposed to north-east winds, in consequence of the non-completion of the south pier.' (I think 'south' here is an error for 'north'.)

The herring fishery, which lasted from September to November and from January to March, was much improved during the Nimmo era, but it had its problems, as the Commission heard. Formerly herring could only be caught when the shoals came into the bay, but now there were three-ton boats that could follow the fish out to sea, shooting their nets in the evening and returning to haul them in the morning; however, there was a need for still larger boats that could stay out at sea overnight. Trawling was not practised, as it was thought to be destructive of spawn, although in the opinion of John Nimmo (Alexander's brother) this was mere prejudice. Salt for preserving the fish was sometimes unobtainable or so expensive that boats had to stay onshore for want of it. Another problem was the piratical ways of the fishermen from the Claddagh in Galway, who regarded the fish of Galway Bay as theirs by ancient tradition. An armed vessel should be stationed in the bay to regulate the fishery, the Commission was told, for 'the Claddagh men come in great numbers in large sail boats and whenever it blows too hard for the small boats of the coast to go out they do as they please with the nets'.

Other fisheries were busy too, and the 1836 account of them shows us the teeming, undepleted seas of those days: cod, ling, whiting and turbot were taken from December to March; gurnet, mackerel, bream and pollock from May to August; sunfish (i.e. basking shark) in May (but this fishery had been in decline for some years); oysters from March to November, or as decreed by Mr Martin, the landlord and owner of the oyster beds; and lobsters and crabs were abundant, about two hundred boats with four men in each being employed in the lobster fishery between Slyne Head, out to the west, and Golam Head, a few miles east of Roundstone.

Alexander Nimmo did not live to see this heyday of Roundstone's fortunes. After his death in 1832 his house in Dublin was occupied for a year or two by John and George Nimmo, described as 'civil engineers' by a general post office directory of 1833, and it is the name of John Nimmo, not Alexander, that occurs here and there in documents relating to Roundstone thereafter. Putting two and two together out of various visitors' accounts from the 1840s, it becomes clear to me that John and George were Alexander's brothers, and that both of them lived in Roundstone, where they were notables of the Presbyterian community. There was also a Mary Nimmo, born in 1815 and perhaps a daughter of John or George, who married the Revd Brabazon Ellis, a curate and one of the early leaders of the Protestant missions in Connemara in the wake of the Famine. According to some local history preserved by the Roundstone Franciscans, John lived in Roundstone from 1826 to 1844, most of the houses were built in his time, and he gave a grant to every man who built a house with an upper storey. One of the Nimmo brothers (John, most probably) was drowned in the upsetting of a small boat in 1849 or a little earlier.

George Nimmo figures as a pious old gentleman in the memoirs of a young Ulster Presbyterian, Henry M'Manus, who spent some time in Roundstone in 1840 while studying the Irish language:

Though advanced in years, yet loving wild scenery, and being of a kind disposition, he sometimes accompanied me in my pedestrian excursions. To beguile our way, he used to relate to me on such occasions anecdotes of what he had seen in foreign lands, having been a great traveller. Of these narratives I may give an example. He had gone to Germany to purchase timber in the 'Black Forest.' While riding about there, his horse rubbed a foot against a tree, severely bruising it. In consequence he could not return home that night, and was obliged to ask lodgings at the first house that came in sight. The owner, after hearing his story, made him welcome, gave him supper, and then showed him to his bed-room for the night. Mr. Nimmo, before retiring to rest, happened unconsciously to pray so loud so to be overheard by the family in another apartment. Instantly, to his surprise, the host rushed to the door; and, in a great passion, ordered him not to repeat again that name in the hearing of his family, – meaning the name of Jesus. 'If you do,' said he, 'I will expel you from my house.' The man was a Jew. Alas! How fearful the undying hatred of that race to

> 'Jesus, the name that charms our fears,
>   And bids our sorrows cease:
> 'Tis music in the sinner's ears –
>   'Tis life, and health, and peace!'

M'Manus also gives us a pleasant portrait of the Roundstone he knew, with which I end this account of Alexander Nimmo's 'tolerable fishing village':

Roundstone then presented the *beau ideal* of a mountain hamlet. It consisted of one street, running alongside the bay of the same name, and flanked on the land side by a dark mountain, rather broad than lofty. The slated houses might be near one hundred. Beside these houses, on the land side were small gardens, producing potatoes and cabbages; and further back were some cultivated fields. All else was an unbroken desert of heath, which, after spreading into vast moors, terminates towards the north in the stupendous 'Twelve Pins,' the finest view of which is seen from Roundstone. Thus the narrow strip of tillage around the town, as contrasted with this ocean of heath, resembled a piece of green selvage on a web of black cloth.

However, he tells us, not all the residents were happy with the new dispensation:

While the district remained inaccessible, it . . . was filled with valuable contraband goods, such as sugar, rum, brandy, tobacco and wine. By stealth these imports were disposed of to the shopkeepers of the neighbouring towns. Still a surplus remained in Connemara sufficient to reduce their price there to a minimum; and so this sterile country abounded in the luxuries of life! Not without truth, then, did an old man tell me in Irish, that 'there was not at that time so plentiful a country for a poor man in all the nine regions!'

And so it was that some of the natives cursed Alexander Nimmo's works. According to M'Manus, their saying was, 'There is no luck in the country since they began to make the roads, and to build the big houses!'

A Cure of Souls

As Nimmo's Roundstone took shape, hungry bodies flocked to the new village looking to be fed. And since they brought their souls with them, the result was a feeding frenzy – among the would-be feeders of souls, more than among those fed. In 1832 the landlord, Thomas Martin, leased a site for a new Catholic chapel to the Revd Patrick Burke, looking out across the mouth of Roundstone Bay from the lofty corner where Nimmo's new road turned west at the south end of the village street. Within a few years the Church of Our Lady Star of the Sea arose there, the splendour of its location reflecting the new status of the Catholic Church in those years so soon after the Catholic Emancipation Act of 1829, and the little chapel in Coogla was abandoned. But Protestant Bible-readers had already been knocking on doors in the district, and when Dr MacHale, the ferocious 'Lion of the West', became Catholic Archbishop of Tuam in 1834 he called in the Orders to stiffen the backbone of Connemara. Five Franciscan Brothers from Mountbellew founded a monastery in Roundstone in 1835 and undertook the education of children. To begin with the Brothers occupied a small single-storeyed house on the village street almost in the shadow of the new church; their own little chapel next door to it still survives, as a holiday home. A finely carved plaque, decorated with the crossed arms of the Franciscan emblem, bore the following announcement:

> This Monastery was Founded by the
> Religious Brothers of Mt. Bellew of the
> third order of St. Francis with the Sanction
> and approbation of his Grace the most

> Revd. Doctor Mc.Hale Lord Arch-
> Bishop of Tuam Dedicated to the
> Blessed Virgin and our holy Father St. Frans.
> To the Greater Glory of God Novr. 18
> AD 1835

This plaque aroused the fury of William Thackeray, who visited Roundstone in the course of his tour of Ireland in 1842. In his *Irish Sketch Book* he writes:

There is little to be seen in the town of Roundstone, except a Presbyterian chapel in process of erection, that seems big enough to accommodate the Presbyterians of the country; and a sort of lay-convent, being a community of brothers of the third order of St. Francis. They are all artisans and workmen, taking no vows but living together in common, and undergoing a certain religious regimen. Their work is said to be very good, and all are employed upon some labour or other. On the front of this unpretending little dwelling is an inscription with a great deal of pretence, stating, that the establishment was founded with the approbation of 'His Grace, the most Reverend the Lord Archbishop of Tuam.'

The most Reverend Dr. MacHale is a clergyman of great learning, talents, and honesty, but His Grace the Lord Archbishop of Tuam strikes me as being no better than a mountebank; and some day I hope even his own party will laugh this humbug down. It is bad enough to be awed by big titles at all, but to respect sham ones! O stars and garters! We shall have his Grace the Lord Chief-Rabbi next, or his Lordship the Arch-Imaum.

No doubt what Thackeray reacted to here was the Protestants' recurrent nightmare of 'papal aggression', the assertion by a malign and scheming foreign power of authority over part of the realm. Within a few years of his visit such fears and resentments would lead to the passing of the Ecclesiastical Titles Act of 1851, under which Catholic clerics were forbidden to use titles derived from places in the United Kingdom, a piece of legislation that was bitterly resented by Catholics.

Br Francis Duffy, formerly Master of Novices in Mountbellew, was the first Superior of the new monastery, but died just two years after its foundation. Two other Brothers died in 1845 and 1846 (whether their deaths were connected with the beginnings of the Great Famine, I do not know), one moved on to Clifden and participated in the establishment of a monastery there, while three or four emigrated to Pennsylvania, where they founded what is now St Francis's University in Loretto, in 1847. More Brothers must have joined the Roundstone community by 1848, when it acquired a two-storey house called Seaview Lodge from a family of middlemen called the Duanes, near the shore a few hundred yards south of the Old Store, in what is now the IDA estate. Later on the Franciscans built a boys' school there, and a chapel, of which the bell-tower survives along with the fine arched gateway and the several hundred yards of ten- or fifteen-foot-high stone walls surrounding the monastery grounds, farm and orchard.

On the Protestant side the winners of the race to net souls in Roundstone were, initially at least, the Presbyterians. The Revd Joseph Fisher, who had been ordained in 1835 and had overseen the completion of the Presbyterian church in Galway in that same year, was an active missioner in both Connemara and the Aran Islands. When the Synod of Ulster proposed sending him to India, his Galway congregation urged their own claims on him:

To the study of the Irish language, the accessible avenue to the hearts and affections of the poor people, he has been sedulously devoting himself with a view to presenting before them in their mother tongue Christ crucified as the only hope of a sinner's salvation . . . To many it may appear almost incredible, but at the present moment, through his exertions in this region there are eighteen Irish schools with about 300 scholars in full operation, all learning to read the Gospel of Christ in the Irish language in defiance of sacerdotal threats and denunciations . . .

At this period there was mutual goodwill among the Galway Protestants; when the cathedral was being repaired, the Episcopal congregation had use of the new Presbyterian church as their temporary place of worship. In Roundstone matters did not work out so harmoniously. Mr Fisher had discovered a little company of Presbyterians there in the course of his visits to Connemara, and in 1838 he brought their needs to the attention of the Home Mission, which later arranged for visits from ministers. But in the meantime a young Church of England man, William Pennefather, then studying at Trinity College, Dublin, and 'burning with desire for the salvation of sinners', heard of the existence of such sinners in Connemara. His brother had been down there on a fishing trip, and reported back that along a great stretch of that wild western coast no Protestant place of worship could be found, and that in Roundstone a little flock of Protestants existed, but in great ignorance, without church or pastor, who would be delighted to welcome a minister. During the long vacation in 1839 William made enquiries and found that the Presbyterians and Anglicans of the neighbourhood would be willing to unite themselves under a minister of either denomination. So he came down to Galway on the top of the Dublin mail coach, in incessant rain, and then took the stage car into Connemara to confer with 'Mr. R., a very intelligent, well-informed Scotchman' (who will have been John Robertson, the Martins' agent at Ballynahinch).

The next morning was Sunday. It was stormy and rainy, and Mr. R. was not sure of my coming, so had not announced it, and the congregation was small, partly hindered by the severity of the day; but the order, the attention, the love which seemed to exist between the members of the little flock, and their apparent interest in the service, made it deeply interesting to me. It is a singular fact that when Mr. R. was urged by the Presbyterian minister of Galway to apply to Scotland for a minister, he answered, 'We are such a small band, it would be a pity to divide us, and perhaps the churchmen would not attend.' He will subscribe largely to our little church, and will superintend the building, and in the meantime, will himself conduct a service.

Mr Pennefather concluded his service with half an hour of sermon; his text was Nehemiah vi. 3, in which the prophet replies

to those who have sent for him, 'And I sent messengers unto
them, saying, I am doing a great work, so that I cannot come
down; why should the work cease, whilst I leave it and come
down to you?' In the evening he spoke again, on Nehemiah ix.
16–17: 'But they and our father dealt proudly, and hardened their
necks, and hearkened not to thy commandments', and distributed
some books he had brought, as a memorial of his coming among
them. The next day an old gentleman presented him with some
stanzas on the occasion. I copy a few of them:

On the Proposed Building of the Church at Roundstone

Amidst the wilds of Erin's Isle,
A feeble flock were left to stray;
No pastor cheered them with his smile,
Within no temple's sacred aisle
Could these poor wanderers pray!

There, mountains form a barrier rude
O'er which few care to roam;
And seldom travellers dare intrude
Where wretchedness and famine brood,
Midst rocks and billows' foam.

At length a pitying stranger came,
Inspired with holy love.
Blest be that gentle Christian's name!
Blest He who gave the sacred flame –
Our heavenly Friend above!

This old gentleman took Pennefather to visit a young woman
who had been bedridden for four years:

Brought up a Roman Catholic, she was hired by an English lady who
invited her in to family prayer, where her mind was awakened; she
became anxious for instruction, and determined to go to church. She

did so, and the next day, as she was going to fetch water from the well, she was waylaid and beaten so violently that she has never since been able to leave her bed; yet she blesses God for her heavy chastisement, prays for her enemies, and says her happiest hours have been spent on that sick-bed.

Returning to Dublin, Pennefather set about raising funds for the building of the projected church. The Church of Ireland Bishop of Tuam offered to pay for a curate at Roundstone, and was hopeful that the Ecclesiastical Commissioners would help with the church. But in the following year Pennefather found that his letters to Roundstone were not being answered, and heard that a Presbyterian minister had arrived there and was about to build a chapel; also, from Mrs Martin he learned that no help was now to be expected from the Bishop. Hurrying down to Roundstone, he went to the house where he had preached:

. . . but, alas! The flock was scattered; there were only fourteen present. The Presbyterians were carrying out their service in another room, and a bitter spirit pervaded the body. However I got leave to meet all together, and after a little difficulty and hesitation in some quarters, we assembled at 6 o'clock in the Presbyterian room. Some were present who had not met for a long time, and between whom unpleasant feelings existed. I preached on Ephesians iv. 4–6, and to my joy Mrs. — and Mr. — shook hands when the service was over . . . Discordant feelings had risen to a melancholy pitch. Both parties were in the wrong; both were injudicious. Mr. —, though anxious for the welfare of the people, and desirous to honour his master, is very weak, low-spirited, and ready to take offence.

Pennefather took the opportunity of calling on the girl who had been beaten for becoming a Protestant, and found her 'in a happy state, but very suffering. A lady had given me a pound for her, and I found she had been three days without anything to eat or drink, but a piece of bread and cold water. Poor creature, she seemed overpowered with gratitude.' Frustrated in Roundstone,

Pennefather now considered pitching his 'little tabernacle' in one of the Aran Islands, and sailed to the biggest of the islands to meet with the teacher of a Protestant school there. At first this new venture promised well, but after much effort his schemes for a church there were not realized, and his thoughts returned to 'those few sheep in the wilderness', his 'little flock at Roundstone'.

However, in Roundstone the Presbyterian cause was for the moment in the ascendant. John Nimmo (himself a Scots Presbyterian) had donated a half-acre of ground on the hillside above the harbour, and in April 1840 the foundation stone of a little kirk had been laid by Mrs Martin herself. John Robertson, who had undertaken to superintend the building of Pennefather's projected church and even to conduct a service in the meantime, was now accounted a leading member of the Presbyterian community. The opening of the Presbyterian church, like Pennefather's first coming, was celebrated in a poem, of which a few verses will give a taste:

> Mid *ocean bays*, where Erin laves
> Her rocky feet in Western waves;
> And, round her ever-winding shore,
> The silvery-crested billows roar:

> Where *Orras beag*, his giant form,
> Opposes to the western storm;
> Whose weather-bleached and naked head
> Hangs frowning o'er the ocean bed:

> Lo! Here, the Gael, with wonder, sees
> A glorious flag float on the breeze;
> CHRIST'S CROWN AND COVENANT stand to view,
> Emblazoned on a banner blue.

This poem was composed by the young Henry M'Manus, who, if he lacked Wordsworth's way with words, had absorbed something of his sensibility. The long walks he took alone or in company with old George Nimmo led to the earliest spiritual appreciation on record of the 'wild desolate moor' now known as Roundstone Bog, the first claim that it had a value above and beyond the productive potentialities Alexander Nimmo had seen in it. The following is from M'Manus's *Sketches of the Irish Highlands*, written some twenty years later during his final illness and, as he notes, 'after his life had been given over by his medical friends'.

My express object on going there, was to test the truth of Dr. Johnson's remark, that a man's feelings in a wilderness are such as could be understood only by experience . . . In truth, such an experience resembles a new window broken into the soul, or a new sense imparted to it. Or, to speak more soberly, it is the waking up of a mental faculty previously dormant for want of its proper stimulus, showing that the human mind is endowed with untold capabilities, which, perhaps, eternity alone can fully develop. Is this the language of aesthetic enthusiasm? We reply that it is not; it is matter of fact . . .

After describing the vast expanse of heath bounded by mountains and the ocean, and inhabited only by carrion crows 'standing moodily on heathery hillocks', he concludes:

But that very desolation itself, being so profound and novel, was deeply impressive; while the less pleasing details were swallowed up in two elements of the sublime. One was – a boundless expanse of surface below; and the other was – a boundless expanse of sunshine above. Instead of hedges bounding your view, as elsewhere, with only a narrow strip of sky visible above you, here you behold at one glance hundreds of square miles, spanned at their extremities by the whole concave heaven, filled of a fine day with a blaze of living light, indescribably glorious . . .

M'Manus was particularly atuned to the solemn, silent play of evening shadows over the Twelve Pins:

Nor was the effect merely aesthetic. Mountains, with their Heaven-pointing summits, are the temples of the Eternal. They lift the soul, unless altogether debased, above the perishable things of time, and point it forward athwart the mists of sense to the ever-during realities of eternity.

And in this striking remark he unites his rather conventional apprehension of Nature as a religious allegory with a fine observation of physical phenomena:

In my past life I have known cases in which a very plain human face looked beautiful, because lit up by a brilliant intellect. The mind within, like a lamp behind a picture, made the features luminous and attractive. Such also is the effect of sunshine in Connemara.

But in Connemara, as he was told, 'it rains thirteen months in the year', and this rather delicate young man suffered much hardship in the still-raw new village of Roundstone.

Finding the inn too public a place to lodge in, I was obliged, for want of a better, to put up with lodgings as miserable as need be. Outwardly the house seemed good enough, being two storey and slated. But it had never been finished inside, and thus resembled a large barn. Of the interior, a part was enclosed for me, forming a small sitting room and bed-room. So far so good; but, alas, the roof was not staunch. Through chinks in it the sky was visible, and when winter set in, I had to 'rough it' in earnest. To keep off the drops, my host covered my bed with plates and dishes; but the moisture would not take the hint that its presence was unwelcome; so, on my awakening some mornings, I saw pools of it on the earthen floor. In this wretched abode I spent four months . . . And yet many Romanists, who saw me endure all this, and more, will not be persuaded that in voluntarily undertaking it for their good, I was not actuated by sordid motives.

Indeed, such missions of goodwill were productive of little but dissension and ostracism among their intended beneficiaries. Like Pennefather, M'Manus was taken to meet Roundstone's first convertite and martyr:

Let the reader visit with me a poor cottage, which then stood in a lane ascending the hill behind the village. This cabin we enter; and within, we find only one apartment, nearly a half of which is occupied by a bed. On the latter lies a female, probably not quite thirty years of age, though she looks far older, being spent with long wasting sickness . . . This invalid, when a stout young girl, had hired as a servant in a respectable Presbyterian family. Brought up a Roman Catholic, she was totally ignorant of God's Word . . . In her new situation, she obtained an opportunity of hearing the Scripture read at family prayer. With all her ignorance she could not but learn from it, that there was one Saviour, not many – one Sacrifice for sin, not a succession of them, called 'Masses' . . . No longer, could she attend the Mass. This bold step set the village in a blaze. Going home one night to her parents' house, she was met in the lane by a tall man, whom she did not recognise. Without speaking a word, he raised his powerful arm, and with one blow felled her to the earth. While she lay prostrate at his feet, he kicked her in the back, and injured so severely her spine, that she could never afterwards stand erect.

M'Manus had been directed to Roundstone by Mr Fisher of Galway to learn the Irish language, as a preparation for missionary work. (As he later wrote, 'Irish is the only way of access to the Celtic heart, which, with its priceless affections, we wish to win for Jesus.' In fact M'Manus prided himself on being the first Irish missioner in Connemara and the first to preach in Irish there, with the sole exception of the locally born Thomas de Vere Coneys, who later became Professor of Irish in Trinity College, Dublin, and who had preached in Clifden in 1838.) Finding that the Roundstone congregation had no minister, M'Manus had volunteered to conduct a service every Sabbath:

Amongst the worshippers on the very first occasion, appeared a middle-aged gentleman and two ladies, who turned out to be the celebrated Thomas Martin, Esq., of Ballinahinch Castle, with his wife and daughter: they were disposed altogether to join our Church, but afterwards drew off, owing, it is supposed, to their aristocratic connections.

And indeed the established Church eventually prevailed over Presbyterianism in Roundstone. Hearing that a suitable minister had been found for the place, William Pennefather persevered with his fund-raising, and his church was built, and consecrated in 1843. (It must have been a plain little building because it was not until it was restored in 1891 that it acquired its tower, porch and chancel.) Pennefather went on to be ordained in 1842 and became, successively, vicar of Wendover, Aylesbury, Barnet and finally of Mildmay Park, Islington, but he was never the vicar of Roundstone. What manner of man was he, this absentee pastor? In a memorial sketch of him a friend wrote:

It would hardly be giving a fair portrait of him in these early years not to mention the power he even then exercised over others – a kind of gentle force, by which he seemed able to lead them to do as he wished, in a way which I never remember to have observed in any one else. We used to smile at and enjoy what we called his '*gift of rule*'. Was it not the foreshadowing of that force and power which came forth in after years, to the admiration of so many, ever connected as it was with such kindness and consideration for all.

Everywhere he showed himself to be a practical and inventive servant of his flock: thus in Aylesbury he ministered to the swarming bargees of the Grand Canal from a boat that he turned into a floating chapel. His biographer writes of him:

He naturally possessed the power of grasping a position at once. The remarkable organ of locality which, to the amusement of his friends, made him at home in the most intricate town, by simply taking the points of the compass, and ascertaining the bearing of the principal thoroughfares, seemed to extend to the moral and physical necessities of a parish. He knew more of his surroundings in a week than many men would learn in a year, and was prepared to grapple with them.

The Revd William Pennefather's works have outlasted him. The Mildmay Conferences on missionary and social enterprise he and his wife Catherine organized have had a wide influence in Germany, France and Switzerland, while the Mildmay Hospital he founded during the cholera epidemic of 1866 became in 1988 Europe's first AIDS hospice. And in Roundstone, though its congregation is tiny, the Protestant church is still open and conserves the memory of its founder; his portrait hangs in the vestry, and a plaque in the porch reads:

> The Parish Church of Moyrus
> Founded by
> Revd. W. Pennefather, M.A.
> Afterwards of Mildmay
> Consecrated Septr. 14th 1843.

As for the Roundstone Presbyterians, they did not acquire an ordained minister until 1843 when the Revd William Crotty, a former Catholic, arrived in the aftermath of the notorious schism in the Catholic congregation of Birr in Offaly. This scandalous affair was the culmination of a bizarre and sometimes ludicrous sequence of events involving William's cousin Michael Crotty. Michael was born in 1795 in Broadford, east Clare, and studied at Maynooth until expelled with the reputation of being 'a fool and a madman'. Back at home he took up the cause of the parish priest, Fr Corbett, who was accused by his housekeeper of being the father of the child she was expecting. She was the deserted wife of a nephew of the Bishop of Killaloe, and the Bishop sided with her, while Michael and many priests of the region believed Fr Corbett to be the victim of a plot. When Corbett was tried and found guilty his infuriated parishioners waylaid the Bishop and would have thrown him into the Shannon together with his carriage, horse and driver, had not Michael Crotty's uncle come to his aid and calmed the mob. It was presumably as a result of this service that Michael was soon afterwards sent by the Bishop to complete his studies in France.

Michael's priestly career was a sequence of rows. As curate in Birr he tried to stop people visiting a fortune-teller or 'cup tosser' called Moll Connors. To expose her as a fraud he called on her disguised in an old torn suit and large overcoat, under which he carried a horsewhip. She tossed the cup for him and prophesied that he would marry a red-haired woman and have a family. He then asked her to toss the cup for herself, which she did, and told him that she was in the presence of a man who was about to give her a severe whipping. As it turned out, both her prophecies proved correct.

While in Birr, Michael became the champion of parishioners who were opposing the parish priest's raising of funds for the building of a new church. Transferred to another parish, he was soon in trouble for beating an Orangeman he found in the embraces of a local prostitute. Revisiting Birr at the invitation of the people, he was ordered out of the old church by the parish priest, but, encouraged by cries of 'Stay with us, Fr Crotty, and we will follow you to Hell', he refused to leave. He remained in possession of the old church until evicted by Lord Rosse at the head of the 66th Regiment, whereupon he took over the unfinished new church and was arrested and jailed for three months. For the next seven years there were two rival congregations in Birr.

It was during this period, in 1832, that William Crotty was ordained and appointed to a curacy in Killaloe. At the dinner given to welcome him to the parish he quarrelled with the parish priest over reports of Michael's strange doings, and decided to take himself off to Birr. But Michael's ministry there was changing: statues of saints were disappearing from his church, prayers were being said in English, and the cult of Our Lady was slighted. Many of the congregation had second thoughts at this stage. After another fracas with the military Michael spent seven weeks in jail, and when it became clear that he would not regain control of the new church he decided to build his own, which was to be a 'reformed church'. He appealed to 'the Protestants of Ireland' for funds, £400 was collected, and his former nemesis, Lord Rosse, donated a site for the building.

When Michael's rival, the parish priest at Birr, became a bishop and denounced him to Rome as 'an open heretic', the Crottys decided to affiliate completely with the Church of England. Michael went to England to raise funds, and there married a lady (who it is said later turned up in Birr saying she did not know where he was, and, while drinking with some of her friends, advised them never to marry a Catholic priest). Upset by news of Michael's marriage, William Crotty persuaded the trustees of their church to hand it over to the Presbyterians. Michael eventually obtained a curacy in Yorkshire, where he remained for a few years; later he was arrested for begging, went to Belgium, was arrested again and committed to a mental home run by Catholic nuns, in which he died, reconciled with the Catholic Church. William stayed on as Presbyterian minister in Birr, married a Miss Dempsey, was transferred to Roundstone in 1843, and remained there for two years before becoming the Revd Joseph Fisher's missionary assistant in Galway. The Crottyite community in Birr dwindled to extinction in the 1850s.

The above rather derogatory account of the Crottys is largely based on a recent booklet on the Birr schism by a Catholic priest. Perhaps a consideration from a Presbyterian perspective should be added – for, having spent some time poking into their writings, I honour a depth of seriousness in those nineteenth-century sectarian controversialists, even if I share not a shred of their passionate convictions. Here is William Crotty's conversion, as recounted by him in later life to a colleague, the Revd Thomas Armstrong:

For some time [after Michael Crotty's suspension by the Catholic bishop] they merely disputed points of discipline and order, but with slow and cautious steps they proceeded to call in question some of the leading doctrines of the Church, and began to preach Christ . . . Having been suspended by the Bishop, they were unable to obtain the holy oil required for one of their sacraments. This caused them to examine the Scriptures as to the orders of bishops and presbyters, and they came to the conclusion that they were identical, and so they consecrated the oil themselves. After a while this rite was given up, the Gospel preached, public worship and the sacraments administered according to the simple and Scriptural forms of our Church. Through the guidance of the Rev. Joseph Fisher, of Galway, they then sought admission into the Synod of Ulster through the Presbytery of Dublin. After due examination and enquiry Mr. William Crotty was admitted into our communion. He was accompanied in this step by a large proportion of his community, to the number of 150 . . . As to his cousin Michael, the people had become dissatisfied with his procedure and doings. He also applied for admission into the Presbyterian Church, but the Presbytery of Dublin did not see their way to receive him.

Mr Armstrong goes on to tell of William Crotty's transfer to Roundstone in 1843:

It was to this remote and romantic, but very wild region that Mr Crotty was first sent after leaving Birr. He describes its religious condition thus: 'This is one of the dark corners of the land; here Romanism is dominant and rampant; here the monster roars without reply, and rages without resistance.' In the prosecution of his work he encountered much trouble, but was able after a time to write, 'A great change has been wrought in the minds of the population. Instead of being actuated by feelings of enmity and hostility towards us, as they seemed to have been when we first came here; they now manifest the kindest feelings to us, and treat us with the utmost civility and courtesy.' . . . He reports that the schools are succeeding beyond expectation. 'I attend five preaching stations beside Roundstone – namely, Clifden, Ballinakill, Orrismore, Recess, and the Isle of Arran. At all these places there is a pretty good attendance considering the small number of Protestants residing in each locality.'

In the town of Galway and as missionary over the whole county, Crotty was indefatigable, according to Mr Armstrong, and had a difficult, if not dangerous, post; he was sometimes violently assaulted, his house was stoned, and he was drummed to and from the meeting house by a ferocious mob. Once he had to be taken out of the church by a window and conveyed to the manse while the police dispersed a mob enraged by one of his Wednesday evening 'controversial sermons'. The Revd William Crotty died in 1856, survived by his wife and ten children.

As to the Revd Henry M'Manus, I have told of his lonely and fruitless evangelizing in the Aran Islands in *Stones of Aran: Labyrinth*. In Galway too he suffered for his faith. An eyewitness describes how he was pelted with mud and stones and threatened with a butcher's cleaver after attending a lecture given by a minister connected with the Irish Church Mission:

When I saw him he had lost his hat, and his grey hairs were streaming behind him with the wind, and his coat all torn. He went to several open doors asking shelter, but was thrust back to the will of the mob. At length Mrs. Thomson, who was well known and respected in Galway, ran out and called Mr. M'Manus to come into her house, which he did, and the mob soon after withdrew. No lasting injury resulted from the treatment. Mr. M'Manus's health was delicate for some time previous to the above painful incident, but he lived for several years after. He died of consumption and exhaustion at his residence, Clontarf Road, near Dublin, October, 14. 1864.

By that time the little community he had known in Roundstone had fallen on hard times, according to Mr Armstrong:

After some time the fishing and other industries failed, and Roundstone rapidly went down, and is now an almost deserted and desolate village. In the year 1883 I visited Connemara in company with the Rev. S. G. Crawford, minister of Westport. The church had been little used for years, and was much in need of repairs. The graves in the adjoining burying-place of Mr. Nimmo and his brothers were in a sad state.

Mr Armstrong obtained a grant to have the church and its grounds put in order, but seemingly it was hardly used until 1918, when, according to an article in the *Irish Presbyterian*, 'a few Presbyterian exiles were found there, and a mid-week service begun for them in the little church, which, thanks to the generosity of an unknown benefactor, was renovated and made moderately habitable'. At this stage its congregation would have consisted largely of coastguards and RIC men, and their time was at an end:

The transfer of government to the Irish Free State, and the campaign of violence with which it was preceded and accompanied, have together driven our people out of the district. So for the present the little church stands closed. A quaint little building, with crow-stepped gables, it looks out over the village nestling below, and over the harbour, to the Twelve Pins, and the mighty Maumturk and Correcogemore Mountains, a witness like them to the everlasting Faithfulness of God.

But nothing is everlasting beneath the moon, and the little kirk, as it was known, was demolished in the mid 1940s. A slight, flat-topped eminence in a boggy field full of rushes and yellow irises, by the lane that climbs inland from the harbour, marks the site of all that fervent sermonizing. There are a few headstones nearby, and a ruined vault, which might or might not once have held the Nimmos' bones.

The Cold of Charity

'Three hundred and sixty-five days a year we have the potato. The blackguard of a Raleigh who brought 'em here entailed a curse upon the labourer that has broke his heart. Because the landowner sees we can live and work hard on 'em, he grinds us down in our wages, and then despises us because we are ignorant and ragged.' So said one of the seaweed-gatherers on Goirtín strand, on May Day 1845, to a good Christian lady, Asenath Nicholson of New York, who was walking about Ireland reading the Gospel to any who would listen. The man was perfectly correct in his understanding of the economy, and the ideology that justified it: the landlords had reduced the peasantry to potato-fuelled machines, all other crops and products being only to pay the rent, not to eat; and because the labourer was lumpen, rough and dirty, he and the potato were perfectly suited to each other. But even as the seaweed-gatherer spoke, the potato crop on which he was so resentfully dependent was doomed and the Great Hunger (so called to distinguish it from the several other periods of dire shortage this man would already have suffered through) was in all probability soon to reduce him to petitioning for public and private charity. In the maintenance of a society based on exploitation, charity has an important role: it blesses him who gives and curses him who takes, warming the heart of the donor and chilling that of the recipient. For this social heat-engine to work, pumping self-satisfaction up the wealth-scale, the lower orders have to be convinced of the shamefulness of accepting what they are denied the means of buying, and the contemptuous look of the Relieving Officer has to be internalized. This ancient lesson, ruthlessly reinforced by the Famine years, was well learned, and still causes many distortions. Those driven by desperation even beyond shame have their inheritors still, while a perverted self-regard makes others refuse the help they need and which in a society of mutual respect would be acceptable with a proud sense of entitlement. In this and other ways, the Famine lingers on into today.

Potato blight, a fungal disease new to Europe, was first noticed in Belgium in June 1845. Spreading by invisible clouds of spore on humid warm days, it reached Ireland by September. The infection fell on the leaves of the flourishing plants, made its way down the sappy stems and rioted in the tubers. Soon an offensive smell was perceptible in the fields, especially by night, and when the potatoes were dug they were found to be black sacs of putridity. Throughout Ireland, about half the year's crop was lost. And, especially in the West where wheat could not be grown, there was little else to eat. In that first season of shortage nobody would have known that it was the beginning of the Great Hunger. There were still some potatoes on the market, most people had a few other resources, however limited, and livestock could be sold or household goods and implements of trade pawned as food prices rose. The authorities' response was tardy, but some public works were inaugurated on which the able-bodied unemployed could earn a pittance, as in 1822 and a few subsequent episodes of 'distress'. But the 1846 crop was totally destroyed by blight, and by that time a much less sympathetic government had come to power in Westminster. In the following year, remembered as 'Black Forty-seven' for its long bitter winter and the onslaught of fever, there was a remission of the blight, but as people had eaten the seed potatoes and were too enfeebled by malnourishment to till the land, the crop was very small. The blight returned in 1848, and in the first half of 1849 cholera followed upon starvation, but that year's potato crop was largely blight-free, and thereafter by degrees the crisis subsided into decades of chronic deprivation. A rhyme once current in Connemara summarizes this history:

> In the year Forty-six build your house of rotten sticks,
> In the year Forty-seven pray to God in Heaven,
> In the year Forty-eight build your coffin straight,
> In the year Forty-nine build your house of stone and lime.

Nevertheless, it seems wrong to treat the Famine as just a period. It was in fact the keystone in a triumphal arch of suffering. Intermittent food shortages had led up to it since the end of the Napoleonic Wars, when agricultural prices fell, ex-soldiers flooded onto the labour market, and the kelp trade, supplier of alkalis to the Industrial Revolution, collapsed as rival sources opened up again; in Connemara even the herring had deserted the coastal waters at this time. And for long after the worst years of hunger, the survivors were further bereaved by mass emigration. So it is not as if the tragic arch of suffering rose up from foundations of a decent competency; rather it was a low squalid affair raised on depleted ground, and none could pass through it unbowed. From the Connemara of today it is hardly visible on the horizon of the past and for most people, the foot-free young and their prosperous parents, it is no longer relevant; but that is not true for all, by any means. There has never been a year in which it would have been appropriate to celebrate the end of the Famine; instead, it has been forgotten while the ragged edges of its shadow still lie around our feet.

Nor do I personally pretend to be a historian of the Famine, even in the restricted field of Connemara and more especially of Roundstone; I rely on a diligently researched book by a Clifden writer, Katherine Villiers-Tuthill's *Patient Endurance: The Great Famine in Connemara*, for the facts and dates and statistics in the following account. Instead I write as a witness, no less appalled for having come too late on the scene to do more than start back from the pitiless, pitiful gaze of a skull I imagine coming across in the shadows of a thicket, and to extend a hand towards it in the respectful silence of writing. There are said to be famine graves in the bushes along Farrell's Road, the lane through the fields behind Roundstone village along which I go blackberrying. They clutch at my ankles like briars stirred by the wind, these demanding dead whose voices I have promised to hear, but who are so numerous as to have overloaded communal memory and who no longer have names. Just one or two individual deaths emerge for me from the well-documented oblivion of famine mortality records, for their stories are so barbed that I cannot shake them off and, when I pull away, the whole dreadful cadaver comes out of the ground, momentarily resuming the aspect of a human being *in extremis* before evaporating into the sunlight. I shall recount these deaths in their places.

A new geography had been clamped on Ireland by the Poor Law Act of 1838. For purposes of famine relief the country had been divided into 'unions', each administered by a board of guardians composed of local worthies, and charged with levying the Poor Rate and building a workhouse. The Clifden Union covered the four westernmost parishes of Connemara, and was one of the poorest and least developed in Ireland. And when the blight struck, this huge diocese of want was still without its high cathedral, for the Board had already proved itself unworthy; its members were of the landed interest and had delayed implementation of the Act so as to avoid payment of the rate and their responsibility for the expenses of indoor relief, and as a result the workhouse was not completed until December 1845 and even then remained closed for over two years more. The North, South,

East and West Roundstone Divisions of the Union rambled into the remotest peninsulas, islands and mountain recesses; for the destitute this hunger-geography was one of long journeys in a nearly roadless land, and long waits for small portions in bare, windy places.

After the Government had received the first official reports of distress, in the spring of 1846, and set up a relief commission, food depots were opened, and small amounts of Indian meal distributed for sale through them. In the Clifden Union the main depot was in Clifden, and the one to serve the widely dispersed population of the Roundstone district was in the village itself. Fr Peter Curran, the parish priest and Chairman of the Roundstone Relief Committee, and the Revd James Ashe, the committee's secretary and the Church of Ireland rector, were horrified at the sight of the crowd that gathered to purchase the meal, which was quickly sold out, whereupon, as they reported to the Relief Commission in Dublin, the people 'retired to their cheerless homes with emotions of gloom and noisy clamour, having pawned and sold their effects to obtain the meal'. But Dublin was deaf to the clerics' request for further supplies and to their suggestion that the meal be given free to the penniless, and in its reply noted the 'total absence of local exertions on the part of the residence in the neighbourhood of Roundstone to provide means of relief'. The committee was urged to raise charitable subscriptions, to which the Government would then add a donation; a list of those proprietors and other 'opulent individuals' in the neighbourhood who refused to subscribe was also to be forwarded to Dublin. But although the gentry, few as they were in Connemara, did make some donations to the Clifden committee, nothing was forthcoming in Roundstone until the beginning of 1847 when the sum of £21 was raised, to which the Government added £22. Fr Curran continued to implore the Relief Commission for deliveries of meal, but was instructed to purchase corn, barley and wheat instead. Once again he endeavoured to explain the realities of the situation to the distant authorities:

Now here in a district in the wilds of Connemara, far removed from the operations of any provision trade, utterly destitute of corn of any description and depending solely on the potato crop, which it has pleased the Almighty to render useless – we therefore earnestly implore of you, sir, as you value the peace of this district, to lose no time in sending a supply of food for the people here . . .

But between those people and the originators of public policy lay the gulfs of distance and social standing that constituted the new geography's direst dimension. Down the degrees from the Prime Minister and his Westminster grandees, through Sir Charles Trevelyan at the Treasury, the Lord Lieutenant of Ireland and the bureaucrats of Dublin Castle, the Board of Guardians of the Clifden Union, the clergy heading the Roundstone Relief Committee, the Poor Rate Collector and the Relieving Officer, came a succession of edicts, variations on the themes of food depots, public works, soup kitchens and workhouses, that must have seemed to the farm- and fisher-folk calculated to play cat-and-mouse with their lives. After Lord John Russell's Whigs, believers in the universal beneficence of the profit motive, came into office in 1846, it was decreed that the food supply even in the starving West was not to be supplemented by the Government unless private traders failed to provide, and then only at prices that would not undercut those pertaining locally. Mr John Robertson, who had a fish cannery near Ballynahinch, became the contractor for supplying the Roundstone food depots, and later on as prices soared and the Union approached bankruptcy, he joined with other traders in refusing to supply Indian meal on credit. As in previous times of distress the Board of Works proposed road-building projects on which the destitute could be employed, but the Treasury refused funds for the schemes put forward in the Clifden Union on the grounds that they were too extensive and might not be finished before the period of distress should be over. It was June 1846 before revised projects were submitted and sanctioned and implemented; soon there were over seven thousand people labouring on them, at 6d. a day, but by the time the blight struck again in August these works were already being wound down as they referred to the previous year's crop failure. A meeting of ratepayers, chaired by Thomas Martin of Ballynahinch, met to propose new road-building schemes, and, under the pressure of an angry crowd vowing to slaughter the landlords' cattle rather than die of hunger, munificently voted £42,000's-worth of works; the crowd was appeased for the moment, but it was October before new works were begun, and then on a much smaller scale. As the able-bodied objected to working with the feeble, who could not keep pace with them, it was now agreed that the old, the women and the children would be employed at 4d. a day in breaking stones and filling wheelbarrows. A fish-curing station was opened in Roundstone to increase the food supply and give employment, but, as the Commissioners of Works reported:

The fishermen themselves, weakened in body from want of food, are still more reluctant from this cause to undergo the increased exertion which severe weather unavoidably requires, and which, from the wretched nature of their equipment, is inevitable.

Another factor was that the fishermen were afraid to give up their places on the public works, and so the Board of Works decided to deny employment to those who had seaworthy boats, a policy that did increase the supply of fish to the curing station.

Access to food or to employment on the roads was policed by the local relieving officers, and, according to Colonel Archer, land agent for the now bankrupt Martin estate, these petty officials were:

. . . not of that class of people in whom I have the slightest confidence, knowing full well that they are very deficient in those principles which would induce them to perform their duty conscientiously and well . . . [They] have obtained land and have purchased cattle at their own prices, and put people off the list, just as they pleased.

One notorious example of such an official active in the South
Roundstone district was commemorated in a song that was still
remembered in Connemara a century after the event. According
to the gossip of the time, John Joyce, or Johnny Seoighe as he
was called locally, having abandoned his wife and family, took up
with the daughter of a bailiff in Carna, stole the relief book from
the legitimate relieving officer and began distributing Indian meal
on his own behalf. This cannot be quite right, as Joyce was in
fact a relieving officer for Roundstone, but it is probably not far
from the truth, as he was eventually dismissed for corruption. The
song, written by a Carna man in 1847, is a touching mixture of
satire and pleading; desperation shows through its good humour.
The translation is by Liam Mac Con Iomaire:

> A Johnny Seoighe tuig mo ghlórtha
> 'S mé 'tíocht le dóchas faoi do dhéin,
> Mar is tú an réalt eolais is breátha lóchrann
> Os mo chomhair ag teampall Dé,
> 'S tú bláth na hóige is deise glórtha
> Dar dhearc mo shúil ó rugadh mé,
> Ó 'gus as ucht Chríost tabhair dom *relief*
> Nó go gcaitear oíche Nollag féin.
>
> Agus lá arna mhárach sea fuair mé an páipéar,
> 'S nach mé a bhí sásta 's mé 'gabháil 'un siúil,
> Ach ní bhfuair mé freagra ar bith an lá sin,
> Ach mo bhean 's mo pháistí bheith amuigh faoin drúcht.
> Tá mé bruite, dóite, sciúrtha, feannta,
> Liobraithe gearrtha le neart an tsiúil.
> 'Gus a Mhister Joyce tá an *workhouse* lán,
> Is ní ghlacfar ann aon fhear níos mó.
>
> 'S nach mór an clú do bhaile Charna,
> An fhad's tá an lánúin seo 'gabháil tríd,
> Mar is deise is breátha scéimh na mná
> Ná an 'Morning Star' nuair a shoilsíonn sí.

Tá an bhanríon tinn is í lag 'na luí
'S deir dochtúiri go bhfaighidh sí bás,
Sé fios an údair de réir mar a deir siad liomsa,
Nuair nach bhfuil sí pósta le Mister Joyce.

Oh Johnny Joyce, heed my voice
As I come in awe to you implore;
You're the guiding light and finest sight
Before my eyes at the chapel door;
You're the finest speaker and youthful leader
My eyes have seen since I was born;
For the love of Jesus give me relief
Until Christmas Eve at least is o'er.

I got the form the following morn
And felt exalted as I went my way,
But throughout that day no answer came
And my wife and wains under wind and hail;
I'm burnt and chafed, bruised and flaked,
Tattered and torn with all I've walked;
Oh Mister Joyce, the workhouse is full
And they won't make room for a man at all.

How great an honour for the Carna parish
That these worthy partners are passing by;
The lady's charm is greater far
Than the Morning Star when it lights the sky.
The Queen is ill and is lying still
And no doctors' pills can her revive;
And the reason for it, as I understand it,
Is that she's not married to Mister Joyce.

Through the activities of Joyce and his like, with their petty
grudges and venal favouritism, the lists of the destitute became
unreliable, and the Guardians decided to have them re-examined.
This meant that all the applicants from a given division had to

attend the food depot on a particular date, with their families, and wait while their exact degrees of misery were enquired into.

By February 1847 many of the public works had closed for lack of funds; those lucky enough not to be thrown out of employment laboured on through hard frosts and heavy snows. The Government's policy was now to set up soup kitchens, so that people could leave the works and apply themselves to preparing the land for the next potato crop. By July over 24,000 people were being fed in the Clifden Union. The Roundstone Relief Committee had requested an 80-gallon boiler, and every day the people waited in line, interminably, while the watery soup was prepared and fever spread among them. A dispensary was opened in Roundstone, serving the district's population of nearly 12,000, and a temporary fever hospital, under a Dr Gannon. But Gannon seems to have been constitutionally negligent, or perhaps just overwhelmed by his duties; in this his record contrasts with that of one or two Clifden doctors who braved the fetor of the workhouse with due diligence. In the following year a visiting inspector found that fever, dysentery and diarrhoea were as prevalent in Roundstone as in Clifden, if not more so. Living, and dying, quite close to Gannon's residence was the Keogh family, whom the doctor had visited only once in some months although they were all sick with fever:

. . . four in the only bed they had, two lying on the floor. The father had been buried that morning; the mother and two children were barely convalescent. Until attacked by this illness, although in humble circumstance, they were decent, and comparatively respectable; even in the abject state of misery in which I found them, they commanded more respect and excited more commiseration than any that I have seen. Fever has completely pauperized them.

The Roundstone dispensary area was huge – parts of it lay twenty miles from Roundstone village – and Dr Gannon was reluctant to undertake long and difficult journeys to visit far-off nobodies. When a Peter Joyce fell sick, his wife, whose father had worked for the Martins of Ballynahinch, obtained a note from Mary Bell Martin and sent it to Dr Gannon, who dismissed it as a forgery. So she obtained a second note and took it herself, but the doctor refused to visit unless she provided a horse. When she came back having procured a horse he said it was then too late to go, but that he would visit on the next day if the horse were sent again. On reaching home that evening Mrs Joyce found that one of her daughters had died in the meantime, and the poor woman abandoned her attempts to get assistance. If Dr Gannon was trying to minimize his exposure to infection, his caution did him no good: he died of the fever in the following year.

The Clifden workhouse opened at last in March 1847, but fear of the fever and of the harsh workhouse regime kept people out of it, and for a time it was only half full. But in the summer new regulations came into force: the depots and soup kitchens were closed, and the able-bodied destitute had to enter the workhouse to become eligible for relief. Under the notorious Quarter Acre Clause of the new Act, occupiers of lands of more than a quarter of an acre were not entitled to relief; this meant that many abandoned their little farms, which were then left uncultivated by the landlords so as not to incur further rates. In the following year, when it became clear that the potato crop was in black ruin once again, the aged and the sick were turned out of the workhouse to make space for the able-bodied, the workhouse diet was trimmed to the bone, and buildings were rented as auxiliary workhouses. In Roundstone a large house and its offices, on the shore just north of the harbour, together with ten acres of land, was leased at £37 a year from a Joseph Reville, the land agent for a north Connemara estate. By the end of October seventy-two boys were lodged there, with an overseer and two tailors to teach them the trade. The buildings were extended, and in December could officially accommodate 175 persons, though there were probably many more crammed into them.

In the summer of 1847 Clifden was declared a 'distressed Union', but the Guardians were informed that it was not eligible for financial aid until every effort had been made to collect the rates.

However, the landlords were already bankrupt, the greatest of them all, Thomas Martin, had died of fever, and no rates were coming into the Union's coffers. The local Poor Rate collectors often came under attack when they attempted to distrain the goods of defaulters. When John Lydon, Collector for the Roundstone Division, seized cattle in the Carna area, they were retaken by the outraged owners, and Lydon was told that the people were ready to lose their own lives and take his too, rather than let him drive away the beasts. Lydon applied for police protection:

I therefore believe my life would be in danger if I were to go there again and have no doubt but that I should not only be unable to impound any of the cattle in that neighbourhood but that I and my assistant would be attacked and perhaps killed if we endeavoured to do so without a strong police or military force . . . no less than 70 to 80 armed men could with safety collect the rates in that remote district.

The Resident Magistrate in Clifden had a low opinion of Lydon and his like, who he felt were overcharging for their services, and the Poor Rate collectors had to complain to Dublin Castle before any protection was provided to him. In the meantime a group of Inis Ní women brandishing sticks recaptured sequestrated cattle from Lydon, and in Murvey a man successfully defended his cow by threatening him with a hatchet. Then in January of 1848 Lydon and his bailiffs, with the backing of the Head Constable of Roundstone and four sub-constables, seized three cows at Leathanach Mór near Cashel, and their owners became so threatening that the police had to load and fix bayonets. The crowd rushed the collectors, two policemen were hit by stones, and one constable accidentally stabbed another in the hand. Two constables were ordered to fire, but seem not to have done so, and were later censured for shirking their duty. The people repossessed the stock, and the Lydon party had to retire. The Resident Magistrate was severely reprimanded when news of this defeat came to Dublin Castle, and had to undertake to attend such expeditions in person in future and to provide adequate police escorts. But when the case against the rioters came before the Petty Sessions in Roundstone, the police were anxious to excuse them: the Head Constable stated that he had never before been obstructed in the course of his duties, that the crowd had no weapons other than sticks and stones, that the tenants had been confused as to whether they were liable for rates, and that in any case they had paid up in the meantime; and so the Collector declined to prosecute, and the Resident Magistrate advised Dublin Castle that it would not be necessary to locate a police station at Leathanach Mór.

Crimes of survival such as sheep-stealing filled the prison in Clifden with what its keeper described as 'half starved, half naked beings in human form', in a letter to Dublin Castle that ended with this prayer: 'May the Lord look to us in the midst of fever and dysentery, overcrowded with felons and beggars. Amen.' In March 1848 a calf belonging to James Cooke, an overseer and brother of the Roundstone Relieving Officer, went missing. Cooke suspected a Bart Flaherty of Cill Chiaráin in the South Roundstone Division, so he went to the house, or hut, as it was described, and looking through a hole in its wall saw Bart and his wife Honora, one of their daughters and another woman lying on the floor, with the hide of the missing calf placed over them. Cooke had the Roundstone police arrest the couple, and the next day he and a constable brought them to Clifden, a twelve-hour journey across the shelterless boglands, part of it on a side-car and part in an open cart. Honora had been very sickly when put on the car, and the day was extremely cold. She was not heard to complain during the journey, and when her husband offered her bread she refused it. According to the keeper of the gaol, they arrived at eleven o'clock at night:

The wife appeared to me to be quite dead, upon which they dragged her out of the cart like a dead sheep, and pulled her to the door and left her and the husband . . . To my astonishment she never moved a hand or foot since that moment, and never uttered a word. Such cruel treatment of human beings is revolting to human nature. Her husband says they were so treated that all their family died of starvation, and shocking to relate that the unfortunate victim, the deceased, cut off the feet from the ankles of one of the children and eat of them.

An investigation established by the Vice-Guardians was told that Bart and Honora had been discharged from the workhouse in the previous December, that their whole family became ill with fever soon afterwards and that three of their children had died. The Clifden doctor looked into Bart's claim that his wife had eaten her own child's flesh; the child's grave, which was close to the Flahertys' cabin and marked only by a few stones, was opened, but the corpse was too far decayed for him to come to any conclusion. Bart's neighbours testified that he had been receiving relief, and that they disbelieved his statement. The authorities concluded that Honora did not die of starvation but of cold and wet during the forty-mile journey; that is, that they themselves bore no responsibility, for the fault was not with the system of outdoor relief; further:

From the inhumanity of James Cooke, exhibited by him having brought the poor creature on a most inclement day in an open cart, without even straw to protect her from the injuries of a long journey, we felt coerced to dismiss him at once from any service under our Board.

Another dreadful case attracted attention to the Roundstone Division in this last year of the Famine. A Peggy Melia was seen by her neighbours walking towards the village, in a very weak state. Later in the day her brother asked one of the neighbours for a shovel to bury her. The neighbours went with him to where Peggy was lying on the shore, and her brother started to dig a hole in the sand, although some thought that she was 'still drawing her breath and groaning'. One woman asked him if he was going to bury his sister alive, and he said that she would die when she was put in the hole, that he could not lose his day's rations by coming back again to bury her. So he put her in the hole and covered her with sand and stones. At his trial the Resident Magistrate was of the opinion that the man acted only 'to save himself time and trouble or probably to put an end to the sufferings of his sister who must have been at the point of death'. He also stated that:

The persons looking on were scarcely less criminal in permitting the thing to be done – most of them women and children. The place of the occurrence is within a mile of Roundstone, in a neighbourhood in which – as well as in other parts of Connemara, I regret to say some of the peasantry are scarcely human.

Thus Humanity, to preserve its good name for humanity, expels the most inhumanely oppressed of its members into the outer margins of its self-definition.

When the 1849 harvest turned out to be largely free of infection the Famine was deemed officially ended. But as late as 1851 the Roundstone auxiliary workhouse still held the almost incredible number of 845 men, women and children, nearly twice the population of the rest of the village – a measure of how severely its effects lingered on after the passing of the blight. Who was to blame for this catastrophe? To certain Protestant clerics it appeared that if God had ordained or at least permitted the Famine it must have been for some worthy purpose, which could only have been to make the Irish 'come out from Rome'. I shall write elsewhere about that second blight visited upon Connemara, the Irish Church Mission Society, for although it blackened minds with sectarianism for decades after the Famine it had little effect in Roundstone, where the Franciscans, with their school and soup-boiler, kept a firm grasp on hungry souls.

Leaving aside the mysterious ways of God, blame then hovers over Humanity, or some section of it. Many English commentators held the Irish landlord responsible, or blamed the common Irish, the feckless potato-gobbling rural idiots, the 'scarcely human'. Nationalists blamed imperialism, both for the vulnerability of the Irish economy and for Britain's niggardly response to Ireland's distress. I still hear from the older National-School-educated generations of Connemara about the £5 Queen Victoria contributed to famine relief; in fact she gave over £2,000, but her five-pound note is a useful emblem of wealthy Britannia's failure to do a hundred times more than she did for starving Hibernia.

The proximate cause of the Great Irish Famine was a natural process evolving in unnatural circumstances. One could rewrite its history from the point of view of the blight fungus, *Phytophora infestans*, which is hardly more than a few strings of genes and a minimal apparatus for their self-reproduction. The innocent creature had the good fortune to be introduced, accidentally, by humans, into an ecology that might have been designed for its delight, the endless crowded acres of the poorest-quality potato, the infamous 'lumper', on which the peasantry subsisted. The parasite revelled and flourished, and in its overweening triumph killed off its host, starved and died, or was reduced to lurking in damp corners and spying for the next big opportunity. But this 'selfish gene' imagery is vicious, whatever the merits of the theory it aims to convey; it blurs the distinction between physical process and cultural behaviour, lending a shred of scientific authority to those who would excuse if not commend self-seeking as a rule of Nature. Thus it is part of the present-day version of the very ideology sanctioning, indeed sanctifying, the laissez-faire policies of Lord John Russell's Whigs, which put Mr Robertson's God-given right to profit by the grain shortage before the lives of the peasantry. The unspoken justification of a class society is that the lesser man deserves less. It was a malignant symbiosis of the mindless potato-parasite and this culture of contempt that left Connemara littered with half-built causeways to islands and roads that peter out in bogs, and strewed the land with bones.

The census of 1851 gives the population of the Clifden Union as 24,349, which is 9,116, or 27 per cent, down on the figure of 33,465 for the census of 1841; what proportion of this loss is due to emigration and what to death cannot now be established, but I suspect that death carried off most, for death demands less effort from exhausted bodies, less hope and less cash, than emigration.

Over the succeeding years many more, weakened and desolated by the Famine, followed them into death or exile. Others survived, half-forgot the past, sang the old songs again, and even prospered, for after all, and most cruelly, the Famine was indeed just a period, and Time turned its back on the victims as soon as they were dead. During the months I spent walking the rocky shores, windy hillsides and briar-tangled boreens of Connemara while making my map, I was shown so many famine graves, marked, if at all, by a few pebbles or a small boulder at head and foot, that I ceased, out of discouragement, to record them all. It was a failing. And despite all my imaginings of voices to be recaptured from them, there is nobody in those graves to hear my apology for it.

The Robinson Era

In the aftermath of the Famine the ruined communities of the Martin estate, quarrelled over by their rivalrous spiritual leaders and deserted by the last representatives of their hereditary patri-archs, fell into the hands of the financiers to whom it had been mortgaged. Whereas the Martins are said never to have evicted anybody, the mortgagees knew that their only hope of selling on the vast desolation they had acquired for little or nothing was to rid it of superfluous human beings, and so they energetically carried on with the clearance the Famine had begun. The Law Life Assurance Society, a faceless, distant abstraction, has left no trace in Connemara lore that I know of, and its representative in oral history is its land agent, George Robinson, Justice of the Peace and Chairman of the Board of Guardians. Even his grim figure is half-dissolved into that of his son Henry, a more genial personality according to report; between the two of them they span the whole period of painfully slow ameliorations from the rapacity of Law Life to the social engineering of the Congested Districts Board, and today's busy and indifferent Connemara scarcely remembers that they were different people.

George Robinson of Thomastown in Mayo had previously been

employed as a civil engineer at Shannonbridge, where he had married Rebecca, daughter of the Protestant minister of Aughrim and a descendant of the Martins and Wood-Martins of Sligo. He came to Connemara in about 1857 with his wife and the beginnings of a large family, and took up residence in the former Martin abode, Ballynahinch Castle, which was then a plain two-storey house looking down through a few trees to Ballynahinch Lake. As a surveyor a few years earlier had reported, its setting was bleak:

There is a good field, not of land, but of rocks and water, to be worked upon, and the scene might be made truly a 'Highland House', but up to the present time the *cutting* and *carving* that has taken place, and the *unfinished* and *poverty stricken* state of everything around the Castle, has only weakened the natural romanticness of the spot.

Although the Law Life Assurance Society furnished the house with battlements in about 1858, the poverty of its surroundings still outweighed its 'romanticness' in prospective purchasers' minds, and the estate remained on their hands until a London brewer, Richard Berridge, bought it in 1872. Thus the Robinsons occupied the Castle up to that date, and probably until 1885 when they built their own mansion at Letterdife, for George became agent to the Berridges, who themselves did not opt for residence in the increasingly dangerous times of the Land War.

The society the family grew up in was as harsh as its setting. A photograph by the well-known William Lawrence of Upper Sackville Street, Dublin, shows the Protestant chapel (now a Catholic chapel, and closed) a mile or so away from Ballynahinch on the Galway–Clifden road. Not a tree or shrub mediates between the pretty little Gothic-revival building and the windswept boglands around it. The occasion is surely the inauguration of the chapel in 1865, for about seventy people line the drive up to the chapel, facing the eye of the future, and behind them a long stretch of the road is occupied by waiting horse-cars and carriages. All the beleaguered gentry of the Roundstone and Clifden area would have mustered for this show of solidarity, for Connemara had been racked by sectarian strife ever since the Revd Alexander Dallas had been blown in by the ill wind of the Famine to fight the priests for the souls of the hungry. One needs a lens to individuate the tiny figures in the photograph: the minister in his shovel hat and cassock, the ladies pyramidal in poke bonnets, mantles and crinolines, the gentlemen all stiffly vertical and extended upwards by tall top hats, the Robinsons' butler Old Burke bringing up the rear with one of his young masters, and three men dressed with propriety but immediately identifiable as 'natives' by the way they sprawl against the gable of the chapel near the bell-rope they have probably just finished pulling. These last remind me of the contemptuous nickname the Catholics of Kingstown near Clifden had for their neighbour who performed the same office for the little Protestant chapel there: 'bell-slasher'.

Another photograph, perhaps taken on the same day, shows the Robinson family posed on a slope one can deduce is that now occupied by balustraded garden steps and hydrangea beds opposite the front door of Ballynahinch Castle. No such charms existed then; patches of stone show through the poor, strawlike grass, and the only other vegetation is a gaunt tussock of hazel scrub further up the slope. George is on the left, Rebecca on the right, and the nine children between them, despite the formality of their grouping, seem to have started from their father's loins in a disconcerting rush. George's body looks undersized, angular, his trouser-leg strained by one acutely bent knee, the other leg doubled uncomfortably beneath him. His top hat has been put aside; one can see his receding hairline and anxious eyebrows and drawn cheeks. His longish beard is frosted. Rebecca seems more settled, matron-formed in her striped blouse and vast dark draperies of skirt, but her face is set and unsmiling. The three teenage daughters − known as the Rose, the Lily and the Ivy, says family lore − are artistically displayed, straw hats in their laps, each with her face at a different angle to the camera. Only the middle one seems happy with her looks, though (and she did become a beauty, as later portraits of her attest). The light tones of the girls' dresses are set off by the dark formality of the two male youngsters behind them. One of them, hand in pocket, manages to lean back in an almost raffish pose despite his tightly buttoned waistcoat and the sharp upward stabs of his collar-points. The other, Henry, who will succeed George as Resident Magistrate and agent to the Berridges, already mirrors his father in attitude and expression, but is as yet unmarked by his cares. And set into this composition here and there are the three younger children and the baby, all glancing askance at the camera in apparent foreboding and mistrust. Despite their architectonic grouping, the family looks fragmented, forlorn. Too much of the surrounding vacancy is shown. The skull-bare mountain top of Binn Leitrí rears behind them.

Were it not for these images, which I have been given by one of his descendants, I would have little idea of George Robinson as a person rather than as that figment of ideological history, the wicked land agent, for the view I have of him from the side of the oppressed is of some absurd, semi-mechanical creature. In his autobiography *Mise*, the nationalist and revolutionary Colm Ó Gaora tells how Robinson was nearly assassinated at Derrypark in the east of the Joyce Country:

It was near this place that *seanRobinson* [Old Robinson] was shot one day. He was coming by pony-car with a couple of policemen when he was fired on. Damned bad luck it was that every inch of him was *plátáilte* [armour-plated] except his head. The shooters were so keen and eager they aimed to put the lead into his heart. The shot didn't touch him there, because he was plated. The police who were there to guard him were so drunk they couldn't draw their guns or get out of the car.

Robinson's own view of the job that exposed him to such dangers is clear from a letter he wrote in 1875 to Dublin Castle, concerning 'an outrage which has been perpetrated on this Estate, near Oughterard'. Certain leases having fallen in, on the tenants' deaths, Robinson had it in mind to 'readjust and square the lands', that is, to put higgledy-piggledy smallholdings together into viable orderly farms. The obstacle to such improvement was the usual one of there being undertenants in possession. Young Henry Robinson had called on them with the sheriff to offer them an arrangement by which they could become temporary caretakers of their farms until new agreements should be drawn up, but their parish priest had refused to let them agree to this proposal, saying that both Isaac Butt, the nationalist MP, and Archbishop MacHale of Tuam had advised tenants not to sign such agreements. So the sheriff had evicted them, but did not put out their furniture, and in one case, 'moved with compassion', had refrained from putting out an infant in a cradle. That night the families all broke into their homes again, and George was advised that, as legal possession had not been obtained (had young Henry been insufficiently forceful in not putting out the furniture?), it would have to be taken again. So George called on the undertenants, accompanied by the sheriff and the local Justice of the Peace:

We went first to the house of John Sullivan of Garranagry a man aged about 80 years. Mr. Jackson, the Sheriff and I strongly advised him to consent to be put in as caretaker & not allow his furniture to be removed. His reply was that he would not sign any caretaker's agreement, that he would pay his rent, & that the furniture might be removed as soon as we liked, he then walked out of his own accord & possession was taken by the sheriff. In the course of an hour or two we received intelligence that the poor old man had died.

In the meantime we went from house to house offering the same terms but receiving the same answer, – they dared not sign caretakers' agreements as the priest had ordered them not, and had moreover taken their money stating that he would settle with me. After having taken possession of all the houses we returned to the village of Garranagry where we found the priest & with him a mob of I should say two thousand men & women. On our arrival he addressed me & stated that the old man had been murdered & that he would swear informations before a Magistrate . . .

The verdict of an inquest, to which Robinson and his colleagues were not called as witnesses, was that John Sullivan had died as a result of rough handling in being put out of his house. Robinson claimed that this finding was contrary to fact, and called on the authorities to hold a sworn investigation into the whole transaction. What the outcome was I do not know, but such incidents must have been part and parcel of George's professional life in those dreadful years of class and sectarian strife. And although the Robinsons might be *plátáilte*, their property was vulnerable: on a November night of 1879 three of Henry Robinson's bullocks were driven over a cliff into the sea at Goirtín, and seventy-six sheep and two rams belonging to George Robinson were killed or injured.

By the time of the Land War, when the peasantry's sporadic and pathetic acts of terrorism were being coordinated into a regular campaign by the Land League, agents and bailiffs had to go about their business with large escorts. In 1880, when ejectment notices were served on a number of Roundstone tenants, forty police under a resident magistrate supporting the process server were confronted by a crowd of three hundred tenants armed with sticks and pitchforks, the Riot Act was read, and eighteen arrests were made. A couple of years later, when thirty-two Roundstone families were evicted for arrears of rent, the echo of cannon-fire from gunboats in the bay underlined the gravitas of the proceedings. According to a letter of protest published in a Galway newspaper by the parish priest, Fr Malone, the shots were fired at the tenants' livestock, which scattered and were chased into the sea by the soldiers, who were later disciplined for letting their ammunition get damp while trying to seize the geese belonging to 'the honest though poor, industrious evicted tenantry'. George Robinson died in 1890, but under Henry Robinson, who succeeded his father as JP and as agent to the Berridges, evictions continued until at least 1894. Henry was also agent for many other estates including that of the Digbys in the Aran Islands, and so he would have ordered the eviction that J. M. Synge witnessed there as late as 1898.

Nevertheless, with the passing of the Land Acts leading to large reductions in rent from the mid 1880s, and the developmental work of the Congested Districts Board from 1891, the worst of times were passing over. George Robinson hardly saw the new age, but Henry is remembered in ways that suggest the good old days rather than the bad, probably because he outlasted the Berridges and became agent to the Land Commission when the estate was bought out in 1914. Mícheál King of Inis Ní tells me that his father was the boatman who used to take Henry Robinson across to Aran in a hooker to collect rents, until the priest there raised an agitation and the Araners refused to pay, so that Robinson came home with nothing for his pains and swore he'd never go there again. On one of these trips to Aran, Mícheál remembers his father tell how 'the crew fried up some fish, and Robinson produced a bottle of whiskey and passed it round. After that they noticed he wasn't saying anything more about the whiskey, so they put down another feed of fish. "We've just been eating!" says Robinson. "Well, the sea makes you hungry," they said, and he agreed, and the whiskey went round again. They had a third feed before reaching Aran too.'

'Peace on Earth Goodwill to Men' is the heading of an illuminated address presented to Henry Robinson, together with a purse, on his retirement. This was probably in 1909; perhaps by then memories of gunboats and constabulary had faded, but I suspect a degree of forelock-tugging in this text:

We the undersigned inhabitants of Connemara and adjoining districts in the Counties of Galway and Mayo are anxious upon this auspicious occasion to express to you our feelings of sincere regard and friendship being amongst us since your early childhood as it is now 16 years since you took upon you the many and onerous duties to which you are instructed and have justly earned the esteem and confidence of all parties with which you have been connected, and while you have promoted the interests and trusts imposed upon you with energy and sound discretion at the same time you have proved a kind and indulgent agent and have never allowed private feelings nor sectarian views to warp your judgement or interfere with proper discharge of your duties . . .

And on his death in 1916 at Letterdife 'after a long and painful illness borne with exemplary Christian patience and resignation', obituaries cast the golden light of sunset on him:

Deceased was widely known and greatly respected in the western counties. His land agency business was the most extensive in the province of Connaught. The work of quite forty estates was carried on in his office at Roundstone. During the land agitation he administered the estates entrusted to him with such wisdom and fairness that he never had any trouble with his tenants, but was held in the highest esteem by all with whom his business dealings brought him in contact. That he was a popular Land Agent in times of trouble and agitation elsewhere speaks volumes for his kindly character . . .

A less sanctimonious and more engaging picture of Henry Robinson, and probably a truer one, is recalled in the memoirs of an eminent civil servant, Sir Henry Robinson of the Local Government Board (a veteran anecdotalist, and yet another Robinson not related to me):

Another instance of queer so-called humour I remember when I was staying on a wet wintry day in Murphy's Hotel, Oughterard. Walter Seymour, the secretary of the Grand Jury, a very peppery gentleman with a wooden leg, was staying in the house, and also a large land agent, a namesake of my own, Henry Robinson of Roundstone. Seymour pulled his chair close in to the fire and, with foot on the fender and the wooden leg on the hob, fell fast asleep, and he snored so loudly that he irritated Henry Robinson, who was trying to wind up the accounts of his day's collection. To put an end to this disturbance, Robinson went to the fireplace and piled the turf sods around the wooden leg on the hob, and then went back to his work. Very soon the leg ignited, burned for a while, and at last with a loud crack split up, waking Seymour, who at first didn't know what had happened, and hopped about the room on the sound leg with the other crackling and burning merrily under him. Robinson proceeded to remonstrate with Seymour, 'Ah now, will you stop your pranks? That's a dangerous thing to do, man; you might burn the house down.'

. . . and so the local carpenter is called in, and replaces the burned leg with a huge hourglass-shaped thing four feet long. Seymour protests he isn't a piano, but the carpenter presents him with a bill for 15s., saying he had to cut down a fair-sized tree to make it. The story goes down well when I retail it in Roundstone, and perhaps when all the Robinsons' oppressions have been forgotten, this contribution to the grotesqueries of Connemara will be relished still.

The plantation of beeches and pines Henry Robinson wrapped around his house has prospered since his day, shadowing it rather too darkly, but mellowing the craggy shoreline of the bay as seen from Roundstone village. One of Henry's daughters, George Doris, married in 1913 into a north Connemara landowning family, the Lushington-Tullochs. She and her husband, Kinmont Willie, had a tea plantation in Ceylon for a while, and later returned to run the family estate at Shanboolard near Kylemore. Henry's other daughter, Olive, turned the family mansion into a guesthouse; I am told that she dressed in a very mannish style, and her clientele had enough of a lesbian tone for the house to be nicknamed 'Sappho's Parlour' by the cattier ladies of our little Connemara Ascendancy.

What piles of accidentally surviving scraps constitute our memorials! To top off this brief memoir of my namesakes, I translate a verse of a song about *carraigín*, an edible seaweed Connemara people used to gather on the shore and sell in Galway market:

Dá mbeadh dhá mhaide rámha
Agus báidín agam fhéin,
Rachfainn ag baint charraigín
Is á thriomú leis an gréin.
Bhéirfinn taoscan dhe go Gaillimh

Agus taoscan ar an traen,
D'íocfainn cíos le Robinson
Is bheadh brabach agam fhéin.

If I only had two oars
And a rowboat of my own,
I'd go and gather *carraigín*
And dry it in the sun.
I'd take a load of it to Galway
and another on the train;
I'd pay the rent to Robinson
and keep the profit for my pains.

So Robinson didn't extort the last penny, at least in the softer, latter times. For the honour of the name, I'd like to think so.

Addendum: The Life and Death of a Robinson

I am not related to the Robinsons of Letterdife, but the reason I know something of their family tree is that I have been grafted onto it, to my surprise. It happened as follows.

One evening some years ago an elderly, portly gentleman of Edwardian demeanour knocked at our door. 'Mr Robinson?' he said; '*I'm* Robinson!', spreading his hand on his chest to indicate himself. He went on to tell me that he was Dr Philip Robinson, retired, of Dublin, grandson of Henry Robinson of Letterdife, that he had heard his forebears described as harsh, evicting, land-lord's agents, and was calling on me as local historian to see if that was the case. I took him down to my studio, opened up files, spread out documents and demonstrated that such, indeed, was the case. Nevertheless we got on well, and although his own stream of family anecdotes had hardly allowed me to say a word, he thanked me heartily for my information. His wife, Edna, a frail and apparently rather bewildered little lady, sat in silence throughout, apart from asking which was the way out when at last Dr Robinson drew himself to a conclusion. It was only later on that we came to appreciate Edna's strength of mind and character.

A few days later Dr Robinson phoned from Dublin. 'Mr Robinson! Tim! May I call you Tim? Well, Tim, I have some old books and papers and family items, and we don't have any offspring. There is my cousin Morton, but . . . Well, perhaps you'll meet Morton someday and then you can judge for yourself, but I'd hate to see these things end up in a second-hand shop in Brisbane. So, would you mind if I sent you a few?' I assured him that I would be very interested to see material relating to Connemara history and that anything he entrusted to me would be carefully preserved in our archive, which was destined to go to the Hardiman Library in NUI, Galway, after our own decease. Thereafter at intervals small parcels arrived: a battered first edition of the Halls' *Tour Through Ireland*, a pair of framed silhouettes of George Robinson and his wife, which I have been told are by the celebrated Frederick Frith, and a fine pencil drawing of their beautiful daughter Lily, by Frank Myles, who, according to Dr Philip, was Oscar Wilde's first lover and had also drawn the fabulous Jersey Lily herself. Incidentally the worst we ever heard about poor Morton was this, from Dr Philip: 'We were staying at the Shelbourne once, and Sir John Horrocks happened to be there. (Sir John was head of the RAF during the war.) One evening Sir John very kindly invited us to join him for breakfast the following day. Well! I was up at seven, and I'm sure Sir John was up even earlier. But Morton! Morton had his breakfast in his room!'

Dr Philip also proposed to take us out to dinner when next he and Edna visited Roundstone, and since our own dining-out is unambitious I suggested we could eat in the nearby bar, O'Dowd's. Then we learned, from a mutual acquaintance, that Dr Philip was one of Ireland's leading amateur wine experts, and so I was not entirely surprised when I met him in the village street on the day we were to dine together, vainly enquiring for walnuts to accompany the 1955 Cockburn's port he had brought with him. 'I suppose O'Dowd's will charge corkage,' he sighed. I doubted that the concept of corkage had reached Roundstone, but assured him that O'Dowd's would do the honours adequately. 'I also brought a bottle of Château Latour 1970,' he said. 'It has a very interesting bouquet, with a slight hint of verbena.' My taste in such matters is so uneducated that I tend to think most wines are improved by a dash of tonic water, but I absorbed this information and trotted home to M with it. That evening we joined Philip and Edna in O'Dowd's, at a table set with their own wine glasses, silver candlesticks and strainer; the port had already been decanted, and happily Edna had remembered that she had packed some walnuts with their luggage. Young Nicky of O'Dowd's sloshed a jot of Grand Vin de Château Latour into M's glass for her to taste. Philip watched her intently as she revolved it with exaggerated nonchalance and took a leisurely sniff. 'Very interesting!' she pronounced at length. 'A slight hint of verbena, I believe!' The effect was electrifying. Philip's jaw dropped and his ten fingers shot out in ten different directions. It was a perfectly gratifying moment. Of course we confessed the fraud, and our companionship was sealed with laughter.

It was on this occasion that we learned that Philip and Edna were staunch atheists, and this created another bond between us. At that period M and I were much obsessed with death, or more accurately with the problem of avoiding the continuation of life into the zone of useless suffering. We were clear about the ethics of it, but not about the practicalities; we had even subscribed to the monthly journal of the Voluntary Euthanasia Society, which was not much use as it was full of descriptions of dire cases we could hardly bear to read; instead, whenever it arrived I would hold it up and intone sepulchrally, 'You don't know how, you don't know when, but it's one month nearer!' Dr Philip – almost Auden's ideal of 'a doctor, partridge-plump . . . who with a twinkle in his eye / will tell me that I have to die' – seemed the right person to consult, and so, on his next visit, I put the question to him. He took it very straightforwardly. 'I don't recommend hanging: it's too grotesque,' he opined. 'Strychnine is effective, but it might give you a nasty jolt at the end. I have to go up to

Dublin for a bit, and I'll make some enquiries for you.' A few days later M and I were surprised to receive a packet of unidentified white tablets through the post. This was taking us seriously indeed! It would seem a pity to waste them, but we were hardly at that extremity of woe yet. What might the shelf life of the product be? It was a relief when Dr Philip called in to collect his heart pills, which he had asked his pharmacist to post down to him, care of us.

But all too soon after that the question of death arose in reality. First, Edna tripped on the uneven stones or piled nets of the quayside and broke her hip. She lay waiting for the doctor and then for the ambulance with great fortitude and dignity, only asking M to assure her that her hair was not in too much of a mess as she was whisked away. Later on I visited her in the hospital in Galway; she seemed diminished, as if she were far away in the perspective of mortality, but she filled out and came back to us as I stroked life into her little hand. Dr Philip strode about the hospital ordering attentions for her with authority. Afterwards he gave me a lift back into Galway; a steady stream of traffic on the main road kept us waiting at the hospital exit gate, until a short gap came along and he slotted the car into it with the precision and dash of a rally driver, and, on seeing my startled look, said, 'That's life!' And indeed that was the tenor of his way with the world: decisive and blithe. Sadly, his own leaving of it did not become him. Soon afterwards he was diagnosed with cancer, and allowed himself to be dragged into the medical mincing machine. In authorizing surgeons to take severe measures uncalled for at his age, I think he was gallantly trying to ensure he would outlive his ailing wife, so that she could precede him through that last door as she had through the many others he had courteously held open for her. But it was not to be, and his life ended in pain and frustration. Edna survived him by a year or so, but was never well enough to revisit Roundstone.

Some months after his death Dr Philip surprised me yet again with a cheque for £5,000, which, his executor explained, was 'a tribute to your work in the west of Ireland', and when in due

course the estate was wound up I came in for a strange fraction
of the residue that amounted to over £10,000. Looking now at
his family tree, of which he gave me a copy once, and half
expecting to find myself lurking somewhere in its leafage, I am
tickled to note that one branch involves the Phibbses associated
with the nineteenth-century Sligo solicitors of immortal name,
Messrs Argue and Phibbs, while a long root of it goes all the way
back to the Emperor Charlemagne.

Dinner at Letterdyfe

The mansion, unostentatious and comfortably-off in appearance, that Henry Robinson built in 1885 on a rise above the road just beyond the northern limits of Roundstone village must have been a more commanding presence in that era of cottages and hovels, until it was hidden from intrusive eyes by his plantation of pines, sycamores and beeches, still known as Robinson's Wood. Only gentlemen could afford to plant trees and to protect them from cattle, goats and sheep by well-maintained fences, and in Connemara such a wood is a certain sign of a history of land-lordism. As the only cover for miles around, Robinson's Wood was, and perhaps still is, a haunt of courting couples from the village; just beyond its gate is a turn of the road nicknamed Flaggers Hotel, where youngsters in search of privacy used to scramble over the wall into a grove of New Zealand flax, whose great sword-like leaves they seemingly equated with those of the common local 'flagger' or yellow iris.

Letterdyfe (the house likes to spell itself with a 'y', and the townland with an 'i') now belongs to a consortium of the friends and colleagues of an eminent Dutch scientist. Professor Victor Westhoff, of the Department of Geobotany in the University of Nijmegen, had been knighted for his services to ecology, and with his students had made important studies of the vegetation of Connemara over a period of twenty years. When I came to know him, in the mid 1990s, he had plans to convert Letterdyfe's hand-some but tumbledown old stable block into a study centre for his students, who were doing very detailed research on the veg-etation of Connemara, but because of his death a few years later that did not come to pass.

Victor was a man of broad literary culture, a poet and a Buddhist for whom the attitudes towards nature we draw from our cultural

roots in the Old Testament and Greek philosophy were ecologically poisonous; he knew where scientific explanation has its place,
and where an exclamation of primal wonder is what is due. I
once had the honour of conducting him on an expedition to
view one of Roundstone Bog's extreme rarities, a little fern called
the forked spleenwort, *Asplenium septentrionale*, known from
northern England and Scotland but unknown in the wild in
Ireland until it was discovered here in 1965. It grows on just two
great knobs of rock known to the sheep farmers as the Hillocks
of Fiodán, which from a distance stand out against the sky like
cottages, on the southern flanks of the swampy saddle between
Cnoc na gCorrbhéal and Letterdife Hill. A *fiodán* is a narrow
watercourse, and here an area of the hillside is named Fiodán from
a little stream that flows from a spring, the Well of Fiodán, to an
oval tarn a few hundred yards to the north, the Little Lake of
Fiodán. The two rock exposures are of the same blackish ultra-
basic igneous rock, metagabbro, as the bedrock underlying the
bog, and each has an almost vertical southern face, smoothed and
bevelled by the glaciers that ground their way over these hills to
the sea many thousands of years ago. These faces are crossed by
some oblique cracks, in which grow a few specimens, only one
or two inches high, of the fern. I took a photograph of Victor
that day, his refined profile intently focused as if in conversation
with one of the tiny tufts of twisted, double-pointed, strap-like
fronds lurking in its cranny like a nest of miniature serpents, or
of serpents' tongues. When I asked him why this species occurs
nowhere else in Ireland but here, he waved his hand comprehen-
sively at the grim wind-scoured outcrops we were standing by,
and the weird surrounding terrain of rocks like great black bulls
erupting out of the bog, and said in his rather grand manner,
'Because there is nowhere else *like* here!'

It was a memorable walk with him. We returned to our human
habitat through the Gleann Mór and the lane down to Roundstone, remarking on every growing thing on the way. The lower
slopes of the hills were glorious in gold and crimson-purple,
plump cushions of the soft little western gorse or furze alternating

almost regularly with tussocks of bell heather. This pairing is a rather characteristic feature of the drier parts of Atlantic blanket bog, a phenomenon frequent and stable and well-defined enough to deserve its own name as an item in our experience of the world. Victor's speciality was the classification not of individual plants but of 'vegetation', of plant communities, ranging from this sparse one composed mainly of a heather and a furze, to the most exuberant and entangled rainforests – an extremely complex and, as I was to learn, controversial matter. 'Plant associations' are the basic units of this taxonomy and play a role analogous to that of the species in the Linnaean scheme of plant names. Associations are assigned Latin names derived according to internationally agreed rules from those of the plant species most important for their recognition, followed by the name of the author and date of the first formal description of the association; for example, the one we were admiring that afternoon, characterized by *Ulex gallii*, western gorse, and *Erica cinerea*, bell heather, has the intimidating name of Ulici gallii-Ericetum cinereae Géhu 1973. Associations are grouped into higher entities called alliances, these into orders, and orders into classes. Thus the association considered above ends up in the class Calluno-Ulicetea Br.-Bl. et Tx. 1943, comprising a range of heathy communities in which ling, *Calluna*, is generally important, and which was first described by Josias Braun-Blanquet and Reinholdt Tüxen – an honourable appellation, since the whole scheme was originated by Braun-Blanquet, and Tüxen was his chief disciple and collaborator. Victor did not try to show me through the vast terminological edifice of the Braun-Blanquet system, but since then I have wandered through a few of its galleries and clambered up its staircases to see how the world looks from its battlements: orderly at every level, inordinately well-ordered, exhibiting so much order that all attempts to capture its order in systems lean towards chaotic collapse and have repeatedly to be called to order. And I have stared up at it from outside, as the forked spleenwort might in some pause in its struggle for survival: the system's proud towers, which, like those of mathematics, are thickly inlaid with the names of the rivalrous human builders of each pillar and buttress, seem to me to touch and sometimes get lost in the clouds.

As Victor and I were walking back along the road towards Letterdyfe House he started to sniff about in the grassy margins like a dog, in search of a little weed called lesser swine cress, *Coronopus didymus*. The specific name, he told me, refers to the seed-pods, only an eighth of an inch across, which are supposed to look like pairs of breasts; but he was relying on smell, not sight, to identify it. 'I have a very keen sense of smell,' he said. 'Several times it has warned me not to enter into relationships that might have been . . . *unfortunate*.' He went on, from the high ground of his seventy-seven years, to offer some wisdom about relationships. 'One has one's wife,' he explained, 'and one has one's *femme inspiratrice*!' As it happened I had met his current muse, a beautiful and intelligent young woman who I am sure was quite unaware of her platonic role in Victor's life. His wife, Nettie, I was to meet that evening.

As we passed into the shade of Robinson's Wood, Victor directed my attention to its peculiarities. It was owing to these rare features, he told me, that the house came into the hands of himself and his Dutch associates. Driving through Roundstone one day he had noted great beech trees growing on the low peaty shoreline – a beechwood on a salt-marsh, an ecological paradox, a community undreamed of by Braun-Blanquet, and only made possible by the copious rains of western Ireland washing the salt spray off the leaves. Intrigued, he explored within, and discovered Miss Olive Robinson's former guesthouse, closed and for sale.

Around the dinner table that evening were two or three other botanists, and Nettie, whose solid properties were, I gathered, necessary ballast to Victor's career. On botanical expeditions, she told me, Victor would have his nose to the ground spotting plants, while she would hold the map and keep track of where they were; so between the two of them they could make geographically accurate contributions to floristics, the study of what grows where. Soon conversation turned to phytosociology, as the study of plant communities is called. The attempt to describe and classify stands of vegetation as wholes, to relate them to their geographical settings and to understand how they develop, decay and succeed one another, goes back at least to Alexander von Humboldt's writings on 'the geography of plants' in the 1800s. By the beginning of the twentieth century Robert Lloyd Praeger was deploying concepts drawn from the new science of plant ecology in an Irish context. For him, a plant association was 'a group of plants, often differing widely in size and appearance, in mode of growth and mode of dispersal, which nevertheless forms a strictly natural group, living together by reason of their being adapted to the particular conditions of life that prevail'. Braun-Blanquet of Montpellier published his classification of associations and higher groupings in 1921 and refined it in succeeding works, and acquired an important disciple, Reinholdt Tüxen of Stolzenau in Germany. The Zürich-Montpellier School, as it was called, gradually wore down its rivals on the Continent; according to the Dutch phytosociologist Van der Maarel, its historical position 'might even be compared with that of J. S. Bach's oeuvre in the history of music'.

But the Braun-Blanquet system was stoutly resisted by British and American authorities. Sir Arthur Tansley, a professor of botany at Oxford and an honorary Fellow of Trinity College, Cambridge, whose great compendium *The British Islands and their Vegetation* of 1939 is still highly regarded, gruffly remarked in his introduction, 'I am unable to form an opinion as to the validity or usefulness of the terminology of plant communities invented by Dr J. Braun-Blanquet, and have therefore had to forgo any attempt to consider its possible application to British vegetation.' When Oxbridge Man professes himself 'unable to form an opinion' as to some French or German thought-construction it is because he suspects that there is nothing in it to have an opinion about, that it is spun out of empty words and as ungraspable as air. I suspect that the whole controversy – which is now laid to rest – was a skirmish in the centuries-old philosophy wars between anglophone empiricism and continental metaphysics. What, to begin with, was the ontological standing of an association? Individual plants exist, but plant associations, are they anything more than highly variable, unstable coincidences? Braun-Blanquet's language was thoroughly idealist. The basic divisions of his system are defined in terms of lists of species; whether an actual given stand of vegetation belongs to such-and-such a division is to be determined by taking '*relevés*', careful censuses of the abundance and coverage of each species present in representative sample areas of the stand, and, he wrote, 'the question of the naturalness of such a division seems superfluous. In the sense of Kant a system is a whole, ordered according to certain principles. Whether nature as such forms a system we cannot decide. This decision is of no significance for science.' To the British cast of mind, more Darwinian and less essentialist, plant communities were too variable and too dynamic in their development to be subjected to the Procrustean bed of the Braun-Blanquet system.

In Ireland the controversy came to a head after an international phytogeographical excursion in 1949. David Webb, who had studied at Cambridge and was then lecturing in Trinity College, Dublin, a pugnacious polemicist and widely recognized as the anointed successor of Robert Lloyd Praeger in the field-studies tradition, described how 'Professor Braun-Blanquet, with the enthusiastic support of Professor Tüxen, expounded and defended his system against some respectful but determined heckling.' His attitude became less respectful after the publication of papers arising out of this expedition, when his own account of Ireland's plant communities was overshadowed by Braun-Blanquet and Tüxen's massive *Irische Pflanzengesellschaften*, which, he felt, dragooned Ireland into the Zürich-Montpellier empire. Webb's rejoinder was a conference paper with the challenging title 'Is the Classification of Plant Communities either Possible or Desirable?' In it he objected to the sharp edges and towering hierarchies and authoritarian imposition of the Braun-Blanquet system, and had fun pointing out an odd feature, the definition of certain associations well known in Ireland in terms of a plant of which no specimen occurs nearer to Ireland than the Alps. This last was a striking observation, but in fact it is a superficial one. Braun-Blanquet and Tüxen were working in southern Europe, where the types of vegetation are more highly defined, being richer in species, than in Britain, and even more so than in Ireland, which has a relatively 'depauperate' flora, as the botanists put it, and it is only natural that the Braun-Blanquet divisions fray at the edges, as it were. Nevertheless, even if all their characteristics are not present, the system, with its scrupulously objective method of *relevés*, does permit less species-rich vegetational units to be referred to those divisions as idealized reference points. And experience has shown, I am told, that with a little tact the system can be usefully extended to these less-favoured realms. Victor Westhoff himself had performed this labour for the Netherlands, and his work there was later to be the model followed by James White and Gerard Doyle's 'The Vegetation of Ireland', of 1982.

More trenchant is Webb's critique of the system's hierarchical structure. As he points out, plant communities can be related to one another in terms of various environmental factors; for instance, bog and heath have in common their acidic, peaty soils, whereas bog and calcareous marsh are both waterlogged, and which relationship is the closer depends solely on the enquirer's interest of the moment. Hence what is needed is a multifactorial classification, as opposed to a hierarchical one based on a single sort of relationship. Webb concludes in thunder:

But to accumulate an ever-growing list of names without precise specification; to arrange these in a hierarchy according to an unspecified principle of relatedness which can, at best, be one out of several possibles; to declare that this is the one and only system of classification and to seek to have it imposed by international authority – this surely is not science but scholasticism out of place.

However, I gather that there are many subtleties in Braun-Blanquet practice, and that the assigning of communities to associations and higher groupings primarily in terms of their floristic content does order them in a way that correlates fruit-fully with many environmental factors, and it has been widely accepted as a helpful basis for ecological studies. Even Britain, pragmatic as ever, has fallen into line, with the publication since 1991 by Cambridge University Press of the successive volumes of *British Plant Communities* edited by J. S. Rodwell, who writes in his introduction that the scientific temperament of British ecologists, shown in their self-conscious avoidance of Braun-Blanquet's type of rigorous taxonomy and their interest in how vegetation actually works, rather than in what exactly distinguishes plant communities from one another, 'has been a lasting hindrance to the emergence in this country of any consciousness as to how vegetation ought to be described, and whether it ought to be classified at all'.

Of all this I was quite ignorant, that evening at Letterdyfe. But perhaps it was some whisper of doubt as to the use of all this grandiose Latinity that made me ask if, just as the Linnaean classification of species into families, classes and orders can be seen, post-Darwin, as a hypothesis about their lines of evolutionary descent, Braun-Blanquet's hierarchical ordering relates to the way in which plant communities develop and succeed one another. Victor looked at me solemnly; this, it seemed, was not a question to be answered over the coffee cups. 'We will go into the drawing room,' he announced; 'Nettie will bring paper and pencil.' So the three of us withdrew, leaving the company to their idle chitchat. Victor settled himself into an armchair with a writing board on his lap. Nettie and I took lesser chairs and watched in silence as he cogitated and from time to time wrote on a foolscap sheet of paper. After a quarter of an hour – it seemed longer – he handed me the result, a diagram of the conceptual relationships of all the botanical sciences, including several I had never heard of, such as chorology and synepiontology. Seven of these sciences bore superscript numbers referring to footnotes on the back of the sheet, but on looking at the precious relic now I see that footnote 7, on syntaxonomy, is missing. Perhaps it held the answer to my question, but I doubt it. The answer, I think, is simply 'No'. The rare heather on Errisbeg Hill that may have come from Spain wrapped round a smuggler's cask reminds me that plant communities recruit their members in an unruly variety of ways and own no laws of genetic descent like those that guarantee a measure of objective reality to species and their affiliations; if it were otherwise, the Braun-Blanquet system would be as nearly natural a scheme as that of Linnaeus and there would be little controversy over it. So, I appreciate the Professor's forbearance; he should have sent me off to do my homework.

In 2001 Victor Westhoff stepped off a pavement in Holland and was struck by a car, and from one moment to the next Connemara lost one of its most devoted friends. I remember him most fondly, not as the great systematist but as a sensuous adorer of nature who pointed out to me the long languorous hip-and-waist-like curve of the skyline of Cnoc Mordáin to the east, which he called the Sleeping Beauty, and who lingered to revel in the charm of forget-me-nots and buttercups and a dozen more of the common sorts of baby-eyed and folksy little flowers gracing a cow-trodden mud-patch, by O'Donnell's mountain gate that day, as we returned from the Hillocks of Fiodán.

Inis Ní in Winter

It often happens that, at the last moment of an overcast day, the sun, hidden from us in Roundstone village by Errisbeg Hill, finds a gap between the cloud cover and the horizon, and reaches across the low-lying bogland north of the hill and then across Roundstone Bay, to touch Inis Ní and feel its way along the island, reading it as a golden Braille of sharply defined little details — stone walls, telegraph poles, bungalow windows suddenly ablaze, cows and haycocks standing in fields, a tractor bumping along the road — while the mountains forming the background to this suddenly enhanced scene remain obscure and fraught with premonitions of rain and night. My mind too tends to finger the island sequentially, place by place, because I have collected so many placenames there, and drawn out the map of it so often. But I can leave it to the sun to tell me where to begin.

In showery weather, clouds coming in from the western ocean tend to trip over Errisbeg Hill and spill their rain into the bay, whereupon we, looking northwards from the village, may see a rainbow spring up from Letterdife woods, span the bay and then shrink away to a many-tinted candle flame guttering and dying on the shoreline of Inis Ní. Sometimes this familiar rainbow looks as artificial and rigid as a girder, so that one could imagine the rasp of wind on its edges, and in the strange clarity that obtains within its arc we can make out the causeway and bridge linking the island to the mainland, although they are over a mile away from our windows and are usually hard to distinguish among the reefs and rocky islets of the bay, Nature's sublime feat of engineering momentarily centring upon the little human construct and presenting it to attention as if it were some precious relic.

The present two-lane bridge, built at a cost of £1,800,000 to the Department of the Gaeltacht and the County Council, was ceremoniously opened in 2001 by the Minister of State for Rural Development, Éamon Ó Cuív. To my eye this new bridge and the broad causeway leading out to it look too large for the island, an aggressive imposition of concrete and tarmac and chain-link fencing on the humble but intricate shoreline of salt-marshy fields and crooked old drystone walls. Just beyond the bridge the way narrows to a country lane with ragged fuchsia hedges and flowery margins, in which cars have to edge into farm gateways to creep by each other, and the logic of the bridge demands that this lane be widened and straightened throughout the length of the island. Several of the few remaining natives of Inis Ní had been campaigning for the new bridge for years; the future of the island, they believe, depends on ease of access, an end to charming moribundity. And even to my recalcitrant mind the bridge soon proved its practicality when a gorse fire went out of control and a holiday home belonging to a friend of ours was saved from destruction by the Clifden fire engine, which would not have been able to negotiate the former eight-foot-wide bridge. The fire had been started by an old reprobate who was a favourite with tourists looking to photograph a traditional wild whiskery Connemara man, and who burned gorse every summer for the good and sufficient reason that his forebears had been doing so ever since the Stone Age. So the rainbow could not span a better instance of the uncomfortable dialectics of old and new in Connemara.

The previous bridge and causeway dated from 1886, but it was not until 1952 that the bridge was given protective railings and the causeway built up high enough to be passable at all times, and the older inhabitants remember sitting in the shelter of a wall nearby on days of wind and high water, waiting for the tide to turn. Before the bridge was built people had to wait for half-ebb before they could go splashing and scrambling across 150 yards of slippery rocks and seaweed to leave the island; then they would hurry to Clifden to do their business so as to get back onto the island before half-tide. The route across the tidal zone was called the Wire, as are two other fords in the Roundstone area; perhaps the word is from the English *weir*, because the falling tide pours over the rocky shallows as over a weir. There is a nasty story attached to the Wire. A beggar and his daughter came into Inis Ní across it one day, and after making an unprofitable tour of the cottages of the island found that the ford was closed by the rising tide. They approached a boatman, who saw that the beggar's daughter was a fine-looking girl, agreed to ferry them out in his little canvas currach, but said that he could only take one at a time. They agreed to that, and the man took the beggar across, returned to the girl, and (as my informant delicately put it), by the time her father got back to her, it was too late. Hence, a phrase for 'poor returns': '*an méid a fuair an bacach ó Inis Ní*' – 'as much as the beggar got from Inis Ní'.

That is not the only connection of this ford with extreme uncharity. Before the island was bought out by the Land Commission early in the twentieth century it was the property of a branch of the Blake family, whose seat was Castle House near Indreabhán and who were accounted the worst rack-renters of Connemara. In the 1830s the Blakes were extracting £200 per annum from a population of close to 400, when, according to a governmental report, the whole produce of the island was not enough to maintain a third of that number. Local tradition has it that, after the Great Famine of 1847–52, Patrick Blake evicted what tenants had not died or fled, and ran the island as a sheep ranch for ten years; when this enterprise failed him, he brought in other tenants from the Carna region, close by to the east of the island. Official records seem to corroborate this oral history: the census of 1841 lists 455 people in 72 households; at the time of the 1851 census there were just 2 households with a total of 21 people, and Griffith's *Valuation* of 1855 states that the island was 'in fee', i.e. there were no tenants, and the only buildings were a herd's house and 'offices', i.e. outhouses. Later on the population increased again. Now, halfway across the Wire is a little islet of rock, largely obscured by the new bridge, called Oileán an Fort; why the English word is used I do not know, but it is said that the 'fort' was a house on this rock, occupied by a bailiff called O'Donnell, in the employ of the landlord, who 'wouldn't let the people pick as much as a *bairneach* [a limpet] off the island'.

Inis Ní (to introduce it formally, having now come ashore on it) is a long, narrow, irregular undulation of marshy or heathy meadows and depleted bog, treeless apart from a few tousled shelter belts of pine, the underlying granite showing through everywhere. It measures nearly three miles from north to south, and consists of three low, roundish plateaus, each about two-thirds of a mile across, linked by sinuous necks so slight that very high tides sometimes run clear across them and make three islands of it. The permanent residents number about thirty-one; summer brings another, fleeting population, the owners of holiday homes and tenants of a few locally owned houses that are rented out. There used to be a gaggle of children crossing the bridge every morning to wait for the school bus on the main road; now there are none attending the primary school in Roundstone and only three in secondary education in Clifden or Carna. Inis Ní is nominally a Gaeltacht, and Irish is still spoken in several households, but what with emigration, the multiplication of holiday homes, and the education of the children in English-speaking Roundstone and Clifden, nowadays one could hardly call this an Irish-speaking community. The meaning of the island's name is uncertain: it might derive from the surname Ó Niadh (anglicized as Nee), which is common in the locality; the islanders prefer to think that it comes from *naomh*, saint, but the linguistic evidence is against them.

However, saints have left their marks on the island. At the most northerly point, on the bare rock sheet just above high-water mark, is a round hole about a foot across, usually full of muddy seawater, with a roughly built semicircular drystone enclosure about four feet high sheltering it on the landward side, and a narrow cairn of similar height close by to the east. Both the cairn and the shelter usually have scraps of withered vegetation stuck in their crevices, for this is Tobar Cholm Cille, Colm Cille's well, and on the saint's day, 9 June, the little monuments are decorated with flowers and a few people come to make their 'rounds', walking around the well clockwise while reciting the rosary, and dropping coins into the water or leaving them with other little tokens on ledges of the stonework. It is not a well in the sense of a spring of fresh water; the hole in the rock is a pothole, full of whatever the last wave to reach it has left there in the way of mud and seaweed and salt water. But so remarkable is the form and finish of the pothole that it is no wonder people take it for a wonder. It is oval in cross-section – almost circular in fact – about a foot across and eighteen inches deep, with a rounded bowl-shaped bottom, and as smooth as if it were sculpted in marble. This is one of the few such seashore 'wells' that are marked on the old six-inch Ordnance Survey maps, which name it and the cairn beside it as St Brendan's Holy Well and St Brendan's Monument respectively. These names would have been assigned by John O'Donovan in the 1830s when he was researching the antiquities of Ireland for the O.S.; in Connemara he was using a seventeenth-century manuscript, Roderick O'Flaherty's *West or H-Iar Connaught*, as his guide, and would have noted its brief mention of Inis Ní: 'This island hath a chapel dedicated to St. Mathias, and another place in memory of St. Brendan.' But O'Donovan was slightly astray in his identification of the place, I believe, for the holy well that Inis Ní people associate with St Brendan lies about fifty yards to the west of the ones he was looking at, which they know as Colm Cille's well. This other well is not marked on the O.S. map, and is very obscure, being lower down on the shore and covered in seaweed, but it is still visited by a few folk at the same time as the more prominent and accessible one associated with St Colm Cille. It is a smooth cylindrical pothole eighteen inches in diameter and two feet deep, and there is a little cairn two or three feet high on its eastern side. It seems – to geologists, at least – that such potholes are formed by abrasion: a stone falls into a cleft and is whirled round and round by the water, especially when waves are crashing on the shore during storms, so that in the course of centuries the stone is worn away and replaced many times, and the pothole is gradually deepened. Connemara folklore ascribes nearly all of them to Colm Cille, who is said to have made them as fonts for the baptizing of the local heathens. ('What sort of boring machine did Colm Cille have?' one old man asked me.)

When I was making my map of Connemara in the 1980s I was shown about forty holy wells of this type, nearly all on the granite shores of south Connemara between Roundstone and An Tulaigh, the eastern limit of my explorations, and including two or three inland ones that must have been formed in the beds of streams no longer extant. I think there are not many more to be found in this district, as my repeated enquiries since then have hardly increased that total. One of them, a Tobar Cholm Cille just west of An Tulaigh, is famous in its parish and Mass is celebrated at it on the saint's day, but most of the others are unknown outside their immediate neighbourhood, and some I had to persuade people to search for and rediscover. I have written elsewhere of the inordinate significance I ascribed to these sacred sites in the mystic underpinnings of my cartography, but my associations with the Inis Ní well are less elevated. I think it was on my first visit to it, when I was still unknown to the people of the area, that a youngish man in a citified but dingy navy-blue jacket came running down the fields, evidently to intercept me. His rather long straw-coloured hair was sleeked back as if with brilliantine, his eyes were sad and restless, his face narrow and pallid. He kept leaping forward to check me out – 'What have you got down in the bag? Books!' – and then dodging behind the cairn to fiddle with himself. I also manoeuvred to keep the cairn between us, keeping up an animated conversation as best I could until I saw my way clear to withdraw along the foreshore without seeming rude. In the years after this episode Larry became a familiar and mournful item of the Roundstone scene; the tolerant landlord of one of the bars used to put up with his silent solitary presence throughout many a long winter afternoon. Once I observed that when a fresh pint of Guinness was passed out to him he automatically and unconsciously dipped the side of his thumb into the froth and gave his glistening locks, his one claim upon style, a lick with it. Larry was generally shunned, but his oddities were hardly remarked upon. Other habitués of the bar never said more to me about him than, 'There's not much weigh on Larry' – a fact I had reason to be glad of, having done the rounds of Colm Cille's well with him. Larry lived with his widower father and found the lonely home intolerable, but it was a weary way on his bicycle from the house to his accustomed perch in the Roundstone bar, and the recurrent logistic problem of his life was to persuade someone to give him a lift to or fro. His masterstroke in this regard was to call on the parish priest one night to say that his father was very ill and in need of the holy oils; the priest jumped into his car, drove out to the house with him and anointed the old man, probably much to his surprise, whereupon Larry immediately cadged a lift with him back into the village. Occasionally when all shifts failed Larry would take a currach from the harbour to row across the bay; he did so very late one winter night, and never arrived. I remember the gloomy sight of boats moving slowly to and fro in search among the shoals and rocks of the bay in the fading light of the following evening, and the solemn moment when they all turned back towards the harbour, and we knew that the body had been found.

There is a third holy well on the shores of Inis Ní, but it is little known and rarely visited as it is exposed only at the furthest ebb of spring tides. It lies in the east-facing bay that almost divides the northern from the central portion of the island. To reach it, leave the road where it enters the narrow neck of land linking the two portions, and walk eastwards along the shoreline for about a third of a mile until you come to a tiny headland with a squarish field on it. The eastern wall of this field is your pointer: walk out from the shore in the direction it indicates, for fifty-seven paces; the well is at the foot of a small pyramid of stones a few paces to your left. However, since the tides pile and unpile stones in ever-changing confusion and all are cloaked in seaweed, and since it is impossible to take regular paces in a straight line in such a squelchy terrain, you are unlikely to come upon the well by following these instructions. Having heard of it, and of how difficult it is to find, I asked a man who was born near the place if he would guide me to it.

Beartla, at that time living in Roundstone in a broken-down mobile home (or 'humbile home' as I once heard him call it) but later of no fixed abode, was a mild and usually silent individual, but his ancient ragged military greatcoat, his raw-edged brows and nose and cheeks, his sparse reddish beard as full of angles as a winter hawthorn bush, his watery blue eyes, his long lips clenched round a reeking pipe, made me think of those figures of ungraspable outline in late oil paintings by Jack Yeats, the more so as Beartla is, as if by nature, of the horse world. He usually had a few Connemara ponies running wild on Roundstone Bog; in spring he would ramble out to see how they were surviving, with a thought of selling the two-year-olds in the usual way, and decide to leave them loose for another season. His stallion occasionally rebelled against its hermit life on an islet off Inis Ní and swam ashore to go on the rampage, gratifying other people's well-bred fillies with its unregistered semen, to the confusion of the stud books. The Clifden Pony Show was Beartla's annual apotheosis; there were usually photographs of him in the local newspapers, as if to prove that he'd been there – archetypal Connemara man, peaked cap low over the eyes, clouds of pipe smoke, fist clenched to the bridle of a rearing horse – but sometimes he would disappear for days on the way home, as if he'd been taken by the fairies. Now and again he would be absent for longer periods, off in Ballinasloe's mental hospital being doctored down into something more like conformity with social norms.

At that period I hardly knew Beartla other than as an occasional bit-part player in Roundstone's repetitive street theatre. I arranged to meet him at his home on a day of spring tides shortly before the hour of low water. He came out as I approached and quickly shut the door behind him, so that I wouldn't see the dereliction of the interior. We cycled to Inis Ní by the bridge and at the head of the little east-facing bay hopped over a few field walls to the shore and struck out into the acres of seabed exposed by the great ebb. We had to grope around in the chaos of orange seaweed and peaty mud for some time before Beartla was sure we were looking at the right puddle of brine, but once we put our hands into it there was no doubt about its singularity: it is a round hole about ten inches across and the same in depth, 'as smooth as a pot', as Beartla put it. That it had ever been found and remarked upon was evidence of how intensively this shore, and indeed the intertidal zone all around Connemara's labyrinthine inlets and archipelagos, was explored by human hands throughout the hungry centuries in which seaweed fed the nearby potato fields as well as the kelp kilns. This repeated laying-on of hands, to me, is the human touch that has made such places holy.

I wanted to photograph the pothole, and asked Beartla to stand behind it to give my picture scale. When I looked through the viewfinder I was intrigued to see that he had picked up a scallop shell and was holding it before him between his two hands in an oddly pious and almost girlish pose. Whether tradition was at work in him I do not know, but I was made to think of the cockleshell badge of medieval pilgrims to the shrine of Compostella, and of the cockleshell-shaped madeleine that is the emblem of Proust's pilgrimage through Time. Later on I gave Beartla a print of this photograph, and he obviously cherished it, for a year or two afterwards, when he returned from being 'away' for a long time and found that his cousins had purged his home of all his belongings, he came to ask me for another copy, so that now I have none, to my regret. Perhaps it was after that absence that he became a man of the roads, doing odd jobs with cattle and horses for farmers, and sleeping in their barns and outhouses. In the year or two before he died I used to meet him very occasionally, pushing his bike from nowhere to nowhere, his worldly goods in a hemp sack on the crossbar. Shortly before he died, I was trying to pinpoint some places local people had named to me up the quiet back road through the woods of Ballynahinch. As I stood looking at a little cliff almost overhanging the road, which seemed to demand its own name, and regretting that nobody lived nearby to tell me it, who should come round the bend but Beartla, walking very slowly, bent almost horizontally over his bike and his sack. 'Beartla!' I cried. 'The very man! What's the name of that cliff?' And Beartla with absolute authority replied, 'That's the

Piper's Cliff!' It was a most satisfactorily positive identification, even if he didn't have a story to account for the name. Then he remarked, 'It's a long time since you and I were in action down at the holy well!' and went on his way down the road as wearily as if he were trundling the load of years for both of us.

The very shape of Inis Ní suggests seaweed; with its three low, roundish hills connected by twisted necks it resembles a frond of the knotted wrack, the 'yellow-weed' as it is called here, that so plentifully cloaks its shores in glowing autumnal colours. From a distance this golden trimming of the island is glorious, but on treading into it one finds a harvest of ugliness entangled in it: multicoloured plastic containers, smashed shrimp pots, bundles of bluish monofilament net. This is a feature of most Connemara shorelines these days, and Inis Ní is not as polluted as the Goirtín peninsula, for instance, where every spring the Roundstone Youth Club organizes a clean-up in preparation for the tourist season, and fills dozens of sacks with rubbish off the famous beaches. A lot of this offensive drift-stuff, so lethal to wildlife, is of distant origin. A habitual strandlooper I know, always the first to patrol Dog's Bay after a westerly gale, has shown me in his shedful of finds a tub that once contained salted navel beef from Paradise in Newfoundland. On Inis Ní I myself was delighted to pick up a green glass bottle embossed '2/5 gallon', which I am told is an American measure, that had been cast ashore with even its moulded glass handle unbroken thanks to a padding of fleshy goose barnacles it had acquired during its years-long voyage. Collectable as some items of it may be, the cumulative effect of this Gulf Stream of garbage is deeply disturbing; it reads as the signature of a worldwide calamity, a breakdown of due process, a resentment of the ocean's superhuman purity. In Inis Ní the ebbtide of communal morale is most marked in the bay of the holy well described above. This bay opens eastwards; from the road, which curves round its head, one sees the almost perfect cone of Cashel Hill, five miles away, centred in its perspective. On a sunny day when the waters, mountains and sky are a thesaurus of synonyms for 'blue' one can overlook the dereliction at hand. There are some spruce whitewashed cottages by the sparkling waters, one of them in local ownership still. A flock of white geese parade in a field, and the halliards of a little white yacht moored close by add random bell-notes to their pompous trumpeting. The place is called Cara Beaga, meaning 'small fords', from the lines of rock by which one could cross the bay when the tide is well out. It used to be a vital centre of island economy, with many boats working out from it; even today a half-dozen open boats moored there, and one with a tiny wheelhouse like a sentrybox, look eager to go off fishing. In spring countless bobbles of sea-pink blossom cover the low ground on either side of the road. But on a grey day these flat expanses around the head of the bay seem only just able to drag themselves out of the sea. Black-bottomed creeks subdivide salt-marsh; at low tide there are wide levels of mud interspersed with eroded turrets of peat and grey stumps of bog deal. One is more conscious of the roofless cottages and outhouses, the craggy gables of granite stonework, empty window frames and gardens full of nettles. By the track that leads along the southern shore of the bay one passes rotting boat hulls, rusty car corpses, clogged-up cement mixers and abandoned fishing gear. It seems an undeservedly poor return, a beggar's portion, for the place's hard-working past.

By chance I have come into possession of the life-story of a former inhabitant of this corner of the island, Darby Gannon, written down by him in 1987 as he lay in a Galway hospital, having lost one leg and the other foot, no doubt to the effects of hardship and long neglect. His grandparents were among the people who came into Inis Ní from the Carna region after the Famine. His father was born on the island in 1857 and was the only one of his generation to stay there; all his brothers and sisters emigrated to Portland, Maine. One sister returned, and inherited half the family's land. Most of the next generation emigrated too. After a few pages on the history of the island and this family background, Darby continues:

I am reluctant to write about myself.

I was born in 1908, and as we had a lot of tillage then, we sowed potatoes, oats, root crop and cabbages, kept two cows, two yearlings and twelve sheep on 13 acres of land, we had hens and geese but we used to sell the yearling when they were a year. My earliest memoires are with all the crops and a little medow we hadnt much pasture, we used to have the cattle and sheep very much on the road side and on that place called the Brinks, the sheep used to trespass on that place where S lives now so, I sat many a long day sitting on the road side there to keep cattle and sheep from going that far If they were routed [chased away] with a dog they might get dround.

I remember the first day I went to school and all the Education I got was all I got in Inshnee I used to go to Roundstone two days a week after school selling eggs. I might be a little more than 14 years when I left school but when my brother Pat went to America I had to stop then

My first job if I could call it a job was on the Inishnee road repair work there was one man from every house on the job . . . We had no rain wear if the day came wet we worked in the rain or went home.

There was a lull in earning then for a few years . . .

We were for many years going to Rosroe [a peninsula east of Inis Ní] to get the turf. We had to carry it on our backs to the shore make a rick of it there, bring it across in the curragh, We used to bring two loads a day one in the morning and one in the evening. We used to be in Rosroe before dawn, and the morning was well advanced after all when we were back we had to take advantage of big tides and calm weather, we had to carry the turf up again and make a stack of it by a wall, an up hill fight

The creek at Carabega was a lively and busy place then when everybody was bringing home the turf, we used to talk to each other across the creek – there was great cooperation The thatching of the house and thresing of the corn were great days the neighbours helped each other we helped them to day they helped us tomorrow.

We never sold wool, my mother used to card and spin it and send to the weaver to make the flannel she knit the socks and the jersey. When she had to give up that work we sold the sheep and bought a bicycle.

In 1934 Darby got word of a beet factory being built at Tuam, so he took the bicycle and went off, unknown to anyone. Failing to get a job on the building, he weeded beet for one farmer and picked potatoes for another, but when the harvest was over he had to come home. The rest, apart from a trip to America to visit a sister, is a tale of hard physical work – stone-breaking for road repairs, turf-cutting in labour camps on the Bog of Allen – followed by years of personal and communal decline.

In the course of my life I have seen a great change come over Inishnee I saw the Hooker and the Gleotog, the pookaun and the row boat disappear until there is only the curragh left and there are no oarsmen every man that has a curragh has an engine

Until I was grown up the people did not go out to the mainland to any entertainment, for them all stage and screen was something immoral if they got paid and free transport they wouldnt go from Inishnee to Roundstone to see 'Quo Vadis' or 'How the West was won' They had their own dance every Sunday night They lived their own way, danced their own dance and sang their own songs, But then Emigration took it toll the young women went to America and the dancing had to stop. The older women gave up the spinning and making of flannel. Most people sold their sheep. People bought clothes of the peg the costume changed, tillage declined very much. Then the bicycle came and the curragh was less used. And when the young girls left off the shawl and put on the pants and took to the bicycle the place was like the island of Tristan the bottom had fell out of it

Worst of all the Language is gone There are some memories that I don't care to recall.

Feature by feature, life lost its character: the currach was pulled up on land and left to rot, the cow was not replaced when she became sterile, his brother died and Darby found himself living alone. Later the electricity came, and piped water, and he got a gas cooker, but the house was in need of repair, and the neighbours had fallen away.

Beartla deserted me altogether. Paddy could do like the Raven from the Ark — go and not come back . . . I used to be afraid when the wind reached storm force, I was not that much afraid of robbers I had nothing to be robbed of. But I could get a crack on the head. My greatest fear was that I might have a seizure and be dead for days perhaps weeks before I'd be found. Whilst lying in bed but not asleep I felt a person trying the door, and going away again and didn't give a shout.

I sold the place and on 3 Nov 1985 I left Inishnee . . .

He ends with a lament for times past and spaces lost:

I missed the landscape the wider view the sea and the boats standing out by the hedge I could see yaghts coming when they were at St. McDaras island. Often on a Summers evening I used to go along the shore from the old house to the big stone at Rusheen and home again across the old Bog in search of birds a hare or a rabbit

I missed the cows and the dog and the Black bird and the Robin that used to come in to the house

One of the finest sights I ever saw was the twelve pins covered with snow on a moonlight night the alps couldn't be more majestic. And above all the fireside chat.

However, fireside chat is not extinct in Inis Ní, and there are families who have made the transition to the modern world and brought something of their old ways with them. Not far beyond Cara Beaga on the road running down the western shore of the island, one passes a neat single-storey house tucked into a shelter belt of pine trees, the home and workplace of Bridie and Pádraic Davis, who returned from Boston some thirty years ago and are well content with the peacefulness of Inis Ní. Pádraic is a gentle person with soft blue eyes and silvery curls. He does some boat-building and maintenance, nowadays a matter of replacing rotten timbers in wooden currachs, in a large barn behind the house. His grandfather Bartly was of the famous boat-building Clogherty family of Leitir Mealláin in south Connemara, and is said to have been the first man to build a timber currach (as opposed to the traditional canvas-covered currachs). With Pádraic's uncle he lived and worked in Ceann Ramhar, the southern portion of Inis Ní, where he built the *Santa Maria*, a 54-foot nobby, for Roundstone's principal shopkeeper, also called Clogherty. The launching of this boat is an event still live in Roundstone tradition; I have been told a hundred men were assembled for it (which I don't believe). On a day of spring tide a winch was attached to a great rock down at half-water mark and the boat was hauled off the shore on a thick bedding of seaweed. Pádraic's grandfather built another boat behind the old family home inland of that shore, and slid it down a good two hundred yards of rocky hillside over a slipway of seaweed; the field in which it was built is still called Cnocán an Bháid, the hillock of the boat. But Pádraic himself never saw a boat built; he graduated without instruction from making model boats to building real boats; it was 'in him', from the family. He represents the end of Inis Ní's rather slight boat-building tradition; the Davis children, all daughters, are engaged in other careers, mainly in the caring professions and city-centred.

Bridie is the island's community activist and represents it on Roundstone Community Council; she lobbied the local politicians remorselessly to have the new bridge built, and now is proud to point out its advantages. Tankers delivering oil for central heating systems, tankers for emptying septic tanks, lorries bringing in building materials – none of these used to be able to squeeze across the old bridge. As we talk I can hear a rock-breaker thumping away somewhere, levelling a site, and Bridie tells me that three houses of local ownership as well as a big holiday home are in building at present. This flurry of construction work is partly due to the fact that it is no longer necessary for concrete blocks, sand and sacks of cement to be unloaded at Inis Ní cross on the main road and brought in piecemeal by tractor, at great expense. The next thing is to get the road improved; it is congested in the summer, and the heavy building machinery is breaking it down. Bridie is upbeat as I go though the island mentally with her, listing the permanent households and the summer homes:

about eighteen of the former and twenty of the latter. The summer folk include a retired Dublin printer who has taken up landscape painting, a retired judge and traditional musicologist, an English ornithologist, an American senator involved in the Northern Ireland peace process (which is why Gerry Adams has been seen strolling the boreens of Inis Ní), a German linguist and a Church of Ireland minister; they are a regular infusion of varied life into the neighbourhood. But as I write down the names of the native-born residents I am very conscious of the fact that several island 'households' consist of one man who will never marry, or of a frail octogenarian.

A few hundred yards further south is the village of Troscaí, by Cuan na dTroscaí, the inlet that almost divides the island's middle portion from its southern one. (These placenames are nowhere officially recorded – I have them only from my Inis Ní acquaintances of that immediate vicinity – and their sense is obscure.) When I was exploring the island in the preparation of my map of Connemara in the 1980s I often called in on Mícheál and Nainsí King here. Their little farmhouse is down by the shore of the inlet. There are snowdrops under the ash trees that shelter it; friendly sheepdogs tussle with each other on the lawn; the granite discs of old querns lean against the stone surround of the spring well close by the front door. The house and its surroundings at that time were lively with the growing-up of their youngsters. Once I found the whole family in a nearby field raking fragrant hay into the little heaps that in western Connemara are pleasantly called *gráinneógs*, from the Irish for hedgehog. If Nainsí happened to be making butter when I dropped in she would insist that I lend a hand, in half-serious, half-joking deference to the traditional belief that if a caller does not take a turn at the churn the good of the butter will be lost. She is from Carna, the strongest part of the Connemara Gaeltacht, across the narrow seaway east of Inis Ní. Confrontational, blackbird-sharp, whenever I meet her in one of the Roundstone shops she throws some observation in rapid Irish at me to see if I can catch and return it. Mícheál, on the other hand, is retiring; a tall, slender man, he speaks Irish fluently but in an unaccented monotone I have difficulty in following, with his face in profile as if addressing the wind.

Both of them generously responded to my passion for salvaging places that were foundering into oblivion. Mícheál walked much of Inis Ní with me, hopping limberly over walls from field to field or along the shore from rock to rock, pointing out where the ancient boundaries of the island's *cartúir* or cartrons run. The cartron is an obsolete land-division of medieval origin, nominally a quarter of a townland. Inis Ní is accounted a townland but for some reason it has just three quarters: Craobh (the literal meaning is 'branch' but in placenames it indicates a thicket or little wood) is the northern lobe of the island plus about a third of the middle lobe; Cill is the rest of the middle lobe and contains the ruins of the medieval chapel or *cill* mentioned by Roderick O'Flaherty, and Ceann Ramhar, meaning 'thick headland', is the broad and relatively high southern portion. On the eastern slopes of the middle lobe of the island the boundary between Craobh and Cill is a little stream draining out of an overgrown patch of bog, part of which is called Muing na Fola, the swamp of the blood. Mícheál had the explanation of this name: it used to be believed that 'bloat', a disease of cattle that makes their stomachs swell up, could be cured by bleeding the poor beasts, and the easiest way of holding the animals for this operation – a cut on the tongue or the tail – was to drive them into this soft place until they sank up to the belly. Another of Mícheál's placename-derivations that seemed unlikely at first disclosed a possible kernel of truth upon examination. Tobar an Rí, the king's well, is a little spring close to the north-western shore of Ceann Ramhar. According to what Mícheál had learned from his forebears, when the King of England used to visit his dominions by battleship his doctor and physician would arrive around a month or so beforehand to locate the best food and drink for him, and this was the well they settled upon in these parts. That sounds like a fairy tale, but there could be something in it, for I note that old charts mark the deep and relatively sheltered waters just off this shore as an anchorage, so the spring may have been used by naval ships and become associated with the forces of the Crown; in fact the Duke of Edinburgh, younger brother of the future Edward VII, may well have been here, when he was taking an interest in the distribution of famine-relief supplies around Connemara by British gunboats in 1880. But if the Duke supped from this spring he may not have enjoyed it: Mícheál says that the water is so full of iron it turns tea blue.

Here and there among the countless little fields, whose lichen-clad walls of granite stones look as old as anything still standing could well be, Mícheál pointed out the remains of still older stony structures. What he called 'the Danes' Fort', near the eastern shore and just north of the little stream forming the border of Craobh, turned out to be an ancient enclosure of some interest, previously unrecorded; later I brought archaeologists to inspect it and take its measurements. It is hard to make it out without a good deal of treading and poking around in bushes because its dry-stone walls have been robbed for the building of field walls, one of which crosses it diagonally, but it is roughly rectangular, about twenty-two paces long and seven to ten wide. Archaeologists tend to get overexcited by placenames involving 'the Danes', as the Vikings are called by rural folk, but in fact many structures of forgotten origins are popularly attributed to them, seemingly through a confusion between Danes and the Tuatha Dé Danann, the mythical inhabitants of Ireland before the coming of the Gael. If to the archaeologists such names sound like evidence of medieval Scandinavian trade and settlement, to country people they hint at buried treasure. Mícheál remembered hearing of a woman living near this Danes' Fort who was visited in a dream by a man who told her that if she went to it at a certain time she would find a bag of gold in its doorway. She never did go, even though the man came again and warned her that she would be too late if she delayed. But many others would not have been so wary of supernatural advice: Mícheál tells me that not only the Danes' Fort but everywhere else in Inis Ní has been 'turned upside down' by people looking for gold.

While some of the newer houses of Inis Ní and especially the

oversized bungalow holiday homes sit in uncomfortable prominence on exposed slopes, most of the cottages, dating from the
era of the Land Commission, are tucked into the lower land and
look as if they understand and respect wind and weather. A few
hundred yards to the east of the Kings' house an old ruin of a
cottage has been restored by a German academic, with the most
painstaking regard to aesthetics and ecology. When we first met
Arndt Wigger, and for a long time thereafter, we were rather wary
of him, he is so forbidding in appearance: tall, unbending, dark-
browed, with a face that works at the suppression of signs of
stormy feelings. But once when I wanted to consult an article by
Heinrich Zimmer on St Enda of Aran, published in 1889 in an
obscure German literary journal, and had rather casually asked
Arndt if he could look it out for me the next time he was in his
university's library, I was surprised to receive from him not only
a photocopy of the whole weighty paper but also his translation,
typed with scrupulous correctitude, of the relevant pages of this
fearfully crabbed text, complete with copious bibliographical references to and quotations from manuscript genealogies in Old Irish.
On the basis of this generous act we became friends. Arndt has
been coming to Inis Ní for many years. As a youngster he was
fascinated by botany and first visited Connemara with the purpose
of seeing its rare heathers and lichens. During one of these early
visits he became aware that, as he told me, 'something else was
going on here', that is, the Irish language. This chance encounter
turned him towards linguistics. After studying Irish and Old Irish
in the University of Hamburg under Hans Hartmann he won a
scholarship to the Dublin Institute for Advanced Studies, and later
spent some years teaching in Al Azhar University in Cairo. Back
in Ireland he attended Hans Hartmann's eightieth birthday, and
on seeing him his former professor ran over to him and asked
him to take over a certain unfinished labour concerning the
dialects of Connemara. In the 1960s Hartmann had collaborated
with Professor Tomás de Bhaldraithe, the lexicographer, in the
recording of many hours of conversations between native speakers
from Ros Muc, An Cheathrú Rua, and other areas of the Gaeltacht

– a unique corpus, of inestimable value to empirical linguists (i.e. to linguists interested in establishing exactly what a given language or dialect actually is, rather than what it is supposed to be according to the prescriptions of grammarians), but which had been left unpublished and indeed largely untranscribed ever since. After some thought Arndt accepted the heavy responsibility, and over the next five years devoted much time to editing the work and in trying to persuade some learned institution to devote time and money to its publication. By then Arndt was teaching in Bonn and Wuppertal universities, and had inaugurated his own foundation, Studienhaus für Keltische Sprachen und Kulturen (School of Celtic Languages and Cultures), in a beautiful eighteenth-century townhouse in Königswinter, on the Rhine. This is a financially independent college of the University of Bonn, and was supported by both the Scottish Office and the Irish Government; in fact Minister Éamon Ó Cuív had flown out to open it in 1999. Sadly, the Irish contribution was contingent upon matching funding from either Scotland or Northern Ireland, and changes in policy and personnel have put that funding into abeyance, so that the school has been forced to part with its lovely old building and is now making do with dispersed temporary accommodation. However, the first instalment of the Connemara Irish corpus has now appeared: *Caint Ros Muc*, two fat volumes, text and dictionary, of rich and lively talk from nearly fifty years ago, preserved for future centuries to wonder at.

Throughout this career Arndt has been settling his cottage into the substance of Inis Ní with the same patient and respectful attention to sky, sea and land that he has shown to the Irish language. It is hidden in a dell near the shore, and the processions of telephone and electricity poles that interrupt the island's stark skylines have not been allowed to approach it; only a grassy track winding down between patches of gorse and granite outcrops from a wooden gate on the side road through Cill reveals its presence. One enters its garden through a tiny gate of wrought iron – it is the head of a narrow old-fashioned bedstead, I note – by the turf stack. Steps half overgrown with delicate wildflowers such as dove's-foot cranesbill and glossy-leaved cranesbill lead down into a sequence of tiny irregular stone-walled enclosures that wrap around the house like the leaves round an artichoke heart. A wind-rounded sycamore tree leans protectively over the roof; there are apple trees hoary with lichen, one of them with a crow's nest in it, a round herb garden, figs and a plum tree, a small stone-lined spring well with a flagstone like a kneeler before it, an outhouse with a couple of small solar panels on its roof and a pair of currach oars leaning against it. From the back garden gate – which is the other end of that old bedstead – a little path runs down to the shore, where the currach sleeps on its back in the grass. The cottage itself is of the traditional western-Irish design, plus a small extension, which is merely the space, roofed over, between the cottage and a natural step in the land just outside it. One enters the cottage by a door into a little kitchen area in this extension, half full of a huge scented geranium and floored with irregular flat stones. The further end of the extension wraps round a corner of the original building to make a little bathroom in which hart's-tongue fern sprouts from the natural rock outcrop into which the bath is set. The main room of the cottage is partly open to the roof beams and has a loft bedroom over one end of it, reached by a ladder, and a big arched fireplace at the other, with another smaller room behind the fireplace wall. A plain old iron candelabrum for six candles hangs over the wooden table; a small neon bulb can be lowered from the ceiling like an evening star to hang over the pages of a book. The low windows look out into the heart of green. Arndt cooks in an iron pot hung over the fire and runs his laptop off batteries charged by the solar panels. The house melds old ways with new; it is a dwelling, in the deep philosophical sense, with technological amenities.

The last cartron of Inis Ní, Ceann Ramhar, begins immediately beyond the village of Troscaí. The road winds along the neck of land between Cuan na dTroscaí to the east and two contrasted bays to the west. The first of these is known to the Ordnance Survey simply as Mud Hole and to the islanders as Na Bruachaí, the brinks, and has little cliffs of black peat four or five feet high around it where the sea has cut into bog that was evidently laid down before the rise in sea levels of the last thousand years or so. The second bay of the western shore here is Cuan Leice, flagstone bay, named from the great bare rock outcrop forming its southern shore. There is a curious construction just beyond this rock sheet, a hollow tower made of granite boulders from the shore cemented together with gaps between them so as to form a filigree cylinder about six feet in diameter, and now standing to about ten feet, though I am told it used to be higher. From the road this little monument can be seen a few hundred yards away to the south-west and when the afternoon sun turns the sea beyond it into a shifting dazzle it is hard to make out what one is seeing; it seems to move a little, and looks almost like a group of people leaned together in sorrow or mutual comforting. This is a memorial to victims of the Great Famine, and was built in 1994 by a Belgian artist, Axel Miret, who, having been directed to Inis Ní, he told me, by mystic and inexplicable coincidences, rented a cottage near this spot, exhibited his paintings and pastels in a Roundstone art gallery (many of them depicting melancholy processions of shrouded female figures, in a style suffused with nineteenth-century Symbolism) and then moved on. Axel used to see such ghostly figures from the Famine times on the shore here, he says. During his time in Inis Ní he kept a lantern lit in his monument by night; we could see it from our windows on the other side of the bay, like a star washed ashore.

Ceann Ramhar stands rather higher than the other portions of the island, and the road climbs slowly and steadily across open boggy ground, disimproving (or improving, depending on one's perspective on such things) into a rough track and then into a narrow path of set flat stones. The half-dozen houses of the cartron (none of them inhabited except by holiday-makers) are set back from the road at the ends of lesser tracks, almost out of sight. Even the path comes to an end, at a fence and a notice, 'Beware of the bull', just short of the summit at 157 feet. The hilltop is called An Maoilín Dóite, the burned summit, a *maoilín* being a slight eminence, usually rather flat-topped, as in this instance; the adjective probably originated with some notable fire long ago. Even today some Inis Ní farmers are the most inveterate arsonists, burning off the invasive gorse and the dead vegetation of the previous year to give a flush of green grass in the spring; it leaves me desolate and furious to see vast billows of smoke rising from the island, in the nesting season and well after the legal limit to this practice, the first of March. A happier fire, one of beneficial power, is commemorated by the name of the very topmost point of the headland: Cnocán Tine Cnámh, the bone-fire hillock, on which the midsummer bonfire used to be lit on St John's Eve. The custom is still upheld in many Connemara villages, with relics of the magical practices once associated with it, but I doubt if today's acrid stench of blazing car tyres does much to bless the fields and cattle with health and fertility.

Beyond these heights the land drops steeply past rock outcrops like breaching whales and astonishing scatters of glacial boulders, to the final south-facing coastline, which is rugged and indented, with low cliffs and narrow inlets full of pale wave-polished shingle. Mícheál is in charge of the little automatic lighthouse at the south-eastern corner of the headland, and when I accompanied one of his occasional visits to it he pointed out many features of this hidden-away land's-end. In a glen immediately inland of the light are traces of a circular stone hut of unknown date, and Mícheál has a story about a man on the run who hid out here. The yeomanry hunting him found his potato ridges in this glen, and kept a watch on them thinking that he would surely return to harvest the crop; but he had put no seed-potatoes into them and the ridges were just 'camouflage', as Mícheál put it, and by the time the soldiers had realized this the man was far away. Mícheál also pointed out a shoal just offshore called Maidhm an tSagairt, the priest's breaker; the name must date from days long ago when Roundstone, to the west, and Carna, to the east, both belonged to the old parish of Moyrus, for the priest was sailing from one part of the parish to the other to say Mass when he was wrecked and drowned here.

To the Inis Ní people Ceann Ramhar evidently stands for extreme distance, being as far as one can go, for they have an old expression: '*chomh fada ó Flaitheas Dé le Ceann Ramhar*' ('as far from Heaven as Ceann Ramhar'). The very southernmost point of the headland is An Coirnéal Sáraithe, the beset or harassed corner, so called because the tidal outflows from Roundstone Bay on the west of Inis Ní and Rosroe Bay on its east meet and fight it out here. The slope of wind-shaven grassland above this point used to be a good place to rest and let the breeze idly turn the pages of the mind. The whole length of the island lies behind one, and, immediately below, its blunt bows butt stubbornly into the waves. The outlook sails away southwards past other low headlands, islands and rocks defining the seaway through which the confluent bays give onto the open distances of the Atlantic. On a recent February visit I heard the croaking of a raven prospecting for a nesting site at Aill na nÉan, the cliff of the birds, a little further round to the east, and saw a splendid chestnut-furred fox slipping away among the rocks. All was peaceful, but I was disturbed by that bull the notice had warned me of, even though my Inis Ní friends had assured me that it did not exist and that I was welcome to go where I liked; it seemed to incarnate the baffled surliness of a declining way of life.

This magnificent headland was open rambling space when I first knew it; now, like many other commonage areas, it is criss-crossed by barbed-wire fences that run right down to the cliff edges, and reaching the point I am describing calls for more rock-climbing than I am comfortable with. There are economic reasons for parcelling out the grazing by such fencing, and it is under-standable that some farmers might want to discourage hikers by loosing imaginary bulls on them; careless visitors have left gates open, and one Inis Ní man had some sheep savaged by uncon-trolled dogs recently. There are also the expenses of insurance cover, for rightly or wrongly farmers fear they could be sued if a visitor, invited or otherwise, comes to harm on the land. But beneath these practicalities, which could all be sorted out by intel-ligent legislation, is a slough of doubts and difficulties concerning not just the future of farming in these ragged fringes of Europe but the survival of the rural population, beset by the conflicting tides of depopulation and development. Inis Ní is already too shrunken to be considered a community separate from that of Roundstone, which itself is much reduced. In a few years' time a large majority of the houses on the island will be holiday homes. Is it the promise of the bridge that Inis Ní will become a holiday village from end to end? What will become of the land as the farming families die out? Will Ceann Ramhar be so treasured by the summer visitors that it will be cleared of fences and preserved in its fierce proximity to heaven? Who is to care for the island's holy places and workaday shores, remember the names of its fields? The tables are strangely turned: Inis Ní goes begging round the houses for its future.

The Catchment

Two hundred and sixty square miles of mountainside and bogland collect the rainwater that is poured into the salt under the old bridge at Toombeola, three miles north of Roundstone. Abundant rainfall and acidic geology make this catchment area a perfect spawning ground for sea trout and salmon, and the Owenmore or Abhainn Mhór, the 'big river', which carries nearly all of this water on its two-mile journey to the sea from Ballynahinch Lake, is (or was) one of Ireland's most renowned salmon rivers, and there are little jetties for anglers, and fishery huts, all along its course. Ballynahinch Lake itself receives the outflow from two main sources: the Inagh Valley with its two great lakes, Inagh and Derryclare, flanked by the Twelve Pins to the west and the Maumturk Mountains to the east; and the lovely series of smaller lakes – Oorid, Cappahoosh, Glendollagh – that greet the visitor coming along the main road south of the mountains. The handsome three-arched bridge under which the river struggles with the tides was probably designed by Alexander Nimmo in the 1820s, but since he was in too much of a rush to set the country to rights to document his own activities, this is not known for sure. Before his time the main crossing of the river was by a ford at its outflow from the lake, and the bridle-way from Galway through the Roundstone area, and eventually to Bunowen in the south-west extremity of Connemara, used to pass Ballynahinch Castle and then follow the western or right bank of the river to Toombeola. But Nimmo's road kept to the left bank, with the result that the bridle-way fell into disuse. There are three ruined cottages in a wooded dell by an inlet (or *airćn*) of the river bank just north of Toombeola, and a sturdy little two-arched packhorse bridge across a stream feeding into the river, and traces of a mill (of an antique design in which the wheel was mounted horizontally) where this stream flows out of Loch Aircín; but otherwise the village of Aircíní has been re-absorbed into the bog, as has the bridle-way itself for much of its length. Instead, business followed the road, and the left bank, the Derryadda and Cashel side of the river, became a remarkable site of commercial activity in the nineteenth century, as we shall see.

Toombeola itself, which once had its post office and National School as well as, in the heady days of religious rivalry after the Famine, a Presbyterian school and a Methodist chapel, is almost deserted nowadays. At the south end of the bridge a track branches off the road and leads past one or two houses to a little grave-yard by the river estuary. The giant Beola, who gives his name to the Beanna Beola, the mountains known in English as the Twelve Pins, is said to be buried here (hence its Irish name, Tuaim Beola, the tomb of Beola — which, having now explained, I shall use henceforth), but I have searched in vain for further news of him. There was also an abbey here, a small Dominican foundation; a raised area in the middle of the graveyard probably marks its site, but I shall tell what is known of its history, and its bloody end, in connection with a place on the other bank of the estuary, when I come to write about Cashel. The only building here now is roofless and ruinous; it looks like a rectangular chapel, with a small arched doorway in one wall and two narrow windows in the east wall, and a fine holly tree flourishing in it. This is prob-ably eighteenth century; John O'Donovan in 1839 noted that it was said to have been built to commemorate the existence of the abbey 'by some gentlemen of the country, whose names I have been unable to learn'. The graveyard is a tranquil place, secluded by trees, beautifully overgrown with foxgloves and wild yellow irises. From my first visit I remember the midday silence of the birds, and a tree-sized *Olearia* covered in little daisy blossoms, like a tree in a child's paradise. Once upon a time, very long ago, one of the monks of the abbey slipped out to enjoy the sunshine and to meditate in the open air for a few minutes. When he went in again he was amazed not to recognize any of the monks within; they too were surprised to see him, a stranger to them. They questioned him; he insisted that he was a monk of the abbey;

they looked up old records, and found that indeed he had been a member of their community, under such and such an abbot, hundreds of years before their time. So I am told, 'and do in part believe it'.

Beyond the graveyard, past cottages that have been deserted these last few decades and tiny ruins obscured by undergrowth from much earlier generations, the track fades out into the rough heath and bog surrounding yet another deserted village, Aill na Caillí. Here a cluster of eight or ten ruined, and two or three still roofed, cottages stands amid old trees, tiny stone-walled plots and rambling, brambly paths, looking out over the narrow straits through which the tides and the salmon come up to Tuaim Beola from Roundstone Bay. There are low cliffs on the shoreline just south of the village, from which no doubt it has its name, meaning 'the cliff of the hag' – the hag here probably being the green cormorant or, in Irish, *cailleach dhubh*, black hag. Aill na Caillí is in appearance an idyllic spot, and the Congested Districts Board put great effort into supporting it, building a small pier and replacing several of the old dwellings with substantial slate-roofed cottages, but the last of its residents had gone by the 1970s, some of them moving up to the road, which passes by a mile or so inland, and one family emigrating to California. Of recent years an imaginative attempt has been made to market the place as 'the Oldest Village in Ireland', but it has found no buyers, and resides in loneliness. A man who used to live there tells me that the old folk of the village used to believe that when the heron shrieks on a moonlit night, it is because it has been frightened by its shadow on the water; somehow this scrap of lore seems to me to speak obscure but eloquent volumes about the place. There are perhaps two more recent stories to be told about Aill na Caillí, one of sanctity and one of devilry, but for various reasons these are not mine to tell. So I will leave the place to the heron, and return northwards by a winding grassy way across the bogs, called the Scholars' Road, because this is the route the children of Aill na Caillí used to take to the National School, and before that to Mr Reddington's hedge school, near the bridge at Tuaim Beola.

The Abhainn Mhór has been famous for its salmon for centuries, as Roderick O'Flaherty, writing in 1684, tells us:

[The river] is shallow and full of wares and stones, from the lake down, for a mile, to Wine Island; on which island is a salmon fishing, worth £30 a year. On this island experience was made how the salmon hath still recourse from the sea to its first offspring; for here eighteen salmon were marked, with a finn cut of each of them at their going to the sea, and seventeen of them were taken next season, in the same place, coming back.

John O'Donovan, writing in 1839, comments on this:

The fishery on this island is now worth £500 per annum. It is let to a Mr. Robertson, a very sensible Scotsman, who cuts up the salmon into pieces of two pounds each and seals them hermetically in tin cases, in which he maintains they will be preserved fresh for seven hundred years!

This Mr John Robertson, a Dumbarton man, came to Connemara in about 1833 to exploit the salmon rivers and also the oyster beds in the bays on either side of the Carna peninsula. During the Great Famine he was contracted to supply the Roundstone food depots with Indian meal, as I have mentioned, and was accused of refusing to allow credit and pushing up prices. (But the people got fish heads, tails and fins from his fishery for free, says oral history.) Thomas Colville Scott, a surveyor who visited the bankrupt Martin estate on behalf of potential purchasers after the Famine, and whose diary I have edited for publication, tells us that when the estate came into the hands of the Law Life Assurance Society, in 1848, Mr Robertson was appointed its agent with a salary of £500 a year and £100 for expenses, 'being the only person resident in the district who had sufficient knowledge of the people and energy to manage them'. He resided in Ballynahinch Castle and had an office near at hand, 'where two Clerks are constantly in attendance to receive rents from the numerous O's on the Estate', while two nephews looked after his interests in the fisheries: 'Mr Wm. Robertson – son-in-law of Mr James Pendlebury of the Dukes Dock, Liverpool, – who manages the Oyster beds, and Mr James Crawford, who attends to the Salmon and river fishing'.

Whether or not John Robertson was a profiteer during the Famine and established himself in this way, his later works were much admired for their contribution to the area's recovery. Several visitors in the post-Famine years commented favourably on his initiatives, including George Preston White, writing in 1849:

To those who are sceptical as to the feasibility of reclaiming bog-land I would recommend a visit to Mr. Robertson's well-managed farm; he has bog-land producing enormous crops of turnips, oats, and potatoes, which he assured me was so wet and marshy in some parts that a person could not walk across it before it was drained. He certainly farms under peculiar advantages, having great quantities of bones, offal, oyster-shells, – the refuse of his establishment, – which are carefully stored up. I cannot give a stronger instance of the security to life and property that exists in Connemara than by mentioning the fact that Mr. Robertson has no locks to any of the doors of his house; indeed the front door is a glass one, so that the precaution would be of no use . . . I could not help reflecting, on leaving Mr. Robertson's interesting settlement, that if such energetic, enterprising men were more frequently to be met with, Ireland would be in a very different position.

Even such an authority as Harriet Martineau, the famous journalist and writer on political economy, echoed these sentiments, in a remarkably sanguine account of Connemara in her *Letters from Ireland* of 1852:

Mr. Robertson . . . has lived in the country for many years and is much esteemed and trusted by his neighbours. It is he of whom we used to hear that he had no locks and bars on his doors, as there was nobody to be afraid of. He is the lessee of the Martin fisheries, and he employs fifty persons, on the average of the year, on the salmon fishery near the Martins' Castle. His bog reclamations answer well, and employ much labour.

Robertson's fish-house was on Wine Island, just upstream of the Tuaim Beola bridge, and linked to the left bank by a narrow iron footbridge. There was a slaughterhouse on the island, and beef was canned there as well as fish. The technology of the cannery in particular amazed the visitors. The Hon. and Revd S. Godolphin Osborne describes it in detail:

In one building, there were all the various descriptions of ingenious machinery, necessary, in the manufacture of tin cases; one boy cuts the body of the case, another, with another machine, punches out the top and bottom; another forms the rims; another solders the sides and bottom together, so as to make a case, only wanting the top. In another building, are a certain number of boilers, superintended by a woman. Presently, a signal is given 'that there are fish,' a boat is manned, and a long net quickly run out, so as to sweep a pool made by the bend of the river; we saw at one haul some twenty salmon, or salmon trout, brought in. They are at once washed, and with very little mutilation, put into tin cases, in certain weights and sizes, as may be: so quickly are they out of the river, into the 'tin,' that as a workman described it, 'you may see them a panting, as we puts the tops on.' The top once on the case, it is instantly soldered on; in short, portions of a fish, or a whole fish, as it may be, are hermetically sealed up in a tin shroud or shrouds before he can scarcely believe he is out of the water; and now into the water, he goes again, but this time 'he is in hot water.' He is tenderly boiled, under the mild superintendence of the boiler woman. After having undergone this ordeal, he is ready for exportation; he may be eat at Liverpool, or on board a transatlantic steamer; he may be eat off Cape Horn, or at the London Tavern . . . Lobsters, oysters, and milk are all here prepared in the same way; and if one can judge from the mass of oyster shells which are heaped up on the spot, the demand for stewed oysters must be very large.

Thus the catchment was transformed into an efficient killing machine.

Some time before 1847 John Robertson built a fishery cottage by the road near Wine Island, and this soon became a hotel: 'He thus avoids the expensive luxury of Irish hospitality in which "the Martins" used so freely to indulge,' as Scott sarcastically noted. Under Robertson's successor it was known as the Angler's Hotel, and was advertised as follows:

Walter Blackadder, manager of the Ballynahinch fishery, having now Rebuilt and Refurbished the above hotel in Connemara for the accommodation of anglers and tourists, trusts by observing a good Cuisine, Wines, Cleanliness and the general comfort of his visitors, that he may solicit a small share of their patronage, as the Hotel is beautifully situated for Salmon and Sea Trout fishing, Sea Bathing and Seal Shooting. The Galway and Clifden Railway, now in construction, to be opened next year, nearest station (Ballynahinch) within ten minutes' walk of Hotel.

After the coming of the railway in 1895, and in particular during the First World War, the fishery prospered. The Berridges had an eel weir built, and on dark winter nights of flood, when the eels were coming down to go to sea, they were netted in their thousands. Daily trains took iced fish and eels direct to Dublin, and thence to Billingsgate. This business fell away during the depressed post-war years. The river was last netted for salmon in 1922, in the short interval between the ending of the Troubles and the sale of the estate by the Berridges to that Maharajah of anglers, Ranjitsinhji. With the development of Ballynahinch as a sporting estate by its later owners, the slaughter of salmon for fun took precedence over their commercial exploitation for food. (I remember an old photograph I saw in a pamphlet history of Ballynahinch, entitled 'Mr. R. J. Jones, "The Killer Jones", lands another one.') The old salmon weir now has a holiday home built on it (though the eel weir, a little further upstream, still occasionally yields some barrelfuls of eels, plus one or two drowned otters).

Ranjitsinhji had the fish-house knocked down and replaced by a bungalow, which itself is in collapse now. The only building still extant of the Wine Island complex is the disused ice-house abutting onto the roadside just north of the bridge and obscured by thick growths of cotoneaster. It is a barrel-roofed concrete construction, half underground, in which ice collected off the lakes in winter, pounded into fragments and allowed to freeze together in big blocks which would last for months, was stored for use in the export of fresh fish. Otherwise all is rust and ruin at Wine Island. A swallow came stooping out of the low door of the ice-house last time I fought my way through the undergrowth to investigate it.

The sporting fishery is in deep trouble too, in the famous river of Ballynahinch as elsewhere, for while 'the salmon hath still recourse from the sea to its first offspring' it does so in greatly diminished numbers. The Angler's Hotel, now a b. & b. known as the Anglers' Return, with its elegant Georgian façade painted a pale lilac, its sunny paved courtyard and the richly wooded gardens climbing the hill behind it, is a delightful place to stay, but these days it sees very few anglers returning triumphant with their catches. The reasons for the collapse of the salmon run are complex and controversial; they include predation by seals, and widespread poaching, but the number of drift-net fishing boats licensed to operate out of Irish ports is certainly a major factor. In the North Atlantic, Ireland is the only state through whose waters the salmon pass on their migration that has not organized a buy-out of drift-netting licences in order to conserve the threatened species. From Newfoundland and Labrador to Norway and England, such compensation schemes are in place, while Ireland still preys on not only the Irish-born salmon but also those that originate in the rivers of Wales, France and Spain. Consultants hired to advise the Government on this question calculate that whereas a netted salmon is worth €22 to the economy, a rod-caught salmon brings in €423, because of the food, drink, air miles and bed-nights consumed by the visiting angler. The netsmen found their case on the need to foster small coastal communities and preserve what they call a traditional way of life. Populist and opportunist politics feeds on such arguments, while the salmon, of both the €22 and the €423 varieties, swims towards extinction.

Sea trout too are facing into a dirty and dangerous environment in their migrations, and are coming back from their time in salt water in a languishing, half-starved state, their scaly coats eroded and their fins eaten ragged by sea lice. Since there are huge fish cages moored in the bays, close-packed with salmon and subject to infestations of lice, it is probable that the sea trout pick up the parasites in passing the cages, especially as sea trout do not go out to sea like the salmon but merely nose around the estuaries and bays for a while. But it is difficult to eliminate the possibility that some other factor is weakening the fish and so making them more vulnerable to lice; the unidentified influence could be as general as global warming, or as particular as the chemicals used to control lice numbers in the salmon cages, or indeed the raw sewage Roundstone and most other small coastal communities pour into the sea. A regime has been introduced of 'fallowing' the cages, leaving them empty for a year at a time, but the statistics about the effect of this on the sea trout run in various catchments are dubious and hard to analyse. These knotty questions have set the sports-fishing interest at loggerheads with the fish-farming industry, which on its introduction in the 1980s was greeted as the antidote to Connemara's chronic ills of unemployment and emigration, and is now foundering in environmental squalor. Meanwhile the sea trout fishery of Ballynahinch, among others, is near collapse.

The river system itself is far from being the natural nursery of fish life that it once was, quite apart from the human predators lining its banks. The practice of scattering fertilizers on mountainsides from helicopters to promote grass growth was encouraged by the farmers' advisory body in the 1990s, and must have polluted the rivers. There are large tracts of coniferous forestry coming right down to the brinks of the great lakes of the Inagh Valley, traversed by hundreds of drains pouring their run-off, always acidified, and periodically silt-laden and pesticide-poisoned, into the delicate chemical balance of the water. Decomposing peat on the blanket bogs, especially where it is being cut for fuel or left bare by overgrazing, is another source of acidity. A tinge too much acid, and the salmon and trout eggs will not hatch; a little more again, and the fish themselves die.

The vast increase in the numbers of sheep on the hills, which is now to some (inadequate) extent being reversed, has been horribly damaging, as I saw recently when the young estate manager of Ballynahinch took me to see some of the detailed conservation work being carried out on the fishery. First we visited a stream that came off the flanks of the Maumturk Mountains, and was in good condition. In one place the outside of a bend had been reinforced with a few big boulders so that the stream would not eat it away when in spate; in another, willow rods had been stuck into the bank and were beginning to show signs of growth. The stream had shape: shallow ripply stretches that would bring lots of dissolved oxygen to the salmon eggs hidden in its gravel beds alternated with deep shadowy pools for the fish to lurk in. Then we looked at a stream that was in such disgraceful form that I will not even identify its location. Admittedly this was in the nadir of a wet winter, but I was shocked by the barrenness of the land, much of which had been reduced to bare mud by excessive grazing. Tea-chest-sized lumps of peat, torn off the eroded bog by recent spates, lay crumbling in midstream, choking the gravel beds with brown silt and forcing the stream to spread out into shapelessness. An attempt had been made to fence the sheep off from the water's edge, but the restless dynamics of the stream, forever altering its meandering course down the valley, and the relentless probing of the hungry animals, had opened up gaps in the fences, which then merely served to channel the sheep along the banks, which were trodden down into quagmires. Loss of substance, loss of form, loss of difference, slippage into chaos, entropic shaming of the land; all this for the sake of grant money, and in a mountain-rimmed valley the grandeur of which, seen from a distance, would seem to proclaim it eternally a fit cradle for the fish that carry the memory of its waters with them on their thousand-mile sea-going, and return to seek it out among hundreds of waters, and fight their way upstream to it again, for generation after generation. What has to be done to end this scandal, by the farmers, the conservators, the fishing industry, the fish-eaters (including myself), the Government and the European Union, has been spelled out by experts in countless reports, and this is no place to rehearse their recommendations; the task is complex and difficult, given the number of interest-groups involved and the short-sightedness of populist politics, but it is not inconceivable that the situation could be remedied. But to what end? Are we to save the salmon from extinction because we enjoy killing it and are willing to pay €423 for the pleasure? The sea trout too; the highest praise of it I have read is that it is 'pound for pound a better fighter than the salmon' – that is, it resists with all its weight and muscle and life-instinct being dragged out of its element by a hook in its mouth.

A catchment area is a naturally defined and functionally integral facet of the world's surface, unlike a parish or electoral division or county whose boundaries may or may not be given by landscape features; as such, a catchment can be taken as a microcosm of the whole. It is an open, self-renewing, dynamic system, supporting and supported by a vast number of life-forms and all their interrelations. Even its basic topography, the most skeletal and reductive representation of its geometry, is profoundly suggestive of a way of looking at the world and caring for it. I have an outline map of the Ballynahinch catchment, showing the two chains of lakes and their interconnecting rivers, the smaller rivers that contribute to them, and the hundreds of little streams feeding into the latter. The whole system of watercourses is firmly rooted into the sea by the Abhainn Mhór, the 'big river'. An ideal outline map would go into further detail of this fractal pattern to show the thousands of tiny trickles draining the basins of each of the streams, and so on. Even without such feathery minutiae the map looks like the wing of some magnificent creature evolved by mythology, or by the future, out of a bird: an archangel, perhaps.

All around its perimeter I could draw a line representing the watersheds that separate this catchment from those of Kylemore to the north, the Maam Valley to the east and the Owenglin that flows westwards to the sea at Clifden. In the mountains this line would run from peak to peak along the high ridges; in the lowlands it might follow the crest of a low rise. But there would also be a branch of this watershed separating any two adjacent subdivisions of the catchment, for instance running down a mountain spur each side of which drains into a different stream, and continued as far as the confluence of those two streams. Similarly the valleys of those streams would be subdivided by still lesser watersheds into the catchments of tiny rivulets – and so on, down to the scale at which gravity-driven water-flows lose all identity in the formless osmotic oozing of the bogs. Thus a tendril of the map of watersheds reaches into each fork, however minute, in the map of watercourses, and vice versa; the two structures are perfect reciprocals. Just by glancing around the mountain skyline from the lowland one can see that the Ballynahinch catchment is held in the arms of a watershed, but this further consideration reveals that watershed and drainage pattern are mutually implicated throughout the entire catchment, that each is delicately and precisely rooted in every detail of the other. And yet they are perfectly distinct; they share no point. Roderick O'Flaherty uses an arresting phrase apropos of a river of the Ballynahinch catchment called the Abhainn Tuaidh (north river) that drains two small lakes at the foot of the Maumturks and adds itself to the Recess, or Sraith Salach, River some miles east of Ballynahinch Lake:

At Balynahinsy, Owantuidhe and Sraith-Salagh rivers, after they meet in one channel, pay their tribute to this lake; and in recompence receive the benefit of its salmons to spawn on them.

This captures the ethics of a catchment. Through its ramified watershed it scrupulously delivers rainwater (and a pharmacopia of other inorganic necessaries), and through the conjugate ramifications of the watercourses receives the salmon (and all the forms of life of the food chain headed by the salmon). The balance is precarious and precious, and becomes a matter of ethics since we, humankind, by the weight of our numbers and demands, are forced to become the managers and conservators of the process.

Another old and weighty word from O'Flaherty, to conclude. Describing the outflow of the Abhainn Mhór at Tuaim Beola, he says the river is 'exonerated' into the bay. To exonerate: to relieve of a burden, physical or moral. A river's ills may be discharged into the sea, but, the way things are, we keepers of the world-catchment cannot be exonerated of our responsibility.

Tales to Lengthen the Road

The seven or eight miles of road running generally eastwards from the bridge at Tuaim Beola to the village of Cashel are narrow, caught between salt waters on the right and rising land on the left. The sea, even after having squeezed through the various straits around Inis Ní and Rosroe, still seems to have had the energy to take a series of small bites out of this coast, so that the road has to swerve and twist like a bicyclist harassed by a snappish sheepdog. The roadside features are remarkably various. Where the shallow rippling estuary of the Ballynahinch River opens out into the deeper water of Cloonisle Bay is a fine old stone quay, one of Nimmo's works, from which the salmon and eels of the Ballynahinch fishery used to be exported, but which is now unused. Then, on the inland side of the road, there are two or three hundred yards of craggy cliff twenty or twenty-five feet high, the last few yards of which are black and glistening where a little stream has been diverted out of a cleft in the hillside to trickle down the cliff-face. Around another bend a low hill of green pasture, very different from the surrounding rough boggy land, appears on the right: a drumlin, that is, a deposit of till moulded and streamlined by the glaciers that dragged this material out of the mountainous interior of the region. It lies half in the sea, forming a little promontory, and the waves have cut into its margins, rimming it with little cliffs of boulder-studded clay. In autumn one sees men making haycocks on its ridge, and a small tractor scuttling to and fro, outlined and miniaturized against the sky.

From here on houses are more frequent, but still scattered. The road deserts the shore for a brief space, or rather the shore makes a long and elaborate detour to the south around the Rosroe peninsula, and then road and shore are reunited along the upper reaches of Cashel Bay itself. On the left, just after the turn down to Rosroe, is the Fireside, which combines pub, post office and general shop. Cashel Hill rears up steeply behind it. The next building to catch the eye is Doon House, formerly Doon Cottage and the residence of Mr Hazell, Connemara's principal kelp-buyer, and now, as the home of an Irish peer and his lady, much enlarged, sober grey but dashed with sparkling quartz and tending to the castle-like. It stands above a grassy rise on which daffodils host in spring, and commands a splendid view down the bay. Their boathouse, a fine old building of uncoursed stone with a wide arched doorway, on the shore opposite the house, used to be Hazell's kelp store. Then, around another kink of the road and inlet of the shore, we pass an elegant and expensive hotel, Cashel House, hidden from the road by the shrubs of its famous gardens, and the pretty little Victorian church of St James daintily perched above a steeply sloping lawn among trees, and finally the village's other big hotel, the Zetland, well known to fishermen, also hidden away among trees and shrubs. And suddenly one is out in bogland again, without having been able to say, 'Here is Cashel.'

A tidemark of tales lies ready for my beachcombing along this way. They are extremely heterogeneous, but every one of them involves contention: between religions, between classes, between animals, between this world and the other. There is none of the optimism of dialectics in these clashes of opposites; antagonisms remain unreconciled and untranscended except by oblivion. I hear them from people born in the area, and write them down to preserve the little asperities and particularities of the way, without which it is just a road one drives along too fast, commending the scenery in watercolour generalities.

The site of the first story, about half a mile from the bridge at Tuaim Beola, is marked by a roundish boulder a couple of feet high set in the grassy margin between road and shore where both make a sudden turn to the left. At this point the river mouth is pinched to a few dozen feet between this angle of the land and a low promontory of the further shore, where a loose stand of trees hides the ruined chapel and the old burial ground, all that is left of the abbey of Tuaim Beola. The angle of the northern shore is called Corr na mBráthar, the friars' point, and the story is simply that two friars tried to escape an attack on the abbey by fording the river, and were caught and shot here. Their graves have since been washed away by the tides, and the stone by the roadside alone remains to mark the spot.

This local lore could well have a sound foundation. The monastery was founded by the Dominicans of Athenry in 1427 with the assistance of the O'Flahertys, the then Lords of Connemara. Like many small foundations in the remoter and still Gaelic areas such as this was, it probably survived the official dissolution of the monasteries in the reign of Henry VIII, but by 1558 or so, at the beginning of Queen Elizabeth's reign, it was deserted, and its stones were taken by Tadhg na Buile O'Flaherty to build a castle on an island in Ballynahinch Lake. Nevertheless, in spite of the penal laws aimed at restricting the Catholic religion, a few friars were present at Tuaim Beola in the 1720s, no doubt with the connivance of the Martins, who had acquired the former O'Flaherty estates in the post-Cromwellian settlements. It seems possible that the chapel dates from this period of relative tolerance. But the existence of the little community was discovered by the notorious priest-hunter Stratford Eyre and along with many other such covert religious establishments it was raided by the soldiery and scattered in 1732. Eyre went on to become Governor of the town of Galway and continued his persecution of Catholic ecclesiastics long after the penal laws had fallen into disuse in most parts of the kingdom. According to his frequent reports to the Government the regions beyond Galway's west gate were seething with rebellious papists and smugglers who at any moment could flood in through the town's dilapidated walls and overpower the garrison with the aid of French officers of Irish extraction, Jacobites and the scheming agents of Rome ever at work among the disaffected populace. The authorities took little notice of his alarms, and he vented his paranoia on the county for years. The bloody deed at the bend of the Cashel shoreline fits plausibly into this man's infamous history.

The next story does not sit in time and space so comfortably.

It concerns the cliff that accompanies the road for about three hundred yards from opposite the old quay of Cloonisle. It has the reputation of being a fairy dwelling, and the fairies of Ireland are not the winsome flower-girl-children captured by English Victorian psychic photography, but malicious, vengeful, appetitive and incomprehensible creatures. At the eastern end of the cliff a diverted stream trickling down it turns the rockface a rather sinister gleaming black. By moonlight it is a looming, intimidating presence, and people used not to like to pass it at night. When the road was widened in the 1930s parts of the cliff were blasted away, and it was rumoured that when the men came to work on it the next morning there was blood on the stones. From several sources I hear a traditional tale of a changeling, with variable details. A boy from a house west of the cliff was taken by the fairies, and something like a black log left in the bed in his place. The parish priest came and prayed over it and recovered the boy. But as the priest on his way back to Roundstone was passing Inis Ní cross, which 'was always and ever a mighty stronghold of the fairies', his horse reared, his mouth was 'put round to the side of his face', and he died soon after.

The Duchess de Stacpoole, whose garden near Roundstone was a resort of fairies, and who was something of an authority on the occult, being often at home to ghosts and poltergeists, had a more circumstantial history of this event. According to a radio interview she gave in the 1970s, Connemara used to be a very psychic place and changelings were not uncommon. Her version of the story concerned a girl called Ann, only daughter of the Conneelys who lived in a cottage the ruins of which can be seen among the trees just beyond the eastern end of the cliff. One night she went out, and when her mother went to call her in the morning she looked slightly different; 'She was Ann, yet she wasn't Ann.' Her mother couldn't wake her, and sent for Fr Moloney. The priest came on his side-car, opened the door of her room and said, 'Ann, where art thou?' There was no response, so he repeated the question, and then once more in a very loud voice, whereupon the girl woke up and rubbed her eyes, and was back again as Ann. But there is always one who has to repay in some sort. The priest went home on his side-car, but opposite the barracks in Roundstone his horse reared up, sweating all over with fear, and a few months later Fr Moloney was changed and he died.

Now, Fr Moloney is someone I can look up in records; he was Roundstone's parish priest from 1873 to 1896. The Duchess's narrative verges on being a rationalization of the traditional changeling story, in which the girl would have been carried off by the fairies into the cliff and a sickly wasted creature left in her place, and the priest would have heroically entered their dwelling place to rescue her. To the fairies the solid rock has doors and windows; the priest too has some access to its interior in his commerce with the invisible, but with extreme risk. The wet cliff gleams like moonlight even on the brightest day, and despite its evident impenetrability I see it as the façade of a palace of lovely impossibilities, an exception to the rule of matter. And I am disappointed to be told that the stream used to lie in the little glen at the end of the cliff, as one would expect, and was only diverted to flow down the cliff-face itself in recent, post-fairy times.

Something of the same permeability of the material world to otherworldly beings is hinted at in the next story, too, which concerns the green promontory a few bends of the road further east. It is called Imleach (according to the dictionaries *imleach* means 'marginal land', but in west Connemara it is the usual term for a drumlin or glacial hill). There used to be a house on it with the anglicized name of Emlagh Lodge, of which no trace remains; its stones were carted away for the building of Ellistrim Lodge a mile or so west of Roundstone, early in the last century. All I have ever heard about Emlagh Lodge concerns an animal brutally misused and casually expended in the war of nerves between human society and the spirit world. The house was haunted, I am told; there was a room upstairs in which nobody would stay. Once a man led his pony up the stairs and left it in this room overnight, and in the morning it was found dead in the field below, having been 'ringed' (made to run in a circle on a long rein) until it dropped. But perhaps there was never anything more behind this cruel little history than the rattling of shutters in the wind off the bay and the pawing of branches at windows.

There is another brief story to be told about the Rosroe headland, but for all its brevity it requires a more elaborate setting for its appreciation, so I shall postpone the diversion down the side road that leads out that way for the moment and continue along the Cashel road. Just beyond the old kelp store opposite Doon House is Fox Island, a few paces of grass and heather and rock, close inshore and accessible by foot when the tide is out. The fox, they say, was picking its way over the seaweed to the island when it saw a limpet that had not completely pulled its shell down onto the rock it was attached to. Hoping to prise it off, the fox stuck its tongue into the gap. But the limpet clamped itself down on the tongue and held the fox there until the tide came in and drowned it.

This disturbing tale is told of several other places in Connemara, such as Carraig an Fox off the western shore of Inis Ní; I have heard it in the Aran Islands too, and I imagine it has its allotted number in the systematic classifications of international folktales. The fox is usually the winner in 'clever animal' stories, but not here. Nor do these Connemara creatures converse in elegant verse like La Fontaine's eloquent beasts. We are familiar here with the eerie voice of the fox, something between a bark and a howl, and can imagine the anguished yelps of this one as the waves ran in among its legs. Also, we know the unbreakable silence of the limpet. (Even Napoleon was impressed by the fixity of purpose of limpets, to judge by Turner's ludicrous painting of the ex-Emperor contemplating one on the shores of St Helena.)

The site of the next story is Meall an tSaighdiúra, the hillock of the soldier; one would hardly notice it unless it were pointed out, among the tip-tilted hummocky fields to the left of the lane to the old cemetery of Caiseal Ard or High Cashel, about a quarter of a mile up the hillside behind the chapel. In the centuries before Alexander Nimmo's road system there was a bridle-path into the Cashel area from the north, which passed the cemetery and then turned west along the lower slopes of Cashel Hill by this hillock. The soldier, an Englishman, was following this old way when he noticed a well near the cemetery. He asked what it was and, on hearing that it was St Connell's holy well, insulted it by urinating in it, and continued on his way. But he had not gone far when he felt terrible pains, his insides fell out (he 'passed his intestines', in the words of one old lady, who must surely have been a nurse in her time), and he died on the hillock now named from his misadventure.

Now, a couple of more modern anecdotes, which claim to be history, and which I can associate with O'Loghlen's Quay at the head of Cashel Bay, and the nearby Zetland Hotel. J. J. O'Loghlen was the owner of the hotel, which used to be known as the Zetland Arms and before that as the Viceroy's Rest; all these names allude to the hotel's distinguished patron Lawrence Dundas, Viceroy or Lord Lieutenant of Ireland from 1889 to 1902, in which year he became the Marquis of Zetland. I can best situate O'Loghlen by quoting an affectionate but patronizing account of his rise by Sir Henry Robinson, head of the Local Government Board. O'Loghlen is lightly disguised under the name O'Flaherty in what follows, but no one who knew Connemara could have been in any doubt about to whom Sir Henry was referring.

Even in the wilds of Connemara there was a wide field for enterprise for any man who could shake himself free of the groove of ignorance and tradition and start trading with the teeming population on the seaboard. Such a one was Mr. Dominick O'Flaherty, the son of a mountainy farmer whose little holding sloped down the mountain-side of the shores of a small inlet of Galway Bay . . . The son, being a man of ambition and opinions of his own, he took the lead in local politics and had little difficulty in being returned as a P.L.G. [Poor Law Guardian] . . . He was a kind-hearted man and in the lean years he never refused the loan of a lock of potatoes or 'yella male' to his neighbours who were without supplies . . . The business included a new line in boots, shirts, groceries, and hardware. It was altogether a credit trade, and after every fair Mr. O'Flaherty collected what he could from his debtors and even accepted payment in the form of eggs, fish, chickens, or pigs. He kept a sort of reckoning of what he was owed, but his accounts were a mystery, and seriously puzzled even himself.

'What I buy I put on one side of the books,' he said, 'and what I give out I put on the other; but the divil of the whole of it is that things go out of the store and I disremember who I gave them to and have no account of them.'

However, in spite of these lapses the shop flourished exceedingly, till eventually his clientele owed him thousands of pounds. With the pride that was in him he sent his family to good schools, and the pretty daughters were initiated into the canons of high society as visualised by the good nuns of the Presentation Convent School. The next step was the building of a house, for it was obvious that delicately reared daughters could not be brought back for the holidays to the long, thatched, cabin. So Mr. O'Flaherty designed himself a new house with a good big parlour and a few extra rooms for travellers. It was found to his surprise that these rooms were never empty; the fact was that the charges were so moderate, the food so well cooked and the beds so clean that the house was a Godsend to fishermen, and it soon became clear to Mr. O'Flaherty that there was a fortune in hotel-keeping. The crowning success came when the Lord-Lieutenant himself, no less, stopped for three days at the hotel and presented his photograph and that of his consort to Mr. O'Flaherty, and caused his elevation to the dignity of J.P. The hotel at once became christened 'The Viceroy's Rest.'

In those years O'Loghlen would have been the most powerful man in Cashel, with the exception perhaps of Hazell the kelp agent. Dependent on the former for credit to tide them over until the latter paid them a pittance for their labours in cutting seaweed and burning it for kelp, the ordinary folk of the neighbourhood would not have shared Sir Henry's appreciation of O'Loghlen's book-keeping. Nor, according to the story I have heard from various Cashel people, were they all as bedazzled by the viceregal condescension as O'Loghlen was, and they demonstrated the fact on the occasion of the official opening of the hotel. The Viceroy himself was to do the honours. The place was decorated with flags and bunting, and O'Loghlen had the red carpet out at the little pier (still known as O'Loghlen's Quay) opposite the hotel. The Viceroy sailed into Cashel Bay in a small cruiser, but when he attempted to come ashore from it in a small boat he was met with boos by a crowd under the leadership of the fervently nation-alist curate from Recess, Fr Michael Murphy. Some say that his landing was merely delayed, others that he was driven off entirely by a broadside of stones, and that Maud Gonne, no less a 'Servant of the Queen' (her loyalty being solely to Romantic Ireland), was the inspirer of this act of rebellion. Afterwards Fr Murphy, rather than pass under a Union Jack hanging over the road, went home to Recess the long way round by Tuaim Beola. But the outcome was bad for Cashel, for favours that were to have been dispensed there by the Lord Lieutenant went instead to a new favourite, Fr Flannery of Carna; hence the construction of Flannery's Bridge near Cill Chiaráin, and the planting of Ireland's first state forestry, at Knockboy.

The lively old gentleman who was my principal source for this story, Willie O'Malley, must have been born in or near the year of the event itself and as a child would have seen O'Loghlen. Willie also remembered the Countess Markievicz staying in the little guesthouse his parents ran near Ballynahinch, and would have been aware, retrospectively, of the political and social force-fields in which O'Loghlen might be characterized by two deeply opprobrious terms that have crept into Hiberno-English from Irish: gombeen-man, one who sells goods *ar gaimbín*, that is, on credit with interest; and shoneen or *seóinín*, one who toadies to the upper classes. The story of O'Loghlen's humiliation in the eyes of the populace makes a crude moral sense, which old Willie O'Malley for one seemed to relish.

Poor O'Loghlen, whatever his deserts, is the butt of tales told by his social superiors as well as by his inferiors. In another of his books of reminiscences Sir Henry Robinson refers to O'Loghlen by his real name (spelling it O'Loughlin), and pokes fun at his overdeveloped sense of loyalty to the Crown and his ludicrous display of it on the occasion of Edward VII's visit to

Connemara in 1903. This royal progress was an uninterrupted series of absurdities, according to Sir Henry's account, and as he was at the King's side throughout he was well placed to observe them. The King and Queen had disembarked from the royal yacht near Leenaun in Killary harbour, were greeted with 'Three cheers for King Henry the Sixth' by the 'Oldest Inhabitant', and were driven by motor-car to Tully, where the curate was capering about with an illuminated address of welcome under a banner reading 'Friend of Our Pope'. Their Majesties were to lunch at the Railway Hotel, and so the motorcade proceeded down the Inagh Valley towards Recess, where, says Sir Henry, O'Loghlen, quite beside himself with excitement, had hit on the idea of honouring the King with a cavalry escort:

The motor swung round the Lough Ina road, turning into the straight for Recess, when we suddenly found ourselves in the midst of an amazing mob of horsemen: farm-horses, cart-horses, ponies, donkeys, of all sizes and descriptions, mounted by men and boys in rags and tatters, black coats, flannels or home-made stuffs. Some had saddles, others none; some had reins, some straw ropes.

There they were all waiting on the high ground up the mountain-side to see the arrival of the cars, and the moment the cars came into sight they were off down the mountainside like an avalanche, yelling, cheering, laughing, knocking each other over and leaping over the ditch on to the road with a speed that sent most of them over the road on to the bog at the other side. The guard of honour of O'Loughlin's Royal Connemara Mixed Cavalry formed a cordon round the hotel to secure the Royal party from intruders during lunch. Afterwards His Majesty commanded Mr. O'Loughlin to be presented to him, who, in his capacity of Commander of the Forces, made a most profound obeisance.

The utterances of monarchs on momentous occasions usually find a place in history, and the notable remark of King Edward the Seventh to the Queen, which just reached the gratified ears of Mr. O'Loughlin, to wit: 'That of all the courtiers he ever had standing around him not one of them ever made him such an iligant bow as Mr. Johnny O'Loughlin,' it is hoped will duly be recorded in the annals of the Irish nation.

Of the stories I have collected along the Cashel road, these of O'Loghlen are the only ones to depend on personal character traits, and this because of their relatively recent origins. All such intricacies have long been worn off the other tales. To make them comprehensible I have had to give each one a sketchy topographical and historical background, of which a local audience would have no need; strip that away, and you are left with a terse telling that is not untrue to the words in which I was told them – words that have been through the mill of folk-memory's translation out of Irish into English. A priest bests the fairies and pays with his life. A foreign invader (understood to be a Cromwellian) profanes a holy well and is literally gutted by the power of its sanctity. A drunken squireen (so I picture him) wagers his pony against ghosts, and the poor creature is driven to death. I hear no comments on these ruthless counterstrikes of the supernatural. It is almost an argument for the historicity of the Tuaim Beola incident that nothing is made of it; unlike the English soldier, the killers of the innocent religious go unpunished and no unseen powers exact their honour-price, as they would in a folktale. At Fox Island a land-creature tries its luck with a sea-creature in the no man's land of the tidal zone, and loses all. If there is a moral (beyond the cautionary 'Be careful!') it is that there is no moral.

The briefest and bleakest of these epiphanies is the one I have put off till last, concerning the population of Rosroe, the townland that comprises the headland of a three-mile-long peninsula separating Cloonisle Bay and Cashel Bay. A narrow, bumpy side road runs down its eastern shore past the usual pretty little fields with twisty thorn trees and lichen-patched walls, creeks with tiny tumble-down quays of loose seaweedy stones, and a few small farmers' cottages. A branch of the road to the left leads away into Canower, a little peninsula budding off the main one; Rosroe begins shortly after this T-junction. An Ros Rua is its name in Irish, meaning 'the reddish headland'; *rua* is a common element in the names of areas of reddish, nitrogen-starved vegetation. Most of the townland's thousand acres are bogland. The ground rises inland of the road to the smooth skyline of the bog a few hundred yards away; here and there a muddy track leads up in that direction. Off the tracks the ground surface is dire, especially in winter and after rain: badly overgrazed, lumpy, sodden, with gnawed-down grass tussocks, mudholes and patches of bare rock. This is cut-away bog; a depth of peat, probably of many feet in places, has been removed by turf-cutting, and now the scraw, the upper layer of living plants, rests more or less directly on bedrock. There is a lake on the bog, called Loch Bharr an Bhaile, top-of-the-village lake, with the ruins of a dozen cottages straggling south from it, only just protected from the worst of the prevailing winds by the ridgeline a few feet above them to the west. Their low walls and gables, some of them serving as sheep-pens or cattle-shelters, still stand here and there among an almost effaced network of old field walls that have no relation to the long straight fences of barbed wire cutting across them. Beyond the ridgeline the land sinks monotonously toward the low, stony western shore facing Inis Ní. There was one man living in an isolated cottage down there until a decade or so ago, but nobody lives on that side of the headland nowadays. Halfway down the slope there are traces of a few more cottages in a place called An Tamhnach Mór, the big arable patch; I hear of a pot of gold buried there, but it is heartbreakingly obvious that nobody ever found it.

'You can't eat the view' is an almost traditional retort of the embittered Connemara native to the visitor enthusing over the beauty of the place; but the huge pre-Famine population was in fact consuming elements of the scenery: the bones of the land were already showing through the bogs where the turf was being stripped away for sale as fuel, especially in the south Connemara coastal zone, and the kelp and fertilizer trades were so demanding that the shores must have been bare of seaweed. Rosroe used to be very populous: there were a hundred houses, most of them cabins built of sods, they say, and dozens of boats in its little harbours. Fourteen hookers worked out of the creeks of its east side alone. The townland lived by hauling turf to the Aran Islands, which, being of well-drained limestone, have no bogs, and seaweed to Kinvara, where the farmers of Clare would buy it in cartloads to manure their land. And that is the basis of the story of Rosroe, as given to me in a sentence by a farmer of an adjacent town-land: instead of planting its own potatoes, Rosroe bought them in Aran and Clare, and so the village went down in the first year of the Famine, while the other villages lasted longer. Went down! He meant that it was deserted, its inhabitants dead or fled. Now, census returns indicate that there were 230 people in Rosroe as a whole in 1841, and 55 in 1851. It seems probable that it was the settlement on the bog that collapsed so abruptly, its remaining inhabitants moving down to the shore where there was some hope of boats bringing in relief supplies of yellow meal. I have been shown traces of a building called 'the Poorhouse' and said to have been a soup kitchen, by a little slip on the eastern shore; there are many famine graves in its vicinity. In any case by 1855, according to Griffith's *Valuation*, the whole of Rosroe was empty apart from a herd's house. On the 1898 Ordnance Survey map no inhabited houses are shown, just a cluster of minute empty rectangles indicating roofless buildings by the eastern shore, a scatter of them on the higher ground south of the lake and a handful near the western shore. While the eastern side was repop-ulated later on by people from Carna and Canower, the settlement on the bog was never reoccupied.

Strolling among its ruins, angling for a good photograph of them, I find myself trying to embrace as much background as possible in the picture, to insist on the luxury of colour enjoyed by those who dwelt here. On a bright day the lake condenses the vastness of the sky into a profundity of blue, the arms of the sea sparkle with silver, sunlight fondles the brow of Cashel Hill. If the wind falls away completely on a summer afternoon the waters begin to reflect every wrinkle of the mountains with such preci-sion that reality and image meet seamlessly along the shores; one could be looking down through great holes and rents in the skin of the earth at the impossibly lovely upside-down land that is the foundation of this one. And when the mountains have once seen themselves with such terrible lucidity, surely they can never change; they know the truth of themselves. The world becomes abstracted, its attention all on its own image. Not a detail of the scene changes, but the earth's unearthly beauty is suddenly terrifying. I have witnessed this awful transformation in the expression of Connemara very often. Perhaps the last person alive in the village by the lake, for whom hope was too far away, behind those mountains scissored out of a hard blue sky, saw it too: the landscape clenched against its reflection like the teeth of a skull.

The Demesne

John Moriarty, mythopoet and religious thinker, used to work at Ballynahinch Castle Hotel during his sojourn in the Thebaid of Connemara. One day after the dishes were washed and the teas sent in, he was leaning over the counter in the still-room watching Bill, the handyman, laying a piece of lino. Worried that Bill was making a hames of it he eventually said with his customary gentleness, 'I'm wondering, Bill, I don't know, is there any chance, Bill, that you're cutting that crooked?' Bill went on working away as if nothing had happened. Then he sat back on his collops and said, 'This is a lovely old castle, John, it's a lovely old place, and in lovely old places like this the only good way to cut anything straight is to cut it crooked.' And indeed when John saw the finished work the next day, the crooked cut of the lino fitted the crooked wall perfectly. For John, this was a lesson in what he would think of as the divine rightness of this crooked old world; for me, a suggestion of a mode of adaptation and accommodation of a book to its subject matter, a hint of a properly devious approach to a place that has come to terms of peace with a disrupted history.

The road running inland from Tuaim Beola follows the windings of the Abhainn Mhór or Ballynahinch River through low boggy hills at first, and then parts from it to plunge into a zone of dark and ragged state forestry, so that the entrance to the hotel grounds when one comes to it on the left lets in a welcome flood of light, further brightened by the smart white paint of a fanciful Victorian gatehouse with a comic little castellated tower in which the disposition of narrow keyhole-shaped windows on the outside mimes the act of climbing the twisty staircase within. The drive beyond opens as promisingly as a nineteenth-century novel, skirting a little water-lily lake and disappearing round a bend between banks of rhododendrons and flowerbeds set in slopes of well-mown grass. A few specimen trees of great nobility soar above it: Wellingtonia or giant sequoia, Lawson cypress, Monterey pine. Evidently this drive is an invitation to a well-mannered enclave, smoothed out and sweetened by money, in the rough and sour land of Connemara. Beyond the bend the drive crosses the river by an old stone bridge, and then, just before it reaches the hotel, passes a slender seven-foot splinter of rock, set up on end in a little lawn of its own, twisted and blackish, like fossilized lightning. This, according to what the travel-writer Richard Hayward was told when visiting the hotel around 1950, is Cloch an Aonaigh, the market stone, by which bargains were sealed, in long-gone days when there was a village nearby. Indeed it may be so, but it is very similar to the gothicky 'standing stones' set up along the approach to Clifden Castle by an antiquarian-minded landlord in the 1820s. What happened to the village of Cillín, as it was called, will be mentioned later, in the history of the creation of this privileged domain.

The hotel itself isn't actually a castle, as several visitors' accounts complain, but a comfortable and unassuming three-storeyed building, grey-plastered, with a wide-arched doorway, ivy clambering around casement windows, a pleasantly asymmetrical roofline of tall chimneys, a stepped gable above the door bay, and decorative battlements on a two-bay extension to the right. A tablet of Connemara marble set in the façade by the door informs one that this was the home of the famous Humanity Dick Martin (1754–1834), founder of the Society for the Protection of Animals; another plaque commemorates a more recent owner, His Highness Kumar Shri Ranjitsinhji, Jam Saheb of Nawanagar. In the entrance hall, roomy enough for anglers to shed their waterproofs and waders in, there are capacious armchairs and old brown portraits and sporting prints, and a log fire blazing in a broad fireplace. For the more enquiring visitors there is a small table covered in maps and guidebooks; I always have a surreptitious look at it to see if my own works are well displayed. In the bar and restaurant, down a passage to the right, there is another good fire, display cases with portly salmon of which the like are not to be seen in these fished-out days, and photographs of gillies holding up mighty fish and of a stout and cheerful Indian gentleman in plus fours and tweed jacket – the Ranji, as he was familiarly known. There is also a portrait of Grace O'Malley, done from a rather etiolated imagination and not at all suggestive of the valiant sea-queen of Mayo who, legend says, faced down Elizabeth of England in her own court at Greenwich. (What Grace's connection was with Ballynahinch will be told in due course.) In the sitting rooms off to the left of the entrance hall are portraits of Richard Martin, and Connemara landscapes, and glass-fronted bookcases. I once gave a talk on the history of the place in one of these rooms, which the listeners seemed to find unexpectedly humorous; afterwards I was told that two little girls had slipped out of the tedious session and run round outside the hotel to the window behind me, where they had been cavorting and pulling faces.

Because of the abrupt discontinuities of its history Ballynahinch is not now a place of memories, but of relevant memoirs there are many. Shevaun Lynam's biography of Humanity Dick is to be found in the bookcases mentioned above, alongside numerous anglers' guides and travel books; ideally these shelves would also provide all the other works I have looked out here and there in researching Ballynahinch, which has attracted the written word more than any other part of unbookish Connemara. The Ballynahinch library would then include medieval annals for their references to the earlier masters of the place, the O'Flahertys and their even more remote precursors the Conmaicne Mara; Hardiman's *History of Galway* for the earlier Martins, several gossipy tomes from the Golden Age of Anecdote for Richard Martin, a foot or two of nineteenth-century travellers for glimpses of his son Thomas Martin, Maria Edgeworth's brilliant letters on Thomas's fascinating daughter the 'Princess of Connemara', two novels of Charles Lever that draw on the Martin myth, and various fictional and biographical works by members of the Martin family themselves; for the post-Famine landlords, the Berridges, not so much apart from family papers, photo albums and ledgers (but I will be suggesting that literature missed an opportunity in the enigmatic life and character of the first Richard Berridge); for the Berridges' successors, Anne Chambers' *Ranji, Maharajah of Connemara*, a richly backgrounded biography, and finally an armful of tourist literature and sporting reminiscences from which invaluable historical trivia can be gleaned.

An old place, worn into comfortableness, a place for eating cress sandwiches with well-dressed ladies, pondering dark-varnished paintings, pacing woodland ways in conversation, watching anglers catch no fish, waiting for a glimpse of the fox that trots out of the shrubberies to be fed sausages at the front door and about which a children's book has been written, Ballynahinch exerts a discreet power of seduction, promising narratives, leading one into slight deviations from one's everyday character. The hotel itself, a four-star establishment, is somewhat out of my star; I have preferred time spent sheltering from the rain with the outdoor staff in a room off the back yard, with tea brewing on a gas ring, tabloid newspapers and a nearly empty milk carton, listening to stories of the river and complaints about the midges that infest the forest rides. But I have eaten in the panelled and mirrored dining room, and well remember a curious occasion there, after the unveiling of the tablet honouring Richard Martin, and the launch of Shevaun Lynam's indispensable book on him (perhaps memory conflates two occasions, but no matter). The book was published by Lilliput Press in its early days when its founder was still working from his family's country home, Gigginstown in Westmeath, and among the invited were a number of his neighbours, ardent bloodsports enthusiasts, as well as representatives from the World Society for the Prevention of Cruelty to Animals and other organizations that stemmed from Richard Martin's historic initiative. I found myself at a table around which members of the two sets had been seated alternately, an arrangement that did not lead to a useful exchange of views. The tender-hearted leaned forward and conversed among themselves in intense whispers – 'Our next campaign really must be for the poor salmon suffering such stress in those dreadful fish farms' – while the hunting and shooting faction sat bolt upright and bugled to each other across the intervening bowed backs about going down to Lady Molly's in Cork for the otter hunting.

From the tall windows of the dining room, at the rear of the hotel, one looks out upon a lovely bend of the river darkly rippling as it withdraws into woodland rich in its maturity. One can walk down to the river bank from the east gable of the hotel by the zigzag paths of a terraced garden. A little island cleaving the current there was named for me as Bear sland by an elderly gardener; Ranji used to keep a bear on it, he explained. Some people say that Bear Island is another island nearer the bank and joined to it by a small footbridge – but they are 'bastard liars', the gardener added, with what might seem unnecessary emphasis. In this belligerent devotion of the old retainer to the minutiae of the place that has given his life its shape and savour I see the last spark of the feudal spirit that made Ballynahinch an inviolable refuge for the Martins from duns and process-servers, as endlessly celebrated in the family's own mythography. It also warns me to be precise and correct in everything I write down, about the relics of former eras to be found here and there in the grounds, lest an atom of fiery indignation from a neglected past burn a hole in my book.

From below the hotel a path leads back eastwards along the river bank and passes under a side arch of the bridge crossed by the drive; old woodland on the left and broad brown ripply reaches of the river on the right, it bends to the north and brings one to a first sight of Ballynahinch Lake, or at least of its broad south-western bay, for the narrow arm of the lake stretching eastwards for a couple of miles is hidden by forestry. The nearest of the Twelve Pins, Binn Leitrí, rears up steeply from the further shore as if looking down into the demesne with a stony, glittering glare, but, as Thackeray noted in describing his ride to Ballynahinch on the Bianconi car in 1842, 'Wild and wide as the prospect around us is, it has somehow a kindly, friendly, look.' And, in the devious way of literature, his confession of failure to capture such scenes is in itself most expressive of them:

But the best guide-book that ever was written cannot set the view before the mind's eye of the reader, and I won't attempt to pile up words in place of these wild mountains, over which the clouds as they passed, or the sunshine as it went and came, cast every variety of tint, light, and shadow; nor can it be expected that long, level sentences, however smooth and shining, can be made to pass as representations of those calm lakes by which we took our way. All one can do is to lay down the pen and ruminate, and cry 'beautiful' once more; and to the reader say, 'Come and see!'

At the water's edge the path divides; to the left it continues around the shoreline, to the right a narrow footbridge carries it across the river where it flows out of the lake. Taking the second alternative, following the path for a few paces into the shade of ancient twisty lichen-festooned trees, and peering down to the right into the twilight of the understorey of the wood, one makes out a little recess holding a gleam of water, a spring well with two or three steps leading down to it from an opening in the low dry-stone wall enclosing it, all so mossy and ferny it is hard to distinguish among the hollows and hummocks of the forest floor. This is Tobar Feichín, St Fechin's holy well, unvisited, its cult long lapsed, but of ancient significance, as I will show later on. A hundred yards or so south of the well is a disused graveyard, but it has been so blasted by recent felling of spruce forest and the collapse of one or two wind-staggered giant broadleaved trees that last time I looked for it I could hardly make it out among the chaos of pros-trate trunks and shattered branches. To find it, follow the path onwards from the well, round the bend of the river, and when you come to a large isolated sycamore with a forked trunk, turn to the left and head into the undergrowth, following a sheep path that is only made visible by the tufts of wool snagged on bramble stems. From earlier visits I remember the graveyard as measuring about twenty by fifteen paces, having the low tumbled remains of a wall about it, with many anonymous graves marked by small boulders, and one small recumbent tombstone. The latter is still to be seen; it is a limestone slab of the sort that used to be imported from the Aran Islands (which are all of limestone and made an industry out of cutting and carving gravestones for Connemara). It has a motif of crossed bones surmounted by a cross and flanked by winged angels' heads at the top, and it is inscribed, as well as I can make out:

> Here lieth the
> Remains of James
> Mulroy Who dep . . .
> this life November . . .
> 1825, aged 6 Months
> 1 day Erect^d by his
> Father Mich^L Mulroy

Some family of means and consequence in the little world of Ballynahinch had this memorial set up to their child; I connect them with a 'major-domo' at the Castle whom Thackeray, visiting it in 1842, discreetly and perhaps slightly mistakenly refers to as Mr J—n M—ll—y. This graveyard or *cillín* gives its name to the little townland of Killeen, on the south bank of the river, which together with that of Ballynahinch on the north makes up the castle demesne. And it too has its story.

If what I am writing here is a guide to the hotel's amenities I should add that the path now turns westwards and delivers one back to the drive and so to the hotel in time for afternoon tea; if I am borrowing that form to establish a sequence of landmarks in the demesne before launching out onto the seas of history, then I must return to the bifurcation of the woodland ways just before the footbridge, and follow the other path, which winds around the southern and then western shores of the lake, climbing slopes knobbly with tree roots and tunnelling through overarching rhododendron bushes. It soon passes a smart-looking new house with trim lawns and black railings with gold spear-heads, incongruous in this tangled setting; it belongs to one of the hotel's shareholders, and is on the site of an old boathouse. When the site was being cleared for it an old cannon was rediscovered in the water close by, a corroded but still massive cast-iron cylinder six feet long, slightly tapered, with a muzzle aperture about four inches in diameter. This has now been positioned on the banks of the lake a little further on, mounted as if to threaten a little island with a squarish ruin on it, which would surely have been far out of its range. The cannon was found on this island in 1910 according to Richard Hayward's book, and the tower house there, from which the hotel inherits the name of Ballynahinch Castle, is the ultimate goal of this devious and divaricating walk.

Beyond this point the lakeside path soon forks again. The left-hand branch climbs along one side of a steep little gully with a stream in its bottom and, lying in tangles of vegetation, some huge old pipes of riveted iron plate. A little further up the path clambers to a stile giving onto a narrow byroad, under which the stream passes by a tall archway half blocked by a collapsed sluice-gate; all this wreckage is the remains of a little hydroelectric station that used to power the Castle's heating system. The other turning, to the right, continues along the western end of the lake and soon emerges onto the well-kept private driveway of the Old Manor, an exclusive time-share development of holiday apartments, facing onto the lake and wrapped away from the commonality by ancient woodland. This used to be Humanity Dick's stables; they were converted in 1994, having lain picturesquely derelict for a long time. Richard Hayward describes them as they were half a century ago:

Built of limestone and Connemara marble, they look as if they'll endure till the crack of doom. Four squat towers stand, one at each corner of a range of buildings which enclose a central court, and when this establishment was in its heyday of hunters and grooms it must indeed have been impressive. No wonder the guide-books of the period say things like: *Marble halls we have heard of in song, but here even the stables are built of marble, and Connemara marble, to boot.*

They did not endure without radical disruption, though, and no detailed description of the former state of this unusual edifice exists.

The Ordnance Survey map of 1819 shows the stables as consisting of two parallel buildings running north–south, but the map of 1898 shows the narrow spaces between the ends of the buildings as built up, completing the courtyard. The intervening ranges of buildings have been almost completely reshaped, but I believe the four corner towers are much as they were: three storeys, battlemented, with the lower third of their walls 'battered', that is, sloping inwards slightly from the ground up. This military aspect of the structure makes me wonder if in fact it also served as a barracks, for Richard Martin, as well as being Colonel of the Galway Volunteers, headed a troop of yeomanry, some of whom were stationed at Ballynahinch and might have been active in its defence during the campaign of the rural terrorists called the Terry Alts, in Richard's son's time. As a historic relic with many questions to answer, these stables, I feel, should have been preserved, or at least thoroughly investigated before their reconstruction in 1994.

On the peninsulas of the lake shore to either side of the Old Manor are patches of oak forest, highly regarded by botanists for their ferns and lichens. These woods were here before the Martins started their planting, and so probably can be said to be aboriginal; in any case they are of an ancientness rare in untreed Connemara. Picking one's way to the shore through them one sees near at hand, between the swags of foliage overhanging the water, the little castle on its island. Sir Bernard Burke (he of *Burke's Peerage*) writes of it in his essay 'Princess of Connemara', on the touching misfortunes of Humanity Dick's granddaughter, in a book irresistibly entitled *Vicissitudes of Families*:

The peasants of the neighbourhood still know these mouldering fragments by the name of *Dick Martin's Prison*, and will tell how the Lord of Connemara used, in somewhat doubtful exercise of his feudal rights, to confine therein such of his tenants as sinned against the laws of humanity towards the brute creation.

This, at last, is Ballynahinch, Baile na hInse, 'the settlement of the island'; the name spread from it to the townland on the lakeside, and then to all the vast western territory between the ridgeline of the Mám Tuirc Mountains and the Atlantic at Slyne Head and Cleggan Head that the Elizabethans denominated the Barony of Ballynahinch. It is the historic kernel of Connemara, and the place from which to start tracing its crooked past.

The Masters of Ballynahinch

The Island

In engravings from nineteenth-century travel books the castle rises in a pale glimmering out of still waters in which its reflection descends to mysterious depths; the romantic perspective captures its symbolic stature as Connemara's navel, but in the physical world it appears from the shore as a brownish rectangular stump. I rowed out to it once in company with researchers who were to measure it up for inclusion in *The Archaeological Inventory of County Galway*.

The island is about thirty-one yards in diameter, and there is enough tumbled stone around its rim to support the tradition, recorded by John O'Donovan in his letters to the Ordnance Survey in 1839, that it is at least in part artificial, i.e. that the castle was built on a pre-existent island cashel. Lake dwellings from medieval times and even as far back as the Neolithic are frequent in Ireland; most of them are crannogs, built largely of wood, but in Connemara about half the known examples are platforms of stone, perhaps based on an islet or a shallow spot, and rimmed by a stone cashel wall. The *Inventory* lists twenty-three lake dwellings in Connemara; one or two more have been found since its publication in 1994, and no doubt several other impenetrably overgrown islands in the area's three hundred or so lakes would turn out to be lake dwellings if they were investigated.

The castle, ragged with ivy, occupies the centre of the island, the rest of which is dense with hawthorn, holly and willow bushes, and a couple of lovely guelder rose trees. It is a simple tower house consisting of four rooms, about nine yards by seven, one above the other. The interior of the ground-floor room bears patches of fancy plastering and a moulded cornice, and large window embrasures have been knocked out of the old masonry. In one corner are the remains of a spiral staircase, like the building's spinal cord, and on the first floor there is a latrine passage in the thickness of the wall. In a two-storey extension built out to the west there are peculiar curved brick-built surfaces, the remains of a kiln and an oven, and above these, on the outside of the tower, more brickwork, perhaps of a flue. Ceilings, garret and roof have long fallen, and in the extension an extraordinary grove of pallid twayblade plants, two or three feet high, struggle up towards the rectangle of sky above. The history of western Connemara, that is, the Barony of Ballynahinch, is summarized in these structures. The decorative plastering and big windows date from the use of the ground floor as a tea room by some of its later owners, prob- ably the Berridges; the extension was a brewery built by Richard Martin probably around the end of the eighteenth century; the tower house itself was used by him as a prison for tenants who maltreated their beasts of burden, but it was built long before his time, by the O'Flahertys when they were lords of Connemara, while the underlying island cashel is thought to have been a stronghold of the Conmaicne Mara, the medieval people from whom Connemara derives its name, and whose own name is rooted in myth.

Indeed, the Conmaicne people claimed that their progenitor was Feargus Mac Roich, the unassuageably lusty owner of the Lia Fál, the great phallus, now turned to stone, which stands on the top of the Hill of Tara. Medieval genealogists held that he had a son, Conmac, by Queen Maebh, from whom are descended the Conmaicne, the 'seed of Conmac', or alternatively that Conmac was the son of Oirbsiu Mór from whom Loch Oirbsen, now corruptly known as Lough Corrib, was named, and who himself was descended from Feargus. In early historic times the Conmaicne dwelled around Dunmore in what is now North Galway, and, perhaps around AD 500, radiated from there into parts of Westmeath, Longford, Leitrim and Mayo, while a branch of them who settled in the Atlantic extremes of Galway became known as the Conmaicne Mara, the Conmaicne of the Sea. Now, although I believe that right living in a place – as I try to live in Connemara – entails a neighbourly acquaintance with those who lived there in previous times, I have found out so little about the very people who gave Connemara its name that to me they are ghosts faded beyond all recognition. References to them are few. It is claimed that Caireach, son of a chieftain of Conmaicne Mara and the first of his line to become a Christian, was baptized by St Patrick himself, whom he invited into his territory to propagate the faith. Their later chieftains were the Ó Cadhla (usually anglicized as O'Kealy or Keeley), one of whom, Carnen, is mentioned in the *Annals of Inishfallen* as having commanded a contingent of the Conmaicne Mara at the Battle of Clontarf in 1014, when Brian Boru defeated the Vikings. Perhaps Carnen marshalled his men on the lake shore here; perhaps it was for his hospitality on the island that one of his successors living in the 1160s earned these praiseful lines, from a *Metrical Topography* composed in about 1350:

> Over Conmaicne Mara great,
> Was Ó Cadhla, friend of feasts.

But if it was so, the venison-reek of his last feast drifted off into the depths of the forest so long ago that not a molecule of it remains. And, since there are traces of other lake dwellings not far away, including one visible after droughty weather as a circle of stones in Ballinafad Lake, a mile to the east, another in Loch Caimín and a third in Lough Inagh; is there any reason to think that Ballynahinch was the central stronghold of the Conmaicne Mara? Well, I can advance an argument to that effect.

According to Roderick O'Flaherty, writing in 1684, there was on the island of Ballynahinch 'a hallowed monument of St. Fechin, to whom there is a well dedicated at Cara-more, where the river parts with the lake'. The remark might suggest the pre-eminence of this island cashel, and hint at the reason for the O'Flahertys' later adoption of it as their own chief place in central Connemara. 'Cara-more' means 'big ford', and the old bridle-way into western Connemara from Galway used to cross the Ballynahinch River where it flows out of the lake, which is about half a mile southeast of the island; nowadays this track is just one of the hotel's woodland walks, and the footbridge near St Fechin's well carries it across the river. St Fechin is chiefly associated with Fore in Westmeath, but he also founded a monastery at Cong and one in Sligo, and is said to have journeyed thence to the island of Omey, off the west coast of Connemara, where he died of the plague in 664, having established monasteries there and on High Island, five miles further out into the Atlantic. A number of holy wells, such as one at the crest of the pass called Mám Tuirc in the Maumturk Mountains, which was the north-eastern gateway of Connemara even down to the early nineteenth century, and this one at Ballynahinch, as well as a stone platform on the shore, the 'bed' he slept in before crossing the sands to Omey, are traditionally regarded as traces of his passage. Perhaps, therefore, 'Cara-more' was a recognized crossing place even in the days of the Conmaicne Mara. So far as I can make out, it is the only ford on the river between the long chain of lakes that stretches far to the north-east from Ballynahinch, and the sea to the south-west at Tuaim Beola; so it would have been a place of military and commercial significance, and the lake island was well situated to watch over it.

The Conmaicne Mara were virtually deleted from history by the O'Flahertys, who moved into Connemara driven by the westward tide of the Norman conquest. Before that time the O'Flahertys had lorded it over the fertile limestone plains east of Lough Corrib. There had been O'Flaherty kings of Connacht in far-off days, but having lost power to the O'Connors they later provided kings to Iar-Chonnacht or West Connacht only (which included territory on either side of Lough Corrib at that period), and they were finally driven west of the lake by the Norman de Burgos in 1238. A branch of them evidently settled at Ballynahinch, as they founded a Carmelite monastery there in the fourteenth century (its site is unknown, and it has been suggested that it lies under the present Ballynahinch Castle Hotel, or that the *cillín* near St Fechin's well marks its site). In the following century they founded the Dominican abbey near the river mouth at Tuaim Beola. The Normans built their characteristic tower houses throughout the former O'Flaherty lands, and by the sixteenth century the O'Flahertys were imitating them. There were tower houses associated with or built by the O'Flahertys along their eastern borders with the de Burgo lands, and spaced out rather regularly around the coast, at Indreabhán, Leitir Mealláin and Aird in south Connemara, at Bunowen, Streamstown Bay and Renvyle on the Atlantic shore, and at one central site, the strategically located island of Ballynahinch. The castle of Ballynahinch was built in the early years of Queen Elizabeth's reign, i.e. soon after 1558, by the chieftain of Aird, Tadhg na Buile (Tadhg of the rage or madness – the O'Flahertys went in for intimidatory nicknames), according to one account; he is said to have robbed the deserted abbey at Tuaim Beola of its stones for the purpose.

The O'Flahertys feuded among themselves now and then; they fought at first with their neighbours to the north, the seafaring O'Malleys of Mayo, but then joined with them in alliances cemented by intermarriage, but theirs was probably a relatively prosperous and settled period in Connemara's history. They had their dependent clans, including the O'Hallorans and the Duanes; the O'Lees were their hereditary doctors and the Canavans their officers. They exported wool to the Continent and shipped in wine and other rich goods, and therefore were regarded by the growing mercantile town of Galway as smugglers and pirates, the 'Ferocious O'Flahertys'. In summer they removed with their herds of cattle to the booleys in the hills and lived in large temporary buildings, accompanied by their ladies, their priests and their wolfhounds. Under their protection the Welsh-Norman Joyces settled in what is still called the Joyce Country, east of the Mám Tuirc Mountains, and the O'Tooles came from Leinster to Omey Island on the Atlantic fringe of Connemara. English law could not reach into these almost trackless fastnesses, and while most of Ireland was being incorporated into the feudal system, under which land was heritable and held as a grant in return for service to an overlord and ultimately to the Crown, the O'Flahertys still lived by the old Brehon Law, their territory being the communal property of the clan, and their chief chosen for his ability out of a small number of eligible contenders. All this eventually came to an end, amid some bloodshed and much paperwork, when it became clear to the Tudor functionaries that diplomacy and bribery would be more effective than soldiery in the conquest of Connemara.

In 1538 Henry VIII's Deputy visited Galway and called upon the nearest O'Flaherty chief, Hugh Óg of Moycullen Castle, to come into town and submit, which he did, whereupon the head of the senior branch of the clan, Dónal Crón of Aughnanure Castle, seized Moycullen and had Hugh starved to death. Then another of the eastern and junior branch of the O'Flahertys, Murchadh na dTua (Murrough of the battleaxes), routed an expeditionary force sent into Iar-Chonnacht by Lord Clanricard, and the English had to buy his loyalty by declaring him chief of all Iar-Chonnacht and helping him seize the castle of Aughnanure and Moycullen. But since the rightful successor to the chieftaincy was the O'Flaherty of Bunowen and Ballynahinch, Dónal an Chogaidh (of the combat), this provoked more feuding, of which Ballynahinch became the epicentre, and Dónal's wife, the young Grace O'Malley, was thus drawn into the tangled history of the castle. In 1584 Murchadh's son captured the castle from the sons of Tadhg na Buile (a later deposition of Grace O'Malley's states that he built the castle, and another source says he built its lower floor, but these accounts must mean that he refortified or strengthened it). He held off the counter-attacks of the western faction represented by Dónal and the sons of Tadhg; in fact, says the *Annals of the Four Masters*, 'he left not a single head of cattle in any part of their country to which he came that he did not kill or carry off'. Then he pursued the westerners to the Aran Islands, and fell upon them at daybreak as they 'lay between sleeping and waking', at a place still called Log na Marbh, the hollow of the dead. 'Unfriendly was the salutation he made them on that shore, and indeed the island [Ballynahinch] was not worth all that was done about it on that one day', is the judgement of the Four Masters on the affair. Later the English made peace between the two factions, and reinstalled the Bunowen O'Flahertys in Ballynahinch.

In 1585 Queen Elizabeth's Lord Deputy in Ireland brought forward a comprehensive settlement known as the Composition of Connaught, according to which the chieftains were to give up the clan territories and receive them back as feudal grants from the Crown. Under Gaelic law these territories were not the chief's either to bequeath or to surrender, but the prospect of becoming a landlord with English protection of his property rights was a strong persuasion to several of the O'Flahertys. Murchadh na dTua had just become Sir Murrough, and he signed up to the sell-out.

It was in connection with this settlement that Connacht was divided into counties and baronies, so that the old territory of Conmaicne Mara – the land west of the Mám Tuirc Mountains and the Inver River near Ros Muc – became the Barony of Ballynahinch. (Nowadays Connemara is informally understood also to include the Joyce Country, east of the mountains, and the lowlands from Ros Muc almost to the city of Galway.) Hardiman, in the magnificently generous appendices to his edition of Roderick O'Flaherty's *West or H-Iar Connaught*, gives this document, so redolent of the English mission of civilization by expropriation, in full; I transcribe some passages relevant to Ballynahinch – for their texture of crackly old parchment as much as for their fascinating content, and noting as I do so that while castles tumble and empires fade away, lawyers' phraseology stands to the good through the centuries.

Indentures of Composition

A.D. 1585

The Country of the O'Fflahertyes called Eyre-Conaght.

THIS INDENTURE made between the right Honorable Sir John Perrotte Knighte, Lorde Deputy Generall of Irlande, for and on the behaulfe of the Queenes most excellent Matie of the one parte, and Sr Moroghe ne Doe of Aghnenure in the county of Galway Knight, otherwise called O'Fflahertie – Donell Crone O'Fflahertie of the Cnocke, competitor for the name of O'Fflahertie – Teig ne Boolye of the Arde, otherwise called O'Fflahertie of both Con o Marrice [and a score or so of other notables] – for and in the behalf of themselves and the rest of the Cheiftaynes, ffreeholders, Gent. Ffarmers and inhabitants, having land or holdings within the countrey or territorie of the O'FFLAHERTYES CONTREY called EYRE-CONAGHT, their heires and assignes, of the other parte:

WITNESSETH, that wher the said whole country of Eyre Conaught is devided into fower barronyes, that is to witt, the barrony of Moycullyn, the barrony of Ballynehynsye, the barrony of Ross, and the barrony of the illes of Arren, which containeth in themselves, as well by aunccient Division as by late Inquisition and presentments hereunto annexed, the number of 318 quarters of land, estemeing everie quarter, with his pastur, woodd and bogge, at 120 acres . . . [here follows a list of 'townes', i.e. townlands, with the number of quarters in each].

The said Sir Moroghe O'Fflaherty, knight, Donyll Crone O'Fflahertie [etc.] . . . for that the said Right honorable the Lo. Deputie dothe promise, covenaunt and graunte to and with the said cheiftaines . . . that they and every of them their heires and assignes, for their lands within the said contrey, shall, from and after the date hereof, be freelie and wholly discharged, acquitted and exonerated for ever, off and from all manner of cesses, taxes, chardges, exaccons, cuttings, ymposicons, purveying, eating, findinge or bearing of soldiers, and from all other burdens whatsoever, other than the rents, reservacons, and chardges here-after in this Indenture specified, and to be enacted by parleament: willingly and thankfully for them their heires and assignes, given and graunted, licke as they hereby do give and graunte, to the said right Honorable the Lo. Deputy and his heirs, to the use of the Queene's most excellent Matie her heirs and successors for ever, one yearelie rent chardge of tenn shillings of good and lawful current money of England, going out of everie q^r of 280 q^{rs} of the aforesaid number of 318 q^{rs} of land, which in the whole amounteth yearelie to the some of £140 ster. payable at the feastes of St Michaell tharchangell and Easter . . .

And further yt is condiscended, concluded and agreed . . . that the names, stilles, and titles of captayneships, taynistships and all other Irishe aucthorities and jurisdictions heretofore used by the O'Fflahertyes, together with all ellection and customarie division of land, occasioning great streefe and contention emongest them, shall from henceforthe be utterlie abollyshed, extinct, renounsed, and put backe within the said countrey of Eyreconnaght, for ever, but that their lands and inherytants shall lynialie discend from the father to the sonn, accordinge to the course and order of the lawes of England . . .

IN WITNESS whereof . . . the said cheiftaynes, gent. freeholders, ffermours, and the rest above named, have hereunto put their seales and subscribed their names, the second of September, anno Domini 1585, and in the xxvii[th] yeare of the reygne of our Soveraigne lady Elizabeth, by the grace of God Queene of England, Fraunce and Irelande, defender of the fayth, &c . . .

SR. MORROGH NE DO O'FFLAHERTIE
    his + mark.

Several lesser gentlemen also signed, but although Tadhg na Buile and the sons of Dónal an Chogaidh and Grace O'Malley were confirmed in the enjoyment of their accustomed castles and lands by it, these western O'Flahertys largely ignored the matter. Making the Barony of Ballynahinch a reality, with all it implied of the acceptance of a new topography and the abandonment of ancient Irish traditions, was to take much time and blood. The aggressive new President of Connacht, Sir Richard Bingham, soon provoked a rebellion by his attempts to enforce the provisions of the Composition; some of the Burkes (descendants of the Norman de Burgos, but long since thoroughly gaelicized) rose against him, including Grace O'Malley's son-in-law Richard Burke, known as the Devil's Hook. Captain John Bingham, the President's brother, made an expedition into Mayo, arrested Grace O'Malley and brought her into Galway, where she narrowly escaped hanging, and had her huge herds of cattle and horses confiscated. Captain Bingham then proceeded against the western O'Flahertys, although they had not joined the rebels. According to a deposition by Grace O'Malley, her son Owen withdrew with his followers and herds into an island (it must have been Omey, a few miles north of Bunowen, which is accessible by foot when the tide is out); Captain Bingham arrived on the shore opposite the island and called on them to provide him with victuals, whereupon the generous but foolish O'Flaherty ferried all Bingham's soldiery into the island and entertained them 'with the best cheer they had'. That night Bingham's men arrested Owen and eighteen of his chief followers, and the next day drove vast numbers of beasts out of the island – 4,000 cows, 500 stud mares and horses and 1,000 sheep, claimed Grace O'Malley – leaving the rest of Owen's men naked on the island. They brought the prisoners and the booty to Ballynahinch, where Owen's fellows were hanged, among them the ninety-year-old Omey chieftain Tibbott O'Toole. (The oak that served as gallows is still pointed out, near the old stable block; sensitive souls have seen apparitions there.) During the following night a false alarm was raised, and Owen was stabbed to death as he lay in bonds in a house nearby.

Bingham's ferocity quieted the western O'Flahertys for a time but aroused Sir Murrough to join the Burkes' intermittent rebellion, in which cause he saw his lands laid waste and his sons and grandson killed. In the end he made an abject submission, was regranted the territory of Iar-Chonnacht, but was left too weakened and wearied to exercise his authority over it, and soon died in his castle of Aughnanure. In the west Grace's younger son by Dónal, Murchadh na Maor (so called from the number of sergeants or stewards he needed to run his wide dominion), whose abode was the castle of Bunowen, also held those of Ballynahinch, Doon at Streamstown, and Renvyle, and thus commanded almost the entire coast of Iar-Chonnacht; he died in 1626 and was succeeded by his son Murchadh na Mart, who owes his name to his custom of feasting his followers on fifty beeves (*mart*) every Shrove Tuesday night in preparation for Lent. The Earl of Strafford, Lord Deputy of Ireland, is said to have made the dangerous journey through Iar-Chonnacht to visit the latter at Bunowen in 1637, was well entertained, and knighted his host.

Nevertheless, when an insurrection broke out in Ulster in 1641 and then spread to the rest of the country, taking advantage of the civil war in England between King Charles I and his rebellious parliament, so hostile to Catholics, the new Sir Murrough joined with the other O'Flahertys in support of the Confederate Catholics. His longboats, commanding the west coast of Ireland, protected the rising against seaborne attack, and in 1642, together with his younger brother Colonel Edmund, he brought hundreds of his clansmen into Galway to assist the townspeople in besieging the English fort there, which had declared for the Parliamentarian side. This act led to the utter destruction of O'Flaherty power once the Parliamentarians had defeated the Royalists in England and sent Cromwell and his army to suppress the Irish rebels. The town of Galway, together with the fort at Killeany in the Aran Islands, held out longer than the rest of the country but surrendered to the Cromwellians in 1652 after a nine-month siege. Aran was briefly recaptured by a body of men from the rebellion's last strongholds, Iar-Chonnacht and Inishbofin, but had to submit when a huge force of footsoldiers was shipped out to the island and another force marched westwards along the coast from Galway. Soon the O'Flahertys were facing charges of treason. A party of soldiers found a terrified Colonel Edmund hiding with his wife in a cave near Renvyle in north-western Connemara, and brought him into Galway where he was tried and hanged. Sir Murrough himself was lucky enough to be allowed to go into retirement in the Aran Islands, but his lands, including Ballynahinch, were forfeited.

The subsequent period in Connemara was one of slaughter, enslavement, famine and plague. The conflicting Acts, and Acts to explain Acts, concerning confiscated lands passed by rapidly succeeding administrations during the rebellion, the English civil war, the Cromwellian Commonwealth, the restoration of Charles II in 1660, and then the war in 1690 and 1691 between Catholic King James II and Protestant William of Orange, produced a legal chaos in which opportunists could flourish. Soon after the uprising in 1641 Charles I's disaffected parliament passed an Act for the confiscation of the estates of those in rebellion, and after the Cromwellian victory another Act laid it down that forfeited lands in Connacht and Clare were to be used to reward the soldiery and the adventurers, that is those who had adventured money to finance the Commonwealth cause. The Restoration raised Catholic hopes of restitution; under the Irish Parliament's Act of Settlement of 1662 Catholics who could prove their innocency of rebellion were to have their estates restored, and the Protestant grantees recompensed with lands elsewhere. An Act of Explanation was soon necessary to resolve the conflicting claims that arose, and the upshot was that the Cromwellian settlements remained largely in force. Under James II the Act of Settlement was repealed, but James was ousted by his Protestant parliament's new defender, William, before much was done to restore their former estates to the Catholics; indeed there wasn't enough land in Ireland to fulfil all the promises that had been made.

In an effort to stabilize this confusion so propitious to lawyers, a series of huge volumes summarizing the changes in land-ownership since the rebellion were drawn up in the 1660s to 1680s. These manuscript *Books of Survey and Distribution* have been edited and published, a record of inexhaustible interest. They are laid out by counties, baronies, parishes and 'denominations', most of which are identifiable by name, with some puzzling and ingenious deductions, as the townlands familiar today. I have a boxful of photocopies of the parts covering Connemara; the breadth of the sheets gives consultation of them the deliberate tempo of a ritual. For each denomination the name of the proprietor in 1641 is given, with a description of the size and quality of the land, the acreages profitable and unprofitable, and the current owner, marked with a little symbol indicating the type of decree or certificate of his ownership. For the present focus of interest, the townland of Ballynahinch in the parish of Moyrus, for instance, the pre-Rebellion owner is given as 'Murragh o Flaherty', as it is for nearly all the denominations of the barony; he would have been the grandson of the Sir Murrough who was granted all of Iar-Chonnacht under Elizabeth, and his ownership of Ballynahinch was paper-thin as the territory was actually in the hands of the Bunowen O'Flahertys and challenged by the O'Flahertys of Aird. The denomination consists of:

1 quar of rough mountain 1/20th pt. profitable
A parcell of Arrable
A parcell of wood and pasture 1/2 profitable

It is curious that the castle is not mentioned, as other castles are; perhaps it fell into disuse at this time. There are 2,713 unprofitable and 143 profitable acres in the 'rough mountain', and the other parcels amount to another 71 acres. (A quarter was 120 acres of standard arable or pasturage, or its productive equivalent in other land, so in stony and boggy Connemara a quarter could be very large.) Finally, the current proprietor is given as Sir Thomas Merredith. Had this part of the record been made a few years earlier the name would have been that of Edmond Fitzgerald of County Cork, who had forfeited his estate of Ballymaloe and was given instead 1,500 acres of the land taken from the western O'Flahertys. But he was restored to his former lands under the Act of Settlement, and the 1,500 acres were divided between Merredith and Trinity College, Dublin. Whether Merredith, who was one of Cromwell's commissioners, ever visited his acquisitions or no, he soon parted with them to a Richard Martin, who also figures as the new proprietor of many denominations in the baronies of Ballynahinch and further east in Connemara. Thus to the Ferocious O'Flahertys succeeded the Litigious Martins (the ancient nickname is recorded by Caesar Otway in 1839 and is mentioned in one or two more recent books by members of this intensely self-aware family). This Richard Martin, a Catholic, came out of the legal whirpool of not only the Cromwellian interregnum and the Restoration but also the Glorious Revolution of King Billy, clutching deeds that made him the largest landowner in fee simple of the 'Three Kingdoms' of England, Scotland and Ireland. Even the learned editors of the *Books of Survey and Distribution* are puzzled as to how he did it

– but he was a lawyer, and his nickname was Nimble Dick. I must go back in time some way to give the new master of Ballynahinch a background.

The Martins were one of the fourteen merchant families the Cromwellians contemptuously termed 'the Tribes of Galway' and who later adopted that name with pride. Other Tribesmen we hear of in the history of Connemara include the Blakes, D'Arcys and Joyces. Norman in origin, they settled in Galway around 1300, under the aegis of the de Burgos. Until their coming, says Hardiman, the historian of the town, it was 'but an ordinary place, with only thatched houses and some castles, but it was by the new colonies and septs, made famous to the world, for trading faithfully, discharging their credit, good education, charities and hospitality both at home and abroad'. The first Martin of Galway was Oliver, a Crusader who had earned his arms (a Calvary cross between the sun in splendour and the crescent moon) with Richard Coeur de Lion in the Holy Land, and had come to Ireland with Strongbow himself. A Peter Martin was one of the town's first two sheriffs, and Martins figure in the list of the town's mayors in the 1500s. Already by the 1620s the family was making inroads into O'Flaherty territory west of the town: Robert Martin, Mayor of Galway, who died in 1622, had bought Ross, which is some sixteen miles north-west of Galway, from the O'Flahertys, and Jasper, who died in 1629, had acquired lands as far out as Casla in south Connemara, by mortgage from Murrough O'Flaherty. Law and credit were by degrees prevailing over muscle and clan loyalties.

The Martins suffered for their Catholicism during the suppression of the 1641 rebellion and the consequent dispossession of Catholics, while the notional redresses made under Charles II after his restoration did the family little good. Their then head, Robert Martin of Ross, who had had his town house confiscated and granted to the Cromwellian Edward Eyre, got an order from the King for the return of his property, but Eyre merely laughed at it and later successfully defended his own claims before the Irish

House of Commons, thus precipitating a feud between their descendants that lasted for four generations. This Robert had three sons: Jasper's offspring formed the senior branch of the family, the Martins of Ross; James died without issue, and Richard gave rise to the Martins of Dangan (between Galway and Ross) and later of Ballynahinch. There was a current saying in their time, 'From Jasper, James and Nimble Dick, good Lord deliver us!' – an echo of the inscription that is said to have stood above the town's northern gate in earlier days, 'From the ferocious O'Flahertys good Lord deliver us'. The Martins earned their reputation as formidable adversaries on the duelling ground as well as in the courts. Nimble Dick especially was a noted swordsman; tradition has it that 'no matter what blow was aimed at him, he would defend it with the sole of his foot'. As a performer on the field of law he amply restored the family's fortunes: he had acquired lands by mortgage from the waning O'Flahertys, been transplanted into others confiscated from the O'Flahertys because of their part in the rebellion, was restored to his previous estates, and somehow managed to hold on to the lot, thus assembling an estate of nearly a quarter of a million acres, most of it admittedly of utter wilderness – all this without compromising his Catholic sympathies. During the war fought out largely in Ireland between James II and William of Orange, Nimble Dick served with Luttrell's cavalry at the historic defeat of the Catholic cause at Aughrim in 1691, but then threw himself on the mercy of the Williamite commander de Ginkle, and helped him draw up the articles of surrender for Galway. These turned out to be surprisingly lenient, but Martin was excluded from them by a technicality, having been elected, but never sworn in, as a freeman of the town. However, during the war he had succoured some Protestant supporters of King William, and on the strength of this he went off to London to plead his cause, and returned with all his titles confirmed; it took him four years and cost him, he said, 'a hatful of sovereigns'.

Nimble Dick then applied, successfully, for his lands west of Galway to be erected into the Manor of Clare (named from a place in the present-day village of Oughterard where the family would later build a house, Clareville), which gave him rights to hold fairs and courts, and to levy fines for his own use. There was perhaps an understanding behind this settlement that he would keep the remnant O'Flahertys under control. The legendarily gigantic Éamonn Láidir (the strong), a grandson of the Colonel Edmund O'Flaherty executed by the Cromwellians, is said to have had frequent hand-to-hand encounters with Nimble Dick; they fought on horseback, with swords, and since Martin was always surrounded by his followers he would get away, leaving the O'Flaherty to hack his way out of his troubles. When the horse of Nimble Dick's eldest son Robert came home riderless one day, it was because the O'Flahertys had murdered the lad. The former and the new rulers of Connemara were to be at loggerheads for generations to come; they even had a little battle in the 1840s, to be mentioned later.

Nimble Dick's other son, Anthony, settled at the house his father built at Dangan, and sent his own eldest son Robert, illegally and secretly, to study at the Catholic University of Louvain. This pious education does not seem to have cooled Robert's head. In records of a court case one reads of how he burst into a billiards room over a coffee house to challenge the man he thought had spat on him as he passed down the street below, and, when one of the company present picked up a chair in self-defence, Robert thrust at him through its framework several times. The man died, but Robert got off; the jury were all from Galway, and Galway juries were, it seems, highly regarded for their broad views on such affairs. A few years later, in 1740, this Robert built himself a house (of which I think no trace remains) at the head of Cleggan Bay in the far north-west of Connemara. In 1745 he set off, disguised as a peasant, to join Bonny Prince Charlie's romantic failure of a rising in Scotland, but was arrested at an inn when he aroused suspicion by ordering a fricassée of chicken. Later in the same year he took out the Protestant certificate in order to ensure his inheritance, while remaining a Jacobite at heart. He married a Bridget Barnewall, sister of Lord Trimlestown, another of whose sisters was married to Lord Gormanston and a third to Lord Mountgarret; all three of these eminent connections were supporters of the Catholic cause. And, at some date unknown, he built a small plain house at Ballynahinch. Perhaps it was a head-quarters for the extensive smuggling trade of the region, and perhaps, as he claimed, it was an inn, for it was by the old bridle-path, just west of the Cara-more. In any case it was the origin of the house that would usurp the name of the old castle on the lake island and become the famous seat of the Martins of Ballynahinch.

Dick Martin Rules

Of all the Martins it is Robert and Bridget's son Richard who has left the brightest after-image on history's retina. As 'Hairtrigger Dick' he was a noted duellist; as 'Humanity Dick' he was the chief founder of the Society for the Prevention of Cruelty to Animals. When questioned on the contradiction between his cavalier atti-tude to human lives and his solicitude for dumb brutes, he replied, 'Sir, an ox cannot hold a pistol!' As a Member of Parliament, his contributions were sometimes drowned in laughter, but he won his point in the end. Dozens of his courageous deeds, high-spirited gestures and genial quips have been preserved in the memoirs of his contemporaries or passed down (and no doubt polished up like the family silver) through subsequent generations of Martins, and he figures in Connemara folklore too. In the 1950s or earlier the writer Richard Hayward was told a story about him by a gillie at Ballynahinch:

A celebrated Continental duellist was engaged to meet Martin on some pretext or another. It became known, as such things always become known in Connemara, that this foreigner, who seemed to bear a charmed life, wore special mail beneath his clothing, and just before the duel one of Martin's servants said to his master, in Irish: *buail é mar mharbhuigheann fear Conamara an mhuc – Hit him where the Connemara man kills the pig.* And Martin, who was a dead shot, took great pleasure in dispatching his deceitful opponent with a bullet behind his ear.

Richard Martin, born in 1754 at Dangan, was sent to school at Harrow; it was understood that a Protestant education would enable him to enter Parliament and fight for Catholic emancipation. He then entered Trinity College, Cambridge, but left without taking a degree. His first election campaign in Galway was not a success as his numerous tenants were nearly all Catholic and therefore could not vote, but he bought a seat elsewhere, and so entered the Irish Parliament for the first time in 1776. Martin naturally gravitated to the grouping known as the Patriots, led by the great orator Henry Grattan. In the following year he married Elizabeth Vesey of Holymount in Mayo, a connection that brought him into relations with a galaxy of eminences including the new Viceroy, the Earl of Buckinghamshire. They soon moved to a rather grand house in Dublin for the Parliament, and plunged into an energetic social life. The American War of Independence had aroused Irish enthusiasm for free trade, and the Volunteering movement was at its height; in 1779 Martin became Colonel of the Galway Volunteers, who were calling for the removal of the restrictions with which England had cumbered Irish trade, and for the repeal of the ancient law under which no bill could be introduced in the Irish Parliament before it had been approved by the Lord Lieutenant's Irish Privy Council and the English Privy Council. Called to the Bar in 1781, Martin accepted a brief, without a fee, for the pleasure of prosecuting a deranged sadist and notorious duellist known as Fighting Fitzgerald, who had shot a wolfhound belonging to Martin's friend Lord Altamount. The consequent challenge, the duel postponed owing to Fitzgerald's imprisonment, escape and recapture, their eventual meeting, Martin's minor wounds, his opponent's survival of two good hits thanks to the armour he had secretly encased himself in, Fitzgerald's arrest and trial for an assassination, and his botched hanging, must have gripped the public mind like the installations of a sensational novel, in which Martin played a noble hero with a dash of comedy in him. In their Galway life Richard and Elizabeth were rather more than amateur actors: they paid for the building of a theatre in town, and appeared on its stage to applause. A young man employed as a tutor at Dangan also joined in these theatricals, and fell madly and not unrequitedly in love with Elizabeth. After a row with Martin the affair was broken off, the young man soon eloped with and married a young girl, and later went to France to find his destiny; his name was Wolfe Tone.

Richard and Elizabeth had a daughter, Laetitia, in 1784, and a son, Thomas Barnewall, in 1786. In 1789, after the birth of another son, George, they happened to be in Paris when the Bastille was stormed; passionate discussions of liberty added a frisson to their enjoyment of salon culture. Meanwhile a possibility of restoring the family fortunes seemed to present itself – for the years of blithe and spendthrift living had left the estate heavily loaded with debt – when promising deposits of copper and lead were discovered near the head of Lough Corrib. It was a delusion; the company exploiting the mines cheated the Martins. Later ventures with a mine on High Island, which flooded when the shaft was sunk below sea level, and a marble quarry at Barnanoraun in the Twelve Pins were no more successful, and money disappeared into them as if flung into holes in the ground. Martin was also shaken by the unexpected elopement of his beloved wife with a rich, elderly Englishman. After a court case in London Martin was awarded ten thousand pounds damages, but, feeling uncomfortable in accepting it, he used it to shoe his horse with silver and changed the rest into small coins which he had his coachman fling to the winds on their way home for whoever might gather it.

In 1793 Richard Martin found it convenient to retire for a time to the house his father built at Ballynahinch, deep in its Connemara fastness, where he would be out of the way of debt collectors. He remarried in 1796; his second wife, Harriet Evans from Cashel, Tipperary, a young woman already with a literary reputation, was to bear him three daughters and a son. In that same year he welcomed onto his estate numerous Catholic exiles from the North, who had been invited to go 'to Hell or Connacht' by their Protestant neighbours, and who arrived in Connemara, in midwinter, in desperate straits. He and Harriet tended to their immediate needs of food and shelter, and settled them rent-free for some years. Connemara became a haven for another lot of refugees after the crushing of the 1798 rising, outlaws from Mayo fleeing the bloodthirsty vengeance of the yeomanry. Again Martin was sympathetic; he offered to intercede for one of the leaders of the rebels, the Augustinian friar Myles Prendergast, who had joined the French invaders on their landing at Killala, been captured after their defeat, and then had escaped from Castlebar Gaol. Father Miley, as he was known, refused to accept a pardon that did not include his companions, some of whom were actually drilling local recruits to their cause up in the Twelve Pins, and when that was not forthcoming from the authorities Martin advised him where to hide himself, in the house of a tenant of his near Carna.

Rumours of these and other extra-legal associations made Martin and his mysterious domain the subject of much speculation in society. Smuggling was part of the Connemara way of life, as a French traveller who called in to Ballynahinch, the Chevalier De Latocnaye, observed:

The safe and deep bays into which this coast is cut, as well as the freedom from fear of customs officials, accounts for the presence of a number of people who are here for what is quite openly the 'smuggling business', as if it were an ordinary trade. I have gone into different cabins and asked, straight away, for brandy or claret without finding any surprise to be expressed. One good woman, like many others, said to me, 'There is nothing at present in the house, but my husband is at sea, and if you come back in a month you can have all you want.'

One of Martin's most highly regarded tenants was a middleman and smuggler, Máirtín Mór Ó Máille, who lived in a permanent state of defence and in lordly style, entertaining his numerous subtenants with ever-open casks of wine, on the peninsula that runs into Galway Bay south of the present-day town of An

Cheathrú Rua. When Ó Máille was killed in a duel arising out of a pointless quarrel, Martin remarked that he had 'preferred a hole in his guts to one in his honour – but there wouldn't have been a hole in either if I'd been told of it'.

A friend of Martin's, the judge and Irish MP Sir Jonah Barrington, once quizzed an old Connemara man, Ned Bodkin, about the ways of Ballynahinch. Ned told him he did a bit of butchering, some smuggling when the coast was clear, burned kelp when he was entirely idle and brewed a touch of *poitín* now and then. 'Anything else, Mr. Bodkin?' asked Sir Jonah.

'Ough yes, plase your honour, 'tis me that tans the brogue leather for the colonel's yeomen (God bless them!); besides, I'm bailiff of the town lands, and make out our election registries; and when I've nothing else to do, I keep the squire's accounts, and by my sowl that same is no asy matter, plase your honour, till one's used to it! But, God bless him, up and down, wherever he goes, here or hereafter! he's nothing else but a good master to us all.'

'Mr. Ned Bodkin,' continued I, 'everybody says the king's writ does not *run* in Connemara?'

'Ough! Then whoever towld your honour that is a big liar. By my sowl, when the King George's write comes within smell of the big house, the boys soon make him run as if the seven devils were under his tail, saving your presence. It's King George's writ that *does run* at Connemara, plase your worship, all as one as a black greyhound.'

'And pray, if you catch the king's writ, what do you do then?'

'Why, if the prossy-sarver is cotched in the territories of Ballynahinch, by my sowl if the squire's not in it he'll either eat his parchment every taste, or go down into the owld coal pit sure enough, whichever is most agreeable to the said prossy-sarver . . .'

. . . and Ned Bodkin continues with a grotesque story of making a captive bailiff drunk twice a day through eating a long parchment soaked in *poitín*. Barrington, as a legal eminence, disapproves of such lawlessness, which he says was widespread and led process-servers to shirk their business, with the result that ruinous judgements were obtained by default against parties who had never heard a word of the claims upon them. Nevertheless, he obviously relishes the picturesque irregularities of Martin's kingdom within a kingdom. Others were less enchanted. A Galway magistrate, Mansergh St George, reported to the authorities that:

Connemara is the asylum of outlaws, deserters and persons escaped from justice, the stronghold of smugglers etc . . . There are at least 2,000 stand of arms dispersed in cabins and two battalions of deserters. Mr. Rich. Martin lives there and conciliates the garrison of Oughterard . . . by presents of liquor and provisions.

When St George sent a constable into Connemara to serve a chancery order on Martin, the man came back wounded in the foot, allegedly by Martin. Soon afterwards Martin interrupted the magistrate in his court, and was arrested and briefly imprisoned, which threatened to precipitate an insurrection in Connemara. To preserve the peace St George marched out with a detachment of dragoons, but when they got as far as Dangan they refused orders, and St George had to fly for his life back to Galway.

All these activities gave Martin's Connemara realm an equivocal allure, especially in the eyes of writers; it was at once dangerous and exotic, and comically old-fashioned. Thomas Moore, in a parody of a Horatian ode, associated it with Irish kingship of old romantic days:

Oh! place me 'midst O'Rourkes, O'Tooles,
The ragged royal blood of Tara;
Or place me where DICK M—RT—N rules
The houseless wilds of CONNEMARA –

Maria Edgeworth, who was to visit Ballynahinch in the time of Richard's son Thomas, sums up the whole of the Martin myth:

My curiosity had been raised even when I first came to Ireland fifty years ago, by hearing my father talk of the King of Connemara and his immense territory, and his ways of ruling over his people with almost absolute power, with laws of his own, and setting all other laws at defiance. Smugglers and caves, murders and mermaids, and duels and banshees, and faeries, were all mingled together in my early associations with Connemara, and I had been much amused by my father's account of Dick Martin . . . Too, besides, I once saw him, and I remember that my blood crept slow and my breath was held when he first came into the room, a pale little insignificant-looking mortal he was, but he still kept his hold of my imagination . . .

The Martins are reputed to have been generous landlords, and Richard is said to have distributed £800 a year among the widows and orphans. But the estate was already debt-ridden; when he inherited it on the death of his father in 1794 the Connemara holdings were providing an income of £10,000 per annum, and the lands east of Lough Corrib, £3,800, but its debts amounted to £20,000–30,000. Richard had only compounded this problem by his misguided ventures in estate management, as De Latocnaye observed:

I have never in my life been in the house of a rich man who appeared to care so little for the things of this world as Col. Martin. He is a man of the best intentions, and thinks of nothing more than how to improve the country which belongs to him. Unfortunately some adventurers have abused his confidence, and have swindled him out of considerable sums under pretext of finding mines on his estate, or of clearing lands for cultivation. The kind of clearing done was clearing out, after they had got the money.

But the Martins' high-handed ways with money was a generational problem. The whole vast antiquated conveyance of Ballynahinch was rattling merrily towards its own ruin and that of its passengers.

On the first day of 1801 Ireland became part of the United Kingdom and its parliament was united with that of Britain. Thenceforth the hotbed of politics and power would be in

Westminster, and Dublin society lost its sparkle. The Act of Union had been strenuously opposed by Grattan and others, but the Government had eventually secured a majority for the measure by means of persuasion and bribery. Martin himself was promised the post of Commissioner of Stamps (which failed to materialize, in the event), and a secure seat as Member of Parliament for Galway, but at the same time he genuinely believed that the Union would lead to Catholic emancipation and to free trade in Ireland. He moved his family to a house in fashionable Cumberland Place in London, and so began the most glamorous, and significant, stage in his career. He and Harriet were passionate theatre-goers, and Harriet published a collection of theatrical criticism as well as a novel. Their daughter, another Harriet, has left a literary portrait of her father in society, an episode that could have come out of a hundred novels of that period:

We will suppose him at an evening party: there has been music – very good, on the part of the young governess of the family – supper is announced, ladies, young, old, and middle-aged, troop off escorted by their cavaliers, but amidst the general movement the young governess has been forgotten. Who perceived that she had been overlooked! Who felt the omission, the discourtesy, the want of chivalry in the young men of the party? Who returned to the drawing room and conducted in the neglected one, taking a seat near her, and ensuring her being attended to? Who would have ventured to do this, after the lady of the house had said, on his observing the omission to her, 'Oh, Miss H— never takes supper'; the tone implying 'I never ask her.' . . . He could feel for the plain girl, the obscure girl, as she sat neglected in the ballroom, while the beauties or the notabilities engrossed all the attention of the younger male portion of the company . . . But then whatever was a source of mortification to another did not appear a trifle to him . . .

The Martins soon became members of a merry circle centred on the Prince of Wales, who was to become the Prince Regent and then King George IV. Once, when the Prince was extolling his avenues at Hampton Court, Martin observed, as one monarch to another, that his own avenue was thirty miles long – meaning the bridle-way to Ballynahinch, measuring from Clareville, the house his father had built at Oughterard, which the Martins used in the winter months and regarded as their gate lodge.

More importantly, Martin as a parliamentarian was earning the nickname the Prince Regent gave him of 'Humanity Martin', which later became the more familiar 'Humanity Dick'. True to his father's intentions, he steadfastly supported the cause of the Irish Catholics, but as a veteran of the Emancipation campaign, having voted for the Catholic Relief Bill way back in 1778, he felt licensed to counsel the Catholic Association against extremism, and had short-lived fallings-out with its leader Daniel O'Connell. He was also active in his friend William Wilberforce's anti-slavery campaign. In 1821 he introduced two bills, one to amend the law under which mere sheep-stealing or petty larceny was a hanging offence and a man charged with such an offence was allowed no defence counsel, the other to remove the death penalty for forgery. Neither bill was passed at that time, but in 1826 the substance of them was incorporated into Peel's Criminal Justice Bill.

At the same time Martin was fighting for the cause closest to his heart, the humane treatment of animals. In his own kingdom of Ballynahinch, two inheritances, the old castle on the lake island, and the right to hold courts won by his grandfather Nimble Dick, had stood to him in this campaign: tenants who beat their donkeys were likely to find themselves being rowed out to the castle by Martin himself and left there to reconsider their behaviour. Now in Parliament he was intent on making the general public reconsider similarly. It was a cause that drew forth all his powers of wit and rhetoric. The House frequently laughed at him and imitated his Irish brogue, but they had to laugh with him as well, and shudder at what he was able to tell them, from personal observation, of the cruelties suffered by stagecoach horses, dogs under vivisection, and various animals set to fight one another in such popular venues as the Westminster Pit. A humorist calling himself the 'Collective' gives us a taste of the mixed response to these parliamentary occasions:

Mr. Martin, of Galway, awakens the sympathy and admiration of the 'Collective,' by recounting a most piteous tale of the beating of a jack-ass in the Lambeth road, opposite the Asylum, to which he had fortunately put a stop, by bribing the cudgelling costermonger with a 'fi'penny;' and how he had been glorious at Smithfield, in triumphing over a butcher, who had struck a bullock in the pith to save the beef, and who, by the honourable member's grappling with him, had been himself kicked into the kennel, and had, in his fall, upset a great basket of potatoes, which had been scattered over the place, and picked up by certain emigrants from Connemara, who called out 'Long life and the blessings of a red cow to your honour!' all the time.

And, late in the evening, when the gallery is emptied of all strangers and the reporters have sunk into apathy:

. . . up rises the honourable member for Galway, and pours out the sympathy of his soul for the brute creation . . . He calls for a division upon some point, in which, forgetting the woes of Erin, he is to secure new privileges and immunities for beeves on this side the channel; but some one moves an amendment 'that the House be counted;' and as the tale does not number two score, the Speaker leaves the chair, and proclamation is made, 'Who goes home to supper?'

After long endurance of the mindless conservatism and racist buffoonery of his fellow MPs, Martin triumphed: the Ill-Treatment of Cattle Bill was passed in 1822. 'Martin's Act', as it was known, is recognized worldwide as the cornerstone of animal welfare legislation. And he was determined that its provisions should be put into action, personally patrolling markets and cab-ranks, and dragging offenders before the magistrates. In 1824 he and various supporters of his continued efforts to extend the scope of the Act came together in a coffee-house to found the Society for the Prevention of Cruelty to Animals, a deeply significant step in our species' foot-dragging progress towards the distant ideal of Humanity.

In the elections of 1826 Martin stood once again for Galway.

The campaign was even more violent than was usual in Galway's notoriously turbulent elections. It was claimed that the tenants of the D'Arcys of Clifden, heading into town to vote for Martin's opponent, were beaten back by Martin's tenants, who held all the roads through Connemara. When Martin's supporters were patrolling the streets of Galway, excited by whiskey and the music of drum and fife, a riot broke out that caused some loss of life. There was a parliamentary investigation into these and other irregularities, and in the following year Humanity Dick was unseated, which meant that he no longer enjoyed parliamentary immunity from arrest for his debts. Now aged seventy-three, he retired to the popular seaside resort of Boulogne, where he lived for seven comparatively equable years until his death in 1834. A late glimpse we have of him is as a benign old gentleman strolling on the beach, picking up the undersized fish the fishermen threw out of their nets, and putting them back into the sea.

'Urbanity towards women; benevolence towards men; and humanity towards the brute creation' was Sir Jonah Barrington's considered judgement on his friend of many years. What then was it that made Maria Edgeworth hold her breath on the one occasion she saw him, and feel her blood creep slow? It was, surely, the frost of death about him. He was known to have 'blazed', as the term was, and to have handled his 'barking irons' with effect. Everyone had heard how, as a young man, he had killed his cousin, a good friend who had forced a slight quarrel to its conclusion much against Martin's wishes. There was therefore a cold glint of menace in his conviviality and wit. Once in Galway, in his sixty-ninth year, his watch was stolen, and later in the evening in a public room he saw a man wearing it on a chain. Martin drew his sword, inserted its point into the ring of the watch and with consummate style neatly picked it off the belly of the terrified thief. His readiness to issue or accept a challenge kept his parliamentary mockers within bounds, and even in his last years in Boulogne, when a young Englishman became quarrelsome and proffered his card because Martin upbraided him for maltreating his horse, the pup withdrew as soon as he learned whom he was dealing with.

Martin's reputation as a deadly shot and his savoir-faire on the duelling ground were often enough to save him the inconvenience of killing his opponent, as in his encounter with a Mr Stowell, who had lent him money and then turned awkward when Martin could not repay it. Martin had offered him bills payable in three and six months' time, but Stowell returned them with a letter saying he would accept nothing but hard money. Martin gave an account of the upshot to his old friend Sir Jonah:

I replied that I had no hard money, nor was there much of it afloat in my part of the country, upon which Mr. Eustace Stowell immediately sent his friend to me, requiring me either to give him cash or *personal satisfaction*; and in the latter event, to appoint time and place. My answer was, that I did not want to shoot him unless he *insisted* upon it; but that as to *cash*, though Solomon was a wise man, and Samson a strong one, neither of them could pay ready money if they had it not. So I prepared to engage him. My friend the Right Honourable St. George Daly, since judge of the King's Bench, assisted in arranging preliminaries to our mutual satisfaction, and pretty early next morning we met to *fight out* the debt in that part of the Phoenix Park called the Fifteen Acres.

Everything proceeded regularly as usual. Our pistols were leaded, and the distance measured – eight yards from muzzle to muzzle. I stepped on my ground, he on his. I was just presenting my pistol at his body, when, having, I suppose, a presentiment that he should go somewhere out of this world if I let fly at him, he instantly dropped his weapon, crying out – 'Mr. Martin! Mr. Martin! A pretty sort of *payment* this! You'd shoot me for my interest money, would you?'

'If it's your *pleasure*, Mr. Eustace Stowell,' said I, 'I certainly will; but it was not my desire to come here, or to shoot you. You insisted on it yourself; so go on, if you please, now that we are here.'

'What security will you give me, Mr. Martin,' said he, 'for my interest money?'

'What I have offered you already,' said I.

Before I had time to finish the last words Mr. Stowell cried out, 'Nothing could be better or more reasonable, Mr. Martin; I accept the offer with pleasure. No better payment can be. It is singular you did not make this offer *before*.'

'I think,' said I, 'you had better take your ground again, Mr. Eustace Stowell, for I tell you I *did* make this offer before, and maybe you don't like so plump a contradiction. If not, I'm at your service. Here is a letter under your own hand, returning the bills and declining to receive them. See, read that,' continued I, handing it to him.

'Bless me!' said he, 'there must be some great misunderstanding in this business. All's right and honourable. I hope the whole will be forgotten, Mr. Martin.'

'Certainly, Mr. Stowell,' replied I; 'but I trust you'll not be so hard to please about your interest-money in future, when it's not convenient to a gentleman to pay it.'

He laughed, and we all four stepped into the same carriage, returned the best friends possible, and I never heard anything irritating about his interest-money afterward.

Perhaps Connemara felt there was something slightly uncanny about Hairtrigger Dick's cool readiness to face and to deal sudden death. I have the following story, which I have never seen in print, from my friend Mícheál Bairéad in Roundstone. One day Martin was out walking when he saw a horse and rider, with a lady riding pillion, coming towards him. He recognized the lady as his sister, who had died not long before. As they galloped past him, she bent down and handed a pistol to him. From then on, that was the pistol he used in his duels, and he never missed his man. But on one occasion his opponent was also using a pistol from the spirit world. Martin took aim, but did not fire. After a few minutes his second asked him what the trouble was, and Martin whispered, 'He's as thin as a hair in my sights.' Then both men fired at the same instant, and the two bullets collided in mid-air.

Romance and Ruin

Richard Martin had made over much of the Ballynahinch estate to his eldest son, Thomas, on the latter's coming down from Cambridge in 1811, but had not been on good terms with him thereafter. The origin of the quarrel was in a question of social rank. Thomas had fallen in love with the daughter of a rich chandler, whose father had been so pleased with the prospective alliance that he had offered to pay off the debts of the estate. Richard could not stomach being bailed out of his embarrassments by a tradesman, however wealthy, and succeeded in having the match broken off. The resentful Thomas took himself off to enlist in the Connaught Rangers, and soon found himself serving under Wellington in the Peninsular War. In his first action, at the Siege of Badajoz, Thomas was to the forefront of a sacrificial assault by ladders against the towering walls of the old Moorish fortress, in which over four thousand men were lost. Thomas was wounded in the shoulder and came home to Ballynahinch covered in glory. He soon fell in love again and married Julia Kirwan of Dalgin on the eastern shores of Lough Corrib. Their daughter Mary, later to be known as the Princess of Connemara, was born in 1817.

The Martin tradition of extravagant hospitality was so well honoured by the rising generation that even Richard was worried by it and felt that Thomas's unreasonable confidence in the fortunes to be made out of the mine on High Island was making him 'more turbulent and outrageous than ever'. But the mining venture failed, and the marble quarries disappointed too, though Thomas had a superb pair of oval tables made for Ballynahinch, and Richard presented a marble fireplace to his friend King George IV. As the economic situation deteriorated after the ending of the Napoleonic Wars the estate fell deeper into difficulties. Soon Connemara, like much of rural Ireland, was in deep distress; Thomas was one of only two resident landlords in the region, and was dispensing relief to his tenants rather than receiving rent from them. By the time Richard had fled his creditors to the Continent, Thomas was in despair. On the eve of a duel (which in the event he survived) he wrote a farewell letter to his father commending Mary to his care: 'Unless some effectual steps are taken the property after your death must be sold for the payment of the debts. On my word I believe that the poor desolate creature will not have her mother's fortune out of the wreck.' Nothing had changed in that prospect by the time of Richard's death in 1834.

After a particularly tumultuous election Thomas had succeeded his father as Member of Parliament for Galway; he was also a Justice of the Peace and a leading member of the Clifden Board of Guardians, and in Ballynahinch, whatever his anxieties about money, he revelled in the role of benevolent despot. One of the Ross House Martins described him thus: 'I never saw anyone who realized my idea of a chieftain so completely as he did. An absolute ruler, but the protector of his people.' And on occasion he could lead them in battle. In his latter years a dispute arose over a strip of bog of no particular value that was claimed both by the Martins and by a descendant of their ancient enemies, George O'Flaherty of Lemonfield near Oughterard. Another member of the Ross branch of the Martins recorded the familial saga:

The belligerents mustered their tenants, and marched down upon the debatable land, where with spades, flails, and graips, a most furious battle was fought. Thomas Martin, who was a man of gigantic proportions and herculean strength, led his forces into action himself. He did not, indeed, avail himself of any weapon save his fists, but with those he dealt sledge-hammer blows upon the enemy.

In the end a boundary wall of the bog collapsed on the O'Flaherty faction, and the Martins triumphed. Thomas Martin had to spend two months in Galway Gaol as a result, but the governor of the gaol placed his own residence at Thomas's disposal, where he gave dinner parties every night to all the neighbouring gentry and claimed he had never enjoyed himself more.

Many such high-spirited traits of Thomas in the role of paternal autocrat have been preserved in the Martin tribe's own treasury of anecdote. A scrap of local lore I have come across suggests another perspective on him. Once a man and a boy were thin-ning a bed of carrots in the kitchen garden at Ballynahinch. The man wanted to take home some of the little carrots he had pulled, and, having no pockets (for in those days men often worked in their *báiníní*, vests and under-trousers of undyed homespun wool), he put them into his loose knitted hat. At the end of the day they presented themselves at the kitchen door to receive their wages. The master came out onto the steps, looked down at them, and noticed a few carrots sticking out through the man's hat. 'I see the carrots are very high this year!' he quipped, and dismissed the man from his employ. I heard this little example of Martin wit from an old man who had it from the grandson of the boy who had witnessed the event. It happened not long before the Famine; what influence losing one of the few paid jobs in the locality was to have on the man's fortunes, I do not know.

The reputation of the Martins as kindly and responsible land-lords who never evicted their tenants has been refurbished in every account of them, but the oral tradition of the neighbour-hood is not wholly in agreement. I am told that Mrs Martin lost a child on one occasion when her carriage was delayed by some mistake or accident with a horse, and that Thomas Martin had the Mannions of Cillín (thirteen families of them, according to one version of the story) evicted because of it. Another bitter folk-memory concerns the ancient graveyard near where the river flows out of the lake, that is, just a quarter of a mile from Bally-nahinch Castle. It is said that Thomas's daughter Mary objected to the wails of local women at funerals there, so they were forbidden to use it, and the graveyard at Ballinafad, two miles to the east, was instituted instead. The Irish *caoineadh* or keening was a traditional art form of stylized lamentation; its discountenancing and suppression, as an atavistic discordant howling, became one of the key moves in the disenchantment of Ireland in the later nine-teenth century, by the end of which it was scarcely to be heard outside of a few refuges of Gaelic culture such as the Aran Islands. Perhaps this episode, if genuine, dates from a later stage in Mary Martin's life, after she had seen something of fashionable society

and perhaps had shed her self-romanticizing fondness for antiquated ways.

To passers-by and visitors of the respectable classes the Martins'
hospitality was inexhaustible, to a degree that sped the estate
towards its eventual ruin. When Bianconi established his public
car service between Galway and Clifden, with one of its 'stages'
on the other side of the lake from Ballynahinch Castle, Thomas
would send his servant to meet the car every evening and compel
any traveller 'of decent appearance' to be the Martins' guest.
Perhaps solitude and time to reflect was the last thing Thomas
needed in this social wilderness. One of the Ross House Martins
remembered visiting her Ballynahinch cousins as a child:

Thomas Martin was wont to declare that the most tedious time of the
day was the quarter of an hour's waiting before dinner; he therefore
appointed that hour for family prayers. Two favourite terriers were always
present, and their gambles and squabbles whilst family worship was
proceeding were sometimes a trial to the gravity of the auditors. If their
goings-on became too obstreperous, Thomas Martin would grasp a dog
with each of his large hands and thrust them one under each arm,
continuing unconcernedly to read the while, unconscious of the struggle
with which we, who fronted him in a long row, had to keep our risible
muscles in control. His servant, who as a Catholic took no part in the
devotions, stood bolt upright at the door whilst they were in progress.
To us upon our knees it seemed that at the end 'Amen dinner Gallagher'
came all in one breath.

Among the many callers at Ballynahinch was William Thackeray,
in the course of his Irish tour of 1842; unfortunately he is too
discreet to tell us anything of the family's private affairs, but he
gives a convincing picture of the servant situation at Ballynahinch:

It will, however, be only a small breach of confidence to say, that the
major-domo of the establishment (who has adopted accurately the voice
and manner of his master, with a severe dignity of his own, which is
quite original), ordered me on going to bed 'not to move in the morning

till he called me,' at the same time expressing a hearty hope that I should 'want nothing more that evening.' Who would dare, after such peremptory orders, not to fall asleep immediately, and in this way disturb the repose of Mr J—n M—ll—y?

There may be many comparisons drawn between English and Irish gentlemen's houses, but perhaps the most striking points of difference between the two is the immense following of the Irish House, such as would make an English housekeeper crazy almost. Three comfortable, well-clothed, good-humoured fellows walked down with me from the car, persisting in carrying one a bag, another a sketching-stool, and so on: walking about the premises in the morning, sundry others were visible in the courtyard and near the kitchen door; in the grounds a gentleman, by name Mr Marcus C—rr, began discoursing to me regarding the place, the planting, the fish, the grouse, and the Master, being himself, doubtless, one of the irregulars of the house. As for maids, there were half a dozen of them scurrying about the house; and I am not ashamed to confess that some of them were exceedingly good-looking.

By far the richest description we have of the Martins of this period is that written by Maria Edgeworth, who drawn by the mystique of this quasi-legendary realm, accepted an invitation to join her English friends Sir Culling Smith and his lady on a tour of Connemara in 1833, and sent a long account of it to her brother. They travelled grandly, in Sir Culling's four-horse carriage, with postillions in jackets of dark-blue frieze, from Edgeworths-town via Athlone to Galway. Then, entering the unknown, they struggled onwards to Oughterard with many delays on the rough road, and with immense difficulties found a tolerable lodging house, in which Maria Edgeworth was treated to her first 'toombler of anti-Parliament whiskey', or *poitín*, which she found detestable. Their next stop was at Corrib Lodge, the little house the Edgeworth family's good friend Alexander Nimmo had built at the head of Lough Corrib as his headquarters when laying out the roads of Connemara, and which had been turned into a hotel after his death. They had intended to go on as far as Clifden that

same day, but now they learned that Nimmo's road was still
unfinished and that they would have to travel by the old bridle-
way, which no carriage had ever attempted. They set off, attended
by a long 'tail' of men and boys who 'dragged, pushed, carried,
screamed' the carriage across various sloughs the horses absolutely
refused to set foot in, but eventually it became clear that they
would not reach Clifden that day, and Maria Edgeworth sent a
lad on ahead to Ballynahinch with a note asking for a night's
hospitality in case of their utmost need. A welcoming reply was
brought back to them as they floundered on through mudhole
after mudhole, and they arrived at the house in the dark. There
by firelight in the drawing room they met Mrs Martin, a lady
who had clearly been accustomed to the best of society, that of
the Dublin of forty years before, and her elegantly dressed daughter
Mary, who made a lasting impression on Maria:

Slight figure, head held up, and thrown back – whether proud or shy
in the extreme, hard to grasp. She had the resolution to come to the
very middle of the room, and made a deliberate and profound curtsey,
which a dancing-master of Paris might have approved; seated herself in
the dark on the sofa, and seemed as if she never intended to speak.

Later in the evening Maria had the opportunity to study her
closely:

With the light of branches of wax candles full upon her, I saw that she
was very young, about seventeen; very fair, hair which might have been
called red by rivals and auburn by lovers. But Miss Martin's is much
finer, in profusion and well dressed. Her eyes blue-grey, prominent; her
nose, I can't deny, snub . . . I could not decide whether she was pretty
or not. But I thought she would make a bust, and that she was like
pictures I have seen of Leonardo da Vinci with that sort of hair and
complexion.

Thomas Martin, whom they met before dinner, proved to be:

. . . a large Connemara gentleman, yes, but coursish, with a Connemara brogue, large white face, altogether massive and heavy-looking, with a stoop forward in his neck, which I was afterwards informed was the consequence of a shot he received in the Peninsular War, into which he went as a volunteer. But his manner was not that of a military man. It was Connemara manner, a sort of brusque cordiality and hospitality, in his particular case struggling against and over-leaping constitutional shyness and reserve.

Thomas was a powerfully built man, well able to keep order in his court by knocking together the heads of the rowdiest disputants and putting them out of the door, 'their legs splaying out as he flings them from him'. Nevertheless, Maria Edgeworth felt that his standing was not what his father's had been:

It is not exactly a feudal state of society – but the tail of a feudal estate, and in a very odd, and not poetical manner the jobbing Irish gentleman and Dublin courtier up at the Castle is here and there joined up (I should not say mixed up) with the Chieftain. The common people used to consider Dick Martin, the father of the present man, as not only the lord of all he surveyed, but the lord of their lives. Now however the laws have come in between them, and he is no longer the unrivalled King of Connemara. There are hundreds who would start up out of the bogs to hazard their lives still for Mr. Martin, but he is called Mister now, and the prestige is gone.

The dinner that first evening was superb: venison 'such as Sir Culling declared could not be found in England except from one or two immense parks of noblemen favoured above their peers', salmon, lobsters, oysters, French wines, champagne. But the rambling, damp and dilapidated mansion gave an impression of the makeshift and temporary. The massive mahogany doors of the dining room admitted icy winds and would not shut except with a slam that shook the house, the windows held 'broken panes, wood panes, slate panes', there were no curtains, no wallpaper, no bookcases. In the morning Maria went out to view the surroundings: a magnificent but desolate prospect of an immense lake and bare mountains in one direction, and in the other 'a boundless sort of common with showers of stones – no avenue or regular approach but a half-made road – no human habitation within view'. And the Castle itself was a disappointment:

. . . a whitewashed dilapidated mansion with nothing of a castle about it excepting four pepperbox-looking towers stuck on at each corner – very badly, and whitewashed; and all that battlemented front . . . mere whitewashed stone or brick or mud, I cannot say which. But altogether the house is very low and ruinous-looking, not a ruin of antiquity – but with cow-house and pig-stye and dunghill adjoining, and a litter indescribable in a sunk sort of backyard . . .

Maria was longing to see more of the family's normal way of life, and as it happened she had her wish, for Lady Culling became dangerously ill, a physician had to be sent for from Oughterard on another night of storm, and it was a good three weeks before they could leave. Mr Martin never flagged in kindness and hospitality, both to the visiting gentry and to their servants:

Mrs. Martin told me that he said to her: 'I am afraid that English man and maid servant must be very uncomfortable here: so many things to which they have been used, which we have not for them! Now we have no beer, you know, my dear, and English servants are used to beer.' So he gave them cider instead, and every day he took to each of them himself a glass of excellent port wine.

Maria especially enjoyed the company of Mrs Martin – 'She is not at all literary; she is very religious – what would be called one of the VERY GOOD, and yet she suited me, and I grew very fond of her, and she of me' – but she continued to observe young Mary Martin as if she were auditioning her for a part in a novel.

While Mrs. Martin was thus refreshing my spirits with anecdotes scandalous and humorous, her daughter Mary was either in her room or on a sofa opposite us with her legs on it and her head back, not hearing or heeding a word that was said, but wrapped in some philosophical abstraction of her own, which I should never have expected, had her mother not let me into her character. 'My dear, you don't understand Mary. She is living in another world and has not the least knowledge or taste or care about this world as it goes. She does not hear one word we say, and the only thing that keeps her here is you as an authoress and celebrated person. She is exceptionally curious about celebrated people, and I know would delight in talking to you about books.' In a dark closet in her own room it seems Miss Martin had books . . . And: 'Every morning,' said Mrs. Martin, 'she comes in to see me while I am dressing and pours out an inundation of learning of all sorts, fresh and fresh: all she has been reading for hours before I was up . . . Now there may be too much of philosophy and science, you know, at least for me: very good all in its place and season, but there must be some relief. You feel that, I am sure, don't you?'

I began to study Mary, and found her one of the most extraordinary persons I ever saw . . . her acquirements are indeed prodigious; she has more knowledge of books, both scientific and learned, than any female creature I ever saw or heard of at her age: – heraldry, metaphysics, painting and painters' lives, and tactics. She had a course of tactics from a French officer, and of engineering from Mr. Nimmo. She understands Latin, Greek and Hebrew, and I don't know how many modern languages.

But Mary's French had a distinct '*ton de garnison*' about it, picked up from the exiled Bonapartist officer who, while in refuge at Ballynahinch, had taught her both his language and his adulation of the Emperor. She had read all of Byron that was fit for a young lady, but had been carefully sheltered from the fact that the poet was 'not a perfectly moral man', and she recited the reams of poetry she had by heart 'so fast and oddly in such a Connemara accent and words so fluid, running one into the other, that at first I could not guess what language it was'. She was well aware of the literary potentials of her life-world and her own role in it; 'Don't you think your friend Sir Walter Scott would have liked our people and our country?' she observed to Maria. One morning the visitors went with Miss Martin to view the green marble quarry with which Mr Martin hoped to 'pay all his father's debts and live like an Emperor sooner or later'. As they admired the huge blocks, several country people gathered round; Mary Martin referred to them as her 'tail' and explained that they invariably accompanied her when she went riding or walking, sometimes to beg a favour but also for the mere pleasure of talking to her. Sir Culling wanted some piece of local information from these people and, conscious that his English tone might be unintelligible to them, asked Miss Martin to put the question for him:

When the question had been put and answered, Sir Culling objected: 'But, Miss Martin, you did not ask the question exactly as I requested you to state it.' 'No,' said she, with colour raised and head thrown back, 'no, because I knew how to put it that our people might understand it. *Je sais mon métier de reine.*'

Maria Edgeworth kept up a correspondence with the Martins after her return from Connemara, following their fortunes and misfortunes with the attention of an enthralled novel-reader, and even playing the author by offering them advice on affairs of purse and heart. Although she felt great fondness for Mrs Martin and was repelled by her daughter's egotism, it was Mary who fascinated her. Maria was agog to see how this flower of the wilderness would transplant to civilization:

Now do think of a girl of seventeen, in the wilds of Connemara, intimately acquainted with Aeschylus and Euripides, and having them as part of her daily thoughts. If she had but tact to know how to manage it all! I am very anxious to know what effect seeing the world and being seen by the world will have upon her. She will come out this season. She is at this instant on her way to London with her father. She has never been out of Connemara before . . .

The Martins called at Edgeworthstown on their return from the season in London. Maria Edgeworth found Miss Martin much improved in manners and dress, and noted that 'books had gone out and men had come into her head – I won't say into her heart'. The interest had been reciprocated: Prince Poniatowski had been charmed by her blushing like a country girl – '*C'est une grâce de la nature qui est hors de mode ici à ce que je vois,*' he remarked; and a Count Werdinski, who had lost his estate through taking the wrong side in the politics of Poland, and had the reputation of 'kissing and cuffing his maids', was so eager to see her again that he actually arrived at Ballynahinch the day before the family themselves returned, and was assumed by the servants to be a dancing master. When his suit was indignantly refused both by the young lady and her parents, he tried to shoot himself in his bedroom, missed and made a hole in the ceiling, fell in a fit, and was packed off to Roundstone in the care of the Church of Ireland curate Mr Foster. Poniatowski himself arrived a few days later; Maria was informed by letter from Mrs Martin what ensued, but unfortunately felt bound by her promise of discretion not to pass on the story to her own correspondent, and so to us.

Mary Martin was by this time a financially interesting proposition, being heiress to hundreds of thousands of acres, and promised riches in green marble that were to wipe out the accumulated debts of three or four generations, for in 1833 Thomas had taken advantage of recent legislation making it easier to break the entail in her favour, which would otherwise have seen the estate go to the nearest male heir, his half-brother Richard, Humanity Dick's son by his second wife. (This act further soured relations with Humanity Dick in his last year of life, and sent the disappointed young Richard off to Canada, where he built a house named after Derryclare Lake. It is the numerous descendants of the Derryclare Martins of Canada who are the present keepers of the Martin flame.)

In the following year Thomas Martin consulted Maria Edgeworth on another matter that was to have tragic consequences for his daughter. Maria detailed it in one of her letters to her brother:

The short of it is this, that a set of Liverpool merchants (by Act of Parliament a company) propose to take the Martins' immense Connemara Estate upon a thirty-one year lease, and to pay all his debts, amounting I guess to upwards of £100,000, and to allow him during the thirty-one years out of his property a sum of £3000 per annum for him to live upon. At the end of the thirty-one years, he to have the whole improved estate . . . also to have the half of the profit made by working his marble quarries during the thirty-one years term.

Maria considered that this would be advantageous to all concerned, given the improvability of the territory, but warned Thomas that he would find his own position, as an 'abdicated monarch', painfully changed. She also urged him to reduce the term to twenty-one years, as a fortune adequate to Miss Martin's 'heiress pretensions' could not be had out of the £3,000 per annum and 'thirty-one years is too long for a lover to look or a husband to wait even for this immense property as it will be when it is improved'. In fact Thomas did enter into some such agreement, with dire consequences for all, including his tenants, the principal victims of the promised 'improved estate'.

Thomas Martin died in the year of Black Forty-Seven, from a fever caught when visiting some of his former tenants in the Clifden workhouse; Martin family lore says that his last words, before turning his face to the wall, were 'Oh, my God, what will become of my poor people?' He was buried in the Franciscan abbey in Galway, and, according to one account that has been passed down the Martin generations, his funeral took two hours to go by the gate of Ross House, the home of the senior branch of the family. However, one of the Martins of Ross who witnessed the event as a child reports that 'Scarcely anyone followed him to his grave; the peasantry who had revered him were dying by hundreds upon the mountain-sides; the gentlemen of Galway were too intent on measures to save those of their people who still remained alive to have leisure to pay respects to the dead, even the last Squire of Connemara, with whose passing an epoch ended.'

And so the Princess of Connemara found herself the queen of

a stricken realm. In the following year, when the estate was foundering in the catastrophe of the Famine and Mary was struggling to maintain appearances on what little income was left after paying out interest on various mortgages, she became engaged. Arthur Gonne Bell, the grandson of her mother's sister, was a good deal younger than herself, a businessman, the son of a Mayo Justice of the Peace. It was said to have been a love match – she could have married someone superior in name and fortune – but on hearing of it Maria Edgeworth felt 'a flat surprise – the sort of surprise one feels at the realisation of what one has always *said* always dreamed would be'. On his marriage Bell adopted the surname of Martin under Royal Licence and was granted a coat of arms, but this was not sufficient to elevate the alliance above Maria's sarcasm, as expressed in a letter to her sister Harriet:

The very day before this note came in we – in the library – had been talking of her and I had ended with saying: 'She will marry you will see whenever she can find a Prince-Consort who will live at Ballinahinch Castle and sit a few steps below the throne.'

A Prince-Consort! Here is an Agent-consort! How lucky! How prudent! Nothing anti-romantic! after all the Princes! And the Polish Count Scampi shooting himself through the ceiling – So very sensible, Miss Martin, and well calculated and achieved! And a journey to London to complete the *business* for a marriage pleasure-jaunt. How the Honey moon will be surprised! – Not *le Mari sylphe*! But *le Mari Homme d'affaires*, saving a thousand pounds by his agency.

How very droll! How very serious!

The coming to power at the height of the Great Famine of Arthur Bell, now Arthur Bell Martin, was not at all droll and was indeed deadly serious for the tenants. By January 1848 Bell Martin owed over £200 in rates, and was using the notorious Quarter-Acre Clause in the Poor Law Amendment Act of 1847, under which anyone occupying over a quarter of an acre of land was not eligible for relief, to reduce his rates by clearing his land of tenants. John Deane, the upright and energetic Temporary

Inspector sent into the Clifden Union by the Poor Law Commissioner to assist in distribution of relief and to ensure that the Board of Guardians was doing its duty as to the collection of rates, reported that Martin's agents were issuing certificates of entitlement to relief to any tenant willing to abandon his home and land, and then pulling down the home so that the tenant and his dependants were driven to take shelter in the already crammed and fever-ridden workhouse. Deane complained 'very decidedly' to Bell Martin 'on the inhumanity of putting so many families as an additional charge on the rates of the union'. But all Bell Martin's thrift was not enough to save the estate. Mary and he had borrowed a huge sum from the Law Life Assurance Society, in order to consolidate their many debts at a lower rate of interest, and when the repayments on this could not be met, the mortgagees sued her in the Encumbered Estates Court, an institution set up in 1849 to facilitate the sale of the numerous insolvent estates of that disastrous period. The court ordered the estate to be sold, and when the sale was an almost complete failure, Law Life themselves bought it in for very little. Mary Bell Martin and her husband retreated to Fontaine l'Evêque in Belgium, where she supported them both by her contributions to the *Encyclopaedie des gens du monde* and other periodicals. She had already published a novel, *St. Etienne*, in 1845, and her autobiographical novel *Julia Howard, A Romance*, which appeared in 1850, told something of her experiences during the Famine (but, as Maria Edgeworth had remarked long ago apropos of the Princess of Connemara, 'Can any romance equal the romance of real life?'). In that same year the Bell Martins emigrated to America, but Mary suffered a miscarriage on shipboard, and died in the Union Place Hotel, New York, soon after their arrival. Another half-dozen of her novels appeared over the following quarter-century; all are unread today.

In 1893 the collaborative novelists Somerville and Ross visited Ballynahinch to enquire into the legend of the Princess of Connemara, and with their lethal sense of humour succeeded in puncturing it with a single word. (Ross was the pen name of Violet Martin, a daughter of Ross House, and Edith Oenone

Somerville was her cousin from Cork; they tell the story in their ruefully comedic travel book *Through Connemara in a Governess Cart*.) A housekeeper showed them around the Castle, and pointed out 'a comfortless-looking stone block' on which Mary Martin used to sit in the terraced garden overlooking the river. After exploring more of the grounds, the cousins came across 'an old woman who had sat down in a tattered heap to rest on the stone bench', and they engaged her in conversation about Mary Martin. 'What was she like in the face?' asked the malicious pair. 'Oh musha! Ye couldn't rightly say what was she like, she was that grand! She was beautiful and white and charitable, only she had one snaggledy tooth in the front of her mouth . . .'

The Reckoning

The policy behind the Encumbered Estates Court was to ease the old-fashioned, unimproving and now bankrupt landlords out of the way, allowing new ideas and new capital to flood in and reinvigorate the land. According to a source quoted by the auctioneer at the opening of the sale of the Martin estate in August 1849:

No colony of Great Britain offers to industrious young men of small or large capital a surer, more profitable, and satisfactory field for investment, either in the purchase or leasing of lands, than Ireland; and in no colony a settler meet with cheaper labour, and with a more willing, docile and tractable race, when justly treated, than the Irish peasantry.

The Martin estate in particular would be an investor's paradise, to believe the sale announcement:

Any description which can be written would fall short of the advantages which would present themselves to the eye of an intelligent person, in his survey of this truly wonderful district. It is impossible for the mind of man to conceive anything necessary but capital, and a judicious application of it, for rendering this vast Property fertile beyond a parallel that this Estate does not contain within itself; facilities for Draining, the formation of Roads, inland Navigation, abundance of lime, sea-weed for manure, valuable kelp shores, innumerable beautiful sites for Buildings, and the soil generally might be designated, to use a homely phrase, as one vast dung-heap . . .

As to the docile and tractable peasantry, the accompanying documentation contained a sinister hint that they would not be too much of an encumbrance:

The number of Tenants on each Townland, and the amount of their Rents, have been taken from a Survey, and ascertained Rental in the year 1847, but many changes advantageous to a Purchaser have since taken place, and the same Tenants, by name, and in number, will not now be found on the Lands.

The five-day sale, at the Mart in London, was well attended, but by the curious – the morbidly curious, perhaps, come to see a great ship sink – rather than the potential investor. The *Farmers' Journal* carried a blow-by-blow account of the proceedings. On the first day, dealing with property in or near Galway, a house and a couple of townlands were knocked down at low rates, but most of the lands offered did not meet the reserve prices. The second and third days' business mainly concerned 'highly improvable bog land' in the Barony of Moycullen; there were no bids at all for most of the lots, and virtually the whole of the property was bought in by the solicitor to Law Life. On the fourth day lands along the western shores of Connemara, including the best arable land of the estate, were on offer. High Island, once the seat of the Martins' delusive hopes of mineral wealth, and two neighbouring smaller islands, were sold to a Revd Anthony Magee, a Catholic cleric who settled at Boolard near Clifden at this period. Two townlands fronting onto Mannin Bay, with its 'large supplies of a very valuable description of sand for manure, called by the inhabitants of the shore "coral sand"', attracted some interest, but 'Mr

Bocket, the agent to the vendors, to the annoyance evidently, of the gentleman who offered 200*l* [£200] for this extensive tract of country immediately exercised the power reserved to him by the conditions of sale, and bid 6,000*l*, at which price it fell again into the hands of the vendors.' There were scarcely any bids for the rest of the lands. The fifth day was no better:

Nothing could well be gloomier than the appearance of the company at the Mart on Monday. There seemed absolutely no disposition to purchase. Not a single sale was effected. Biddings were indeed, given for four out of the 17 lots put up, but they were all, except in one solitary instance, so small, and at so cautious distance from the marketable value of the land, that the bidders incurred no risk whatever, supposing they were idle spectators merely, of having two or three Irish townlands knocked down to them.

The idle spectators witnessed the death of the heart of the Martin kingdom that day; among the lots were:

. . . the Demesne of Ballynahinch, with the Residence and picturesque grounds called Ballynahinch Castle, surrounded by 60,545 acres of Land, embracing the beautiful Lakes and Rivers, and extensive and valuable fisheries, the 'Twelve Pin Mountains,' with the inexhaustible Quarries of Marble of great variety, beauty, and value, rendering it the most compact, desirable, and improvable, Estate which can be found within the shores of the United Kingdom.

This tempted not a single bidder; nor did the district and town of Roundstone with its seventy slated houses and the rights to hold four annual fairs and a weekly market. The sum outcome of the five-day wake was 3,982 acres sold, at an average price of £3 2s. 7½d., out of a total of 196,540 acres. Thus virtually the whole of the estate fell into the hands of the mortgagees, Law Life, at a price of £12,465, some £60,000 less than their claims on it, while the Bell Martins and their other creditors got nothing.

Of course, to profit from the investment, Law Life had then

to make it saleable, and to this end set about simplifying and rationalizing the jumble of disconnected patches of the traditional 'rundale' pattern of holdings. By the time the land was put up for sale again, at the Encumbered Estates Court in Dublin in July 1852, the vendors could claim that 'the greatest possible care has been taken to allot, square, and otherwise improve the holdings of the several tenants throughout the estate'. These 'improvements' involved evictions. The travel writers Mr and Mrs Hall commented on Law Life's 'wholesale clearances':

They have driven humanity out of their way – alas for the miserable thousands who have perished – and alas for those who, at distant day, purchasers of these very lands, will look in vain for hands to till them. Much have they to answer for whose vices – or recklessness hardly less criminal than vice – led to these appalling results.

It seems that this attempted sale came to nothing at the time, but very soon afterwards a company of gentlemen represented by a London solicitor, Mr Coverdale of Bedford Road, proposed to buy the estate, and sent an energetic and enthusiastic young man over to survey, value and report upon it. Thomas Colville Scott's diary of this, his first commission, came to light at an auction and was published recently. His dismay at his findings was profound. 'At present the face of this country, & of its people,' he wrote, 'look as desolate as if the whole region was about to be abandoned.' Visiting the remotest headlands and islands and penetrating the inmost valleys of the Twelve Pins, he came across horrible marks of what had happened to those tenants who, in the words of the sales announcements, would 'not now be found on the Lands':

In going and returning from Roundstone, I looked at many of the rude graves in the Bogs, Quarry holes and even on the ditches, into which the unfortunate people were flung in the time of the famine of '47. The very dogs which had lost their masters or were driven by want from their homes, became roving denizens of this district & lived on the unburied or partially buried corpses of their late owners and others, and there was no possible help for it, as all were prostrate alike, the territory so extensive, and the people so secluded and unknown. The luxuriant tufts of grass and heath show the spots where they lie.

Concerning the townland of Glinsce in the Carna peninsula he noted:

Saw some hundreds of forsaken cabins – *sepulchres* of those who had tenanted them, while living: the fallen thatched roofs were in many cases, their only covering, in others the walls had also fallen in upon them, but all this did not hide from our view the whitened bones of many of the old and young who had huddled together, in these lone spots, to wait for death.

Worse, in that snowy and frosty February of 1853 he found that famine still ruled. At Ballynew, on the northern coast of Connemara:

. . . we were surrounded by a swarm of the poor squatters, about *30* in number, with their wives, sons, daughters, sisters and brothers, making about a hundred in all, who kept up a constant chatter in Irish as to the object of our visit. A spokesman amongst them put this pointedly to us, and having satisfied him so far that we had no sheriffs' warrants, we were assured, 'by dad', that it was 'all right' & the whole mass seemed to breathe more freely. Hundreds of these poor tenants have been driven from this part of the property by a combination of Soldiers, Revenue Officers, and the Constabulary, and hundreds perished in the time of the famine.

A townland called Aughrusbeg, on the western shoreline, was 'covered with unrecognized subtenants':

I saw these subtenants at work, most of them widows, forsaken wives, and young women, carrying peat on their backs. They were nearly in a state of nudity, and appeared from actual want, to be reduced to a state of Idiocy. There is no Irish animation and buoyancy here, but a stealthy and timid look, as if these poor souls were ashamed of their condition, and lost to the faintest hope of escape from wretchedness and misery, Good God! Where are their landlords & the responsible power that rules over them: have they never looked into these all but vacant faces only animated with a faint imploring look – have they never seen the bent back of the aged, and the sunk cheek of the young? then let them come here and see what neglect has done.

These pages were written for Scott himself and his family, but no doubt his report to the London businessmen reflected the truth behind Law Life's hopeful prospectus. We hear no more of potential purchasers for another decade or so, when an ambitious scheme for the development of Roundstone, based on a projected railway from Galway, was initiated and then abandoned. According to a newspaper report of 1871:

A vast deal of building and railway materials are now lying at Roundstone, having been collected there by two gentlemen who were for some time in treaty with the Law Life Company . . . The magnificent schemes which [they] conceived for the development of the resources of Connemara have given place to more moderate and perhaps sounder projects. There is to be no grand hotel to be built at Roundstone on speculation, nor terraces of fashionable villas and lodging houses run up in anticipation of a population, fixed or migratory, which may or may not make its appearance in the locality for years to come . . .

This early proposal for a railway along the densely populated coast, necessitating causeways across sea-inlets, has left a few traces in local lore. In Rosroe, the peninsula running south from Cashel, an old house known as the Toolhouse was connected with the project, and I am told that a boat bringing in machinery sank in the approaches to the little bay nearby called Rosroe Harbour, and its cargo was never salvaged. However, the article quoted above goes on to hope that a railway would be built and that 'Roundstone will not long lag behind the rest of the country, and a line of steamers will ere long find traffic in that port.' It was in fact to be another forty years before a railway was built, and then it followed an inland route by Maam Cross and Ballynahinch, not far from the line of the present Galway–Clifden road, which was less costly but on the other hand ran through almost unpopulated countryside, and perhaps for this reason it did not prosper for long.

At the time of this newspaper article Law Life was in negotiation with a gentleman of the name of Berridge, and in the following year, 1872, the company conveyed to him the 160,000 acres it still held of the Martin estate, including the Castle, the fisheries, oyster beds, rights to hold fairs, etc., plus Clare Island and another five small estates in Mayo, for a sum of £230,000. Neither written nor oral history retains much about the Richard Berridges, father and son, who were to be the largest landlords of Connemara for over forty years, and what information I have about them comes mainly from thumbing through documents – wills, conveyances, newspaper clippings, notes from censuses, a few letters – lent me by their descendants, who still have many ties to the area and revisit it each summer. The first Richard Berridge is especially obscure, to the point of being mysterious, in both his doings and his motivation.

To begin with it seems that the new master of Connemara was not originally surnamed Berridge but McCarthy. His father is thought to have been a Florence McCarthy from Kerry, an officer in the 60th Regiment of Foot who served in the Leeward Islands and married an Anne Berridge, whose nephew Charles James Berridge Aldis is a name in the history of London's sanitation. Their son Richard, born in Lambeth, Surrey, in 1809 or 1813 (the sources disagree), for some unknown reason renounced his father's name and took that of his mother, who disowned him on that account; at some stage he also left the Catholic Church for the Church of Ireland. By 1859 he had an address in Great Russell Street, London, and was a member of the Reform Club. He made his money through his partnership in Meux Brewery; according to family lore, Lady Meux offered him the Meux fortune if he would change his name to Meux, but he declined to do this. In fact it was said that he made three fortunes in his life, and lost two of them. He married twice; the name of his first wife is unknown, but there was a daughter of this marriage. His second marriage was to a Mrs Wilson, née Laura Isabella Dove, and took place after they had had four children, of whom the one son, Richard, was born in 1870. There is a scintilla of doubt as to whether this Richard was indeed Berridge senior's son.

Having spent a fortune to acquire the Martin estate (although only half the agreed price was paid at the time, and it is doubtful if the balance was ever paid), the first Richard Berridge seems to have done little to improve it. The Castle itself was handsomely refurbished, but, probably because of the threatening state of the country, he was an absentee landlord and was reported to be ready to resell the estate. This was that tense period in which gunboats went up and down the coast alternately supporting evictions and delivering relief supplies, of which I have given some account in connection with Berridge's estate agent, George Robinson. William Edward Forster, the Chief Secretary to Ireland, regarded Berridge as a specimen of the worst type of rack-renter, his tenants being genuinely poor and unable to pay. Towards the end of that decade there were dreadful years of potato blight and of fuel shortage caused by torrential rains that ruined the turf; reports of the sufferings of Connemara were as distressing as they had been in 1847, and a catastrophe comparable to that of the Great Famine was averted only by the dedication and energy of the Mansion House Fund and other private charities, from the records of which the Berridge name is conspicuously absent.

Richard Berridge died in September 1887, in the Midland Grand Hotel, St Pancras, London, having survived his wife by only two months. Reporting this under the heading 'The Great Landowner of Connemara Dead', the *Tuam Herald* had some relative good to say of his regime:

In justice to him it must be said that as things go his property was not a rack-rented one, and although considerable reductions were allowed by the Land Commission in the cases that went before them, they bear creditable comparison with the high-pressure rentals of other neighbouring lands . . . As far as we can learn there have been no evictions on this estate in these past years and few, indeed, at any time, which is a fact worthy of honourable mention.

Richard Berridge junior naturally inherited the estate, plus £200,000, and the daughters were left £15,000 each. But other provisions of his father's will, presumably influenced by his relative Charles Aldis, under which £172,000 went to London-based institutions concerned with sanitary education, caused much comment and made the *Tuam Herald* change its tune:

Although an Irish landlord drawing large revenues from this country for years he devotes over £200,000 to the improvement of the sanitary science in Great Britain, studiously omitting any mention of this poor country which helped support him and his for over a quarter of a century. He might show a little gratitude to poor Connemara. Had he given some of the money for the railway to Clifden he would have done something to redeem his memory from the stain of injustice and he might then die with the consciousness that his money was being devoted to a useful cause and not to the furtherance of an ideal.

Details of the will are intriguing. The National Society for Promoting Education and other societies providing voluntary schools received £50,000; £5,000 went to the National Training School of Cookery, Kensington (which later established itself in Hampstead, in premises known as Berridge House, now part of Westfield College of the University of London); the Queen Victoria Jubilee Institute for Nurses received £5,000 for instructing the sick poor in making their homes more healthy and comfortable according to simple sanitary principles; the Mansion House Council on the Dwellings of the Poor, the Worshipful Company of Plumbers, the Sanitary Institute of Great Britain and seven other bodies were left some thousands each for similar purposes of sanitary education; the Lister Institute of Preventive Medicine, in Chelsea and Elstree, was built largely on the strength of a donation of £46,000. And finally, a note of obsession seems to obtrude:

To the National Health Society (53 Berners St. W.), the objects of which are to collect and diffuse sanitary knowledge, and all other knowledge bearing on the physical and moral welfare of all classes of society; to call public attention to the serious pecuniary loss and injury to the health and comfort which arise from defective sanitary arrangements, to investigate the facts and diffuse by publications, lectures or otherwise, knowledge respecting any of the following matters, that is to say, clothing in relation to health, prevention of disease, spread of fevers, house sanitation, foods, cookery, temperance, ventilation, cleanliness, diseases, disinfectants, the supply of pure water, drainage and sanitation of houses, appliances for the sick room, home nursing and home education – £4,000.

It was a bizarre codicil to fifteen years of absenteeism, this sanitizing of London with monies wrung out of the reeking cabins of Connemara. Had Dickens, creator of the Golden Dustman who made a fortune by collecting London's 'night soil', not died before his work was done, he would have been the man to give us the interior world of the first Richard Berridge, to fill up that strange absence. But Dickens's last, great novel, *The Absentee*, is the one absent from all bookshelves.

The Sportsmen

In its obituary of Richard Berridge senior, the *Tuam Herald* looked forward to better times with the advent of his son:

He is succeeded in his estates by his son and heir, Mr Richard Berridge, a promising and clever young gentleman who was among his tenants not long since, and was everywhere well received, making a good impression and giving people the idea that he was a reasonable and intelligent man with no territorial prejudices and a good deal of sense . . . The young owner we hope will continue to take a still deeper interest in the affairs of this vast estate and give some time and thought to its intimate management.

Young Richard, who seems to have disliked his father and had very little to say about him, was a resident landlord from the beginning and took the estate in hand. In 1889, urged on by Fr Flannery, he offered a hillside of bogland called An Cnoc Buí, near Carna, to the Government for a relief-work scheme of afforestation. The offer was accepted 'as it was felt that, if planting succeeded there, it might be tried anywhere!' This early experiment in forestry soon fell foul of the western gales, but the gesture on the part of the new landlord was appreciated, as were his plans for improving the oyster fishery and developing Ballynahinch as a sporting estate. Richard soon became a local Justice of the Peace (he had studied law at Queen's College, Oxford), and in 1894, at the age of twenty-four, he was made High Sheriff of County Galway; later he joked that he had been appointed so young in the hope that he would buy all his officers new liveries.

By this period the Congested Districts Board had begun its work in the territory, and the *Tuam Herald* felt able to announce that Connemara was on the high road to prosperity. The railway was in building, with up to six hundred men employed on it between Oughterard and Clifden. In the vicinity of Ballynahinch work on the railway included bridging the river and blasting two long and deep cuttings through great ridges of rock. The men, in groups of three, spent endless hours in boring holes for the explosive charges, one man holding the iron bar and two others smiting it alternately with sledgehammers until the hole was the necessary three feet deep. The Berridge household would have enjoyed the anecdote about a local man who was promoted to be foreman over this activity and swaggered into a Clifden shop saying, 'I want the longest three-foot rule in the house!' Richard had donated the site for a railway station just west of the Castle's south gate, and was rewarded with a free ticket for life. When the railway was opened, in 1885, it made the west of Connemara easily accessible for sportsmen. Ballynahinch, blessed with the finest salmon and sea-trout fishery of Connemara and endless square miles of rough shooting, was a foretaste of heaven for the gentry of that great age of the gun and the rod. Albums of photographs and shelves of meticulously kept daybooks record the glorious slaughter. Richard himself varied the delights of Connemara with the thrills of big-game hunting in Africa.

One of these sportsmen was Arthur V. Willcox, a wealthy American who first came to Connemara in 1897 with his wife, Marion, and their son and daughter, and rented Glendollagh House, half a dozen miles east of the Castle, from Richard Berridge, for his fishing and shooting holidays. It was at Glendollagh that Richard met a young society girl, Arthur Willcox's niece, Eulalia Willcox Lesley. They married in 1905 at the Lesleys' 'handsome residence' in Haverford, Pennsylvania, 'under a canopy of white roses, smilax and lilies of the valley', according to a local newspaper. The bride wore 'a magnificent gown of white satin covered with duchess lace with court train', and to add to the picturesqueness of the occasion Richard had to forgo 'a delightful automobile trip in Italy' and 'hurry back to his estates in Ireland with his wife in order that he may be with his peasants during the famine that has broken out there'. Photographs of this happy return show a celebratory arch decked with the Union Jack, the Stars and Stripes and a banner reading 'Céad Míle Fáilte' (a hundred thousand welcomes) over the north gate of the Castle grounds, as well as a great concourse of people on horseback before the Castle door, as if assembled for a hunt, and 160 'peasants' seated at long tables in the back yard eating bread and drinking porter served from watering cans; this feast must have gone some way to relieving the famine, of which no more is heard. Richard converted to Catholicism, his wife's faith, at the time of his marriage, and took out a coat of arms (it features three dolphins and three anchors, with the motto *semper fidelis*). By 1909 a third storey was being added to the Castle, and his uncle-in-law Arthur Willcox was building Lisnabrucka, an impressive mansard-roofed mansion, on a site he bought from Richard overlooking the eastern end of Ballynahinch Lake.

Nevertheless, outside of the Ballynahinch demense there were signs that the era of the Berridges was drawing to an end. One of the functions, indeed a great historic task, of the Congested

Districts Board, in conjunction with the Land Commission, was to arrange for the transfer of landownership from the landlords to the tenant farmers. Compulsory purchase of the Berridge estate had been under discussion for years and there were complaints about the Board's laggardness; in 1910 the Roundstone parish priest Fr Gleeson claimed that the estate had been offered to the Board five years earlier; the Board denied this, but revealed that Mr Berridge and his agent, Mr Robinson, had now agreed to supply maps to facilitate valuation of the lands, for which the Board would then offer a price, calculated as the equivalent of so many years' rental income. Two years later the Nationalist MP Mr O'Malley, a native of Ballyconneely, speaking in the House of Commons, castigated the CDB again for its slowness in coming to an agreement with Berridge, and added a threat:

He was sorry that the Board should see fit to haggle over two or three years above the 14 years' purchase, because he was convinced of this – that unless the Berridge Estate was purchased they would not be able to restrain these people from some drastic action of their own. He had always condemned cattle-driving, but if this estate was not purchased he should not hesitate to advise the people to go cattle-driving.

In 1914 the CDB finally took over the estate, 143,325 acres, at a price of £95,441. The *Tuam Herald* commented rather sourly, in the course of a rather garbled account of the estate's history:

The famous and historic Martin estate of Connemara . . . has changed hands for the last time . . . It knows an owner of the old style and stamp no longer. It is now possessed by the people, and much good may it do them. The present representative of the Berridge family is a most popular gentleman, and did all he could to facilitate the transfer of the land to the tenantry. Mr Berridge will continue, of course, to live in his beautiful and picturesque castle – one of the finest situations in Ireland.

Indeed the Berridges did keep on the Castle and its immediate demesne, though some land was sold to the Forestry
Commission; hence the spruce and pine woods that rather darken
its setting these days. However, they occupied a rented house in
Killiney near Dublin in subsequent years, and then one in Kent.
These were troubled times in Ireland, and the quiet countryside
of Connemara was not exempt; during the War of Independence
Ballynahinch was raided by the Black and Tans, who removed all
its sporting guns, and then, in the Civil War, it was raided by the
IRA, who commandeered the Castle's horse and cart, and with
great politeness searched the place for warm coats, guns and binoculars. The Berridges were present on that occasion, and Mrs
Berridge was frightened that the grenades with which a local lad,
Charlie Cummins, was festooned might go off. During that period
the IRA were in control of most of Connemara and burned
several large buildings such as coastguard stations and barracks to
prevent them falling into the hands of the Free State forces
advancing from Galway. When the Railway Hotel at Recess was
burned out, the IRA then came to do the same to Ballynahinch,
but were dissuaded, perhaps by the housekeeper, who was a
Cummins. She wrote to the Berridges describing the event:

Dear Madam

I am sure you will excuse my liberty in writing to let you know
that everything is alright so far We had the IRA here since Monday.
They occupied the yard I had to give them Beds & Boarding
They certainly were very nice and & are now after leaving. The
National Army are somewhere between this & Maam Cross They
assured me before they left that nothing would happen to this
place so my mind is ever so much easier We are just longing to
get a letter Im so surprised that Nurse did not write I hope you
all are well & please tell Master Jimmie that his pets are on good
form. I hope you will excuse this letter and believe me to remain
    Your obedient servant
        Mary Cummins.

Nearby Glendollagh House was taken over for a while as the local headquarters of the IRA, but after its narrow escape Ballynahinch was regarded as a place of safety, and valuables belonging to other landed families were stored there; Oliver St John Gogarty, whose house at Renvyle was burned in 1923, sent his wife's jewellery there for safe keeping. Berridge himself was apparently seized by the IRA on a train between Dublin and Galway, but was released after a railway guard or porter had a word with his abductors. All this points to the high regard in which the second Richard Berridge was held. After the Troubles ended in a truce the Berridges returned to Ballynahinch for a while, but they rented out the Castle and its fishery for the summers of 1924 and 1925, and finally sold them in November 1925. They moved into a fishing lodge they owned at Screebe in south Connemara, which remained the family home until about 1960.

The new owner of Ballynahinch, 'the Ranji', was the most exotic person Connemara had ever seen, and was to become the best-loved of all masters of the Castle. Ranjitsinhji was, on one side of his life, the Jam Saheb of Nawangar, an independent princedom on the east coast of India, about four times the size of Connemara and home to 350,000 people. As a child he had been informally adopted by its ruler, a distant relative, and given hopes of the succession, which came to fruition, after many years of complex and perhaps even murderous intrigue, in 1907. On the other side of his life he was Ranji the famous, but now retired, cricketer, for, having been given a public-school type of education in his native state he had been sent to Trinity College, Cambridge, and had shown such talents on the field that he was selected for Sussex, and then for England, and soon rivalled the legendary W. G. Grace in the public's estimation. He brought some potent magic to the game, it seems, that won him adulation despite the racist prejudices of the time:

Graceful as a panther in action with lean but steely muscles under his smooth brown skin, wrists supple and tough as a creeper of the Indian jungle and dark eyes which see every twist and turn of the ball, he has adopted cricket and turned it into an oriental poem of action.

His life was a vivid mosaic of those of the Edwardian playboy, celebrity and sportsman, plus those of an eastern potentate and a self-seeking politician. He fished and shot and had affairs in England; in India he built palaces, shot tigers and bought fabulous diamonds, and on the twenty-fifth anniversary of his accession he processed in a silver chariot wearing the costume of legendary kings of old and had himself weighed against silver ingots; he schemed and negotiated, fruitlessly in the end, to preserve the independence of the multitude of tiny princedoms out of the vast democratic nation his contemporary Ghandi was campaigning for; he brought a touch of modernity into his little state, and colluded in swindling it to support his extravagance. Cricket had to be abandoned when he was accidentally shot in the eye on a Yorkshire grouse moor, and fishing took its place; that was the main attraction of Ballynahinch for him.

Ranji made his first visit to Ireland in July 1924, having been assured that as a head of state he and his entourage would be met on the dockside by the Minister for External Affairs, President Cosgrave's aide-de-camp and a troop of the National Guard, and wafted unexamined through Customs. The arrival of such a prominent sportsman was the best possible way of assuring the world that, after the painful interlude of the Troubles, Ireland's countryside was open for business again. Having been shown around the capital, and having wined and dined the President and members of the Free State Government at the Shelbourne Hotel, Ranji proceeded by train to Galway, in a private carriage supplied by the authorities, and then in the Clifden train to Ballynahinch. As soon as possible he was out by the river that was to become the focus of his Connemara days for the next seven summers. He enjoyed the spontaneity and informality of the locals, and he himself often told the story of one of his first outings on the lake, with a gillie who was very dubious of Ranji's skills. When, with his first cast, he hooked a huge salmon the gillie advised, 'Take him easy!' and then, 'Let him run, let him run! Now wind him in again, your Highness!' and as excitement mounted, 'You're doing mighty, your Majesty!' – until the line snapped and the fish was gone: 'Ye bloody black bastard, ye lost him!' But Ranji soon became an expert; he is recorded as having caught twenty-two salmon in the eel-weir pool on one occasion, and boasted of having landed two hundred sea trout in one night's fishing. Ranji's friend and constant companion the cricketer C. B. Fry was as enthusiastic as himself, and claimed to have caught sixty salmon in three weeks, while the Indian staff too took to the sport with fervour. Ranji became friends with a fellow sportsman, Roundstone's parish priest, Fr White, and through him was invited to open the first Connemara Pony Show, held in the grounds of the Franciscan monastery. A guard of honour received him there, and among the eminent guests were Richard Berridge and the former Lord Lieutenant of Ireland Lord Dudley, another keen fisherman, who was renting Screebe Lodge at the time and became a life-long friend.

During his next visit, in 1925, having been assured that he would be exempt from taxation in Ireland, he started negotiations with Richard Berridge to buy the Castle, its gardens and pleasure grounds, the 800 acres of its demesne, virtually all the lakes and streams in the Ballynahinch watershed, together with Glendollagh House and its grounds, Inagh Lodge, five miles north of Recess, and shooting rights over 16,000 acres of bog and mountain; the price was agreed at £30,000. Richard Berridge was invited out to India that following winter, and the sale was concluded despite his fears that accepting Ranji's dazzling hospitality might make it difficult to insist on prompt payment. Over the next few years the Castle underwent a comprehensive refurbishment: sixteen bathrooms were put in, and a central heating system powered by the water turbine in the grounds, and a splendid mix of antique and modern, eastern and European furniture and carpeting. The grounds were enhanced by flowerbeds and plantations of trees, the salmon and sea-trout runs were improved by blasting the riverbed in places and building cascades in others, and angling was facilitated by rustic bridges, luncheon huts (I'm told they had thatched roofs, which all blew away in the gales), miles of waterside paths and no fewer than eighty little stone jetties. Ranji's eagerly awaited spring arrivals by train with tons of luggage to be carted to the Castle were announced by a merry banging of fog detonators placed on the railway line. Then there would be interesting new faces in the vicinity: Ranji's two nieces, who later went to school with the Benedictine nuns at Kylemore Abbey in northwest Connemara, were to be met, shyly smiling, walking into Clifden in their costly saris and veils; his enigmatic and unexplained companion Mrs Williams, in her white dress, spent the summers reading in picnic huts while her lord and master fished nearby; a guru walked the circuit of road by Tuaim Beola and Cashel every day carrying 'a god in a box', and it was believed that he walked to atone for his master's sins, so that when he was seen as far afield as Clifden it was surmised that Ranji had been sinning more than usual. The Indian servants ('smoked Irishmen' to the local wits) soon picked up some Irish; there were flirtations and assignations, and inevitably, despite the fulminations of a new and repressive parish priest, Fr Cunningham, a couple of babies. On Ranji's birthdays his staff and their families were feasted in the courtyard, and then delivered merrily home by lorry.

So for a few summers the sun rose and set in the east, and Ballynahinch remembers them yet, as the last of Ranji's gillies died only in 2004 and his anecdotes still circulate. In the perspective of the past, the Maharajah of Ballynahinch eclipses the improving landlords, and the disimproving ones, the duellist gentlemen, the rebellious clan chieftains and their mythic ancestors. But in his last seasons, 1931 and 1932, the sunshine was visibly waning. Ranji was tired and preoccupied, and a gillie had to hook the fish for him to play. He was overweight and going blind, he suffered from malaria and bronchitis, his debts were mounting and financial scandal threatened, he faced political defeat in the affairs of India and his obsolete statelet. Ranjitsinhji died, back in the East, on 2 April 1933, and because of the difference in time zones the news arrived by telegraph in Ballynahinch on the evening of April Fool's Day, and was not at once believed.

A great clearance sale soon followed. Inagh Lodge and Glendollagh House and their rights and lands went to Sir William Arbuthnot Lane of London, and Derrada Lodge (now the Anglers' Return) with its sporting rights to a Captain Algernon Crowe; Athry Lake near Recess was acquired by the owner of the Zetland Hotel in Cashel, and five other small lakes around Recess were bought out by a local guesthouse owner, Thomas Lyons, who had been leasing them. The auction of contents took four days; everything was dispersed, from boats to books, of which last Galway County Council bought over nine hundred. The Castle and its 1,132 acres, its river and shooting rights, were bought by a Dublin businessman, F. B. McCormick, for £8,000; thirteen years later it was sold to the Irish Tourist Board, and as a hotel has passed through several hands since then. So now it is an inn, as it was in the days of the muddy bridle-way by the Cara-more; all who can put money in their pockets may enjoy its carefully maintained old-fashioned charms. More readily than for any other place in Connemara, a simulacrum of its past – or at least a paperchain of silhouettes of its former masters – may be snipped out from the pages of past commentators. In its drawing rooms the guest, who may be the next to write on Ballynahinch, will find some of the vociferous and opinionated old books I have drawn upon, and, I hope, this book now in hand.

Walking the Skyline

Sometimes the Twelve Pins seem to sleep all day, a pride of tawny beasts slumped together, breathing just perceptibly, their fur ruffled by cloud-shadows. Then in the evening they rigidify, revert to the inorganic. Once when I was lying on the terrace of our house overlooking the bay, listening to music from the room behind me and watching a summer night subvert the scale of all things, I felt I could raise my hands and spread my fingers over the mountain range, solidly dark against the still wine-flushed sky, as if over the keyboard of a piano, and produce one tremendous, definitive Connemara chord. But Connemara tends to undefine itself from minute to minute, and this Beethoven moment quickly passed. The range of peak became sheet iron, two-dimensional, a serrated rim to the floor of the world, dangerous to the imagined touch. A few little dots of light appeared at its base, some of them moving horizontally: houses and cars on the lowlands around the head of the bay. Soon there was nothing to say the mountains had ever existed, except for one of these sparks climbing slowly and apparently uncertainly into the night, a late homecomer to a farm up in one of the two great valleys opening on our side of the massif.

We can see eight of the twelve highest summits from our windows; all are between 1,900 and 2,400 feet high, as are the ones hidden from us. They are bound together by high ridges, and from the air or on a map they show their unity, like a condensed spiral galaxy or five-armed sea monster. The Twelve Pins are the mandala hub and round-dancing heart of the Barony of Ballynahinch, the old Conmaicne Mara. In the classic, much-painted and photographed view from Roundstone the peaks are splendidly disposed in a group with outliers, a body with wings outspread as if to shelter the glens on either side. Of the central heights, two stand forward: Binn Leitrí, the peak of the *leitreach* (a word that only occurs in placenames now, and according to John O'Donovan means 'a wet or spewy hillside'), rears up very steeply from the lowlands, with the more gently rounded Binn Ghleann Uisce, the peak of the glen of water, to the west of it. Binn Gabhar, the peak of the goat, just overtops Binn Leitrí and is almost hidden behind it, while the craggy top of Binn Bhraoin (the meaning of which is uncertain, but it might be from an old personal name) shows above the ridge between these two. From Binn Ghleann Uisce a long smooth slope falls westwards and then rises again in a perfect catenary curve, forming a sill to the upland glen of Barr na nOrán, top of the springs, and apparently cradling the three mountains around the head of the glen, which constitute the western wing of the range. There used to be a great rectangle of coniferous forestry on that lovely sweep of land, like a sticking plaster on the face of a high-cheekboned beauty, and it was becoming more obtrusive with each year of growth until in 2004 it was felled, although still immature, under an EU scheme for removing unsightly plantations. The drainage channels have been blocked and the land is already healing, toning back into its surroundings. Coillte, the Forestry Board, has long stopped expanding its plantations on Connemara's blanket bog; they were undertaken in the 1960s in response to political pressure and a demand for jobs, and showed little promise of profit, the land being so wet and the topography so intractable. Several sublime prospects in the Twelve Pins have been degraded by forestry, and the restoration of this one is the best environmental news to come out of Connemara during the years I have known it.

Those mountains of the western wing, behind Barr na nOrán, are Binn Bhán, white peak, the highest of the twelve but the furthest away and half withdrawn behind the central group; next to it the green rounded summit of Meacanacht (from another obsolete word, *meacanach*, meaning 'a lumpy thing'), and Binn na Caillí the peak of the hag, which shows us its precipitous southern flank hung with acres of a silver-grey scree called Clochar na Caillí. Lesser summits continue the range in diminuendo westwards. To the east, the majestic Gleann Chóchan (again probably from an old personal name) is rimmed with very steep slopes including those of the second wing of the mountains: Binn Chorr, pointed peak, which rears up and jabs at the sky with two summits like the budding horns of a goat-kid, and Derryclare (a name I will unpick in a later chapter), which from our viewpoint is a great shoulder blade of rock, the remains of some vast famished foundered beast sinking down into the bogs. The Mám Tuirc Mountains look like a continuation of the Twelve Pins beyond Derryclare, but are in fact separated from them by the two- or three-mile width of the Inagh Valley. Both ranges are of the same general height and are in fact the remains of a single broad plateau that has been deeply cut about by the Ice Age, as their scarred mountain faces and boulder-strewn valleys attest.

Although they only just qualify in height as mountains, the Connemara hills are not to be approached lightly; the Alpine and Himalayan climber Joss Lynam tells me that the trickiest situation he ever found himself in was when a sudden winter shower swept over the Twelve Pins and lacquered every facet of the bare rock slopes with ice, so that he had to creep down from the heights on all fours. I used to love being alone up there, and still appreciate it as a luxury to have a landscape to myself, but nowadays I arrange to have a companion, and a mobile phone. A popular route with hill-walkers is the Gleann Chóchan horseshoe, a circuit of the six peaks and the ridges linking them into a dizzy parapet around the dramatically scenic glen that gapes down at Ballynahinch Lake. According to Joss Lynam's guide, *The Mountains of Connemara*, which we (Folding Landscapes) published with a contoured map in 1988, this is a six- or seven-hour walk involving a total of 5,450 feet of ascent, with 'an awful lot of steep rough ground and, if there is mist, several navigational booby traps'. I have never done it as a whole – my favoured mode of walking being not a single-minded goal-bound linear advance but a cross-questioning of an area, or even a deliberate seeking out of the *fóidín mearaí*, the 'stray sod' that is said to put anyone who treads on it wandering – but I have visited most points of the circuit at one time or another, and will take it as the framework for an account of the mountains.

Joss suggests starting from the Ben Lettery Youth Hostel on the main road, opposite Ballynahinch Lake. However, a problem immediately presents itself: between the main road and the bare mountainside is a zone of fields in private ownership, and there is no right of way across it; further, the open land beyond that is commonage, which in the Irish context means that a number of farmers share grazing rights to it, some of whom may not be happy to facilitate walkers. One is advised to contact the relevant farmer for permission to cross cultivated land or commonage, which seems reasonable but is impracticable in many cases, most obviously so when there are perhaps six or ten farmers in question. In fact access to the mountains has become so problematic and fraught with contention that we have abandoned the idea of updating and reissuing Joss's hill-walkers' guide despite a steady demand for it. It was fortunate that I researched my own maps of the Aran Islands, the Burren and Connemara, in the 1970s and 1980s; I would not embark on such a project today as I could not rely on the warmth of welcome I enjoyed then.

The reasons for the great souring of the Irish countryside are many. The number of people taking walking holidays has increased hugely (on a fine day there might be a rambler, or a group of them, setting out on the Gleann Chóchan horseshoe every twenty minutes or so); the farmer sees these happy folk, led perhaps by a well-paid guide, revelling in the joyous freedom of the land the farmer knows too well in its dark and laborious aspects, and foresees the trampling of easily eroded slopes, gates left open, wire fences trodden down, and compensation claims in case of accident. Some of the farmers' fears are largely imaginary or exaggerated and have been exploited by their ignorant and obstructive leadership, but they are symptomatic of the deep malaise of a fading way of life. The matter is important not just because walkers bring their wallets and credit cards to the local economy but because of the inestimable and mysterious grace that mountains have in their gift for all who can seek it out. The practical, democratic and responsible solution of the access problem – which at the time of writing amounts to a stand-off – is up to the politicians and community representatives. For the moment, let the reader use a space-time wormhole or trick of the loop to avoid the obstacles of fences and resentful farmers, by slipping back to the days of freedom I enjoyed without knowing how exceptional they were, crossing the fields and then coming up to date again on the skirts of Binn Leitrí.

But wait: the approach itself is of great interest. The little fields all along the foot of the mountain range lie in what the geologists call the 'steep belt', because the strata dip to the south so steeply that they plunge into the earth almost vertically and one walks on their ragged edges, which run approximately east–west. There is a band of similar rocks dipping to the north, on the further side of the Twelve Pins. These rocks are of schist and marble; that is, they are of clayey and limey materials originally deposited in layers on an ocean floor and later metamorphosed and upended by geological forces. The Dalradian ocean in which they were born once stretched from what is now the Shetlands to the west of Ireland, and it lay within a vast supercontinent that comprised most of the Earth's present land masses, for this was long before the Atlantic came into existence. This supercontinent was under tension due to the slow upwelling and outspreading of molten rock in the mantle beneath it. As it thinned and sagged in the middle to form the Dalradian ocean basin, great river systems were carrying material into it, eroded from the surrounding land surfaces. At first these sediments were dumped in shallow water, where ocean currents washed the mud out of the sand, which was slowly consolidated into sandstone. Then the crust collapsed further, and unconsolidated sediments avalanching down into deep, still waters built up into strata some miles thick. Eventually the stretching and rifting of the continental plate culminated in the birth of the Iapetus Ocean, the predecessor of the Atlantic, which lasted for some 100 million years and began to close up again around 510 million years ago. The Dalradian sedimentary rocks were caught up in the reunion of the continents; they were crumpled and torn, pushed down into the hot depths of the Earth and thrust up into mountain chains of Himalayan proportions. Where the Twelve Pins now stand became a gigantic anticline, a complex ridge running roughly east–west and arched from north to south. The sandstones were pinched in the middle of this fold and metamorphosed into the tough and resistant quartzite, while the mixed muddy stuff overlying them was stretched and thinned and became today's beds of soft schists and rough marbles. These ranges, produced in what is called the Grampian orogeny, or period of mountain-building, were subsequently weathered down and reduced to an almost plain surface over many millions of years, exposing the quartzite that had lain in their depths. When the land was uplifted once again, much more gently, in the last ten million years, and then attacked by the Ice Ages, the schists and marbles succumbed more rapidly, so that the highly resistant quartzite that had formed the roots of the old mountains was left upstanding as the peaks of the new.

Out of these cataclysms, Earth-shaping in their cumulative effects but so slow that they would have escaped observation had anyone been around to observe, arose a difference, an enrichment of potential experience, worth noting and lingering over, in these little fields of the steep zone: on the near side of the last drystone wall, one enjoys close-up views only, in a detailed terrain of humps and hollows, friendly little fields and mossy dells and scrubby woodlands, robins and wrens, primroses and ferns and herb robert, and the half-tumbled basins of old limekilns next to undergrowth-filled holes where marble was once quarried for burning to lime; and on the far side of the fence, wide outlooks across the boggy foot-slopes of hills that lift one up into spaces fit for eagles.

Binn Leitrí rises from 200 feet to 1,902 feet at forty-five degrees, steepening towards the top. The bog is soon left below, the shiny little leaves of bearberry begin to show among the heather, and then as the vegetation thins out the furry-looking green fingers of a curious plant adapted to high exposed places, the fir clubmoss, grope among scatters of angular pale-grey stones, and at a touch release clouds of spore – lycopodium powder, that mysterious ingredient of school physics. The final few hundred yards seem to stand on end; one has breath for nothing but one's pounding heart. Then, sitting on the summit to rest aching thighs, one can triumph over the low country to the south. The agitated crest of Errisbeg outlined against the vaporous sea-horizon gives the vista a centre, around which all the rest is flattened and map-like: the apparently random or wilful complications of water in Roundstone Bog, the arms of Roundstone Bay elbowing their way around Inis Ní and reaching into the land to meet the Abhainn Mhór, and, nearer, steeply below, Ballynahinch half lost in forest, with its island castle adrift in the dreamy sky-mirroring lake. A general could plan strategies of advance and encirclement from up here; I could plan a book, and from this height it looks as if it would be achievable, all the sticking points of that contentious, foot-dragging, ankle-twisting subject matter being ironed out by distance. I can just distinguish individual houses in the village of Roundstone; could M see me, elevated and courageous, if she happened to look out this way? Hardly, for I am only one three-hundredth of the height of the mountain; but I wave anyway, and cry, 'Excelsior!'

Down below to the east of this first summit is the deep gulf of Gleann Chóchan, with a ribbon-like stream making a hundred twists and turns to find its way down through bogs and boulders, and a little road that looks as if it were made of a few lengths of tape laid end to end coming up from the main road, bridging the stream and climbing the further side of the glen to the last few houses. This topmost hamlet, dwarfed by Aill an Torann, the cliff of thunder, soaring above it, is Baile an Lotaí; the word *lotaí* or loft occurs in the names of several high places in Connemara. Towards the end of the Civil War the last members of the IRA hid out in a house up there, and were surprised and rounded up by the Free State forces when their lookout went to sleep, as I am told. When one walks or drives up the road to it the village does seem very high and remote, and perhaps they enjoyed a false sense of security up there because of this; but seen from the mountain tops the constructions and dimensions of settlement are minute in comparison with the crushing bulk of rock around them; politics too, and even civil war, are petty concerns. Up on the heights one is under the examination of the sky, heaven's vast eye, and if not humbled by the experience may be puffed up with the afflatus of the Divine, charged by revelatory lightning, burdened with wisdom carved in stone, and sent cascading down the screes like Moses or Zarathustra to fulminate and castigate and make oneself ridiculous in the valley of human affairs. Whereas, on the mountains, it is best to focus on the next step, the nearest handhold, to be aware of oneself as a physical object with a precarious centre of gravity, limited reach and fragile bones.

There is a short scramble down between great blocks of stone to the ridge connecting Binn Leitrí with Binn Gabhar, three-quarters of a mile to the north and 280 feet higher. The summit here is a desolation of frost-shattered quartzite that glitters fiercely if the sun is out, and running down a buttress of the mountain to the south-east is a vein of white rock that stands proud of the ground like a thick crystalline wall some four to six feet high. This dyke is the result of hot aqueous solutions from deep in the Earth forcing their way up a fault and depositing pure silica on its walls as they cooled, to form a great vertical sheet of quartz, which has evidently withstood subsequent ages of erosion better than has the less-pure silica of the quartzite on its either side. Seen from the main road some miles away, the 'Bengower Fault' so marked out is a very conspicuous feature, a rough seam or knotty tendon in the flesh of the mountain. It is one of several major faults cutting south-south-eastwards or south-westwards through the Twelve Pins that originated in the shock of Connemara's forced voyage along the margin of the Iapetus Ocean and its final ramming into place against Mayo as that ocean closed, about 450 million years ago. A pointer into deep time, this white reef is also a handy pointer for a relatively easy descent into the valley bottom if one decides to abandon the horseshoe at this point.

Next on the circuit of the peaks comes Binn Bhraoin, approached by a ridge that dips by about five hundred feet to form Mám na Gaoithe, the gap of the wind, before climbing about six hundred feet to the summit. A *mám* is the amount one can scoop up between two hands, and, seen from the valley, the skyline here looks as if Beola or some such giant being had taken such a scoop out of it, as it does in many high mountain gaps of similar names; in some cases these are hardly to be called passes as the ascents to them on one or both sides are sheer precipices. From Binn Bhraoin one looks down tremendous drops into the uninhabited and afforested valley of Bearna na nEang, the gap of the angles, to the west and north-west, and beyond that more mountains, with glimpses of the Atlantic along the glens between them. From Roundstone we often watch dirty weather brewing up in these great cauldrons, and slow turbulences of cloud mounting their brims to overflow into Gleann Chóchan, so I keep a wary eye on the high ridge running northwards from Binn Bhraoin when I am exploring the upper parts of that glen.

This ridge terminates in a steep rocky descent into a genuine but complex pass, Mám Eidhneach, which links both Bearna na nEang and Gleann Chóchan with the magnificent glacial valley of Gleann Eidhneach or Gleninagh, the ivied glen. It would be easy to go wrong here, though very rewarding, and find oneself scrambling on the gigantic scree slopes of Binn Bhán to the north, or the strange crumbly cliffs of schist with their rare montane flora on the north face of Meacanacht; but here I'll turn eastwards and continue with the Gleann Chóchan circuit. Binn Dhubh, black peak, is the next summit, reached by a stiff climb out of the pass, after which one descends a few hundred feet onto a rocky plateau linking it to the soaring peak of Binn Chorr. This plateau is Mám na bhFonsaí, a name I learned from the people of the glen, meaning 'the gap of the rims' and referring no doubt to the cliff-like scars running across the ascent to it from Gleann Chóchan and the vertiginous precipice on its other edge, dropping into Gleann Eidhneach. The latter crag is famous among climbers for its testing routes, one of them being the longest rock-climb in Ireland, Carrot Ridge, so named by Joss, he tells me, because it took more carrot than stick to get a certain novice up it; no amount of either would persuade me to attempt it.

This awesome precipice is the back wall of a corrie, from which in the last Ice Age a glacier flowed down, excavating the glen and giving it the characteristic U-shape of a glacial valley, and then, joining with other tributary glaciers from the Mám Tuirc Mountains, ground its way down the broad Inagh Valley to the southern lowlands, and so to the sea. One can clearly visualize the process by which the corrie came into existence: snow blown inland from the Atlantic and across the mountain heights settles on this sheltered north-east-facing slope, accumulates and packs down into ice; under its own weight the frozen mass begins to inch downhill, plucking rocks out of the slope behind it, so that a crevasse opens up between the ice and the mountainside; more snow falls into this gap, welding the glacier to its bed again; the ice moves again, pulling more stones out of the slope, cutting it back, steeper and steeper into the mountainside, and so on. For tens of thousands of years the vast river of ice, studded with boulders, rasps away all before it, digging out the long troughs of the Inagh Valley lakes and the lake of Ballynahinch; then comes global warming, the ice dies back, dumping its load of stone and clay in rampart-like moraines such as the one that almost closes the mouth of Gleann Eidhneach, clearly visible in the almost apocalyptic timescape one may scan from Mám na bhFonsaí.

Joss describes Mám na bhFonsaí as the most desolate part of the Pins, and in my mind too there is something terrible about it. If, in imagination, I approach its northern edge and look down into Gleann Eidhneach, I feel myself, for reasons I will explain, caught in a gaze that shrinks me to nothing. There are, on the crest of that heather-covered glacial moraine lying athwart the bogs of the valley bottom, six boulders set a foot or two apart in a line, the largest, at the southern end of the row, about three foot six high and the others rather smaller. I noticed them one day in 1986 when I was walking up the track on the further side of the valley with a friend who was researching the breeding birds of the Connemara mountains; we were on our way to see the ravens and the peregrine falcon pairs nesting on the great corrie cliff. The six little tabs sticking up on the profile of the moraine ridge had caught my eye, because I had been rambling all over Connemara with the Galway Archaeological Survey that year, and had learned to recognize the sort of thing they were looking for. We splashed across the bog to examine them more closely; clearly, a Bronze Age stone alignment. There is a well-known alignment in north-west Connemara and several standing stones in the Clifden and Ballynakill regions, but as this was the first such monument to be identified in central Connemara, it was an exciting find. However, I failed to notice the crucial fact about it, later ascertained by the archaeologist Michael Gibbons: the stones are aligned on Mám na bhFonsaí, which from that angle looks like a steep-sided notch in the skyline, and, further-more, at about 2.15 of the afternoon of the midwinter solstice the sun sinks into this notch and shines through it for a few minutes before disappearing behind the mountain wall. The spectacle is blindingly magnificent; the concentrated blaze of light bites into the skyline, and in its turn is quickly swallowed by the dark edge. Some three thousand years ago to the minute there would have been a congregation at these stones to observe and celebrate an event that had great practical significance, as marking the begin-ning of the year's cycle of plenty and want, and was surely a profound religious experience. Who knows anything of the religion of Connemara three thousand years ago? Perhaps some shamaness was storing the last rays of the sun in her belly, to bring them forth as golden corn in nine months' time; perhaps some fierce-eyed priest was facing the dying sun, desperately seeking an assurance of its return, or pretending to command its obedience. If someone, if I, had appeared up on the lofty rim of the gap at that moment, would I have cast a shadow into the valley and along the sacred stones? No, the radiance would have engulfed and nullified me, the dazzled eyes below would have been unaware of my microscopic blasphemy. Near annihilated, ant-sized, I creep away from the holy place.

A man died waiting for a lesser light near here once. He was a sapper of the Royal Engineers, employed in the first Ordnance Survey of Ireland. The first stage in mapping the island was the primary triangulation, the measuring of angles between directions from hilltop to hilltop throughout the island, by observation of signals from powerful lamps by night and from heliostats (sun-reflecting mirrors) by day. The process began in 1822 with the setting-up of poles on such heights as Divis Mountain near Belfast, and their observation from various Scottish mountains such as Ben Lomond, to link the Irish survey with that of mainland Britain. Gradually the trigonometrical skeleton was extended to cover the whole of the island of Ireland. In the 1830s the sappers were peri-odically at work on Binn Chorr, sending and receiving signals from Slieve More in Achill, Nephin in Mayo, Knockalongy in the Ox Mountains of Sligo, Keeper Hill in Tipperary, and Baurtregaum and

Mount Brandon, ninety miles away in Kerry. The greatest obstacle to the survey was 'the inveterate haze and fogginess' of Ireland, according to its director Thomas Colby, and Gleann Chóchan people tell of how the sappers on Binn Chorr had to wait seven weeks for a clear day to receive a heliograph signal from 'the Kerry man'. Their sufferings in wind and rain must· have been dreadful, and one of them fell to his death; from him the mountain gets its altern-ative name of Binn an tSaighdiúra, the peak of the soldier.

As the list of mountains the sappers observed from here suggests, Binn Chorr is, in the words of Joss Lynam's guide, 'a magnificent belvedere', and at 2,336 feet it is the high point of the circuit. Its western flank falls appallingly steeply into the glen, scored by the deep runnels of winter streams that the local people call Na Trinsí, the trenches, which are even visible from Roundstone. To the east it descends in a long ridge between two mighty corries that termi-nates in a cliff looking down on Loch Eidhneach. Four miles away across the wide Inagh Valley is the long quartzite-glittering wall of the Mám Tuirc Mountains, the eastern boundary of the old Conmaicne Mara. Its skyline, as grand and lofty as that of the Pins, is broken by the high passes of Mám Tuirc itself, the gap of the boar, which used to serve as a route into Connemara before roads were built through the lowland bogs, and, further south, Mám Éan, the birds' gap, a site of immemorial legend, where I intend to stage the conclusion of this book.

From the summit of Binn Chorr the way now lies southwards, down along a broad ridge and then up again to the next peak, Derryclare. At the lowest point of the ridge there are the slight remains of the sappers' encampment: hut foundations, or – since the people of the glen call the place Tinteannaí – more probably just low surrounds to pitch tents in, to prevent them being whirled off into the abyss. Then, from Derryclare, a wonderful walk down the narrow spine of a descending ridge eventually delivers one onto a tract of craggy reefs and reedy quags by the shore of Derryclare Lake, tiring to cross, but with the main road not too far ahead. However, I shall end this account of the uplifts and downthrows of the mountain experience at a point only about two-thirds of the

way down this last descent, as it gives me a last chance to arrive at
a just estimate of my – or any individual's – relationship to the physical scale of our planet. One day some twenty years ago, coming
down this ridge, I happened to look at Cashel Hill, four miles away
to the south, standing out like a small dark pyramid against the blue
of the sea beyond. As I shed height the hill seemed to grow a little
and adjust itself until at a certain moment the straight hard line of
the sea horizon looked as if it were exactly balanced on its summit.
Surely, I thought, the diameter of the Earth could be worked out
from this observation. I saw myself as in a diagram, with a straight
line drawn from my eye to the top of Cashel Hill and onward to
graze the curve of the Earth, a tangent. I dimly remembered a
theorem from Euclid about the length of a tangent to a circle from
a point at such-and-such a distance outside the circle. Back in my
library that evening I disinterred the theorem, and with a little alge-
braic fiddling arrived at an approximate formula for the diameter
of the Earth in terms of the height of Cashel Hill, the altitude of
the point I had been standing at on Derryclare and the distance
between them. Those data could be read off a map, but it pleased
me to realize too that, had I set up a pole at my station on the
ridge of Derryclare, like the sappers of old, and taken observations
of it and of Cashel Hill from two points so many paces apart on a
level and straight stretch of the coast road north of Roundstone,
with a homemade theodolite, or even a pair of straight sticks hinged
together, I could have found by trigonometry, or simply by drawing,
the three quantities I needed, and thence arrived at the diameter of
the Earth, in terms of the length of my own stride – all this without
recourse to a compass, the stars, a map or anything outside the realm
of naive locality. That the result would be wildly inaccurate, and that
I had not thought to mark that point on the ridge of Derryclare,
was irrelevant. I tried the calculation, using the map data and making
a guess as to where I had stood on the ridge, and arrived at a figure
of about eleven million paces – a distance I could walk in a couple
of easy-going years. Thus the cool regime of geometry gives me a
number, a measure, emblematic of a just and modest relationship to
the Earth, that all my haunting of precipices refuses me.

The Cuckoo of the Wood

No sooner had I written that paragraph of my preface in which I made Cuach na Coille, the cuckoo of the wood, a spokeswoman or spokesbird for all those Connemara people to whom history has not lent a voice, she herself being unremembered except for her voiceful nickname, than I unexpectedly came upon information about her from two or three sources. I was not entirely pleased about this, as the facts are relatively humdrum and I had fallen in love with her mystery, as shadowy as the wood she haunted. But ultimately I accept the complication, the obstacle to writing, with gratitude; it widens the boundary region between established truth and unstable imaginings that is my preferred territory and through which my book prowls to its conclusion.

To get the facts out of the way, Cuach na Coille was one Bid Delia Conneely; she was born in Derryclare Lodge, which was a herd's cottage and later a gamekeeper's cottage, in the wood on the west shore of Derryclare Lake, and she had a lovely singing voice. Since I am told that the Conneelys were succeeded as tenants of the lodge by the Shaughnessys, and the Shaughnessys by the Cumminses, who were there until it was deserted in the first decade of the last century, it seems probable that Bid lived in the time of the Martins, before the Famine. And if so, we may even have a glimpse of her in Thackeray's account of a fishing expedition from Ballynahinch Castle during his stay there in 1842. He describes with ecstasy the way one had but to cast and immediately a big trout would spring at the fly and soon be in the net. The single rod in the boat, he says, caught enough fish in an hour to feed the crew of five and 'the family of a Herd of Mr Martin's who has a pretty cottage on Derrycleer Lake, inhabited by a cow and its calf, a score of fowls, and I don't know how many sons and daughters'. Since the east shore of the lake was not Martin territory (it belonged to Trinity College, Dublin), he was certainly referring to Derryclare Lodge, which according to the Ordnance Survey map of 1841 was the only habitation on the west shore. Later in the day it began to rain, and the party resorted to the lodge for shelter, and Marcus the boatman cooked the fish in turf ashes from a fire 'on which about a hundred-weight of potatoes were boiling'.

When the gentlemen had finished their repast, the boatmen and the family set to work upon the ton of potatoes, a number of the remaining fish, and a store of other good things; then we all sat round the turf-fire in the dark cottage, the rain coming down steadily outside, and veiling everything except the shrubs and verdure immediately about the cottage. The Herd, the Herd's wife, and a nondescript female friend, two healthy young herdsmen in corduroy rags, the herdsman's daughter paddling about with bare feet, a stout black-eyed wench with her gown over her head and a red petticoat not quite so good as new, the two boatmen, a badger just killed and turned inside out, the gentlemen, some hens cackling and flapping about in the rafters, a calf in a corner cropping green meat and occasionally visited by the cow, her mamma, formed the society of the place. It was rather a strange picture; but as for about two hours we sat there, and maintained an almost unbroken silence, and as there was no other amusement but to look at the rain, I began, after the enthusiasm of the first half hour, to think that after all London was a bearable place, and that for want of a turf-fire and a bench in Connemara, one *might* put up with a sofa and a newspaper, in Pall-Mall.

The bare-footed girl-child? The stout black-eyed wench? There is a possibility that if Thackeray had broken the silence by asking for a song, he would have heard a marvel, even if he might have derided it as caterwauling. Of course error may have crept into the oral record of the lodge, and my deductions may be all unsound. But in any case it seemed worth my while to revisit the place recently, to see if anything of the girl has transcended the world of fact and still haunts the wood, and to drink in the scent of the place itself – an aboriginal Atlantic oak wood, to encapsulate it in three words that resonate in my mind.

Aboriginal: its trees being direct descendants of those in the first forests to establish themselves after the last Ice Age had wiped the land as bare as the tops of the Pins are now. Birch and willow were the light and swift outriders of the forest, advancing as the glaciers retreated, and they still form thickets wherever they get the chance in Derryclare, but they were largely replaced by hazel and the heavier troops, oak, elm, Scots pine. Alder and ash arrived with the warmer and wetter Atlantic period of five thousand to seven thousand years ago, completing the present woodland association. What with a deteriorating climate and the advent of humankind with fire and axe, the woods by degrees gave place to bogs except in a few sheltered corners. In Connemara Derryclare is the best-preserved relic of the forests of pre-human millennia. The sessile oak (the species of oak in which the acorn cups have no stalks and sit directly on the twigs) is the main player, but because of the mild and humid Atlantic climate the supporting cast of trees, shrubs, herbs, ferns and lichens is quite different from that of continental oak woods. Hence Derryclare is treasured by ecologists; Victor Westhoff loved it, and with his younger colleague, David Ferguson of the University of Antwerp, wrote a paper analysing it as an assemblage of various plant communities, which has helped me to discriminate its complex tones and textures.

Driving up the Inagh Valley, one first sees the wood about a mile away to the west across the placid waters of Derryclare Lake, a wind-rounded unity, like a low-lying cloudbank. Derryclare is the anglicized form of Doire an Chláir; *clár* often signifies a plank bridging a river, and as the track to the wood crosses the river flowing into the north end of Derryclare Lake, I think that the placename derives from some simple predecessor of the present broad wooden bridge. *Doire*, oak wood, is a common placename element, but still one of the weightiest, harking back to times before Ireland lost its immemorial forests. Through its Indo-European root *derew* it is related to the Greek *drys*, oak, and hence to *dryad*, the nymph of the oak tree. The harsh bare flank of Derryclare Mountain used to look as if it rose steeply from immediately behind the wood, but in fact there is some intervening hillocky land which in the 1960s was afforested with Sitka spruce and lodgepole pine, a dark surround that showed off the changing tints of the deciduous woodland and especially its new-budded green in spring. The wood is quite small, about half a mile long and 150 yards or so in width, and very vulnerable. It was nearly sacrificed to the rage for forestry, which at the time was being promoted by politicians as the answer to the old question of what to do with Connemara, but in the event it was saved and kept as a nature reserve in the horny hands of Coillte, the Irish Forestry Board. Nowadays rangers from the Connemara National Park visit occasionally and try vainly to keep marauding sheep out of it.

The arrival of the conifer plantation, overnight, as it were, relative to the slow ways of oak, was a physical shock to the wood and put it in danger. The resinous flimsy branches of conifers are so much kindling awaiting a match, a lightning strike or a discarded bottle focusing the sun's rays, and the plantation came right up to the margins of the old wood with no intervening firebreak; also, the drifts of fallen needles from the conifers must have further acidified the streams coming down off the mountainside to water the wood. And recently the old trees have suffered another brutally sudden change of environment, for the coniferous forestry has nearly all been clear-felled, and trees that had grown tall in its shelter are now exposed to the blasts that hurtle up and down the valley. The aftermath of felling is, for some years, an appalling sight, while the heaps of lopped-off branches left *in situ* mulch down into the soil to feed the newly planted saplings poking up through them. One used to walk down from the Inagh Valley road to the old wood by a forestry track leading around the head of the lake, between the hushed depths of the pine woods on either hand. Stepping off the track and passing between the first two stately trunks was like being admitted by an invisible gate into a domain defined by a geometry as regular and never-ending as the system of whole numbers, with a dry, sound-absorbing sponginess underfoot, and a scent that prickled like champagne in the nostrils. Now the track crosses a catastrophic bone-bright landscape of bleached and shattered timber that looks as if it were frozen at a moment of maximum horror: trees collapse into each other's arms, smashing their branches together; torn limbs hang by slivers; here and there a splintered birch shrieks and totters like a bereaved girl searching the battlefield. On my most recent visit my companion and I rashly took a short-cut along a quarter of a mile of the lake shore to reach the oak wood; but the forestry had come right down to the water's edge and we found ourselves clambering, hesitating and back-tracking among piles of rotten branches covered in swathes of dead *Molinia* grass and intricately threaded through with brambles. It took us an inordinate time to get out of this disaster-zone, but when we dragged ourselves free from the last paroxysms of the carnage and looked at last into Derryclare Wood, a mere step over a strand of barbed wire away, we were immediately aware of an atmosphere too complex and unfamiliar to be captured in a word, having been five thousand years in the distillation.

This northern end of the forest is spacious; each tree has room to face in all directions (which is what distinguishes the presence of a tree from that of an animal). The limbs of the first oaks that we stepped between flowed up and out through the air with slight bends like those of a slow river. The upper surfaces of their branches were deeply furred with moss, out of which the foot-long fronds of hundreds of polypody ferns stood up. The visit I am remembering now took place in early March, and there were deep drifts of crisp brown oak leaves around the tree roots. The ground sloped to the left, down banks of moss-wrapped boulders, to where the lake gleamed through hanging screens of branches. One tree had been riven into two great fragments from near the base, perhaps by a lightning strike, one half still upright but gaunt and dead, the other resting several massive elbows on the ground, living, and each half so full of its own histories, places and denizens the event must have been as momentous as Byzantium's falling away from the Roman Empire. Along the lake shore were dark rocks water-worn into ragged crests: the marble or metamorphosed limestone that outcrops throughout the Inagh Valley. Further into the wood the oaks were mixed with ash and undergrown by hazel, and there were some swampy hollows where downy birch and common sallow sprawled in sphagnum moss.

The lodge faces the lake shore from a few dozen paces inland, its ruins almost obscured by the dense growth around and within them. In her days, when the forest was more frequented and the gamekeeper's family kept a few grazing animals, Bid Delia Conneely would have had a glimpse between the tree trunks from it of the water and a rough little stone quay. It was a comparatively large stone-built, slate-roofed cottage of the usual Connacht design: about twenty-one yards long, of three rooms, with doors into the middle one and a fireplace in the wall between that and the north-western one; no doubt the central room would have been the kitchen, and open to the rafters, with a ladder or stairs to lofts above the other rooms. A fallen sallow tree now occupies the south-eastern room, having grown there for the seventy years or more since the roof fell in. There are the remains of a couple of outhouses close by, a small limekiln, and traces of field walls. A grove of sycamores and horse chestnuts stands around the lodge, and close by to the north there used to be a mighty beech, reputed the largest tree in Connemara, probably dating from before the Famine and planted in the time of the Martins, who built the lodge. Victor Westhoff found that this beech measured four and a half metres around the trunk at eye level; that was in the 1980s, and the tree had even then shed some huge branches, exposing its heart to rot and beetles and fungi; later it was deliberately ring-barked and is now a mouldering horizontal bulk like a rampart across the forest floor. Someone has had to make the difficult decision as to whether to remove the introduced trees (beech is not native to Ireland) in order to favour the aboriginal elements of the forest — but I remember Victor's distress when he heard of the death of this king of the forest.

There have been more recent losses too. A huge oak has split in two from a rotten base, one half of it lying in the lake and the other a twisted chaos on land, both still leafy, but doomed. South of the lodge is a zone in which one has to clamber over criss-crossed trunks of slim young ash trees, fallen because the bark has been nibbled off near ground level by the half-dozen sheep that infest the wood, some of them ferried across the lake, I have heard, and others pushed in under the wire fence by local farmers who like to know where their sheep are and are unaware of or indifferent to the wood's rare status. A few hundred yards south-west of the lodge a single very ancient yew, laden with polypody fern, great woodrush and the saxifrage known as St Patrick's cabbage, hangs over the lake water, as extravagantly crooked as a tree in a Japanese print. At the time of Westhoff's researches (published in 1987) there was another mature yew about 140 yards to the south, where a stream off the mountainside comes down through the wood and tumbles into a narrow inlet of the lake shore; it was female and the other male, and between them they were producing a few seedlings. These trees were probably the oldest members of the wood; the male, he determined from a coring, is certainly more than 130 years old and probably more than 200 years old; the female was too precariously sited on the sheer side of a ravine for him to be able to core it, but he thought it was even older than its mate. Since then, as I discovered on a recent visit, this antiquity has dropped off the rockface and is rotting away upside-down in a deep pool of the stream, and so the male is a widower.

By coincidence there is a fine description of this stream in a letter by Maria Blake, wife of the landlord of Renvyle in north-western Connemara; it was written to her English friends in 1823, when evidently the lodge had not yet been built and there was only a 'cabin' in the woods. Like Thackeray a couple of decades later, the Blakes were overtaken by rain during a lake fishing trip from Ballynahinch, and had to make for shelter:

We approached the shore at a place where a little sparkling streamlet comes tumbling down amidst the rocks, forming, about twenty yards before it falls into the lake, a pretty natural cascade. There was just breadth enough to allow our boat to enter its narrow channel, and we advanced, the dark rocks closing in on us on every side, and the lofty oak and graceful birch meeting in a canopy over our heads. It was a sweet spot, which Nature seemed to have taken delight in adorning with every miniature beauty, while resting from the labours of her more majestic works around.

Although the rain still continued to fall, we left the boat, and supporting ourselves by the overhanging branches, clambered over the slippery rocks, which were covered with ferns and mosses, and wet with the sparkling foam that the brawling streamlet dashed about on every side. The interior of the wood, entangled in all the wild exuberance of nature, was enchanting to the Cunnemara eye, which can so seldom rest on a tree unbent by the western blast . . . After sheltering ourselves for a while under a spreading thorn, and gathering the delicate blossoms of the Enchanter's nightshade (*Circaea lutetiana*) with the *melampyrum pratense*, and others of our old woodland friends, we took refuge in a cabin . . .

. . . where they had to amuse themselves for some time by watching the raindrops chase each other off the thatched roof, while their brawny boatmen tried their strength by trying to lift a block of marble lying nearby. (Thus our only two literary witnesses to Derryclare Wood concur on its dominant feature: rain, rain, rain.)

Maria Blake was well informed botanically: the *Circaea* is listed among the present-day flora of the wood, but not the *Melampyrum* (cow-wheat), which, however, is common enough in the region. Westhoff and Ferguson list 124 species of flowering plants from Derryclare Wood, 16 ferns and 40 mosses, and of course all this richness does not occur in an amorphous mixture but in a number of more or less well-defined vegetal communities. Chief among these is an association characterized by the sessile oak and the hard fern, which grows profusely on the forest floor. The typical form of this association occurs on the acidic metamorphic rock that outcrops in steep slopes just behind the old lodge and makes up much of the mountain range; on the lime-rich Lakes Marble that underlies much of the forest, hazel is an additional component.

Two central areas of the forest, around the lodge and beyond the stream, also underlain by marble, bear an association of hazel and ash, and at the junction between the two rock types, where lime-rich water wells up, there are patches of an association headed by ash trees and a sedge, *Carex remotum*, so called because its flower spikes are spaced out along its stem. Westhoff and Ferguson also noted the swamp community growing in patches fed by nutrient-poor water running off the mountainside and the conifer forestry, of common sallow, downy birch and the moss *Sphagnum palustre*, but did not designate it formally as an association as its occurrence elsewhere is unknown. Thus the patient eyes of science disentangle the chaos of phenomena, naming, classifying, hypothesizing causal connections, reconstituting it as a highly individuated organic whole, fragile but adaptive, simultaneously rivalrous and convivial. Some may feel that this intellectual process distances one from reality, or reduces it, drives the spirit out of it, frightens the cuckoo out of the wood. But I have always found it a form of awareness, an introduction to wonder.

For many botanists the glory of Derryclare would be its lichen flora – ninety-eight species known by 1970, and no doubt quite a few added to the list since then; the huge populations of certain species, and the presence of a handful of the greatest rarities, make this the richest site for lichens in Connemara. The lichens of Derryclare were first studied by a Charles Larbalastier, who was employed as tutor to the children of Mitchell Henry at Kylemore Castle in north Connemara from 1874 to 1878; the Revd W. A. Leighton published 'the marvellous discoveries of Mr. Larbalastier in the west of Ireland' in his *Lichen-flora of Great Britain, Ireland and the Channel Islands* of 1879. Several other heavyweights of the lichenographical world have investigated Derryclare since then, notably during field trips of the British Lichen Society.

Looking to learn something about lichens, I tagged along with one of these expeditions, organized by Harold Fox in April 1998. We approached the oak wood through the forestry on the slopes above it to the west, and by chance I was almost the last to reach the rim of the wood, as I had waited to help an elderly member of the party over some tricky fences and ditches. When I looked down into the first dell, into which they had preceded me by just a few minutes, I was surprised to see no sign of them; it was as if they had all vanished into the enchanted wood of a fairytale. Then I made them out: each was standing motionless, forehead close to a tree, magnifying glass in hand, deep in study of a lichen. When one of them began to move away, the spell was broken. As they dispersed I followed them around, and they showed me their finds: crustose lichens like bits torn out of maps or illegible parchments, on rocks and tree trunks; filamentous and fruticose or bushy lichens, hanging in tangled masses from branches; foliose or leafy lichens like patches of peeling wallpaper. A lichen, they explained, is composed of an alga and a fungus, the cells of the alga being layered between or dispersed among the internal structures of the fungus, in a symbiosis, a being-together, closer than the sexual. The fungal partner is the housing that prevents the alga drying out and channels nutrient-bearing rainwater to its cells, and it controls the metabolism by which the alga produces the sugars they both live on. Nevertheless the fungus is the more dependent; lichen fungi are not found living alone, while some lichen algae can survive by themselves. Lichens reproduce from fallen fragments of themselves, or produce fruiting bodies that disperse the spore of the fungus, which may or may not be lucky enough to alight on the right species of alga. It seems like a precarious mode of existence, but the combination of fungus and alga is highly viable and resistant; lichens can live for a century or more, and in apparently extremely unpropitious environments.

In Connemara's clean air and equable, humid climate, lichens flourish, and nowhere more so than in Derryclare Wood. I heard the lichenologists' excitement as they exclaimed over their finds. *Lobaria pulmonaria*, the lungwort, once prized as a herbal cure, growing in great cabbagy bundles up in the treetops! The biggest colonies of the rare *Sticta canariensis* known in Ireland! The fairytale-pretty *Lecanora chlarotera* that forms a pale greyish crust on twigs and has fruiting bodies like minute Bakewell tarts! And then, the fungi that live on other fungi's lichens, parasitically or independently: these little black dots on the fruiting bodies of the lichen *Pannaria conoplea* are *Stigmidium mitchellii,* known from nowhere else in Europe and named for Michael Mitchell, the lichen specialist from NUI, Galway, while these dots on the *Sticta* are the rarest of Irish fungi, *Hemigrapha astericus,* found for the first time in the northern hemisphere right here in Derryclare Wood! . . . I am thoroughly caught up in this search-and-record mission; in its drive to make new finds, to augment species lists, it might appear to be egocentric, competitive, intrusive on the cryptic life-ways of the wood and disruptive of its endlessly self-productive wholeness, a part of modernity's reprehensible dis-enchantment of the world – but really what we want is for Derryclare to be at its best and most fecund, to exist in all plen-itude; we want every detail of it to command awestruck attention; and when we go elsewhere, perhaps to the next wood on our schedule, we will want the same for that. I understood why the lichenologists had momentarily disappeared as if enrapt into the wood: they were listening to its ecology as to a singer, on one of those rare occasions in which audience and performer are united by the spell of the music and gifted to render and receive each note in the fullness of its relationship to the song.

Nevertheless, I soon left them to it and wandered off by myself, for no single science, nor even all the sciences put together, can read the score of a wood. And a note was missing, or two notes: those of the cuckoo. Where was Bid Delia? Could this robustly named Connemara wench haunt such a delicate place? Would the slow passage of time in the wood have fined her down, rendered her as elusive as that other bird-girl, Rima of the Amazon's green mansions, or those other fantasies dreamed into existence by huntsmen lost in medieval forests, amnesiac Melisande of Allemonde, snaky Melusine of Colombiers in Poitou, or the dryads that watched over every single oak of the classical world, and each of whom died with her oak? Might Bid have been dispersed throughout the wood and become one with it, like the algal cells in the lichen? I ducked under boughs that seemed to be weighted down by their ferns and mosses, parted hazel stems, hopped from stone to stone across the stream, until I came to the end of the wood and looked into the coniferous twilight beyond. I turned back, moved more slowly and carefully. The breeze had dropped away and the wood was utterly silent; it absorbed all my thoughts – my attempts to apply the scientists' disenchanting schematas, my vague mythological re-enchantments – echolessly into the depths of its being.

'What is the finest music in the world?' asks Fionn Mac Cumhaill, in one of the profoundest tales from the time of the great woods of Ireland. 'The cuckoo calling from the highest tree' is Oisín's answer, and others of the Fianna suggest the belling of a stag across the water, the baying of a pack of hounds in the hunt, the laughter of a girl. But Fionn's own answer, which has become a foundational utterance for the contemporary version of Celtic spirituality, is all-embracing: 'The music of what happens – that is the finest music in the world.' Fionn, though, was not to know what was to happen to his beloved woods. What happened to the conifers around Derryclare was not music. Oisín's answer, the cuckoo's ringing defiance of eventuality, is the best. But Bid is dead a hundred years or more, her wood is in deep distress, and on that day of the lichen-hunt I heard no cuckoo in it.

Glass, Marble, Steam, Fire

It was the children of one of our regular summer visitors to Roundstone who first told me about the Glass Mountain, which can sometimes be seen from a point on the road just under a mile north of the village, but from nowhere else. When the light is right, the south-facing slope of one peak in the distant Mám Tuirc range appears to pass in front of the north-facing slope of its neighbour, so that the two of them outline a V-shaped notch in the skyline; at other times, though, it is the north-facing slope that appears to pass in front of the other; and occasionally, most mysteriously, one can see the profiles of both mountains continued below their point of intersection, as if one were visible through the other. Move a hundred paces to the north or south, and nature's trickery is revealed: there is a conical hill between us and the Mám Tuirc Mountains, and when seen from the magical spot its summit is exactly aligned with the bottom of the notch in the horizon behind it; the distribution of sunlight and cloud shadow on the hill and its mountainous background does the rest.

This hill is Cnoc Lios Uachtair, the hill of the upper *lios*, and a *lios* is an ancient mound or ring fort, of the sort often regarded as a fairy dwelling; however, no such thing is known to the inhabitants of the townland of Lios Uachtair itself, who are also unaware of the otherworldly appearance of their hill as seen from the Roundstone road. In reality the hill, under a skin of bog, is of the same obdurate quartzite as the Twelve Pins, except on its western face where marble, more amenable to human needs, being rich in lime and susceptible to solution in water, underlies a spider's web of little stone-walled pastures and tillage plots. This marble originated as a limestone, and there are flat outcrops of rock on the hill that look much like the bare limestone clints of Aran or the Burren. The greenish streaky decorative marble that has come to be associated with Connemara occurs here and there among the less useful sort, a buried treasure laid up for the digging some hundreds of millions of years ago. There is a quarry in the village itself, not very active nowadays – it supplies small amounts to a Dublin factory making worry-stones and other little knickknacks – but formerly important enough to have been honoured (or dishonoured, according to some) by a royal visit, as I shall tell.

The other village of the townland, Recess, or Sraith Salach, is strung out along two and a half miles of the Clifden–Galway road, which passes the southern foot of the hill. The bed of the railway, dismantled in 1935, is still visible as a low embankment all along the other side of the road, with occasional gaps where a bridge over a stream has been removed. Immediately south of the railway bed is the Recess River, flowing westwards into one of the larger lakes of the Ballynahinch system. (A *sraith* is a stretch of low-lying riverside land, and *salach* here means, not 'dirty', as is often supposed, but 'of the sallies or willows'.) From the opposite bank of the river an immense bog stretches away to the hills and shores of south Connemara. My garrulous old friend the late Mr John Barlow, of the newspaper shop in Roundstone, was brought up in Seanadh Chaola, or Shannakeela, not far to the east of Recess, and once drew me a map of the area on which the bogland was marked 'morasses, quagmires, unsafe to walk without ropes or plank!' and 'swampy ground, bottomless!' Indeed, it is an intricately watery terrain, and the foresters curse the politicians who insisted they plant a large portion of it in the 1980s.

Because of the underlying schists and marbles, Recess always wore a more welcoming face than the frowning quartzite mountainsides and bleak wetlands travellers would have passed on the road from Galway, and from the mid nineteenth century and earlier a few members of the gentry, resident or regular summer visitors, had villas around Garroman Lake, at the west end of the townland. The adjective 'pretty', unusual in the context of Connemara, recurs in early reports of these developments. On the north side of the road, opposite the east end of the lake, William Wakeman in about 1850 took note of a farm called the Recess, 'the property of

Mr Andrews, who has displayed much taste in his improvements. One of his tenants has converted a pretty cottage into a rural hotel.' William Andrews was a Dublin alderman and presumably so named his farm (and inadvertently gave the present village its name) as he came down to it during the recess between terms of the official calendar. He claimed that he had a hundred-year lease of it dated 1846 from Mr Thomas Martin of Ballynahinch, but Mr Martin's mortgagees, the Law Life Assurance Society, who were virtually masters of Connemara by that time, asserted that Bell Martin had no right to make such an agreement and regarded Andrews as a tenant from year to year only. Nevertheless Andrews held on, subletting to a Mr McTaggart who opened the little hotel, on the north side of the road, the later history of which was to be determinative for the neighbourhood. On the south side another subtenant of Mr Andrews, a Robert Macredy, leased a small farm in 1857 and built Lissoughter Lodge on a little rise overlooking the east end of the lake. (He later became a local worthy, active on the Connemara Relief Committee in the 1880s, and the oppressive landlord of the unfortunate island of Inis Leacan near Roundstone.) And next door to McTaggart's hotel was the post office, Rose Cottage, obliquely tucked in under a bluff that must always have been sheltered and verdant, and that nowadays is a vast cumulus of rhododendron blossom in summer. Somerville and Ross were charmed by it when they came jogging by in their governess cart in 1893: 'We splashed along the road, past the little post and telegraph office, where you write your telegrams in an arbour of roses, and post your letters between the sprays of clematis.'

Further west was Strasalliagh Lodge, which later became Naughton's Hotel and then a police barracks, while on the opposite side of the lake, in a patch of ancient oak forest extended by recent plantations, stood Glendollagh, the pretty 'cottage-house' of a Dean Mahon of Westport, who had leased the land from the Martins as far back as the 1830s. ('Gleann Dealbhach', handsome valley, was John O'Donovan's educated guess at the Irish origin of this obscure placename, and although this is not likely to be correct its connotations are apt.) After the Dean's death in the

1840s the house became his son's shooting lodge, and then was sold to a German gentleman called John Strutzer, who, according to the surveyor Thomas Colville Scott, writing in 1856, was expending about £50 a week on improvements to the house and on reclamation of bogland, but of whom nothing was known locally: 'some say he is a Professor in the University College London, others, that he is a returned Convict, and between these two extremes, it is hard to come to a conclusion.'

Of these various buildings, Lissoughter Lodge still stands, discreetly withdrawn behind its little plantation, as does Rose Cottage, which only ceased to be the post office in 2004, after 157 years of service. The former Naughton's Hotel has acquired a long roadside extension housing a pub and an extensive crafts shop specializing in Connemara marble, the headquarters of the Joyces of Recess and known after the present proprietor's father as Paddy Festy's. Kevin, son of Paddy, son of Festy, tells me that Festy's grandfather Old Festus secured the family's future by sensibly marrying a woman from the *poitín*-making village of Doire Rois, across the bogs to the south, and selling the illicit spirits to the workmen building Kylemore Castle in the 1860s. The Joyces of Recess own the most productive of the Connemara marble quarries, the one up in Barr na nOrán in the Twelve Pins that the Martins had such delusive hopes for, and which is now a huge pit, and their marble works is on the site of McTaggart's long-gone hotel and its successor, the Railway Hotel. Thirty-ton blocks of marble stand in the yard there, the green zigzags visible in their faces condensing millions of years of geology. In the factory are gaunt dusty machines for slicing, splitting and polishing the blocks, and for impregnating the resultant panels with resin to strengthen them (for after their frantic geological past they are full of cracks), a technique developed in partnership with their international distributors, Antolini Luigi and C. Spa, which has transformed what was a local souvenir craft into a heavyweight commercial enterprise.

On the other side of the lake Dean Mahon's little lodge has had a troubled history and no longer exists. Glendollagh (or

Glendalough) House, a boxy two- and three-storey structure with flat roofs, little corner turrets and battlements, was built next to it, probably in the time of the Berridges, and was leased to Arthur Willcox before he built Lisnabrucka, and then to a cavalry officer, Captain Forrester, who left when it was taken over by the IRA as their local HQ during the Civil War. The Misses Mongan, sisters of Joe Mongan of the hotel in Carna, later ran it as a fishing hotel until about 1944; but it was then left unoccupied and was demolished when it became unsafe and was camped in by hippies. Little trace of it or the lodge remains, but the damp, shady (and private) woodland rides lead one past intriguing survivals: a moss-cloaked limekiln, two high-walled gardens, an antique sundial inscribed with the terse motto 'Look' (which I am tempted to borrow as an epigraph for this book), and finally a symmetrical hillock by the lakeside, presumably of glacial origin, half shrouded in birches and known as the Fairy Hill.

As to McTaggart's little hotel, when the railway came past its door in the 1890s, it was acquired by the Midland Great Western Railway Company and enormously expanded. Flourishing with the sporting tourism of the Edwardian era, the Recess Railway Hotel became the economic engine and proud focal point of central Connemara. Old photos show it as a rambling three-storeyed building of many gables with scalloped fascia, and tall bay windows looking onto a lawn bestridden by croquet hoops. In its heyday the hotel boasted amenities previously unknown in Connemara:

. . . spacious drawing, coffee, writing, billiard and smoke rooms, private sitting and bath rooms and about 35 bedrooms. Improved heating system: electric light throughout. Darkroom for amateur photographers. Postal and telegraph office adjoining the hotel. A special platform has been provided opposite the hotel for passengers arriving and departing by train. A hotel porter, in uniform, meets all trains.

The zenith of the hotel's history was the visit of King Edward VII and Queen Alexandra in 1903, already mentioned in connection with Mr O'Loghlen of Cashel. The royal party, accompanied by the Viceroy, Lord Dudley, having visited Dublin and Belfast, sailed down the west coast of Ireland and disembarked in Killary harbour for a tour of Connemara, ending at Recess where they were to visit the marble quarry and lunch at the Railway Hotel. Sir Henry Robinson, who was in charge of some of the arrangements, observed the proceedings with his customary eye for the absurd:

Chamberlain, the new head of the Royal Irish Constabulary, was very nervous about his responsibility of the King's safe conduct through the west . . . He had collected an enormous force of constabulary from all over the country. He spread them all along the roads disguised as tourists, under the impression that as the King's visit might be expected to attract tourists this guard would not be noticed. But what rather spoiled this precaution was that every man was dressed alike; straw hat, Norfolk jacket, watch-chain from breast pocket to button-hole, knickerbockers and bicycle. Every man was exactly the same distance apart, 100 yards or so, and all were lying in a carefully rehearsed loose and careless attitude beside the road in the character of the weary cyclist. But what further spoiled the effect was that when the King's car was passing each man sprang to 'attention,' clicked his heels and saluted smartly, and then resumed his full-length attitude until the King was out of sight.

Mr Barlow, at my request, wrote an account that preserves the local memory of the royal presence in Recess:

After lunch which consisted of salmon and sea-trout, caught in Lough Inagh, there was a pair of horses and a carriage provided by the proprietor of Naughton's hotel, to take the Royal party to the quarry. There was some difficulty in negotiating the steep incline leading up the hill-side. The men decided to un-trace the horses and push and pull the carriage themselves. There was an elderly couple who were cheering themselves hoarse. The woman shouted, 'Three cheers for the King,' while the old man shouted, 'And Mrs King, too!' When the Royal party arrived at the Marble Quarry there was slight tussle between Reverent Father Gleeson, the Parish Priest in Roundstone, and the right Reverent Mr McCormack the Church of Ireland Minister, as to which of them took the Queen's arm as she went into the quarry. Fr Gleeson, it seems, won the race. I was talking to an old man, who was working there that day. He was a young man at that time. He said that there was a man from Glasgow in charge of the gang. He ordered the men not to dare look up from their work. This man who told me was holding a steel drill, while two men, one on each side, were striking it with seven pound hammers, while old Jack the foreman was shouting, 'Down on it, Down on it,' without cease. He only saw their shoes, and a lovely scent of perfume permeated the whole atmosphere, as they passed him by on that hot June day.

On their return to the Railway Hotel, says Mr Barlow, the King was presented with a sample of the 'local brew', and took a drop too much, so that the royal physician had to prescribe an hour's rest. As the loyal subjects waiting outside were becoming impatient to be addressed, the King's equerry pulled a man out of the crowd who had a striking resemblance to the King, got the royal barber to trim and shape his beard, dressed him up in the King's naval uniform and pushed him out onto the balcony with a speech in his hand. His voice could not be heard over the cheering of the crowd, which was so thunderous that it woke up His Majesty. On learning what had happened the King demanded to see the man, examined him from all angles, pronounced him a perfect likeness, and asked, 'My good man, has your mother ever been to England?' The man answered, 'No, Your Majesty, but my father has!' – on which the King said, 'Take him away!' (Needless to say this figment of collective memory forms no part of the official accounts of the royal progress.)

That evening the King and Queen travelled to Galway by train. The royal carriage was the most splendid vehicle ever seen in Connemara, according to newspaper reports:

The saloon carriage constructed by the Midland Great Western Company of Ireland for the use of the King and Queen during their present visit . . . is a most sumptuously-appointed vehicle some fifteen yards in length. The accommodation includes an entrance hall, reception-room, smoking-room, dining-room, dressing-room, and kitchen. The furniture, carpets and curtains used are all of Irish manufacture. The reception-room is panelled in satinwood framed in teak. Fluted Corinthian columns, with carved satinwood capitals, support the roof. The floor is covered with specially-woven Donegal carpet, the furniture being upholstered in sage green brocade. The smoking-room is panelled in polished oak, and has a parquet floor. Through bow windows at the back a perfect view is offered of the country traversed. The dining-room is panelled in fumigated oak, and the furniture includes two dinner tables and a carved sideboard. The carriage is lighted by electricity, electric bells communicate with the kitchen, and in the smoking room are electric cigar lighters. The ventilation is supplied by means of electric fans, and the coach can be artificially warmed in cold weather. Externally the carriage is coloured royal blue, with white panels, the royal arms being emblazoned on each side. It will be strange to see a vehicle of such magnificent appearance in the wilds of Connemara.

And so the gorgeous apparition faded from sight in a cloud of steam. But not all of Connemara was so bemused by a whiff of royal perfume as Recess. Ros Muc, where Patrick Pearse was already visiting and trying to counteract the influence of Lord Dudley, who had a fishing lodge nearby, was bitterly divided, and a schoolchild of that time and vicinity, Colm Ó Gaora, later wrote about the event with deep contempt for Connemara's '*seoiníní agus lucht galldachais*' (toadies and anglicized folk):

The spirit of nationalism was never so weak in all life as it was then. I say this because of the hullabaloo in the parish when Edward the Seventh, the King of England, visited Connemara. There wasn't a person with the sign of a pound on him who didn't go to look at him. There were a couple of bigwigs who boasted afterwards that they had rubbed shoulders with him. If there weren't English flags on hill and hillock, and bonfires on height and hummock, there's no God in Heaven. People – if you could call them people – pulled his coach from Sraith Salach railway station to the marble quarry in Lios Uachtair and back again,

with pride and joy. 'Wasn't it great for him,' said my father soon afterwards, 'that the tyrant saw the slavishness that he and each generation
that came before him has left them in deeper than ever.'

Out of such resentment came the spark that burned the hotel
to the ground nearly twenty years later, to the unassuageable loss
of the locality. Mr Barlow, whose mother had the contract for
curtaining the hotel (his father was the local Singer sewing
machine representative), used to be my memory-well for the
Recess area and especially for the hotel; for him it was the centre
of the world, and its destruction by the IRA an unforgivable
crime:

I remember it before it was destroyed. There was a full-time gardener
employed. During the Summer season, there were two part-time men
employed. The Hotel had a generator for electricity. At night the electricity was switched on, for the arrival of the late train from
Galway–Clifden at the Hotel's private platform. The Hotel had their
own electrician. They had also two cars for taking guests to their different
lakes. I remember coming home from Galway with my mother and
seeing the Hotel all lighted up for the train. There was a beautiful orna-
mental double entrance gate, with two shaded glass domes on each
pillar, and also an Automobile Assn sign with full lighting. The Hotel
platform was also well lighted and a line of shaded lights from the platform all the way up to the Hall-door of the Hotel. It was a sight that
I will never forget.

Mr Barlow was a schoolchild at the time, and in his old age
he wrote me 'A Boy's Eye View of the Anglo-Irish and Civil
Wars', a vivid memoir of the terror inflicted by the Black and
Tans, and then by the IRA, on the countryside:

I remember a very hot and humid day in May 1921. I was a fourth
standard pupil at Derryneen National School [which was a few miles
east of Recess]. As we were preparing to go home, our teacher asked
us boys to remain with him, on our way home to Shanakeela, where

he also stayed. We were about halfway between the school and our homes when we heard the distinctive 'zoom' of lorries approaching from the direction of Maam Cross. Our first reaction was to run, only for the teacher who said, 'Don't run, stand your ground!' The two 'Crossley Tenders' came around the bend. One of them passed us, while the second lorry pulled up in a cloud of dry dust. We all felt petrified with fear. Next, a 'Tan' pointed a rifle straight at my head. I remember being fascinated by that bright round little hole in the barrel of his rifle. Immediately an R.I.C. man pushed the 'Tan's' gun to one side, saying, 'Not that, Bill!' Since that time I have always been under the impression that my life was saved by that R.I.C. man.

In the following year, that of the Civil War, Connemara was dominated by the Republican forces, who occupied Glendollagh House and Ballynahinch Castle, broke down the road and rail bridges east of Recess, and burned the Railway Hotel to prevent it being used by the Free State Army.

There was a rumour going round Recess at the time, that a young local man, who had been employed full time on the Hotel farm and who had been dismissed by the Manageress for some irregularity, was present at the October Maam Cross fair, where he met a soldier who said that he was stationed in the old workhouse in Oughterard and also that they were going out the following week to occupy Recess Hotel, on their way to take over Clifden. The local man went immediately to Glendalough House and reported what he was after hearing. A Despatch rider was sent to Leanane, to report the matter to the O/C, West Galway Brigade I.R.A. The answer he sent back was an order for the destruction of the Hotel. The man that carried the message from Maam Cross fair was often heard to boast about this when he had a few drinks taken.

And so the hotel was burned to the ground. The people of Seanadh Chaola had wondered at the smoke blowing in the wind through their village, until a passer-by told them that the hotel was in flames. Some carpets and the grandfather clock were salvaged by the railway ganger, and taken away to Recess Station for storage. The manageress, Miss Mai McCarthy, and the book-keeper, Miss Healy, were conveyed on a railway bogey pushed by two or three men as far as the broken bridge, and thence by train to Galway; young John saw them passing his house, Miss McCarthy reading a book. (I picture them both bolt upright and dignified, and still incensed by the way the local IRA men used to swagger into the hotel and put their feet up on the furniture, as Mr Barlow has described to me.)

Years afterwards Mr Barlow learned from an army officer who was a young lieutenant in Galway at the time of the Civil War that there had never been any intention of taking the hotel, as it was too close under the rise of the hill behind it to be defensible. Whatever the truth of this, the heart had been burned out of the locality. Mr Barlow records what it meant to the suffering country folk:

There were large numbers of local people employed in different ways at that Hotel. There were boats-men or gillies. There were owners of horses and side-cars for driving visitors to the various lakes. There were men employed in cutting and saving turf. The Hotel had its own bogs. There were men looking after the cows which gave milk. There were women selling rolls of home-spun tweed and also knitting long stockings. The local women were rearing geese, ducks and chickens and selling them to the Manageress, to supplement the Hotel's own stock of poultry. When Recess Hotel was destroyed, those were the people who suffered. They were thrown into a world of unemployment, where there were no payouts from any sources. The government paid out no soft monies. Emigration was at an end . . .

The winter of 1922–23 was a most hard and difficult one for everyone. There was a great scarcity of supplies and especially flour. All this hardship occurred during the time the bridges and railway line were broken. Connemara received two-thirds of its supplies on the S.S. *Dun Angus*, which ran from Galway to Roundstone about once a fortnight. Two horse-carts from Shanakeela used to travel to Roundstone, each capable of carrying fifteen cwt of flour. It used to be late, around 8 p.m. on a dark night in November. An I.R.A. sentry halted the carts, asking them to identify themselves. They said they were on their way home with flour and that it was badly needed by the large families. The answer to that was a 303 round sliding into the rifle breech and 'Each cart put down one cwt of flour. We need it equally as bad!'

Young John had been especially distressed by the sufferings of a pony the IRA commandeered from Ballynahinch.

It was completely worn out as a result of privation caused by hunger, tiredness, lameness, loose shoes, cut breast, anything that could happen to a poor animal that was driven without food or water for days or nights on end, by people that knew nothing about kindness to the poor dumb animal . . . I heard afterwards that they tied that poor animal to a pole in a field in Ballynahinch. It died shortly afterwards. I remember staying awake that night thinking of that poor horse.

The hotel was never to be rebuilt. But the ceasefire came soon afterwards, and eventually the bridges were reinstated. John, aged a mere handful of years, went along to inspect the Barony Bridge, so called because the stream under it marks the eastern boundary of the old Connemara, the Barony of Ballynahinch. An army officer was on duty at one end of it, and on seeing the child hesitating at the other, waved him on with the resounding words, 'Come on, little boy! This bridge was built for you!' And John Barlow marched across the Barony Bridge. The smallest possible procession, this is the event that stands in my mind for the inauguration of independent Ireland.

Curse and Blessing

Records of the pilgrimage to Croagh Patrick in Mayo go back nine centuries, and there is no reason to doubt that for just as long people have visited Mám Éan for the same purpose, to honour the patron saint of Ireland. Indeed it is likely that the origins of this Connemara 'pattern', as such a festival in honour of a patron saint is called, and of the nearly two hundred other recorded annual gatherings that used to take place on a Sunday close to the beginning of August, long pre-date St Patrick and even the foundation of Christianity. Many of these patterns were held in high places otherwise rarely visited, places whose topography lent them a weight of meaning.

Mám Éan, the pass of birds, is one of the two main passes through the Mám Tuirc range, the other being Mám Tuirc itself, the boar's pass, six miles to the north-west. The saddle-point of the pass is at a height of about 1,200 feet, and the mountains on either side of it rise steeply to over 2,000 feet. The boundary between Connemara proper, that is, the old Barony of Bally-nahinch, and the Joyce Country, runs from peak to peak along the mountain chain, but where it crosses the hummocky and boggy little plain at the top of the pass there are no natural features to define it. Boundary disputes between the townlands to the west and to the east were noted in the *Books of Survey and Distribution* at the time of the post-Cromwellian settlements, and although the nineteenth-century Ordnance Survey ruled a definitive line across the map of this vague terrain they still added a zest to the stick-fights that were part of the ritual of Mám Éan Sunday until the suppression of the pattern in the 1920s. Nowadays there is a little chapel, built after the pilgrimage was re-established in clerically approved form in 1980, perched exactly on the boundary as deter-mined by the official maps, but if one ambiguity has thus been scotched and expelled, as St Patrick did with the snakes, I am glad to report that others are still wriggling around the site, rite and legend of Mám Éan. To climb to a summit like that of Croagh Patrick is to go as far as one can go in the dimension of transcendence, of certainty, of faith; to climb to a pass is also to leave the lowland of wordly concerns behind, but without going all the way over or choosing between the peaks to left and right of the way. This topography of doubt, of judgement or decision suspended, lends itself to my purposes in this final chapter; in short, it suits my book.

I have been beaten back by shrieking gales and teeming rain in ascending to Mám Éan from the east, felt faint on a heavy afternoon on the mountain above it to the north, and poked about its ancient holy well and pilgrim stations on several occasions, but the only time I have visited it on the festive Sunday was just a few years after the revival of the pilgrimage, when a Connemara marble altar had been built there, together with a makeshift wooden chapel that would soon be replaced by a stone-built one. Domhnach Mhám Éan, Mám Éan Sunday, is very much a festival of Irish-speaking Connemara, and I had persuaded my friends from Inis Ní, Nainsí and Mícheál, to come with me, as they had the Irish language, and a car. We left the main road just east of Recess and took the turning up to Bun na gCnoc, the foot of the hills, as the Gaeltacht area along the western base of the Mám Tuirc range is called. Bun na gCnoc consists of a number of townlands strung together by a rambling little country road, each consisting of a handful of cottages and a large tract of steep sheep-grazing land rising to the mountain tops above it. They have rich names: Doire Bhéal an Mháma, the wood of the mouth of the pass, referring to Mám Éan itself; Doire Bhó Riada, not so easily made out, but the local understanding is that a *bó riada* is a tame cow; An Uillinn, the elbow or bend (of what, is not clear to me); and Fionasclainn, which would at first glance mean white recess or nook, but which P. W. Joyce's untrusty old warhorse of a book, *Irish Names of Places*, says is from a long obsolete word, *inesclund*, a strong or swift stream.

When we arrived at the foot of the steep stony path up to Mám Éan there were a score or so of parked cars by the road-side, and a stall selling sweets. We fell in with a group of south Connemara people, to whom Nainsí introduced me; they knew of me through reading a column I was writing for the *Connacht Tribune* in those days, detailing my finds, townland by townland, throughout the territory I was mapping, and one man immediately started to tell me the legend of a certain holy well, which I guessed he had recently read up in my column. But then, continuing the religious theme, he went on, half in Irish and half (for my benefit) in English, to give me a story that was new to me then, about *Rún Diamhair na Tríonóide*, the deep mystery of the Trinity. 'This man,' he said, 'was going round the coasts of Ireland trying to understand the deep mystery of the Trinity. He saw a lad making a hole in the sand and pouring water into it. The water all drained away but the lad continued to pour more in, until your man got irritated. "You'll never fill that hole," he said – and immediately an angel appeared and said, "He will have filled that hole before you understand *Rún Diamhair na Tríonóide*."'

And so we climbed, discoursing of sacred matters like the pilgrims of old, until after twenty minutes or so we came to the top of the pass, where a crowd of about 250 were assembled. The Stations of the Cross had recently been installed on small cairns of stones spread out over a wide arc of the rough ground, each station marked by a rudimentary white timber cross with a metal house number screwed onto it. I know that some locals resent the imposition of this rite, which, as one of them said to me, 'has nothing to do with Mám Éan', on an occasion that has had its own forms of worship for centuries; nevertheless, most of the congregation was participating in it, following a fine-featured elderly priest and his young crucifer from station to station, as directed by another priest with a loudhailer from the altar up on the northern hill slope overlooking the site. The sound was torn away by gusts of wind and came bouncing back strangely from the cliffs of the opposite hillside. Other people were making their devotions at the nearby holy well, Tobar Phádraic, a little spring within a U-shaped stone enclosure, by walking round it seven times, with prayers and Ave Marias, throwing a pebble into the enclosure at each round.

The legend of Mám Éan is that St Patrick climbed up to the top of the pass from the Mám Valley below it to the east, blessed the land spread out before him from that height, and spent the night in a little hole in the hillside known as Leaba Phádraic, Patrick's bed, but ventured no further into Connemara. People of the Mám Valley specify that he came here after his sojourn on Croagh Patrick, and was accompanied by St Martin. The episode is not mentioned in the writings ascribed to the saint, nor in other early sources, and indeed all certainty about the first missioners to Ireland whom tradition has collectively embodied in the person of St Patrick remains lost to history. Nevertheless, the eminent Jesuit scholar Fr Mac Gréil states that the saint's visit took place in AD 441, and, being himself a native of the Mám Valley and the prime mover in the resurrection of the Mám Éan pattern, he should know.

The saint's outlook on Connemara must have been very restricted by the slopes on either side of the pass, and so, when the Mass began, I drifted off and climbed northwards, scrambling around rocky bluffs and steep heathery knolls, picking up a few lovely crystals of quartz, and peering into the low tunnel of an ancient and possibly prehistoric mine I hadn't come across before. By degrees an overview of the territory to the west opened up: the pyramid of Lissoughter Hill a few miles away, and beyond it the clustered peaks of the Twelve Pins, the glinting levels of Roundstone Bog, and the ragged back of Errisbeg on the dim horizon – roughly speaking, the whole of the parish of Roundstone. Looking back now, from the present moment of writing to that moment of retrospection, I see that, as it has worked out, I was looking at the ground trodden by this book and which I have come to regard as my neighbourhood, for I can see nearly all of it from my windows in Roundstone. Have I dealt fairly with the land and its people? Sometimes the problems of Connemara make me cantankerous and bitter. The saint himself seems to have been troubled by ambivalent feelings, according to a folktale of his visit to Mám Éan that begins to reveal some matter deeper and darker than does the usual simple and pious account, and that could be read as a diagnosis. I translate the Irish version collected early in the nineteenth century from a renowned *seanchaí*, Pádraic Mac Con Iomaire of An Coillín, a village near Carna that abounded in stories and storytellers:

When Patrick was at Mám Éan there was a lad with him. There was a bed there, and St Patrick was asleep in it. This day he stood up by the bed on the side of the hill and spread his two hands and looked down south to the sea, for he knew he wouldn't be going any nearer it, and he prayed to God that there would be twice as much benefit on the land to the south as on the part that he had walked.

When evening came and he went to rest he said to his lad, 'While I am asleep let you be awake.'

He fell asleep, and after a bit he began to talk. He was dreaming and soon he said out loud that he put his curse on Ireland.

'On the foam of the river!' said the lad.

Soon after that he put his curse on Ireland again, and the lad declared that it would be on the tip of the rush. The tip of the rush is withered ever since.

The third time St Patrick put his curse on Ireland, the lad declared it would be on the tip of the bracken.

St Patrick woke up with a jump and asked the lad if he was asleep.

'I'm not,' replied the lad. 'It was as well for you.'

'What did I say?' asked St Patrick.

He told him.

'That is why I told you not to fall asleep. I knew I had to say it, but in the end I couldn't stop myself saying it. The third time I said it I woke up. I knew I would have done a bad deed if you hadn't been awake and laid the curse on something else.'

So the quick-witted youngster, presuming on the naming-rights over all creatures vested in us by the Genesis story, diverts the curse from humankind onto what we call, in a stale word, the environment. The rush the lad has in mind would be the black bog-rush, with its little head of blackish flower-spikelets; it infests Connemara's soggy pastures, as does the bracken its drier slopes, to such an extent that the farmer sprays the land with poison to get rid of them, and the poisons together with many other noxious chemicals are washed downhill and carried away in the foam of the river, which splashes us as it churns against the invisibly infected tide at the bridge of Tuaim Beola. Such are my gloomy and vengeful imaginings. But on that long-passed Sunday when the conflictual aspects of Connemara had yet to force themselves upon me, I revelled in the purity of the scene, the sun-crisped legibility of the nearer territory, which was beginning to become familiar to me, and the romantic shadowiness and airy dilution of the realm beyond it, the savage Atlantic peninsulas, where Wittgenstein found 'the last pool of darkness in Europe', and which my restlessness will drive me to write a book about too, if time allows.

When I had sated myself with distances and turned to look down into the pass I was disconcerted to find that the crowd had mysteriously vanished and not a soul was to be seen; for a moment I wondered if everyone had gone home and I had been wandering for much longer than I knew, for the air was grand and elating up on the heights. But then I saw the line of parked cars down on the road glinting in the afternoon sun, and realized that the congregation had all gathered around the altar and were hidden from me by the scarp that rises sharply behind it. By the time I came lurching and sliding down, the official ceremony was nearly over and right next to the altar there was a dense crush around Leaba Phádraic, which is a shallow recess with an overhanging roof in the almost vertical scarp face. One by one people were clambering up into this hollow, balancing themselves on a knob of rock in its floor and steadying themselves by touching its roof or holding on to the shoulders of the people nearest them while turning around seven times, in the magically beneficent sense: *deiseal*, sunwise. There seemed to be a reciprocal obliviousness between the rugged faces intently turned up to the craggy niche in the rock, and the priests with their embroidered vestments, stately gestures and silver vessels at the marble altar; it was as if the two rites, although taking place only a few yards apart, occupied different streams of time.

After that the assembly broke up and by degrees, amid much talk and many goodbyes, separated peaceably into two streams, each of which flowed slowly down its own side of the watershed. In the past it would not have been so: even though the pattern would have begun with a Mass celebrated by a priest, it would have been incomplete without an almost ritualized battle – perhaps incorrectly regarded as a faction fight – between the men of the Joyce Country and those of Connemara. Two nineteenth-century visitors have left accounts of the pattern as it was in its heyday before the Famine, the fullest of which is that of the early tourist, H. D. Inglis, who attended it with the Joyce Country folk (all called Joyce, he says) in 1834:

The ascent to the spot where the pattern was to be held was picturesque in the extreme. Far up the winding way, for miles before and miles behind too, groups were to be seen moving up the mountainside – the women, with their red petticoats, easily distinguishable: some were on foot, some few on horseback, and some rode double. About half-way up, we overtook a party of lads and asses, beguiling the toil of the ascent, by the help of a piper, who marched before, and whose stirring strains, every now and then prompted an advance in jig-time, up the steep mountain path. Some few we met coming away, – sober people, who had performed their station at the holy well, and had no desire to be partakers in the sort of amusement that generally follows.

When I reached the summit of the pass, and came in sight of the ground, it was about four in the afternoon, and the pattern was at its height: and truly, in this wild mountain spot, the scene was most striking and picturesque. There were a score tents or more – some open at the sides, and some closed; hundreds in groups were seated on the grass, or on the stones, which lie abundantly there. Some old persons were yet on their knees, beside the holy well, performing their devotions;

and here and there apart, and half screened by the masses of rock which lay about, girls of the better order, who had finished their pastimes, were putting off their shoes and stockings to trot homewards or were arranging their dress; or perhaps – though more rarely – exchanging a word or two with a Joyce, or a Connemara boy.

All was quiet when I reached the ground; and I was warmly welcomed as a stranger, by many, who invited me into their tents. Of course I accepted the invitation; and the pure potheen circulated freely. By and by, however, some boastful expression of a Joyce appeared to give offence to several at the far end of the tent; and something loud and contemptuous was spoken by two or three in a breath. The language, which, in compliment to me, had been English, suddenly changed to Irish. Two or three glasses of potheen were quickly gulped by most of the boys . . . and taking advantage of a sudden burst of voices, I stepped over my bench, and retiring from my tent, took up a safe position on some neighbouring rocks.

I had not long to wait: out sallied the Joyce and a score of other 'boys', from several tents at once, as if there had been some precon- certed signal; and the flourish of shillelaghs did not long precede the using of them . . . The shillelaghs, no doubt, do sometimes descend upon a head, which is forthwith a broken head; but they oftener descend upon each other: and the fight becomes one of personal strength . . . On the present occasion, five or six were disabled: but there was no homicide; and after a scrimmage, which lasted perhaps ten minutes, the Joyces remained masters of the field . . .

Most of the women had left the place when the quarrel began, and some of the men too. I noticed, after the fight, that some, who had been opposed to each other, shook hands and kissed; and appeared as good friends as before. The sun was nearly set when the pattern finally broke up; and, with the bright sun flaming down the cleft, and gilding all the slopes, the scene was even more striking now, than when we ascended . . .

With the post-Famine triumph of Irish Catholic miserabilism, such behaviour was increasingly condemned, by the clergy and by the law, as a Joyce Country song-maker, Seán Seoighe complained, having been pursued by the police from glen to glen of the surrounding mountains:

> . . . Thar éis nach coir náireach bhí ariamh mo dhiaidh;
> Ach buille 'bhata a bhualadh Domhnach a' Mháma,
> Mar isé bhí gnásamhail ariamh sa tír,
> 'S gan cuimhne bheith agam-sa lá'r na bháireach,
> Ach iad a bheith 'baint sásta amach an bhliadhain dár gcionn.

(. . . although I'd never done anything shameful / but striking a blow with a stick on Dómhnach a' Mháma / as had always been the custom here / and not remembered the day after / but to get satisfaction the following year.)

The Revd Henry M'Manus, the Presbyterian who lodged in Roundstone while studying the Irish language in the 1840s, also described the pattern. Having discreetly damned the religious (and of course Catholic) part of the ceremony with a tendentious image – 'the lighted candles, with their feeble glimmer, forming a strange contrast to the summer sun; like an age of ignorance outshone by a brighter era' – he goes on to tell of the ensuing amusements:

The piers struck up their merry tunes in the tents, and the dancing began. Nor was there any lack of 'creature comforts.' Bread and cake were abundantly supplied by pedlars, and whiskey flowed on all sides. Under such circumstances, we may conceive the uproarious hilarity of an excitable people. Not did it cease till the Sabbath sun 'sought the western wave.' But it seldom ended well; like all other unhallowed joys, it left a sting behind. In the words of my informant, "*S annamh lair bith nach mbeidh troid ann*' – 'Seldom a day that there was not a fight in it.' At length these fights became so serious, that influential parties were obliged to interpose; and finding all their means for their suppression ineffectual, they got the pattern removed to Tullochbee.

His 'Tullochbee' must be An Tulaigh Bhuí, where the main road crosses the Abhainn Tuaidh east of Recess. All the same it seems the Mám Éan festivities persisted into the 1920s, until the clergy condemned it from the pulpits, especially after a drunken Inis Ní man went astray on the mountains and was found dead two days later. Individuals continued to make their rounds at the holy well, however, and by degrees the pattern was revived in soberer form. An altar was made by Mícheál Coyne, Fr Mac Gréil's grandfather, in the 1930s, and Mass was served there at one time by no less a devotee than the former President of the Executive Council of Ireland and Knight of the Grand Cross of the Order of Pius IX, William T. Cosgrave, and his two sons. In 1979 the ceremonies were attended by several hundreds, especially from the Irish-speaking areas. Fr Mac Gréil brought a youth camp from Finney in Mayo for Mass at Mám Éan, and with the proceeds of the collection built a new altar (or Mass Rock, Carraig Aifrinn, as it as termed, in an echo of Penal Law days) of Connemara marble, which was consecrated by the Archbishop of Tuam, Dr Joseph Cunnane, in 1980. A small wooden chapel like a woodcutter's hut in a pantomime, Cillín Phádraic, was built, and then replaced by a neat stone one with simple Gothic-arched door and windows, which was consecrated by Dr Cunnane in 1985. Stations of the Cross by the stone-carver John Coffey, more acceptable than the previous wooden ones, were erected, and when the holy well proved insufficient for modern demands a new one was engineered further up the slope. A limestone statue of the saint, 'Pádraic Mór na hEireann', carved by Cliodhna Cussen and helicoptered up to the site in 1987, stands square and stolid on his pedestal and with prayerfully folded arms looks gravely out across the place of assembly.

Following the saint's gaze, one notices a small tarn lying like a sunken eye below the fierce brows of rock of the formidably steep opposing slopes, which are always sombre against the afternoon light. This is Loch Mhám Éan – also known as Loch an Dá Éan, the lake of the two birds, and as Loch an Tairbh, the lake of the bull – and its gloomy waters (bottomless, says legend) reflect something deep and dark about this place, which has not succumbed to clerical modernization. There are always two birds to be seen afloat on it, one is told, but whether they are the birds the pass is named from, or what sort of birds they are, I have not heard. I know of a Loch an Dá Éan in the Burren too, another dark lake haunted by two birds, and I believe the placename and the associated belief occur elsewhere. It is said that St Patrick fought with a monstrous serpent at Mám Éan and imprisoned it in the lake; alternatively that there was a bull that used to kill all who ventured into the pass, until St Patrick drove it into the lake to drown. And one version of this story holds that the bull was called Crom Dubh – a name that links Mám Éan with a vast echoing arcanum of mythology.

Crom Dubh Sunday, Domhnach Chrom Dubh, is the old countryside name for the last Sunday in July, or in some places the first Sunday in August, a day marked by popular festivities that often involved climbing to high places and gathering the *fraocháin* or bilberries that grow among the heather. The Mám Éan pattern of the old days was on the July date, as is the ritual ascent of Croagh Patrick, while in its revived life it has sometimes been scheduled for the August date, perhaps so as not to conflict with the more widely known Mayo pilgrimage. Crom Dubh (which means something like 'bent dark one') figures sometimes as a bull and more often as a pagan chieftain, the owner of a bull, whom the saint overcomes and confines to some narrow place, in the legends connected with dozens of traditional gatherings held around the end of July and associated with the beginning of the harvest season. And beneath these folktales and practices of popular religion lies a much more ancient stratum of Celtic myth, as the folklorist Máire MacNeill has shown in her magisterial study, *The Festival of Lughnasa*. It seems that the conflict between the champions of Christianity and paganism restages the Battle of Moytura in which the radiant host of the Tuatha Dé Danann defeats the grim and sinister Fomhóire, and in particular the duel between Lugh, who has all the talents, and whom the Romans identified with their god Mercury, and Balor, whose single baleful eye was his fearful weapon. What sort of a being was Lugh is indicated by the eleventh-century Irish text *Cath Maige Tuiread*, 'the Battle

of Moytura', which gives an account of his joining the Tuatha
Dé Danann.

One day when Núadu their king was feasting the Tuatha Dé
Danann at Tara, Lugh Samildánach (the all-talented), a handsome
young warrior, arrived out of the unknown, gave his name and
told the doorkeeper to announce him. The doorkeeper asked,
'What art do you practise? For no one without an art enters Tara.'
'Question me,' he said. 'I am a builder.' The doorkeeper answered,
'We do not need you. We have a builder already, Luchta mac
Lúachada.' But Lugh persisted: 'Question me, doorkeeper: I am a
smith.' The doorkeeper answered, 'We have a smith already, Colum
Cúaléinech of the three new techniques.' In answer to successive
questions Lugh also claimed to be a champion, harper, warrior,
poet and historian, sorcerer, physician, cup-bearer and brazier.
When the doorkeeper had affirmed that they already had men
with each of these skills in their number, Lugh said, 'Ask the King
whether he has one man who possesses all these arts: if he has I
will not be able to enter Tara.' So the doorkeeper went into the
royal hall and told the King, 'A warrior has come before the court
named Samildánach; and all the arts which help your people, he
practises them all, so that he is the man of each and every art.'
In the meantime Lugh called for all the *fidchell*-boards of Tara
(*fidchell* being a precursor of chess) and won all the stakes on
them, inventing the '*cró* of Lugh' (presumably an encircling tactic,
a *cró* being a small enclosure). 'Let him into the court,' said Núadu,
'for a man like that has never before come into this fortress.' Then
the doorkeeper let him past, and he sat in the seat of the sage,
because he was a sage in every art.

After Lugh had performed other feats of strength and skill,
Núadu gave him command of the Tuatha Dé Danann in their
forthcoming battle with the Fomhóire. During that battle, Cath
Maigh Tuired (or the battle of the plain of towers), Lugh met the
enemy's champion and his own grandfather Balor, who had a
destructive eye which was never opened except on a battlefield,
when four men would raise its lid by a polished ring set in it.
'Lift up my eyelid, lad,' said Balor, 'so I may see the talkative fellow

who is conversing with me.' But as soon as the lid was raised Lugh cast a sling stone which knocked Balor's eye through to the back of his head so that it glared upon his own host. Thus the Fomhóire were routed; Lugh spared the life of one of their leaders, Bres, in exchange for his knowledge of the arts of ploughing, sowing and reaping, but as for those that died, 'until the stars of heaven can be counted, and the sands of the sea, and flakes of snow, and dew on a lawn, and hailstones, and grass beneath the feet of horses, and the horses of the son of Lir in a sea storm – they will not be counted at all.' Near the village of Cong in Mayo there is a prehistoric circle of standing stones which tradition holds to be the Fomhóire petrified by Balor's backwards gaze.

Lugh's name is still around us, in such European placenames as Lyon, Leiden and Loudon, and the Irish Louth and Dunlooey (and perhaps, it occurs to me, in a tiny islet of Lough Inagh called Illaunloo). The benignant god's festival, Lughnasa, one of the four high points of the Celtic year, marked the juncture between summer and autumn, when the first of the new crop was ripe and the hungry month of July had been survived. With the coming of Christianity and the waning of the old gods, Lugh, who gave us the arts of crop-farming, and his antagonist Balor were replaced by St Patrick and Crom Dubh, and Lughnasa became a pattern celebrated at Mám Éan and many other sacred sites. If Balor was Lugh's grandfather they are to a degree the same being; perhaps the whole *agon*, from the battle of the gods down to the saint's dream-struggle with his own destructive impulses, can be read as a myth of the sun's fructifying influence winning out against its withering power. And among the messages wrapped into this bundle of old tales is the assurance that as a species of all the talents, as warriors, cup-bearers, poets and chess-champions, we can countermand the curses we have laid upon the earth. I take it as a good omen that I find a positive significance in this ancient site, the saddle-point of the pass, the provisional resting place of my imagined journey through the troubled times and windy spaces of Connemara.

*

And now where? I remember my first visit to Mám Éan a score of years ago. I had come to consider whether it was the right place at which to begin, not end, a book on Connemara (a premature project that came to nothing). Having inspected the holy stones at the saddle-point I turned to the mountainside to its south. It looked rather daunting, but an hour of foot- and handwork brought me to the top, where the vague vastness opening up around me overwhelmed my intention of making a few notes towards a preface. All the colours omitted from the rainbow had been thrown aside here. To write a book about these spoil heaps of eternity? Even the lowland to the south, fragmented by a web of seaways, that pre-eminent land of talk, as I now know it to be, seemed to demand a book to itself and made me fear cluttered footnotes and tangled cross-references. To find the content of the saint's blessing and curse upon Connemara would evidently be the work of many years. I began to pick my way down towards the main road, which looked like a piece of string forgotten on the valley floor below. The first few hundred yards of descent were of bare, angular stones glinting with crystalline veins. Then came hundreds of yards of heather-cushions embroidered with tiny, vivid flower-motifs. I strolled down a glen by a stream with fingerling trout in its pools, to the village of Seanadh Chaola, where there were children riding a donkey, who waved to me. The grown-ups were in the fields beyond, turning hay in the sunshine; they paused from their work and waved to me too. It was a moment left over from Eden. I followed the lane down to the main road, and waited hopefully and wearily for a lift back through the little bit of the world I am only now, after so many years, beginning to know as home.

Bibliography

Airy, Alan, *Irish Hill Days* (Manchester, n.d.).

Andrews, J. H., *A Paper Landscape* (Oxford, 1975).

Anon., *The Collective Wisdom, or Sights and Sketches in the Chapel of St. Stephen*, by a Member of the Upper Benches (London, 1824).

Armstrong, Revd Thomas, *My Life in Connaught* (London, 1906).

Arnold-Forster, Florence, *Irish Journal*, ed. T. W. Moody and Richard Hawkins, with Margaret Moody (Oxford, 1988).

Barrington, Sir Jonah, *Personal Sketches of His Own Times* (London, 1827).

Berry, James, *Tales of the West of Ireland* (Dublin, 1966; republished as *Tales of Old Ireland*). Berry's tales originally appeared in the *Mayo News*, 1910–13.

Bigger, F. J., 'Prehistoric Settlements at Portnafeadog in the Parish of Moyrus, Connamara', *Proceedings of the Royal Irish Academy*, 3 (1895).

Blake Family, *Letters from the Irish Highlands* (published anonymously, London, 1825; republished Clifden, 1995).

Blake, Martin J., *The Blake Family Records* (London, 1902 (1)).

——, 'The Abbey of Athenry', *Journal of the Galway Archaeological and Historical Society*, 2 (1902 (2)).

Bourke, Austin, *The Visitation of God? The Potato and the Great Irish Famine* (Dublin, 1993).

Braithwaite, Revd Robert (ed.), *The Life and Letters of Rev. William Pennefather, B.A.* (London, 1878).

Braun-Blanquet, J., *Plant Sociology* (New York, 1932).

Burke, Sir Bernard, *Vicissitudes of Families*, vol. I (London, 1883).

Burke, William P., *The Irish Priests in the Penal Times (1660–1760)* (Shannon, 1969).

Callwell, J. M., *Old Irish Life* (London, 1912).

Carney, James, *The Playboy and the Yellow Lady* (Swords, Co. Dublin, 1986).

Chambers, Anne, *Granuaile: The Life and Times of Grace O'Malley, c.1530–1603* (Dublin, 1979).

——, *Ranji, Maharajah of Connemara* (Dublin, 2002).

Chapple, Fred. V., *The Heather Garden* (London, 1960).

Commissioners of Inquiry into the State of the Irish Fisheries, *First Report* (Dublin, 1836).

Cullen, Louis M., 'Five Letters Relating to Smuggling in 1737', *Journal of the Galway Archaeological and Historical Society*, 27 (1956–7).

D'Alton, Right Revd Monsignor, *History of the Archdiocese of Tuam* (Dublin, 1928).

de Courcy, J. W., 'Alexander Nimmo, Engineer: Some Tentative Notes', paper for the National Library of Ireland Society (November 1981).

De Latocnaye, Le Chevalier, trans. John Stevenson, *A Frenchman's Walk Through Ireland 1796–7* (Belfast, 1917).

de Stacpoole, Duke, *Irish and Other Memories* (London, 1922).

Doyle, G. J., 'The Vegetation, Ecology and Productivity of Atlantic Blanket Bog in

Mayo and Galway, Western Ireland', *Journal of Life Sciences*, 3, Royal Dublin Society (1982).

Eager, Alan R., and Scannell, Mary J. P., 'William M'Calla (c.1814–1849), Phycologist; His Published Papers of 1846', *Journal of Life Sciences*, 2, Royal Dublin Society (1981).

Edgeworth, Maria, *Tour in Connemara (1833)* (first appeared in an unpublished memoir, 1867; reprinted with additional material, ed. H. E. Butler, London, 1950).

Feehan, John, and O'Donovan, Grace, *The Bogs of Ireland* (Dublin, 1996).

Ferguson, David K., and Westhoff, Victor, 'An Account of the Flora and Vegetation of Derryclare Wood', *Proc. Koninklijke Nederlandse Akademie van Wetenschappen*, series C, vol. 90, no. 2 (22 June 1987).

Folan, A. C. M., and Mitchell, M. E., 'The Lichens and Lichen Parasites of Derryclare Wood, Connemara', *Proceedings of the Royal Irish Academy*, 70B (1970).

Foss, P. J. and Doyle, G. J., 'Why Has *Erica erigena* such a Markedly Disjunct European Distribution?' *Plants Today*, 1 (1988).

Fox, Howard F., *Field Manual of West Galway (H11) Lichenology*, prepared for participants of the British Lichen Society Spring Meeting (1998).

Gibbons, Erin, Report 56 in *Excavations 1991, Summary Accounts of Archaeological Investigations in Ireland* (Bray, 1992).

Godwin, Sir Harry, *The Archives of the Peat Bogs* (Cambridge, 1981).

Gosling, Paul (ed.), *Archaeological Inventory of County Galway*, vol. 1, *West Galway* (Dublin, 1993).

Gray, Elizabeth A. (trans.) *Cath Maige Tuired: The Second Battle of Mag Tuired*, Corpus of Electronic Texts Edition (online) (Cork, 2003).

Griffith, Richard, *General Valuation of Rateable Property in Ireland, Union of Clifden* (Dublin, 1855).

Hall, S. C., and Mrs Hall, *The West and Connemara* (London, 1853).

Hardiman, James, *The History of the Town and County of the Town of Galway* (Dublin, 1820).

Hayward, Richard, *This is Ireland: Connacht and the City of Galway* (London, 1952).

Hogan, Patrick, 'The Migration of Ulster Catholics to Connaught 1795–96', *Seanchas Ardmhacha*, 9:2 (1979).

Inglis, H. D., *Ireland in 1834*, vol. 2 (1835).

Jessen, K., 'Studies in Late Quaternary Deposits and Flora History of Ireland', *Proceedings of the Royal Irish Academy*, B52 (1949).

Joyce, P. W., *Irish Names of Places*, vol. II (London 1912; republished Wakefield, 1973).

——, *Irish Names of Places*, vol III (Dublin 1913; republished Wakefield, 1976).

Knowles, M. C., 'Notes on West Galway Lichens', *Irish Naturalists' Journal* (February 1912).

Larkin, William, *Map of County Galway* (1819; reprinted Phoenix Maps, Dublin, 1989).

Leake, Bernard E., Tanner, P. W. Geoff, and Singh, D., 'Major Southward Thrusting of the Dalradian Rocks of Connemara, Western Ireland', *Nature*, 305: 5931 (September 1983).

Long, Richard, *Walking in Circles* (published in connection with his 1991 exhibition in London by Thames and Hudson).

Lynam, E. W., 'The O'Flaherty Country', *Studies* (June 1914).

Lynam, Joss, May, Justin, and Robinson, Tim, *Slí an Iarthair or The Western Way in Connemara; A Walkers' Map and Guide* (Roundstone, 1997).

Lynam, Shevaun, *Humanity Dick Martin 'King of Connemara' 1754–1834* (London, 1975; pbk edn Dublin, 1989).

Macalister, R. A. S. (ed. and trans.), *Lebor Gabála Érenn* (Dublin, 1938–56).

McClintock, David, 'Further Notes on *Erica ciliaris* in Ireland', *Proceedings of the Botanical Society of the British Isles*, 7:2 (1968).

Mac Con Iomaire, Liam (trans.), *Camchuirt Chonamara Theas*, and Robinson, Tim, *A Twisty Journey: Mapping South Connemara Parts 1–59* (Dublin, 2002).

Mac Giolla Choille, Breandán (ed.), *Books of Survey and Distribution*, vol. III, *County of Galway* (Dublin, 1962).

Mac Giollarnáth, Seán, *Peadar Chois Fhairrge, scéalta nua agus seanscéalta d'innis Peadar Mac Thuathaláin* (Dublin, 1934).

——, *Annála Beaga ó Iorrais Aithneach* (Dublin, 1941).

——, *Conamara* (Cork, 1954).

MacLysacht, Edward, *Irish Life in the Seventeenth Century*, 3rd edn (Cork, 1969).

MacIntyre, James, *Three Men on an Island* (Belfast, 1996).

M'Manus, Revd Henry, *Sketches of the Irish Highlands* (London, 1863).

MacNeill, Máire, *The Festival of Lughnasa* (Oxford, 1962).

Mannion, Karen (ed.), *Croí Chonamara, The Heart of Connemara, The History of Ballinafad, Recess and Bun na gCnoc* (Recess, 1998).

Martin, Archer E. S., *Genealogy of the Family of Martin of Ballinahinch Castle in the County of Galway, Ireland* (Winnipeg, 1890).

Martin Estate Sale, *The Third Section of the Galway Estates of the late Thomas Barnewell Martin, Esq.*, particulars of sale (August 1849). Also: 'Auction of the Connemara Estates', *Farmer's Journal* (November 1849). Also: *In the Court of the Commissioners for the Sale of Incumbered Estates in Ireland. Connamara. Martin Estates*, particulars of sale (July 1852). (Public Records Office)

Martineau, Harriet, *Letters from Ireland (reprinted from the 'Daily News')* (London, 1852).

Micks, W. L., *An Account of the Congested Districts Board of Ireland, 1891–1923* (Dublin, 1925).

Mitchell, Frank, *The Way That I Followed* (Dublin, 1990).

Moriarty, John, *Turtle Was Gone a Long Time*, vol. I, *Crossing the Kedron* (Dublin, 1996).

Morris, J. H., Long, C. B., McConnell, B., and Archer, J. B., *Geology of Connemara*, Geological Survey of Ireland (1995).

Nelson, E. Charles, 'William McCalla – a Second "Panegyric" for an Irish Phycologist', *Irish Naturalists' Journal*, 20:7 (1981).

——, 'Historical Records of the Irish *Ericaceae* . . .', *Irish Naturalists' Journal*, 20:9 (1982).

Nicholson, Asenath, *Ireland's Welcome to the Stranger . . .* (London, 1847).

Nimmo, Alexander, 'Report on the Bogs of Galway, West of Lough Corrib', in *Fourth Report of the Commissioners on the Nature and Extent of the Bogs of Ireland*, House of Commons (London, 1814).

Ó Concheannáin, T., *Dinnsheanchas*, vol. II (*c.*1967; on the placename element *trosc*).

O'Connell, Michael, *Connemara: Vegetation and Land Use Since the Last Ice Age* (Dublin, 1994).

Ó Cuaig, Seosamh, 'Fáisnéis aimsithe ar an "Playboy"', *Stáitse* (Camus, 2000).

O'Donovan, John, *Ordnance Survey Letters, Co. Galway* (1839). Typescript copy in National Library of Ireland.

Ó Duilearga, Seamus, *Leabhar Sheáin Í Chonaill* (Dublin, 1977).

O'Flaherty, Roderick, *West or H-Iar Connaught* (written 1684), ed. James Hardiman (1st edn Dublin, 1846; reprinted Kenny's Bookshop, Galway, 1978).

——, *Ogygia; or, a Chronological Account of Irish events . . .* , (in Latin) (London, 1685; trans. Revd James Hely, Dublin, 1793).

Ó Gaora, Colm, *Mise* (Dublin, 1943; new edn 1969).

Ó Gráda, Cormac, *An Drochshaol: Béaloideas agus Amhráin* (Dublin, 1994).

Ó hEochaidh, Seán, 'Builteachas I dTir Chonaill', *Béaloideas*, 13 (1943).

Ó hÓgáin, Dr Daithí, *Myth, Legend and Romance* (London, 1990).

Ó Máille, Tomás, *An Gaoth Aniar* (Dublin, 1920).

——, *Micheál Mhac Suibhne agus Filidh an tSléibhe* (Dublin, 1934).

Ó Máille, T. S., '*Meacan* i nÁitainmneacha', *Dinnsheanchas*, 2:4 (December 1967).

Ordnance Survey Field Books (MS notebooks of placenames recorded in the 1830s for the first Ordnance Survey, with, for Co. Galway and elsewhere, anglicized forms due to John O'Donovan; microfilm copies in National Library of Ireland).

Osborne, Hon. and Revd S. Godolphin, *Gleanings in the West of Ireland* (London, 1850).

Otway, Caesar, *A Tour in Connaught* (Dublin, 1839).

Pain, Wellesley, *Richard Martin (1754–1834)* (London, 1925).

Petrie, George, 'Military Architecture', MS, National Library of Ireland, and in 'Aspects of George Petrie, V', *Proceedings of the Royal Irish Academy*, vol. 2, section C, no. 10 (1972).

Póirtéir, Cathal, *Famine Echoes* (Dublin, 1995).

Praeger, Robert Lloyd, *The Botanist in Ireland* (1934; reprinted Dublin, 1974).

——, *The Way That I Went*, (1937; reprinted Dublin, 1969).

——, *Natural History of Ireland* (1950; republished London, 1972).

Purton, Louise, *An Investigation of the Evolution of the Dog's Bay / Gorteen Tombolo*, Earth Science Moderatorship Thesis, Trinity College, Dublin (1993).

Report of the Commissioners of Public Instruction (1835). Available in National Library of Ireland.

Robinson, Sir Henry, *Memories: Wise and Otherwise* (London, 1924 (1)).

——, *Further Memories of Irish Life* (London, 1924 (2)).

Robinson, Tim, *Connemara: Part 1, Introduction and Gazetteer; Part 2, A One-Inch Map* (Roundstone, 1990).

——, *Setting Foot on the Shores of Connemara* (Dublin, 1996).

——, *Stones of Aran, Part 2, Labyrinth* (Dublin, 1995; Penguin edn, London 1997).

——, *My Time in Space* (Dublin, 2001).

Rodwell, J. S. (ed.), *British Plant Communities* (Cambridge, 2000).

Rundle, Dr Adrian, 'Sand Sample from Dog's Bay, Connemara, Ireland', *Geologists' Association Earth Alert Festival* (August 2002).

Salmon, Mary, 'Sméaróid', in Gannon, Paul (ed.), *The Way It Was* (Cloonluane, Renvyle, 1999).

Scannell, Mary J. P., and McClintock, David, '*Erica mackaiana* Bab. in Irish Localities and other Plants of Interest', *Irish Naturalists' Journal*, 18:3 (1974).

Scott, Thomas Colville, 'Journal of a Survey of the Martin Estate, 1853', in *Connemara After the Famine*, ed. with introduction by Tim Robinson (Dublin, 1995).

Simington, Robert C., *The Transplantation to Connacht 1654–58* (Dublin, 1970).

Somerville, E. Oe., and Ross, Martin, *Through Connemara in a Governess Cart* (London, 1893).

——, *Irish Memories* (London, 1917).

Synge, J. M., *The Aran Islands* (1st edn London, 1907; reprint ed. and introduced by Tim Robinson, London, 1992).

Tansley, A. G., *The British Islands and their Vegetation* (Cambridge, 1939).

Thackeray, W. M., *The Irish Sketch Book of 1842* (London, 1843; often reprinted).

Thompson, D'Arcy Wentworth, *The End of the World* (Galway, 1945; reprinting a lecture reported in the *Galway Vindicator*, 24 March 1866).

Tohall, Patrick, 'The Diamond Fight of 1795 and the Resultant Expulsions, *Seanchas Ard Mhacha*, 3:1 (1958).

Uí Mhurchadha, Brighid Bean, *Oideachas in Iar-Chonnacht sa Naoú Céad Déag* (Dublin, 1954).

Villiers-Tuthill, Kathleen, *History of Clifden, 1810–1860* (Clifden, 1981).

——, *Beyond the Twelve Bens, a History of Clifden and District 1860–1923* (published by the author, 1986).

——, *Patient Endurance: The Great Famine in Connemara* (Dublin, 1997).

Wakeman, William, *A Week in the West of Ireland* (Dublin, n.d., [c.1850]).

Wall, Mervyn, 'Along Many a Mile', RTÉ radio talk, 20 February 1959.

Webb, D. A., 'Is the Classification of Plant Communities either Possible or Desirable?' *Bot. Tidsskr*, 51 (1954).

——, 'Notes on Four Irish Heaths: Part I', *Irish Naturalists' Journal*, 11 (1954).

——, '*Erica ciliaris* L. in Ireland', *Proceedings of the Botanical Society of the British Isles* (September 1966).

Webb, D. A., and Glanville, E. V., 'The Vegetation and Flora of Some Islands in the Connemara Lakes', *Proceedings of the Royal Irish Academy*, 62B (1962).

Webb, D. A. and Scannell, Mary J. P., *Flora of Connemara and the Burren* (Cambridge, 1983).

Westhoff, V., and Van der Maarel, E., 'The Braun-Blanquet Approach', in *Classification of Plant Communities*, ed. R. H. Whittaker (The Hague, 1978).

Whilde, Tony, *The Natural History of Connemara* (London, 1994).

White, George Preston, *A Tour in Connamara, with Remarks on Its Great Physical Capabilities* (London, 1849).

White, James, 'A History of Irish Vegetation Studies', *Journal of Life Sciences*, 3, Royal Dublin Society (1982).

White, James and Doyle, Gerard, 'The Vegetation of Ireland', *Journal of Life Sciences*, 3, Royal Dublin Society (1982).

Whyte, Revd Edward, *The Crotty Schism at Birr (1820–1850)*, n.d., n.p. [published by the author in 1991 or earlier].

Sources

Scailp

This essay was first published in the *Dublin Review*, 13 (Winter 2003–4).

Pages

8–9   (Mediterranean heath) Chapple, 1960. Foss and Doyle, 1988. Nelson, 1982.
10   (Mass) Mac Giollarnáth, 1941.
        (post-Cromwellian settlement) Mac Giolla Choille, 1962.
12–17   (booleying) O'Flaherty, 1846. John Dunton's letters, in MacLysacht, 1969.
        Ó hEochaidh, 1943.
13–14   (Mac Thuathaláin) Mac Giollarnáth, 1934 (my translation, with advice from
        Liam Mac Con Iomaire).
17   (ghost crossing the bog) Information from Noel King, Roundstone.

Dead Man's Grave and Halfway House

Pages

24   (crannogs) Gosling, 1993.
25   (blanket bog) Feehan and O'Donovan, 1996. Doyle, 1982.
31–3   (lake islands) Webb and Glanville, 1962.
36   (Tulach Lomáin) Ordnance Survey Field Books, 1839.
38–40   (Mackay's heath) Webb *(INJ)*, 1954. Scannell and McClintock, 1974. For the
        airport controversy see Robinson, Tim, 1996 and 2001.
39–41   (McAlla) Nelson, 1981. Eager and Scannell, 1981.
41–2   (Dorset heath) Webb, 1966. McClintock, 1968.
42–3   (Liam Dearg) Mac Giollarnáth, 1941 (my translation).
43–5   (Halfway House) Berry, 1966.

Superincumbent Intellect

Pages

47–52   (Knud Jessen) Praeger, 1937. Jessen, 1949. Mitchell, 1990. Godwin, 1981.
        Tansley, 1939. For another consideration of the meeting in the bog see 'The
        Echosphere', in Robinson, Tim, 2001.
52–5   (recent studies of vegetational history) O'Connell, 1994.

Climbing Errisbeg

This essay first appeared in *Irish Pages*, 2:2 (2004).

Pages
70   (butter) Mac Giollarnáth, 1941.
72–4   (Roundstone Bog) Nimmo, 1814.
75   (Mannin Thrust) Leake, Tanner and Singh, 1983.
76–8   (geological history) Morris, Long, McConnell and Archer, 1995. I thank
          Professor Paul Mohr for his guidance in geological matters.

Murvey

Pages
80   (*The Book of Invasions*) Macalister, 1938–56.
82   (*machair*) Whilde, 1994.
84–5   (William O'Malley) Ó Máille, Tomás, 1920. Irish Folklore Commission,
          Schools Scheme material, quoted in *Connemara News*, July 1992. Ó Cuaig,
          2000.
86   (J. M. Synge) Synge, 1992.
87–8   (James Lynchehaun) Carney, 1986. The reference to his teaching in Murvey
          is in Uí Mhurchadha, 1954.

The Boneyard

Pages
95–6   (children's burial ground) Salmon, 1999.
101–3   (prehistoric remains) Petrie, 1972. Bigger, 1895. Gibbons, 1992.
103–7   (dyestuff) Murray, Ph.D. thesis, Queen's University, Belfast, 1999.
106   (Creagacorcron) Mac Giolla Choille, 1962.
107   (grazing rights) Information from Joe Rafferty, Roundstone.
108–9   (tombolo) Purton, 1993.
112   (foraminifera) Praeger, 1937. Whilde, 1994. Rundle, 2002.
113   (maze) Long, 1991.

Ogygia Lost

This essay first appeared in the *Dublin Review*, 14 (Spring 2004).

Pages
117   (*Ogygia*) O'Flaherty, 1793.
118   (Cruagh Coelann) O'Flaherty, 1846.
119–20   (bailiff and wife) O'Flaherty, 1846. Mac Giollarnáth, 1941.
122–3   (soldiers marooned) Hardiman's notes to O'Flaherty, 1846. Mac Giollarnáth,
          1941.
123–4   (Na Sceirdí) O'Flaherty, 1846. Mac Giollarnáth, 1941.
124–5   (Fairhaired Merchant) Ó hÓgáin, 1990. Ó Duilearga, 1977.
126   (wind farms) *Connacht Tribune*, 28 September 2001.

Holiday Island

Pages

130   (time) From a logbook kept by Alex and John Findlater.

132   (Northern Ireland artists) MacIntyre, 1996.

133–5   (island history) Mac Giolla Choille, 1962. Commissioners of Inquiry into the State of the Irish Fisheries, 1836.

134   (Broughtons) Griffith, 1855. Thompson, 1866. Congested Districts Board records (CDB 3225).

The Wind Through the House

Pages

141   (lace school) Information from the late Kitty Barlow, daughter of Margaret Cosgrove.
For an earlier portrait of the house see 'A House on a Small Cliff', in Robinson, Tim, 2001.

The Neighbours

Pages

159–60   (de Stacpoole history) de Stacpoole, 1922.

Forgotten Roundstone

SMUGGLERS AND ASYLUM SEEKERS

Pages

167–9   (smuggling) Cullen, 1956–7.

170–72   (Coogla) Wall, 1959. Tohall, 1958. Hogan, 1979. *The Times*, 16 July 1824.

NIMMO AND HIS BROTHERS

Pages

174–7   (Alexander Nimmo's career) de Courcy, 1981.

175   (report on bogs) Nimmo, 1814.

178–9   (harbour) Donnell's evidence to Commissioners of Inquiry into the State of the Irish Fisheries, 1836.

179   (Nimmo's lease) Nimmo's coast survey, 1826, in Commissioners of Inquiry into the State of the Irish Fisheries, 1836. Martin estate sale documentation, 1849.

181   (Mary Nimmo) Her lease on a house in Roundstone is detailed in the Law Life Association Society's conveyance of the former Martin estate to Berridge, 1872.
(John Nimmo's drowning) White, George Preston, 1849.

181–3   (George Nimmo) M'Manus, 1863.

A CURE OF SOULS

Pages

183   (lease of Catholic church site) Martin estate sale documentation, 1852. (Franciscan monastery) D'Alton, 1928. Thackeray, 1843. The plaque is now on the tower in Killeen Park, the former monastery grounds.

185   (Franciscan Brothers) From a typescript history of the monastery by Br Ambrose O'Connell, in possession of Fr Cosgrove, parish priest, Roundstone.

185–6   (Revd Joseph Fisher) *Irish Presbyterian*, January 1924.

186–9   (William Pennefather) Braithwaite, 1878.

189   (John Nimmo) *Irish Presbyterian*, January 1924.
(lines on opening of Presbyterian church) *Orthodox Presbyterian*, November 1840.

190–92   (Henry M'Manus) M'Manus, 1863.

193   (William Pennefather) Braithwaite, 1878.

194–8   (Revd William Crotty) Whyte, 1991 or earlier. Armstrong, 1906.

198   (later life of M'Manus) Armstrong, 1906.

THE COLD OF CHARITY

Pages

199   (Raleigh) Nicholson, 1847.

200   (potato blight) Bourke, 1993.

201   (rhyme) Póirtéir, 1995.

202–13   (history of the Famine in Connemara) Villiers-Tuthill, 1997.

206–7   (song about Johnny Seoighe) Ó Gráda, 1994. I am grateful to Liam Mac Con Iomaire for his translation.

211–13   (deaths of Honora Flaherty and Peggy Melia) Villiers-Tuthill, 1997.

THE ROBINSON ERA

Much of the following, on George and Henry Robinson, formed part of *Secret Connemara*, a talk given at the Canadian Institute of Irish Studies Conference in Toronto, 1994, and was incorporated in 'Four Threads', in Robinson, Tim, 1996.

Pages

215   (George Robinson's family) Information from the late Dr Philip Robinson, Dublin.

216   (Martin residence) Scott, 1995.

218   (shooting of George Robinson) Ó Gaora, 1943, my translation.

218–19   (his letter to Dublin Castle) Documentation kindly lent by Dominic Berridge.

220   (killing of Robinsons' stock) *Galway Vindicator*, 12 June 1880.
(evictions) *Galway Vindicator*, 5 May and 12 June 1880. Villiers-Tuthill, 1986.

221–2   (address to Henry Robinson, and obituary) I thank Patrick Gageby for supplying this document.

222–3   (wooden leg anecdote) Robinson, Sir Henry, 1924 (2).

Dinner at Letterdyfe

Pages

230   (forked spleenwort) Webb and Scannell, 1983.

231   (plant associations) Braun-Blanquet, 1932. Westhoff and Van der Maarel, 1978.

233–5   Tansley, 1939. Webb, D. A., 1954. White and Doyle, 1982. White, James, 1982. I am grateful to Dr White of the Botany Department, University College, Dublin, for guidance on this subject.

Inis Ní in Winter

Pages

240   (story of beggars) Information from Mícheál King, Inis Ní.
       (Blakes) Blake, 1902 (1). Commissioners of Inquiry into the State of the Irish Fisheries, 1836. Congested Districts Board records (CBD 3225).
       (fort) Information from Paddy Folan, Inis Ní.

248–51   (Darby Gannon) I am grateful to Sigrun and Armin Quester for this unpublished text.

255   (Duke of Edinburgh) *Galway Vindicator*, 17 April 1880.

The Catchment

Pages

264   (Tuaim Beola schools) Uí Mhurchadha, 1954.
       (chapel) O'Donovan, 1839.

264–5   (legend of monk) I heard this from John Moriarty, who had it from local residents.

266–9   (Robertson) Scott, 1995. White, George Preston, 1849. Martineau, 1852. Osborne, 1850.

269   (advertisement) I am grateful to Lynne Prynne of the Anglers' Return for this document.

274   (Abhainn Tuaidh) O'Flaherty, 1846.

Tales to Lengthen the Road

Pages

278   (abbey) O'Donovan, 1839. Blake, 1902 (2). Gosling, 1993. Burke, William P., 1969. D'Alton, 1928. Local lore from Margaret Keaney, Canower, and Annie Conneely, Doire Fhada Thiar.

280   (Imleach) Local lore from Bernie O'Toole, Roundstone.

281   (Fox Island) Folktale from Tom MacDonagh, Tamhnach Bán, Cashel.

281–2   (Meall an tSaighdiúra) Local lore from Patrick Nee and Mrs Keaney, Cashel.

282–3   (O'Loghlen) Robinson, Sir Henry, 1924 (2).

283–4   (Viceroy's reception) The late Willie O'Malley, Ballinafad.

284–5   (royal visit) Robinson, Sir Henry, 1924 (1).

288   (Rosroe famine) Local lore from Joe Joyce, Canower.

The Demesne

Pages

290   (linoleum) For John Moriarty's very different development of this incident see Moriarty, 1996.

291   (market stone, stables) Hayward, 1952.

298   (castle) Burke, Sir Bernard, 1883.

The Masters of Ballynahinch

THE ISLAND

Pages

302   (Conmaicne) Hardiman's notes to O'Flaherty, 1846.

303–10   (O'Flahertys) Lynam, E.W., 1914. For a fuller account see 'The Ferocious O'Flahertys', in Robinson, Tim, 1995.

305, 308 (Grace O'Malley) Chambers, 1979.

305   (Log na Marbh) See also 'Backwaters', in Robinson, Tim, 1997.

311–13   (post-Cromwellian settlements) Mac Giolla Choille, 1962. Simington, 1970.

312   ('Litigious Martins') Otway, 1839. Callwell, 1912.

313–15   (Galway Martins) Hardiman, 1820. Martin, 1890. Lynam, Shevaun, 1975.

DICK MARTIN RULES

Pages

316–7   (duel) Hayward, 1952.

317–28   (Richard Martin, life and times) Lynam, Shevaun, 1975. Pain, 1925.

319   (French traveller) De Latocnaye, 1917.

319–20   (smuggler Ó Máille) Mac Giollarnáth, 1941; see also 'Tales from the Hill', in Robinson, Tim, 1997.

320   (Ned Bodkin) Barrington, 1827.

321   (Thomas Moore) Horace, Ode XXII, Lib. I, in *Poetical Works of Thomas Moore* (Paris, 1827).

321–2   (Maria Edgeworth) Edgeworth, 1950.

322   (estate management) De Latocnaye, 1917.

323   (Harriet Martin's description of Richard Martin) *Animal World* (September 1871), quoted in Pain, 1925.

324–5   (Collective) Anon., 1824.

326–8   (Richard Martin's urbanity and duelling) Barrington, 1827.

ROMANCE AND RUIN

Pages

329   (Thomas Martin's early life) Lynam, Shevaun, 1975.

330   (battle with O'Flahertys) Callwell, 1912.

331   (Cillín evictions) Local lore from Kevin Joyce, Recess.

332   (Bianconi, and family prayers) Callwell, 1912.

332–3   (servants) Thackeray, 1843.

334–40   (Mary Martin) Edgeworth, 1950.

340   (Thomas's death) Callwell, 1912.

(his funeral) Somerville and Ross, 1917. Callwell, 1912.
341   (Bell–Martin marriage) Burke, Sir Bernard, 1883. Martin, 1890. Edgeworth, 1950.
341–2   (Bell Martin evictions) Villiers-Tuthill, 1997.
342   (Mary's death) Burke, Sir Bernard, 1883.
343   (her snaggledy tooth) Somerville and Ross, 1893.

THE RECKONING

Pages
343–4   (Martin estate sale) *Farmers' Journal* (November 1849).
346   (clearances) Hall and Hall, 1853.
346–8   (survey) Scott, 1995.
348   (railway project) *Irish Times* (?), December 1871. Rosroe lore from Josie Keaney, Canower.
349   (Berridges) This history of the Berridges is based on family papers kindly lent to me by Dominic Berridge.
350   (William Edward Forster) Arnold-Forster, 1988.
350–51   (death of first Richard Berridge) *Tuam Herald*, 8 and 22 October 1887.
352   (Dickens) *Our Mutual Friend*.

THE SPORTSMEN

Pages
353   (forestry) Micks, 1925.
         (railway) Villiers-Tuthill, 1986.
         (cuttings) Local lore from Willie O'Malley, Ballinafad.
354   (Arthur V. Willcox) Information from Pam Reid, Lisnabrucka.
         (wedding, refurbishing of Ballynahinch Castle) Documents and photographs lent by Dominic Berridge.
         (Congested Districts Board) *Tuam Herald*, 12 May 1894. Congested Districts Board record (CDB 9751).
355   (O'Malley) *Irish Times*, 23 May 1912.
357–61   (Ranjitsinhji) Chambers, 2002.

Walking the Skyline

Pages
366–7   (geological history) Morris, Long, McConnell and Archer, 1995.
368   (IRA) Information from William O'Brien, Gleann Chóchan. Ó Gaora, 1943.
371   (stone alignment) For further details see 'Through Prehistoric Eyes', in Robinson, Tim, 1996.
372–3   (primary triangulation) Andrews, 1975. Airy, n.d.
373   (Tinteannaí) Information from Pat Joyce, Gleann Chóchan.
374   (diameter of Earth) The theorem is Euclid, Book 3, No. 36 (to the effect that if a line from a point P outside a circle and passing through its centre meets the circle at A and B, the length of the tangent to the circle from P is given by $d^2 = PA.PB$). The actual diameter of the Earth is just under 13,000 km. For another development of this theme see 'Taking Steps', in Robinson, Tim, 1996.

The Cuckoo of the Wood

Pages

375–6   (Bid Conneely) Information from Pat Joyce, Gleann Chóchan. Thackeray, 1843.

377   (plant communities) Ferguson and Westhoff, 1987.

381–2   (Blakes' visit) Blake Family, 1825.

383   (Charles Larbalastier) Knowles, 1912.

384–5   (lichens) Folan and Mitchell, 1970. Fox, 1998.

Glass, Marble, Steam, Fire

Pages

388–9   (Recess) Wakeman, n.d. Hall and Hall, 1853. Martin estate sale documentation.

389   (Robert Macredy) Berry, 1966. The Law Life Association Society's conveyance to Richard Berridge, 1872.

(Rose Cottage) Mannion, 1998. Somerville and Ross, 1893.

(Gleann Dealbhach) Ordnance Survey Field Books, 1839. Information from Dónal Mac Giolla Easpaig, Ordnance Survey Placenames Department, County Galway.

(Paddy Festy's) Mannion, 1998.

390–91   (Glendollagh) Wakeman, n.d. Hall and Hall, 1853. Martin estate sale documentation. Griffith, 1855. Scott, 1995. Information from Mrs Pam Reid, Lisnabrucka.

391–5   (royal visit) Robinson, Sir Henry, 1924 (1). Ó Gaora, 1943.

393–4   (royal railway carriage) Unidentified newspaper report, kindly supplied by the archivist, Buckingham Palace.

Curse and Blessing

Pages

399   (boundary dispute) Mac Giolla Choille, 1962.

400   (recent developments) Mannion, 1998.

401   (*Connacht Tribune*) These articles were collected in Mac Con Iomaire and Robinson, 2002.

402   (Fr Mac Gréil) Mannion, 1998.

(St Patrick's blessing) Mac Giollarnáth, 1954.

403   (his curse) Mac Giollarnáth, 1941, my translation.

405–6   (faction fight) Inglis, 1835. M'Manus, 1863.

407   (song) Ó Máille, Tomás, 1934.

409   (Crom Dubh and Lughnasa) MacNeill, 1962.

409–11   (Battle of Moytura) Gray, 2003.

Index

Mammals, birds, insects, etc. are listed under 'animals' and all plants except seaweeds under 'plants'.
Members of the Martin and Robinson families are listed in approximate chronological order.
Translations of Irish placenames and words are given where this can be done concisely.

He just wanted a decent book to read ...

Not too much to ask, is it? It was in 1935 when Allen Lane, Managing Director of Bodley Head Publishers, stood on a platform at Exeter railway station looking for something good to read on his journey back to London. His choice was limited to popular magazines and poor-quality paperbacks – the same choice faced every day by the vast majority of readers, few of whom could afford hardbacks. Lane's disappointment and subsequent anger at the range of books generally available led him to found a company – and change the world.

'We believed in the existence in this country of a vast reading public for intelligent books at a low price, and staked everything on it'
Sir Allen Lane, 1902–1970, founder of Penguin Books

The quality paperback had arrived – and not just in bookshops. Lane was adamant that his Penguins should appear in chain stores and tobacconists, and should cost no more than a packet of cigarettes.

Reading habits (and cigarette prices) have changed since 1935, but Penguin still believes in publishing the best books for everybody to enjoy. We still believe that good design costs no more than bad design, and we still believe that quality books published passionately and responsibly make the world a better place.

So wherever you see the little bird – whether it's on a piece of prize-winning literary fiction or a celebrity autobiography, political tour de force or historical masterpiece, a serial-killer thriller, reference book, world classic or a piece of pure escapism – you can bet that it represents the very best that the genre has to offer.

Whatever you like to read – trust Penguin.